Out and About
with
Winsor French

Out and About with Winsor French

James M. Wood

The Kent State University Press · Kent, Ohio

© 2011 by The Kent State University Press, Kent, Ohio 44242
ALL RIGHTS RESERVED
Library of Congress Catalog Card Number 2011016830
ISBN 978-1-60635-060-7
Manufactured in the United States of America

LIBRARY OF CONGRESS CATALOGING-IN-PUBLICATION DATA
Wood, James M., 1939–
Out and about with Winsor French / James M. Wood.
    p. cm.
Includes bibliographical references and index.
ISBN 978-1-60635-060-7 (pbk. : alk. paper) ∞
1. French, Winsor, 1904–1973. 2. Gossip columnists—Ohio—Cleveland—
Biography. I. Title.
PN4874.F65W66 2011
070.4'49092—dc22
[B]

                            2011016830

British Library Cataloging-in-Publication data are available.

15 14 13 12 11   5 4 3 2 1

To The Women Who Waited

and Waited

and Waited

Peggy

Martha

Anne

and

Jane

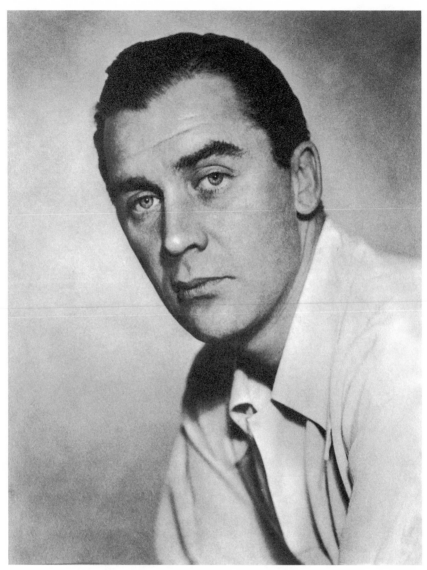

During Winsor's cruise aboard the MS *Kungsholm*, a portrait of him in casual dress appeared with his column. The absence of jacket and tie was unusual for a man who observed 1930s masculine fashion standards by attending local nightclubs in black tie and velvet evening slippers. Courtesy Martha Eaton Hickox

No effusive paeans of praise. Every man has some little feature, shall we say, he likes to hide from the camera. . . . Seek these out. But please don't mistake me. Scandal and character surgery are not the point, neither is sensationalism. Mirror-clear portraits are, however, with no retouching of the obvious scars.

Winsor French
Cleveland Press,
November 20, 1953

Contents

Preface and Acknowledgments

The idea for *Out and About with Winsor French* belongs to the late Margaret Halle Sherwin, who loved Winsor French and for a very short time— not more than an hour or two—was engaged to marry this remarkable man. Her friends called her "Mag"; she was a scamp like Winsor and could imitate the columnist making a theatrical entrance to a private party. In a voice that all agree was as deep and penetrating as Winsor's, she would utter the words with which he announced his arrival and began the stories with which he would regale listeners: "You won't believe it!"

With his phrase, let me introduce my extended family of collaborators, because you won't believe the year Mag first suggested a conventional biography of Winsor. It was 1985 or 1986. As a result, you will notice a slightly defensive tone to these words of appreciation. Several of my collaborators, including Mag Sherwin, never saw the results of their effort. I take very small comfort in the fact that it wasn't until 1997 that research on Winsor's life began in earnest, through the generosity of the late Frank Taplin, a philanthropist, author, and husband of Winsor's sister Margaret Eaton Taplin. Martha Eaton Hickox, another of Winsor's sisters, provided additional help.

Over the next four years, however, the conventional biography became the problematic partner of Winsor's anecdotal history of urban nightlife. In 2001, John Hubbell and Joanna Hildebrand Craig of the Kent State University Press read several chapters. They expressed cautious interest in reading more material—if the entire manuscript was at least "90 percent complete." I didn't satisfy that requirement until 2007, when scholars and the Press's editorial board expressed concern about the combination of biography and anecdotal history. After deliberating, I realized that Winsor's life and reportage were legitimate partners as American newspaper history. Will Underwood, on behalf of the Press, accepted a refocused manuscript; Joyce Harrison, Mary Young, and Erin Holman, exceptionally helpful editors, led me through the final editorial tasks. Christine Brooks and Darryl Crosby gave our efforts panache.

Persevering is tedious, but I was never on my own. Winsor's sisters— Peggy Taplin, Martha Hickox, and Anne Parker—as well as his nieces and nephews lent pictures and stories. Ann provided letters she had saved from Winsor, written between 1942 and 1970, and Martha had saved her father's file on Winsor, which included correspondence from the 1920s and 1930s. Both collections amplified and clarified miles of microfilmed copies of Winsor's columns.

Over several years, Evelyn Ward, the retired head of Cleveland Public Library's literature department, found all sorts of esoteric material in her own and others' libraries. Four of her colleagues in the library's photography collection—Margaret Baughman, Venchor Boyd, Patrice Hamiter, and Elmer Turner—found and processed many of the images that illuminate *Out and About with Winsor French*. Their work was enhanced with more photographs and drawings from Cleveland State University Library's *Cleveland Press* collection, where Lynn Duchez Bycko searched the files and Vern Morrison prepared copies for publication. In an era of heightened concern about copyrights, Randy Siegel, the current owner of *Parade*, a magazine Winsor founded in 1931, gave permission to use early photographs and drawings. Kara Darling, on behalf of Irving Berlin's estate, and Nick Janssen, on behalf of Cole Porter's Trust, guided me through the process required to quote both composers' lyrics.

There is another group—I'll call them wheedlers—who stayed the course. Winsor's sisters and my wife, Jane Semple Wood, the women to whom *Out and About with Winsor French* is dedicated, suffered the longest. Jane read and corrected two different book-length drafts. Our two sons, the Wood Brothers (Jim and Bob), learned to avoid the question, "What's Dad writing?" for the answer was the same for about twelve years. Ann Halle Little, Mag's sweet sister, provided photographs and encouragement; the Arcadians (Ed Walsh and John Brandt) read drafts and provided advice as did an innocent bystander, John O'Connor. Marco Ciccarelli and James Duber, principals in the architectural firm of StudioTECHNE, provided desks in three different offices that included a cubicle, a computer, printers, ink cartridges, and reams of paper. The Trepal brothers (Ladd and Norm) took my photograph for the back cover, a chore they last performed twenty-five years ago, for my first book of Cleveland history. Rosemary Merchant, former neighbor and steadfast friend, was never afraid to ask, "How's the book coming?" and a newcomer, Steve Friedman, said at least twice with only the slightest hint of impatience, "I wish he'd finished it, so I could read it."

Well! You won't believe it. The book is finished. Please accept *Out and About with Winsor French* as a token of my love and gratitude.

"Walks quivering on an empty stomach"

Out and About with Winsor French is illuminating reportage by a singular journalist: Winsor French. From 1932 to 1968 he wrote for two Cleveland daily newspapers, the *News* and the *Press,* as well as *PARADE* and *Harper's Bazaar* magazines. During Winsor's career he reviewed film, stage plays, and books, but his finest achievements appeared in an about-town column consisting of a dozen vignettes, or, in newspaper lingo, "items." Some were only a single sentence long; most documented social behavior that occurred after dark.

Winsor did not invent the about-town column, a public version of the private diary. In the twentieth century, the format proved ideal for covering café society, that mixture of old-money socialites and new-money celebrities that emerged in the 1920s. Newspaper columnists observed them in American cafés—urban nightclubs and restaurants. Maury Paul, who wrote an about-town column for the *New York American* under the name "Cholly Knickerbocker," coined the term "café society" and polished the format. His New York City imitators included Lucius Beebe in the *Herald Tribune* and Walter Winchell in the *Mirror.* Winsor chose another model, which he first read as an impressionable, twenty-year-old novice writer: the eccentric short, short stories in "The Talk of the Town," the editorial section that has opened each issue of the *New Yorker* since 1925.

Winsor worked harder than his New York City counterparts did. Beebe's column appeared once a week; Winsor's six. Winchell had a full-time assistant; Winsor was a one-man show. He loved to scoop his competitors, and on slow news days worried that his column "walks quivering on an empty stomach."

Readers unfamiliar with newspaper beats sometimes referred to Winsor as a "society" or a "gossip" columnist. He was neither, although grandes dames and rumors appeared under his byline. Winsor called his turf the "smoke and music" beat and redefined "town" to include places like Havana, Hollywood, Paris, and Pago Pago, as well as Cleveland. At first, he watched and listened to patrons in Prohibition-era speakeasies; later, he collected items in nightclubs, honkytonks, theaters, movie houses, railroad club cars, and steamship smoking lounges. His sources included bootleggers, crooners, debutantes, fan dancers, hoboes, gangsters, millionaires, torch singers, diplomats, waiters, redcaps, and deckhands. Notably, several of the twentieth century's most celebrated stage, film, and literary artists phoned Winsor with items: playwright Noël Coward, singer and actress Marlene Dietrich, movie star Cary Grant, author W. Somerset Maugham, and songwriter-showman Cole Porter.

In Cleveland, Winsor occupied desks in two newspaper city rooms where the language reflected a masculine culture. Ambitious reporters competed for assignments on the police or city hall beats, where they asked "tough" questions and wrote "hard" news about murder and corruption. The smoke-and-music beat was for journalistic softies.

Winsor, a self-described "effeminate young man," not only endured his colleagues' condescension, he risked losing his job by using his articles to defend unconventional behavior. He repeatedly ignored newspaper taboos about covering liquor laws, "sepia" entertainers, Jewish baseball players, schoolchildren in wheelchairs, and men—including Winsor—who found males more romantically exciting than females.

When vocabulary acceptable to his employers inhibited descriptions of controversial topics, Winsor found a way to inform his readers. If they could read between the lines, he could write between them. Two legendary editors in American newspaper history—A. E. M. Bergener, reportedly the model for the rascally editor in *The Front Page,* a 1928 satire on no-holds-barred journalism, and Louis B. Seltzer, who directed the sensational coverage of Dr. Sam Sheppard's murder trial—enabled his defiance.

Winsor began writing for newspapers in 1932, the last year of Prohibition, a lawless era that banned the sale of beverage alcohol and nurtured unconventional behavior. He retired in 1968, a year before the Stonewall riots, which launched a national movement protesting discrimination and police harassment of homosexuals. With the noteworthy exception of George Chauncey's *Gay New York,* contemporary historians have often described the three decades between Prohibition and Stonewall as exceptionally repressive, an era that forced "fairies" and "pansies" to be sexually vague or anonymous, especially if they aspired to be prominent figures in their communities.

Winsor's life and career contradict the conventional interpretation, confirming Chauncey's proposition that gay men weren't "isolated" or "invisible" and imprisoned in a metaphorical closet of their own construction. Winsor never hid his sexuality, yet despite his personal honesty, he achieved and maintained journalistic leadership and unchallenged influence over Cleveland's cultural and social life.

To explain his unusual clout, *Out and About with Winsor French* avoids two book-length clichés: a verbatim collection of published columns or a conventional biography. While Winsor's unpublished letters and my interviews with his family, friends, and colleagues reveal his personal life and how it influenced his work, excerpts from columns make his telling anecdotes accessible to a wider audience, from curious cultural historians to amateur film and drama buffs. *Out and About with Winsor French* documents the power of about-town columnists and re-creates an illuminating episode in the raucous history of twentieth-century American newspapers—which is entering what former *New York Times* media critic Frank Rich called "the post-newspaper era." The business of printing news on paper is quickly becoming a symbol of obsolescence comparable to nineteenth-century buggy whips.

"The plot is very, very daring"

CLEVELAND, OHIO

Monday, January 2, 1933, 8:25 p.m.

Five minutes before stagehands were to pull the curtain for the world premiere of a mysterious new play by Noël Coward, the Hanna Theatre was
almost empty. Outside, the night air hovered just above freezing. Hundreds
of anxious ticket holders, unable to get inside, sought shelter under the
hot white lights of the Hanna's marquee. Sunday's coal-colored snowfall
was puddling in the gutters of East 14th Street, where a steaming queue
of chauffeured limousines grumbled, filled with fretful passengers searching for openings in the crowd. There were none. People were jammed to
the curb. Somewhere in the crush, Winsor Brown French, the new movie
critic for the *Cleveland News,* greeted friends. None of them had trouble
hearing him.

Winsor had once belonged to an acting troupe whose players pursued
vocal splendor. He burnished his baritone: "Every time a cork in a bottle
of champagne goes 'bowp,'" a female newspaper colleague wrote, "I am
reminded of Winsor French. He can say 'Oh!' and make you think the mil-
lennium is at your elbow."

Although he was only five feet, seven inches tall, he was easily distin-
guishable among the men outside the Hanna. A male newspaper colleague
wrote of the opening night audience, "There were hard high hats and col-
lapsible high hats and black velour hats. . . . All the hats that were worn
were worn by the men." Not by Winsor. He was bareheaded, which was
unconventional for men in the 1930s. He combed his straight brown hair
back from an intellect's brow. As he inched toward the theater's entrance,
his blue-gray eyes searched for amusement. While he did not record his
emotions on this particular night, the twenty-eight-year-old writer had
every right to feel smug. He had created this clamorous mob. It was the
first, but not the last crowd he would inspire in a rollicking career of provocative journalism.

In 1933, newspapers and magazines were the only viable commercial news media. Radio broadcasting, just five years old, was struggling to build an audience and secure advertisers. The Radio Act of 1927 had created a federal commission that licensed and regulated local and network stations, but news broadcasts still featured announcers reading stories from newspapers and wire services. Radio programming in Cleveland, according to Winsor, included the "nasal twanging" of "cooking specialists" with "new recipe[s] for rice pudding" and announcers who read "setting up exercises at five in the afternoon." Television? The transmission of live, moving images was an eight-year-old invention with commercial potential.

Three daily newspapers vied for the attention of nine hundred thousand Cleveland residents. The *Plain Dealer* was published in the morning, the *Press* and *News* in the afternoon. The *News* charged eighteen cents a week for home delivery but sold more single copies from street vendors. If someone needed the news between 11 P.M. and 2 A.M., Winsor recommended a woman at Euclid Avenue and East 55th Street, who "has never missed saying 'thank you,' when you slip her three cents."

When Cleveland's newspaper reporters were seen at events, scribbling notes, their presence provoked curiosity. The number assigned to cover any particular occasion was a direct reflection of its potential news value. Local editors sent twelve writers to the Hanna Theatre that night. In addition, the Associated Press and United Press sent reporters who would wire dispatches datelined "Cleveland" to newspapers throughout the United States. One amazed observer noted that the world premiere was given the same importance as the scene of "some shooting or race or notable accident."

In addition to Winsor, the delegation at the Hanna included some of the city's most illustrious journalists: three drama critics, two feature writers, two society editors, and five about-town columnists. Two of the columnists could be read on editorial pages, prime newspaper real estate, and the remainder appeared in entertainment sections, second-class territory in the minds of news professionals. At the *News,* the urban turf that included nightclubs and theaters was referred to as the "smoke and music beat"; at the *Plain Dealer,* it was dismissed as the "whoopee beat."

The about-town column was a relatively new development in Cleveland news coverage, designed to build readership in the city's "younger set," whose members were bored by accounts of old money's debutante balls and wedding ceremonies, the staple of traditional society pages. The new generation entertained itself on "Euclid Avenue between E. 6th and E. 17th Streets, where the theaters, music stores, style shops and restaurants" clustered. About-town columnist Eleanor Clarage, who wrote "Main Street Meditations" for the *Plain Dealer*'s editorial page, got most of her items about "the bright sophisticated things of the moment" along those eleven city blocks. Typically, she began her day with a "luncheon at a new tearoom," followed by "a matinee, tea, or dinner with a celebrity or near-celebrity," then "a concert, a dance or party in the evening." The Hanna anchored the east end of her newspaper beat; a world premiere intrigued her readers.

Clarage, thirty-four years old, was one of four women assigned to cover the occasion; this was a far larger percentage of females than one would have found among all of Cleveland newspapers' editorial employees. The "free and easy life of a newspaper office" was considered unsuitable for women, according to one survey of editors. According to another respondent, the profession's "dreadful sense of freedom" often led "into all sorts of license of language and behavior," which often had "a harmful effect upon a girl's health." Of the female reporters at the Hanna that night, Clarage was the only one who had married. She chose a husband who understood newspaper life: Rodney C. Sutton, a *Press* sports editor. While more of the men had spouses, only one was a father. In the 1930s, journalists considered newspaper careers and families a risky combination, a historic attitude reinforced by the era's economic uncertainty.

Both males and females in this unscientific sample of local journalists were largely self-educated, acquiring their newspaper skills through on-the-job training. Only two were college graduates. For more than thirty years, media critics had advocated structured journalism education at the college or university level to improve news-reporting quality. By 1930, more than two hundred colleges and universities were offering structured journalism education, yet only one of the Cleveland reporters covering the world premiere held such a degree.

The reporter at the Hanna with the least formal education was George Davis, the bespectacled, fifty-four-year-old drama critic for the *Press*. He never finished high school, but it was he who perfected the short, simple sentences (subject-predicate-object) prized by the editor of the *Press* for their "force, virility, sparkle and pungency." At the *Plain Dealer,* Clarage disdainfully referred to Davis's style as "journalese." Nevertheless, she adopted similar syntax for her "Meditations."

Cleveland readers didn't know that two of the male about-town columnists used noms de plume: "Jake Falstaff" and "Noel Francis."

Falstaff was Herman Fetzer, a thirty-three-year-old poet, whose work for the *Press* was called "Pippins and Cheese." William Shakespeare wrote the same phrase for Jack Falstaff in *The Merry Wives of Windsor:* "I will make an end of my dinner; there's pippins and cheese to come." By taking the name of a renowned Shakespearean glutton, Fetzer acknowledged his weight (250 pounds) and appetite. At the Hanna that night, it was Falstaff who commented on men's hats.

Francis was none other than Winsor French. In addition to reviewing movies, he was also writing "The Night Parade," an about-town column for the *News,* the smaller of the two afternoon dailies. He had chosen "Noel" because he was born on Christmas Eve, "Francis" because it was another form of "French."

All twelve journalists were competing with each other to be the first to break significant news about Coward's play. Two of the drama critics, both veteran reporters, had achieved national scoops, coveted trophies of newspaper journalism. Twenty years earlier, Davis had broken the news that Teddy Roosevelt would run for president as the candidate of the Bull Moose Party. Thirty years earlier, Archie Bell, the fifty-five-year-old drama critic for the *News,* had uncovered a smallpox epidemic public health officials were trying to hide.

Yet, two weeks before the opening, Noël Coward had stymied the entire local press corps. Reporters had uncovered exactly four facts about his newest play: its title, *Design for Living,* and the names of its three leading players. Coward would reportedly appear on stage with two of his closest friends, Alfred Lunt, forty years old, and Lynn Fontanne, forty-five years old, husband and wife—two handsome, dark-haired perfectionists who created the illusion of spontaneity on stage and film through relentless rehearsals. In 1931, after starring in *The Guardsman,* a romantic movie about a famous actor and actress who were married, Lunt and Fontanne had become America's most popular acting couple.

A world premiere starring national celebrities in a play written by a brilliant, thirty-two-year-old Englishman was a first for Cleveland. Reporters and columnists were eager to publish rehearsal anecdotes. At the *Press,* the larger of Cleveland's two afternoon dailies, Helen Allyn, a twenty-eight-year-old feature writer and the only newsperson at the Hanna with a journalism degree, was forced to confess her inability to crack Coward's silence. "The plot and story," she wrote, "are so far a secret to the world at large."

Normally, press agents hired by theater managers, producers, and performers would be swarming about newspeople offering complimentary tickets in return for a mention that would boost box-office sales. The Hanna was competing with two dozen downtown theaters presenting vaudeville, moving pictures, burlesque, and legitimate stage productions. Every night tickets for about thirty thousand seats were for sale, more than anywhere else but New York City. More important, the lack of publicity about *Design for Living* had reduced the number of mail orders at the Hanna Theatre, especially after management raised the top price for a single ticket from two dollars to three. The decision seemed foolhardy; everyone else was lowering prices.

That very morning, the Standard Oil Company of Ohio, the petroleum giant that had made John D. Rockefeller the richest man in the United States, announced that to increase sales, it had cut the price of its premium grade gasoline, the fuel required by the limousines idling in front of the Hanna, by two cents a gallon, to seventeen cents, the lowest ever in Cleveland history.

Ruthless deflation had the world's economy in a tailspin. With hindsight, Winsor realized the first signs of trouble had begun appearing in February 1929: "Man after man being laid off work; family after family reaching their last few dollars, being forced to give up their homes and storming the charities for help." Relief organizations were swamped. On Public Square in downtown Cleveland, where Winsor watched "hundreds of hungry and homeless men" gather daily to listen to speeches urging violence "against the government and capitalists," Alice Schmid, a "strange, short hatless woman with an enormous head of red braids" organized the city's first breadline. The number of persons seeking food became so large, the breadline was moved to the foot of East 9th Street, where "early every morning, rain or shine, a long, tragic line of ragged men stand patiently in single file outside a huge brown tent." Inside Winsor found "a small group of old women sitting in broken-down rockers waiting for their daily bread and milk."

As economic conditions worsened, many newspaper columnists "questioned whether the capitalist system could revive and return the country to prosperity." A few promoted communist or fascist solutions. Winsor eschewed revolution in his public columns and private conversation, but he did recommend to readers "a concise and brilliant arraignment of Capitalism" published by the *Saturday Review of Literature* and written by Archibald MacLeish, a prolific, forty-one-year-old poet and playwright, "the one really outstanding American poet who has appeared since Walt Whitman," in Winsor's opinion.

MacLeish charged capitalists with mismanaging the economy that had generated their wealth and power and bungling the job of defending the system by assigning the job to their publicity agents and advertising firms. As a result, "voices of a thousand copy writers went throbbing and blurbing through the land creating a picture of America so mawkish, so nauseating, and so false that the magazine which eventually appeared to satirize it became a journalistic triumph overnight." That "magazine" was *Fortune,* a monthly publication conceived specifically to cover the affairs of American capitalists, to which MacLeish was a regular contributor of critical essays.

"Ask yourselves," he wrote in the *Saturday Review,* "why a man earning five dollars a day should believe in capitalism in any of its forms." Capitalists had "ignored the necessity of giving the economic order shape and structure" so it could compete with alternative systems. MacLeish applauded "attempts to give capitalism human hope" and "a fairer distribution of wealth without the laborious and dangerous bureaucracy of state control," positions with which Winsor agreed.

In 1933, however, national unemployment rates were stuck at 25 percent, and in Cleveland conditions were worse. Officials estimated the local workforce numbered half a million. In early 1933, 219,000 individuals—more than 40 percent—couldn't find jobs. President Herbert Hoover's inability to reverse national unemployment rates led to a landslide victory for his opponent in November's election. Franklin Delano Roosevelt would be inaugurated in March.

During this same period, press historians noted that "bleakness" permeated most writers' prose. While acknowledging "the gaunt and ugly shadow of the depression," under his Noel Francis byline, Winsor was essentially optimistic, dispensing advice on how to cope with a drastically reduced income: "If you can't afford to rent a summer house . . . ask some lonely farmer permission to pitch a tent on his property. . . . Scatter sand on the road and then dance to an automobile radio." He cheered deflation when it lowered prices for males who made weekly visits to barbershops. In December, Francis had gleefully announced, "Fifteen-cent haircuts have arrived."

Under the circumstances, workers gave the highest priority to holding their jobs, yet in Winsor's first month at the *News* he risked losing his by allowing Francis to violate American newspaper propriety with an item about unconventional employment for men. While the road company was performing *Show Boat* at the Hanna, Francis wrote, "One of the highest kickers in the . . . feminine chorus is a man."

Albert Edward Myrne (A. E. M.) Bergener, managing editor at the *News,* tolerated Winsor's journalistic misbehavior. He hired Winsor and authorized his use of the nom de plume. Bergener, fifty-eight years old, was the "most sworn-at and sworn-by newspaperman" in Cleveland. Although reporters had tremendous respect for the man, his decision to hire Winsor rankled certain male employees. In the 1920s and 1930s, newspaper offices did not accept openly gay men, as compared to restaurants, department stores, hotels, and the theater. "Polly Parsons," nom de plume for society editors at the *News,* documented the profession's intolerance. She wrote that Winsor "created a raised eyebrow department among the hard-boiled reporters (they like to think so, anyway) of the *News* city room when he fluttered into an about-town column and movie reviews."

Bergener ignored the eyebrows and innuendo of his homophobic reporters and allowed a young man some thought effeminate to infiltrate an American daily newspaper's city room, traditionally a rumpled, smoky den of masculinity with liquor on its breath. George Davis and William F. McDermott, the forty-one-year-old drama critic at the *Plain Dealer,* wrote their reviews while smoking cigars. During a single workday, Falstaff smoked a hundred cigarettes. Sydney Andorn, the twenty-six-year-old about-town columnist for the *Press,* recalled that many reporters facing deadlines fortified themselves from flasks hidden in their desks. He claimed, "Every reporter had to be a character in those days to make it." His column, "The Minute Review," had the tagline "Read it while you boil an egg." Winsor claimed Andorn had pasted a picture of stage and film star Rudy Vallee over the photo on his press card.

In this droll atmosphere, Bergener and his new columnist-critic did share some attributes. They were both short and fastidious. Bergener set unusual hygiene standards for reporters: "Before coming to work, every man on the *News* must take a shower and put on a clean collar." (In the 1930s, most men's shirts had detachable collars and had made Winsor's maternal grandfather, George P. Ide, a wealthy man. He manufactured "soft" and "starched" models in Troy, New York. Winsor preferred the "Idehaven," one of his grandfather's patented "starched" collars.)

Although Winsor had the least newspaper experience of any journalist covering the world premiere, he thought he could reveal the "secret" plot of *Design for Living* under the Francis byline, if he could only talk to Coward personally. He had met the playwright at least twice: in March 1926, when Coward played Cleveland in another of his shows, *The Vortex,* and later that same summer in England, while Winsor claimed to be studying at Oxford. Winsor's Cleveland friend Leonard Converse Hanna, who was an acquaintance of Coward's, had arranged both encounters.

For introductions to celebrity playwrights, Hanna, the portly nephew of deceased U.S. senator Marcus Hanna, possessed impeccable credentials. Worth at least $20 million in 1932, he occasionally invested in plays, plus his cousins owned a theater (the same one where *Design for Living* would premiere) and a newspaper (the one that had recently hired Winsor). More important, Hanna, Coward, and Winsor shared an uncommon desire. For sexual partners, they preferred men like themselves: handsome, hard-drinking, cigarette-smoking, articulate, and amusing night people. Neither Hanna nor Winsor tried to hide these desires. Hanna, who had celebrated his forty-third birthday in December, played the role of a wise, generous older brother among Winsor's homosexual friends and news sources, an unorthodox circle that often provided the columnist with the private phone numbers that gave him an advantage over his competition.

With Hanna's help, Winsor tried to reach Coward in New York City, where *Design for Living*'s cast was rehearsing. His pursuit of the playwright is the first recorded account of an attempt by Winsor to turn a celebrity acquaintance into a quotable news source. Convincing a person of Coward's stature to tattle on himself in print requires immense charm and discretion. For a man like Winsor, who was making his debut as a newspaperman, words attributable to Coward were of enormous value. Editors would grin. Readers would tell their friends. Competitors would curse. Yet, when Winsor finally reached the playwright over a crackling long-distance phone line, he heard a cautious man. Coward's many biographers have insisted he was loath to discuss this particular play in advance of its opening for fear the subject matter might offend potential audiences. For the world premiere, he chose the United States rather than England because he suspected Lord Chamberlain, Britain's official censor, would not approve the script. Although Coward knew Winsor would applaud *Design for Living*'s theme, a rousing call for sexual liberty, the playwright still demanded that Winsor not publish details until after the opening.

Though the terms would appear to have defeated Winsor's purpose, he accepted them. While there is no record of the exact language the playwright used to explain *Design for Living*, it is a comedy about a ménage à trois, two men and a woman. Coward wrote the play for himself and the Lunts to fulfill a promise he had made the couple in 1921, when they were all living in New York City and before Lynn had married Alfred. In Manhattan, the playwright and two actors shared a cook and the dinners she prepared. In *Design for Living*, a playwright and two artists share more than a cook. Each is in love with the other two. During the course of three acts, the action and dialogue suggest that each has enjoyed the others sexually. The play was one of a handful in the 1930s that implicitly referred to homosexuality.

Because those couplings included two males, neither Winsor nor any of his contemporaries writing in American daily newspapers could have been explicit about the play's plot. There was no acceptable vocabulary. "Gay" still meant "excited with merriment" to most newspaper readers, although some men, who proudly identified themselves as "queers," used "gay" to describe the flamboyant behavior of men they dismissed as "fairies," "faggots," or "queens." Derogatory slang—"nance," "pansy," and "buttercup"—was in the same taboo newspaper lexicon as racial or ethnic slurs. The term "bisexual" was evolving and didn't necessarily mean "attracted to both males and females." For some, it implied a person who was both male and female. "Homosexual" was not in common use. When Winsor hung up the phone, he had a scoop, yet both Coward's skittishness and the lack of a benign noun or adjective to describe the play's male characters prevented him from breaking his startling news. Winsor French was not to be deterred. On Tuesday afternoon, December 20, 1932, the following paragraph appeared, as the fourth item under the Francis byline: "Noël Coward is wondering what the reactions of the public will be toward his new play, *Design for Living,* which has its premiere at the Hanna one of these days. The plot is very, very daring."

Despite a depressed economy and higher ticket prices, broad hints opened checkbooks. One week after "very, very daring" appeared in the *News,* every seat on the theater's main floor for opening night had been purchased via mail order. It was a record for the Hanna. Mimicking Francis, Archie Bell, the *News* drama critic and Winsor's colleague in the entertainment department, described what happened: "Somehow, by a sort of underground telegraph, word had filtered through that [*Design for Living*] would be very, very naughty. This whetted curiosity. There was much speculation and gossip."

Apparently, the hullabaloo initially worried the play's producer. After *Press* drama critic George Davis printed "a wildcat report that the play now being launched here is so daring in its theme that many who see the play would object to it on that account," a press agent who claimed to have read the script told Davis "it wasn't so." The public ignored the press agent's denial. The Hanna box office, according to Bell, had "so many unfilled mail orders for opening night, they would practically have filled another house to capacity."

On the night before the world premiere, after the final dress rehearsal, Coward did tell a reporter for the *Plain Dealer* that his play was about "three rather peculiar characters who loved each other very much but who found, after play of emotions between pairs, that they were incapable of division, that they were individuals who fitted into no ordinary human pattern."

For a playwright known for crisp repartee, this description was very, very abstruse. The *Plain Dealer* reporter clarified Coward's quote by citing Francis, albeit without attribution. "The theme," the reporter added, "is rumored to be ultra-sophisticated and daring." Bell's "very, very" and the *Plain Dealer*'s "daring" testify to the impact Winsor's language had on his colleagues. Yet the word "rumored" meant the *Plain Dealer* questioned the authority of Winsor's source. Readers waiting to get inside the theater believed he had inside information. For the Hanna, Winsor's words were as good as gold.

After opening night sold out, theater management satisfied pleas for tickets by flouting fire laws and renting gilt chairs, which were lined up and down the four aisles on the main floor. The illegal chairs meant there were 1,550 tickets for sale every night—200 more than the Hanna's legal capacity. Coward accepted the scheme for increasing income while endangering the audience. In a letter to his brother Erik, the playwright boasted about the demand for tickets in Cleveland. "The play is a wow here and we have to have extra chairs in the aisles."

On opening night those golden chairs, literally and metaphorically, prevented people from taking their seats. Francis fingered a member of Cleveland's City Council who took advantage of the lawbreaking: "Although chairs are verboten in theater aisles, Ex-City Manager [William R.] Hopkins sat in one."

When 8:30 finally arrived, there were more people standing than sitting, so Coward held the curtain. While he waited for the house to fill, he sat in his dressing room with Jeffrey John Archer Holmesdale, at thirty-six, the Fifth Earl of Amherst, who had traveled from England to attend the world premiere. While the audience sidled past the gold chairs, Coward and his short, blond, blue-eyed friend smoked cigarettes. Lord Amherst was the great-grandson and namesake of Sir Jeffrey Amherst, commander-in-chief of the British army during the French and Indian War. Amherst College was named for Sir Jeffrey, as well. Coward's titled pal had dabbled in American journalism. In 1927 he wrote drama reviews for Alexander Woollcott, powerful and outspoken critic at the *New York World*.

That morning the *Plain Dealer* had introduced its readers to Lord Amherst with a photograph and caption that described the aristocrat as Coward's "intimate" friend, an adjective some reporters used to suggest a romantic relationship between two males. In Amherst's account of his travels with Coward, he characterized their friendship as a "sort of two-pronged mutual admiration society." Philip Hoare, Coward's authoritative biographer, suggests that the playwright was disappointed because they had not become lovers. On matters of sex and sexuality, 1930s newspapers were notoriously unreliable.

Noël Coward's biographers agree, however, that of all his plays, *Design for Living* was the playwright's personal favorite. So at 8:45, when he finally stubbed a cigarette, smoothed his blond hair with the palm of his hand, and told the stagehands to pull the curtain, he was beginning what should have been a high point in his career.

Coward had set Act 1 in a squalid Parisian garret shared by a painter named "Otto" (played by Lunt) and an interior decorator named "Gilda" (Fontanne). Otto wasn't home when the curtain rose. Instead, Gilda had spent the night with a playwright named "Leo" (Coward). (Note the occupational and name-spelling similarities between Noël and Leo.) Early in the act, Coward announced the theme through Gilda: "Everything's glandular. . . . All the hormones in my blood are working overtime. They're rushing madly in and out of my organs like messenger boys."

Members of the audience who bought tickets based on Winsor's "daring" were to be rewarded with a witty discussion of sex and, as the play unfolded, a critique of traditional marriage. Coward's lovers grappled with their ménage à trois:

GILDA: What's the truth of it?
LEO: The actual facts are so simple. I love you. You love me. You love Otto.
    I love Otto. Otto loves you. Otto loves me. There!

More than an hour later, the curtain fell, and according to Amherst, Coward "stormed off the stage in a blind rage. It was a serious comedy. The oafs had laughed all through the first act; he'd be damned if he would go on with the play. Alfred Lunt was near to hysterics, Lynn Fontanne was in tears."

What caused the playwright's emotional outburst?

Although local drama critics and reporters sensed something was wrong on stage, they attributed any problems to opening-night jitters and acting technique. Davis claimed Coward and Fontanne had "mumbled most of their lines." In the *Plain Dealer*, McDermott wrote, all three actors were "too low pitched."

Francis published another possibility on the following afternoon. "People will tell you, by the way, that *Design for Living* is Coward's own life story."

If Winsor was correct, the playwright had just spent an hour trying to explain his love and lust for both Lynn and Alfred. When the oafs laughed, Coward could only assume they found his confession, including an implicit reference to homosexuality, absurd or depraved. The audience didn't seem to understand how seriously he felt about the passions that drove his plot.

When *Design for Living* eventually opened in New York City, two drama critics gave credence to Winsor's item as the reason for Coward's outburst. Brooks Atkinson, drama critic for the *New York Times,* sensed the playwright's desire to justify his character's emotions in the first act: "Mr. Coward writes as earnestly as a psychologist." After seeing the play twice, John Mason Brown, drama critic for the *New York Evening Post,* cited the play's first act as "a serious, though giddy, study of the intricate emotional relationship existing between two men and one woman, all of whom are deeply fond of one another."

In Cleveland, however, Coward remained adamant. He would not return to the stage. As the ten-minute intermission neared its end, Gladys Calthrop, a longtime friend of the playwright's and the artistic designer for most of his productions, approached Coward "shaking her finger." "Small of stature," according to Amherst, "but strikingly handsome . . . she upbraided Noël, reminding him that he was not . . . Sarah Bernhardt." He finally surrendered and agreed to finish the show. Stagehands dimmed the house lights, calling audience members back to their seats.

When the curtain rose on Act 2, Gilda was living with Leo in London but reviving her affair with Otto, who summarized their predicament: "Our lives are diametrically opposed to ordinary social conventions. We've got to find our own solution for our own peculiar moral problems."

By the end of Act 2, Gilda's "solution" was to leave both men to each other and a bottle of brandy.

LEO: (Resting his head on Alfred's shoulder) Will you forgive me for every-thing?
OTTO: (Emotionally) It's I who should ask you that. . . . Thank God for each other, anyhow!
LEO: That's true. We'll get along, somehow—(His voice breaks)—together.
OTTO: (Struggling with his tears) Together . . .

The curtain fell on Act 2, leaving the audience with the image of two tearful, tipsy men embracing, a stage image emphasizing intimacy. According to a *Plain Dealer* feature writer, the audience had been "astounded . . . in spots, but it was still a moot point in the lobby . . . whether everything that had been seen was a coherent understandable whole."

Design for Living was only "understandable" if you could discuss romantic love between two men, and you couldn't do that in a newspaper. For sheer irrelevance, nothing topped the chatter of the traditional society-page editors who attended the opening. Despite economic chaos, Dorothy Harman of the *News* observed a stable social order in women's clothes. "Dress, of course, featured smart winter models which always precede those of the mid-season opera styles."

If a member of the "younger set" did not know exactly what "a smart winter model" was, Cornelia Curtiss told her in the *Plain Dealer*. "Nearly every smart gown has fur trimming." To prove her point, she selected two exemplary models. The first was Mrs. Lawrence Lanier Winslow, a Cleveland heiress with an international reputation as a hostess, who "was handsomely gowned in brown velvet cut with a square neck and having short puff sleeves of beige ermine." The second was Miss Katherine Halle, an attractive blonde and oldest daughter of Samuel Halle, who owned local department stores that served Cleveland's carriage trade. The Halles were Winsor's childhood neighbors and lifelong friends. Katherine, called Kay by family and friends, had recently returned to the United States to work on Roosevelt's presidential campaign. She had been living in London and dabbling in newspaper journalism with a weekly column for the *News*.

According to Curtiss, who was considered the arbiter of traditional Cleveland society, "Miss Halle was very lovely in a black velvet gown, the shoulder straps of which were made of tiny ermine tails which extended to the waistline in back."

Yes, but what did she think about *Design for Living?* None of the society editors quoted her. Under the Francis byline, Winsor's about-town column did. "Kay Halle gaily bon mots that *Design for Living* is conclusive proof for her that three is not a crowd." Joking about a ménage à trois in a newspaper is a classic illustration of the license that was granted about-town columnists in the 1930s and denied society page editors.

Toward the end of Act 3, Leo and Otto made a spectacular entrance from the top of a Bauhaus stairway, dressed in "two of the most astounding pairs of pajamas ever seen on a stage."

Winsor saw Leo and Otto arriving on stage in risqué satin bedclothes, two handsome bon vivants only a few years older than he. They were sexually attractive to a bright and beautiful woman, as well as to each other. And they were manly! They didn't flounce. They were the antithesis of lisping, limp-wristed, supposedly comic "horticultural lads" (men called "pansy" or "buttercup") who pranced across the sets of American plays and movies in the 1930s.

On a couch with Alfred's arms around him, Leo held Gilda's hands as he defended their ménage à trois: "We have our own decencies. We have our own ethics. Our lives are a different shape from yours."

The *Plain Dealer* counted eight curtain calls, but how many people really grasped what Coward was advocating, especially those who couldn't afford three-dollar tickets and had to rely on the explanations of newspaper drama critics? In Tuesday's editions, these critics were opaque on a subject as critical as the ménage à trois.

Davis at the *Press:* Coward's comedy poses situations which couldn't be acceptable if they were presented seriously.
McDermott at the *Plain Dealer:* An unconventional variation of the triangle that would have shocked Queen Victoria and may even disturb some of her descendants.
Bell at the *News:* A strangely different triangle, with a wavering hypotenuse and two curved sides.

Because personal experience with married life might influence a critic's opinion, readers should know that Bell never married; McDermott was divorced in 1933; and Davis was in love with a woman who lived with him twenty years before accepting his marriage proposal.

Using Bell's term, what were any "curved sides" in the audience's think-ing? The newspaper critics did not write about the reaction of men for whom *Design for Living*'s "situations" were not only "acceptable" but utterly desir-able. That afternoon, Winsor didn't waste any space describing the ménage à trois. Instead, for all who had seen or would see the show during the week it played in Cleveland, the columnist made his startling announcement that Coward's friends thought *Design for Living* was autobiographical.

The playwright didn't object in print, although he was quite concerned about his press coverage in Cleveland. He dispatched his personal manager to the city room of the *News* to demand a correction from Archie Bell, who had overestimated Coward's weekly earnings. (They were $5,200 a week, not $7,500.)

Unfortunately, Winsor's candid items and Coward's silence were unknown to scholars studying this singular play in Noël Coward's oeuvre. Thus, a gen-der studies academic, Samuel D. Abel at Dartmouth College, wrote, "What has gone unmentioned, though, is the possibility of reading [*Design for Liv-ing*] as autobiography." No, Winsor French mentioned that specific "possibil-ity" about twelve hours after the curtain descended on the world premiere.

In John Lahr's book *Coward the Playwright,* the distinguished theater critic and historian writes that *Design for Living* is "Coward's comic revenge . . . , the victory of the disguised gay world over the straight one." "Dis-guised" is not the right word to describe Coward's script. Barry Day, author of *The Letters of Noël Coward,* who also helped Coward's companion Gra-ham Payn write *My Life with Noël Coward,* insists the playwright "always believed that suggestion is more interesting than statement." He was pro-viding teasing glimpses of gay relationships, not hiding them. Coinciden-tally, when Francis described the play's subject matter as "daring," it was his broad hint about unconventional sexuality, never stated explicitly, that provoked the "speculation and gossip" among newspaper columnists and the public that increased ticket sales.

Limited to innuendo, Cleveland journalists in 1933 still struggled to report a topic that their publishers, reflecting what they understood to be the public's taste, considered taboo. American newspapers exemplified Oscar Wilde's definition of homosexuality: "The love that dare not speak its name." Yet, following the premiere none of Cleveland's about-town col-umnists printed items about politicians or clergy who thought the play indecent or sinful. Instead, the public's curiosity established local records for ticket sales. Cleveland newspaper sensibilities were at odds with many readers' attitudes.

When Cleveland drama critics are compared with those writing for New York City newspapers, the local men seem positively permissive. At the *New*

York Times, Atkinson smelled the "odor of sin" hovering about *Design for Living,* while Percy Hammond at the *Herald Tribune* complained about the play's "silken obscenities." Euphemia Van Rensselaer Wyatt in the *Catholic World,* called the production "essentially rotten." Because New York City drama critics are considered the most powerful (their verdicts can close a show) and their articles are indexed in accessible publications, they are cited more often than their colleagues in smaller cities. As a result, scholars studying *Design for Living,* Coward, gender, and the media reached oversimplified and erroneous conclusions.

In Cleveland, newspaper readers discovered a new authority buried in the entertainment section of the *News,* the city's smallest daily newspaper. He was willing to amuse and inform with discreet sexual innuendo. In his column, "queers" received a subtext and local theater owners found a place to boost their income. In less than six weeks, Winsor's Noel Francis had become the most powerful and talked-about columnist covering the city's nightlife.

One drama critic, Davis at the *Press,* reminded readers about the press agent who claimed to have read *Design for Living*'s script and denied it was "daring." Davis contradicted the agent and confessed that "the wildcat report" was "correct," acknowledging Winsor's "scoop."

While basking in mutual notoriety, Winsor and Coward were invited to supper on Sunday, January 8, by Mrs. Winslow of the "beige ermine cuffs." Her parties were considered "one of the two existing bona fide salons" in the United States by no less an authority than the country's most patrician newspaperman: Lucius Beebe, a thirty-one-year-old author, playwright, and journalist. In 1933, he was writing a weekly about-town column for the *New York Herald Tribune* that was widely syndicated and which helped establish him as a national arbiter of social rank. Income from a family trust subsidized his writing career, allowing him to indulge a gourmet's appetite and a spectacular wardrobe. The young man was a member of both the National Council of the Wine and Food Society and Les Amis d'Escoffier.

The closets in his Manhattan apartment held two mink-lined overcoats. In recognition of his sartorial splendor, a trade association of merchant tailors elected Beebe "the greatest dandy of his time." Despite his aristocratic taste, Beebe had demonstrated his suitability for newspaper work in the 1930s by failing to earn a college degree. Undergraduate incidents involving alcohol had led to his being asked to leave both Yale and Harvard. Given Beebe's eccentric credentials, and lack thereof, his five-star rating of Mrs. Winslow's Sunday suppers meant Winsor and Coward accepted her invitation.

"Rudderless in a . . . sea of hospitality"

NUTWOOD FARMS, OHIO

Sunday, January 8, 1933, 7 p.m.

Mrs. Lawrence Lanier Winslow received supper guests in the drawing room at East House, which rambled room after room along a ridge overlooking Lake Erie's forested shoreline. In Cleveland's social hierarchy, the tall, slender, thirty-eight-year-old widow was very, very old money. She had inherited bundles of railroad securities from her late father, Henry K. Devereux.

Originally, East House had been her family's country place, one of several residential buildings on Nutwood Farms, where her father raised and trained world-champion trotting horses. The family's town house, and Mrs. Winslow's birthplace, was one of the most elaborate stone mansions ever erected on Cleveland's upper Euclid Avenue, the fabulous Millionaires Row. When she was eighteen years old, Aileen Devereux married diplomat Lawrence Lanier Winslow and left Cleveland for postings to U.S. embassies in Berlin and London, where she became fluent in German, Spanish, and French. When her husband died in 1929, Mrs. Winslow returned to Nutwood Farms with a son and two daughters, whom she called "Peter, Patter and Petsey." (The first names on their birth certificates were Lawrence, Mildred, and Aileen.)

In Winsor's opinion, East House was a "Victorian museum," where Mrs. Winslow maintained an enviable schedule. "She went to bed when she was tired, got up again when she felt rested, ate when she was hungry." As a hostess, she would "plan to sit down to supper at eight o'clock with half a dozen guests, and end up wandering into the dining room at midnight with fifty." Winsor attributed the success of her salon to Binnie Corrigan, "a beautiful, militant Irish woman," who ran East House. "Without Binnie," he wrote, "Mrs. Winslow would have been rudderless in a tempestuous sea of hospitality."

Of her supper guests, Mrs. Winslow "asked only that they shouldn't be boring." In her drawing room, they sat on "somewhat battered settees" or "sofas done up in horsehair." Winsor recalled an "inlaid rosewood grand piano" stood in a bay window, where Mrs. Winslow would invite someone like Coward to play his latest compositions. On this particular occasion, however, that was not how her weekend guests amused themselves. Instead, according to Francis, they played the "latest parlor game to sweep the polite circles."

Participants selected a famous person, then asked the others to guess who it was by giving them hints in the form of a flower, animal, car, time of day, or music. When it was Coward's turn, he asked the group who was a "cut tiger lily, a half-tamed eagle, a fast and snappy roadster, three o'clock in the morning, and the music of Gershwin and Berlin." After numerous wrong answers, Mrs. Winslow's guests admitted they were stumped. When asked whom he had chosen, the playwright answered, "Noël Coward."

Why would he describe himself as a "half-tamed eagle," a winged predator? Coward biographer Philip Hoare offers a possible explanation. "Noël was staying with a family in Cleveland" and "fell hopelessly in love with the young son of the household." Peter Winslow, by all accounts a handsome youth, was seventeen in 1933. Mrs. Winslow may have been the only mother in Ohio who would have shown no signs of alarm at Coward's infatuation. She "was truly a tolerant woman," Winsor wrote. "Nothing disturbed her."

But was the playwright disturbed? His gaming skills evaporated. During the late afternoon, Peter's mother "calmly nicked Noël Coward, who is a glutton for punishment, of $15 at backgammon, and then took $40 more away from him during the evening." The sum was almost twice the average salary—$30 a week—paid newspaper reporters and schoolteachers in 1933. "Don't feel sorry" for Coward, Francis wrote. "Think of the $26,000 business his play did last week."

Coward's intriguing autobiographical confession and the details of his gaming losses, extravagant in a depressed economy, appeared in a single newspaper: The News, under the byline of Noel Francis. Eyewitness accounts of celebrities at play in private homes seldom appeared in American newspapers. "Private parties were truly private," according to journalist and critic Brendan Gill. "Reporters and photographers were not expected to mingle with guests."

Mrs. Winslow did not invite Winsor's competitors to her salon. He alone had access to the hostess and her guests, an international circle in 1933 that included Edward, the Prince of Wales and heir to the British throne. Her friends, according to Winsor, "provided her with so many interesting things to say"—the perfect source for an about-town columnist.

The ability to charm a wealthy, smart, sophisticated woman was a talent Winsor began developing in his teens. He trained with a partner, his childhood friend and neighbor Jerome Zerbe. They both "detested school," had crushes on other boys, and were destined to play key roles in Cleveland newspaper and magazine history. Winsor would document café society with an about-town column, Zerbe with a camera. Before embarking on their careers, each acquired a skill critical to his future success: how to crash private parties in a manner that delighted their surprised hosts.

According to Gill, Zerbe's acquaintance and biographer, the young men knew how to present themselves to society. They cherished "first class . . . dinner clothes." Their evening shirts were "spotlessly laundered and ironed." During one Christmas holiday, by Zerbe's account, he and Winsor found themselves "without an invitation to a dance, but the morning's *Plain Dealer* noted that evening Mr. and Mrs. Whosebaum were presenting their daughter to society at the Union Club. As my friend Winsor French and I had nothing better to do, we dined at his house and went to the club, where we were both so well known that no one even thought to check the list. We went down the receiving line, gave our correct names, saw quick glances between debutante and parents, along with shoulder shrugs, and knew we had clear sailing. . . . I even gave the deb a twirl. As she was neither a good dancer nor amusing, we never put her on our own lists."

For those who were worthy of being added to their lists, especially those whose wealth far exceeded Winsor's and Zerbe's own earnings, there was another set of rules. To enjoy the company of wealthy persons, Zerbe insisted, "You don't have to be really rich, but you must make the effort within the limits of your pocketbook to reciprocate hospitality and make gestures toward maintaining your friendships." As a result, both young men launched what Gill called "exceptionally strenuous" social lives. As adults, both lunched and dined out "some eight or ten times a week."

In 1925, when Winsor and Zerbe were twenty-one years old and still polishing their social skills, Calvin Coolidge, a notoriously taciturn Vermonter committed to doing nothing that would disturb the national mood of self-satisfaction, occupied the White House. At the same time, two men hell-bent on revolutionizing American magazine journalism became Cleveland residents. Briton Hadden and Henry Luce, the founders of *TIME*, moved their two-year-old newsweekly's editorial and production offices to the city's warehouse district.

In comparison to local newspaper journalists, Hadden and Luce, both twenty-seven years old, were American aristocrats. They met at Hotch-kiss, one of America's most expensive boarding schools, and attended Yale, where they were elected to the university's most exclusive secret society, Skull and Bones. At graduation, classmates voted Luce the "most brilliant," Hadden, the "most likely to succeed."

Their weekly newsmagazine was one of a half-dozen general circulation magazines launched in the 1920s that responded to the interests of a growing middle class and changed the content and style of American print journalism. *TIME* sorted, condensed, and interpreted national and international current events in simply written stories with colorful details and a style of "flippant urbanity." The best of the new publications helped raise journalism standards with "serious and entertaining writing" about public affairs.

Despite *TIME*'s unique content, when its staff arrived in Cleveland in August 1925, the magazine was losing money. Luce had been desperately searching for ways to reduce production costs and the time required to mail the magazine to subscribers. His solution was to transport the publication from New York City to the Midwest, where it would be closer to most of its readers. Luce traveled alone to Cleveland and signed a contract with John Penton, an industrial printer. When Hadden discovered his partner's actions, he vehemently opposed leaving New York City and objected to Cleveland because it was "devoid of news sources" and advertising executives who could buy space in the magazine. Luce fought back by seeking support from *TIME*'s business and circulation manager, Roy Larsen, a twenty-six-year-old Harvard graduate, whose priority was profit. The magazine's "sole purpose was to make money," Larsen declared, so he backed Luce, forcing Hadden to acquiesce.

In Cleveland, Luce and his first wife, Lila, who was expecting a child, set up housekeeping in Cleveland Heights, where they "lived quietly," according to Winsor, and "moved in country club circles." Hadden, "lost and lonely . . . roared and bellowed" in a downtown "bachelor apartment." Late at night, Hadden prowled the "speakeasy and honky-tonk district" where his only friends were "a few carefully chosen" individuals that he "regarded as traitors to their own environment." Their behavior was "outlandish, questionable or wicked." Two young men who satisfied Hadden's requirements for friendship were Zerbe and Winsor.

During the spring of 1926, Hadden organized an amateur baseball team, the Crescent Athletic Club. He recruited nine hard-drinking, rowdy young male athletes in their twenties and dressed them in gaudy green uniforms. Winsor was the tenth team member, the club's twenty-one-year-old batboy. The men competed in a sandlot league, and Winsor claimed they compiled a twenty-game losing streak.

Winsor saw even more of Hadden when the editor began dating Zerbe's sister Margaret and attempted to persuade Winsor's stepfather, Joseph O. Eaton, a wealthy manufacturer of truck axles, to invest in *TIME*. In 1927, when Winsor was looking for work, Hadden told him to apply for a job in the magazine's research department, run by a Faith Willcox.

So Winsor made an appointment with the woman and recalled that she handed him "a written examination on national and foreign affairs, science, religion and so on, that would have staggered a college professor. It staggered me to the point I explained I had parked my car by a fireplug and would have to move it. Move it I did, right back into the family garage."

A few days later, over drinks, Winsor told Hadden the news quiz was "a stupid way to hire anybody. There are geniuses running around the world who haven't the faintest idea who some obscure prime minister is." Subsequently, Winsor received "a call from Miss Willcox and was put to work in the research department. Not because I was equipped for the job, as she carefully pointed out." On *TIME*'s masthead, Winsor first appeared as a "weekly contributor" on May 23, 1927, one of an editorial staff that totaled seventeen people, including Hadden and Luce. Winsor's accounts of his employment made him an important source for both *TIME*'s historians and Hadden's biographers.

When she hired her boss's batboy and drinking buddy, Willcox broke her department's gender barrier: Winsor was her only male employee. He checked facts and wrote occasional articles. "Everyone was on everyone else's neck," Winsor recalled, "everyone was always shouting at someone and Faith Willcox . . . was always on the verge of tears."

Hadden's temper was "quick" and "violent," and he hated tears. He "thought nothing of putting in twenty-four-hour days when the pressure was intense and consequently saw no reason why anyone else, male or female, shouldn't and couldn't do the same."

A month after Winsor joined the research department, Hadden suddenly promoted him to "chief of research with orders to fire everyone on the existing staff." The reason? "They were a jittery, chattering bunch of women who cried."

Winsor thought the decision "practically amounted to madness, as the magazine was just going to press." But he did what he was told. To proofread the magazine at the printer, Winsor hired several secretaries who worked for his stepfather. His resourcefulness earned Hadden's respect.

After two years in Cleveland, Luce's midwestern strategy worked. Mailing time was reduced, circulation increased; the locally owned Central National Bank provided a short-term, no-interest loan for working capital; and *TIME* began earning profits. Yet despite financial success, Hadden had become increasingly depressed in Cleveland and spent most weekends in New York City. During this same period, his *TIME* colleagues claimed that he had become a "full-blown alcoholic." He broke up with Margaret Zerbe, who began dating the circulation manager, Roy Larsen. Within six months they were married, and TIME Inc. became a permanent part of the Zerbe family.

Confident about the magazine's future, Luce and his wife sailed to Europe for a vacation. While his partner was abroad, Hadden decided *TIME*'s stronger finances meant he could end his Cleveland exile and return to Manhattan. He bullied his reluctant partner, and they rented space at 25 West 45th Street, one floor below the *New Yorker.*

In July 1927, Winsor followed Hadden and explained his decision in a letter to his friend Kay Halle. "Mad as I get with Brit—unbelievably disagreeable as he is most of the time, I could never leave this job because it is an inspiration to work for the man—and you can't help admiring him and being fond of him. . . . *TIME* is certainly the absolute expression of everything that he stands for. . . . The damn magazine is his mind, his personality—his very existence."

Winsor's admiration had its limits, however. When he arrived in Manhattan, he asked Hadden for a raise. The editor replied, "Take it or leave it." Winsor accepted his existing salary and told his family why. "He can always get people to work for even less than I am. . . . I have letters from all over the country from people who have had great experience that will take any salary at all." One of those individuals who caught Winsor's attention was "a high school dropout from Pottsville, Pennsylvania who arrived at the office in a moth-eaten raccoon coat." John O'Hara, the future novelist and author of *Pal Joey,* would become Winsor's lifelong friend.

Winsor wrote his family telling them how he supplemented *TIME*'s tiny paychecks. "I am working graft with the theatre man and the book editor." The book editor was Hadden's cousin, Noel Busch, who also wrote "insulting movie reviews" that amused Winsor. Whenever he wanted a book, he told Busch, who called the publisher, claiming he'd misplaced a review copy. Of course, the publisher sent him a replacement. For theater tickets, Winsor used the name of a drama critic who no longer worked for *TIME* but still reviewed "shows for several New Jersey papers and so I make the various press men crash through with tickets and we split them."

In New York City, Winsor's relations with Hadden improved. "B.H. and I are getting along much better, in fact had dinner twice last week," Winsor wrote his stepfather. "I think he is simply awfully worried, although now I am really quite encouraged about the state of the magazine. Clearing out all that old wood was perhaps after all a pretty good thing."

In addition to cadging books and theater tickets, on at least one occasion Winsor put a hotel supper on his stepfather's account. "You must have been desperate and very hungry when you ate $6.05 worth of food at one meal," Eaton wrote after receiving the invoice. "Perhaps you had a starving friend with you. At any rate I am paying the bill."

Subsequently, Hadden made Winsor his "confidential" secretary. "I was put at a desk outside Hadden's office with orders that I was never to have as much as a piece of paper or pencil in evidence. 'Executives,' said Brit, 'should never work. Only give orders.' So I never worked."

From his privileged position, Winsor learned that Hadden was borrowing $2,500 to buy a cooperative apartment in a posh East Side neighborhood. According to a typescript of an interview with Winsor in *TIME*'s archive, "French thought Hadden was living over his head and told somebody about it." Hadden eventually learned about his "confidential" secretary's indiscreet tongue and was "incensed."

"Some time later," Winsor wrote, "I took a phone call for Hadden from a man wanting to lunch with him several days later. Consulting his engagement pad I saw the only appointment that day was one with me. It was for 12 noon and read, 'Oust French.' The day and the moment arrived, the buzzer buzzed and I walked into the office and was offered a chair. It wouldn't be necessary, I told him. What I had to say would only take a second. I was quitting. Hadden's roars could have been heard for blocks." But Hadden treated Winsor to a "two-hour lunch of Martinis" at the Yale Club, "during which he talked about nothing except baseball and possible candidates for my former job."

Winsor liked to boast about getting the axe from a founder of *TIME*, yet he always ended the accounts with Hadden picking up their bar tab. He did not want a listener to have the impression that their relationship was trivial. Yes, Hadden fired Winsor, but the two-hour lunch proved that the pioneering editor, "one of the few authentic geniuses it has ever been my good fortune to know," respected his callow ex-secretary. Winsor considered Hadden a "rebel" among *TIME*'s executives and appreciated his "robust curiosity," which "attracted him to unusual and odd people." Others, including cofounder Luce, had not taken Winsor seriously. He felt belittled as an "effeminate young man."

Coupled with the published accounts of "raised eyebrows" at the *News*, Winsor's experience testifies to the homophobia he encountered among America's journalists in the 1920s and '30s. Newspaper and magazine editorial departments were not bastions of tolerance; they reflected prevailing public attitudes. Winsor's name disappears from *TIME* after September 1928.

After Hadden lubricated his departure from *TIME*, Winsor did not retreat to Cleveland but enrolled in writing courses at Columbia University with the goal of improving his skills as a novelist or playwright. He eventually ran out of money, returned to his family's home in Cleveland Heights, and took a job as an "advertising agent" for a local firm. Less than a year later, he quit and joined Stuart Walker's Stock Company, an acting troupe that performed at the Portmanteau Theater in Cincinnati and toured throughout Ohio.

Every year, Walker auditioned ambitious acting students for the position of "disciples," his term for trainees who filled small parts in his summer productions. Walker minimized scenery, costumes, and props. Instead, he taught his disciples to emphasize "charm of expression . . . , an appeal to the imagination by the very simplicity of the ensemble." An actor's voice was his most important tool. In developing vocal talent, according to one former disciple, Walker was a "bully" who used "sarcasm as a lash, working himself into frightful rages."

Walker's priority and personality, as well as the timing of Winsor's membership in the acting company, may explain a dramatic change in the columnist's persona. At least one *TIME* employee remembered Winsor as a "soprano," an affectation that some young homosexuals during the 1920s "used to express their feminine side." After a summer with Walker, Winsor had developed a deep, sometimes explosive baritone, a masculine voice that he used, according to friends, to dramatize his repartee.

Yet neither advertising nor acting was Winsor's future. His melodramatic introduction to journalism at *TIME* had determined his career. Every time Roy and Margaret Larsen visited the Zerbe family in Cleveland, Roy would regale his brother-in-law and Winsor with stories about how TIME Inc. was making him wealthy and influential. He also told them that Hadden was not the whirlwind personality they had known in Cleveland. He lacked energy, was physically weak, and ran a constant fever. In late 1928, Hadden was admitted to a hospital and diagnosed with a bacterial infection of the bloodstream. For a few weeks, he edited *TIME* in bed, but his condition steadily worsened, and in February 1929 he died at the age of thirty-one.

Winsor had lost his genius mentor but not the desire to follow his example. Later that year, Winsor began talking to Zerbe about starting a biweekly magazine in Cleveland that would combine the "cultural attributes of *Vanity Fair* and the *New Yorker*." Winsor named the publication *PARADE*. As Hadden had tried to persuade Winsor's stepfather to invest in *TIME,* Winsor began pitching *PARADE* to potential financial backers. In late 1930, he approached W. Holden White, the twenty-five-year-old heir to a local manufacturing fortune (steam-driven automobiles, sewing machines, and screws), who agreed to provide the capital. With money to pay staff, Winsor convinced Zerbe to accept the position of art director at $35 a week and set about recruiting a handful of male writers. Several were recent Ivy League college graduates, decidedly better educated than the reporters employed by the city's daily newspapers.

Two noteworthy examples, who helped establish *PARADE*'s irreverent tone, were Joseph Bryan III and Alan R. Jackson. They gave up jobs with *TIME* and *Fortune* in New York City and moved to Cleveland to work for *PARADE*. Both men were twenty-seven years old and graduates of Princeton (Class of 1927). Bryan had been voted "the most entertaining and wittiest member of his class," and *Vanity Fair* had published his article titled

"In Philanderers' Fields." For *Fortune,* Jackson wrote "Budget for a Speakeasy" and "Budget for a Debutante." Winsor preferred writers with a flair for satire. (*PARADE*'s office boy was apparently the direct descendant of English royalty: "Lancaster Plantagenet.")

The first issue was published in March 1931. The masthead listed Winsor French and Noel Francis among several associate editors. Francis wrote an about-town column provocatively headlined "The Pointing Finger." Francis coyly compared himself to George Francis, a handsome reader, who reportedly had "been complaining bitterly lately because people continually insist upon mixing his name with ours and giving him the credit, or blame— whichever way you want to take it—for writing this column. . . . But we really feel we ought to put you straight. It isn't George, although we're young and blond too, but then, not quite so young, no—nor so blond either."

Winsor's former associates at *TIME* took note of the new publication, calling it a "trim, well-mounted magazine which came creditably close to its aim: a smartchart for Cleveland." ("Smartchart" was a term *TIME* coined for a bright, sophisticated printed journal.) *TIME* compared *PARADE* to two magazines with national circulations. "In vitality of photograph it easily equaled *Town & Country,*" a monthly that slanted its editorial content to the peculiar needs of white, Anglo-Saxon Protestant readers of wealth and social pretension. *TIME* also thought *PARADE*'s "text and drawing exhibited well the *New Yorker* technique but missed the master's polished cough and sigh." French was described as "a vivacious adman, versifier, socialite"; Zerbe was identified as "an able sketcher" and given credit for the "excellence of photography and art."

In fact, it was at *PARADE* that Zerbe traded his pencils and sketchbook for a camera and film. With the charm and chutzpah he used to crash debutante balls, he convinced prominent women to sit for portraits in *PARADE*'s studio, violating a Cleveland tradition that there were only two times a woman's picture should appear in a newspaper: her engagement and wedding. Zerbe persuaded women to use their portraits to publicize their charitable work, the first step in his remarkable career as a photographer.

While Zerbe was soothing women's egos, Winsor enraged one. In *PARADE*'s third issue, Francis ran an item about "rumored" romances between well-known Clevelanders in what appeared to be a satire on kiss-and-tell items that were the staple of some newspaper gossip columns. For one of his unlikely couples, the columnist paired Margaret Cotton, a slender, socially ambitious, and single member of Cleveland's Junior League, with Phil Selznick, the stocky, married owner of the Club Madrid, a popular speakeasy in "a large down-at-the-heels brick house" on Euclid Avenue. Selznick thought he was the spit and image of the handsome heavyweight boxer Luis Angel Firpo, Wild Bull of the Pampas. As the emcee of his own floorshow, Selznick would strip to the waist and throw punches à la Firpo. Francis thought readers would laugh at the absurdity of a society miss flirting with a déclassé exhibitionist.

Miss Cotton was not amused.

In the magazine's fifth issue, Winsor apologized. "*PARADE* sincerely regrets that the intent of the item . . . was misinterpreted . . . and as evidence of the seriousness with which her protest was regarded, announces that Mr. Noel Francis no longer is a member of the staff." Winsor fired his nom de plume. (Hadden had used a similar device at *TIME*. He listed "Peter Matthew" on the masthead, a nonexistent editor named for two apostles. Hadden blamed him for all of *TIME*'s errors.) Winsor continued to write the about-town column, under a more subdued headline: "So I've Heard." At first, he used his own name, but as the economy continued to deteriorate, he changed his byline to "Hobo."

Winsor's use of pseudonyms raises a question. Did he use "Hobo" or "Noel Francis" as a mask to protect himself from homophobes? The evidence at *PARADE* suggests the opposite. His most explicit discussions of sexuality occurred in book and drama reviews signed "Winsor French." In a review of Virginia Woolf's *The Waves,* a book he admired enormously, he wrote about the psychological impact of unconventional sexual desire on the personality of a fictional character named Neville. He was "dreamily poetic," but "too homosexual to face realities courageously, finding life bewildering, suffocating."

On another occasion, he reviewed *The House of Men,* a "manuscript play" by Charles Price Green, produced by the University Players of Western Reserve, a group specializing in work by "inexperienced but sincere beginners."

In Price's play, a mother decides that her fourth son will "be anything except what his brothers were." She "kept him close," producing a boy who was "sensitive and poetic," but also "timid and introspective. . . . No one understood him or bothered to try—and other children made his life hideous with their teasing and bullying. In the end . . . he throws himself into the swollen river and drowns."

The playwright's "mama's boy" embodies a classic stereotype of the homosexual male. To make his character more believable, Winsor suggested the boy's "timidity and sensitiveness" should be "more questioning and less cowering." He also objected to the actor's portrayal of "a rather wretched, weak sort of person, utterly incapable of standing up for himself. On the slightest provocation he would run, tail between his legs, to clutch at his mother's frail apron strings. He would have been far more sympathetic a character if he had been a little less dependent."

In addition to literary and dramatic criticism, Winsor also wrote two-thousand-word articles about local personalities and institutions, loosely following patterns set by *Vanity Fair* and the *New Yorker*, but filled with details and historical context Winsor had personally observed in the 1920s and early 1930s: "Broken-down old troupers . . . went wearily through their routines, forever hopeful of finding a way back to the 'big time,' even through so ignominious a rear door" as Luna Park.

"From the very beginning of its sickly existence," the Cleveland Zoo "has been a constant, pricking sorrow to imaginative children."

Although he was only twenty-six, his reportage reflected skepticism about early-twentieth-century progress: "Radio, aviation and the automobile have come to make life hideous."

In "Airport 1931," for example, Winsor documented the public's fascination with aviation and attempts by entrepreneurs to exploit that interest. He recalled how on Sundays during the summer of 1925, "great crowds of people thronged curiously through the potholed streets of west side Cleveland to stare in dumb wonder as planes landed and soared again by the scores." A school of aviation "hired fantastic barkers to stand before their hangar and in true circus style beg the passers-by to discover for themselves the fascination of flying. Like sideshow screamers they shouted incredible aeronautical news to delighted crowds, sometimes true, sometimes not—all depending upon the special embroidering talents of the individual as he yelped his glowing account of famous flights and records."

Despite Winsor's unusual profiles and criticism, *PARADE* did not thrive in a ruthlessly depressed economy, and it ceased publication in July 1932. Winsor's friend Roy Larsen at TIME Inc. eventually purchased the name, then sold the title to another publisher. Several owners later, *PARADE* still exists as a magazine supplement distributed with Sunday newspapers.

That summer, however, Winsor joined Francis in the ranks of the unemployed. In November, they were offered and accepted jobs at the *News*, where they soon generated items in competing newspapers' about-town columns. In the *Plain Dealer*'s "Footlights and Bright Lights," Glenn C. Pullen exposed Francis as the creation of Winsor French, calling him a "humorist," a patronizing term for "one who has some peculiarity or eccentricity of character, which he indulges in odd or whimsical ways." How did Winsor allegedly indulge his "peculiar character"? At a local nightclub, Pullen observed Winsor trying "to start a new style by wearing bedroom slippers."

Pullen, a twenty-eight-year-old high school graduate found his formal education was insufficient for a successful newspaper career, as had many of his newspaper colleagues. To qualify for assignments as a drama critic, he had begun reading the plays of August Strindberg, Henrik Ibsen, and

Anton Chekhov. For the subtleties of men's evening dress, however, Pullen was given a crash course by friends of Francis, who sent him "clippings of photographs of evening slippers" so that he could "differentiate between them and bedroom slippers." Low-heeled velvet pumps were de rigueur for Winsor at nightclub and theater openings because he wore evening clothes, the sort that he and Zerbe cherished. His hard-boiled competitors wore dark wool business suits and black leather brogans.

A snickering, unsophisticated local columnist could not derail Winsor's career. He aspired to a national audience and boasted about scooping America's most famous about-town columnist: Walter Winchell. "W.W. announced in his column yesterday that Warner Brothers' New York studios would close. So did I—only days ago"; and "Ruth Cambridge, Winchell's 'good girl Friday,' finally married [actor] Buddy Ebsen. I told you she would months ago."

The *News* bought Winchell's syndicated columns and published them a few pages in front of Francis. For Winsor, the least attractive items were the ones where Winchell baited "queers." Everyone who knew the man, according to the columnist's biographer Neal Gabler, agreed, "there wasn't a discriminatory bone in his body—except when it came to homosexuals." In the *News,* Winchell's columns were often littered with coarse jokes:

> Among the current quips amusing the Broadway fraternity . . . is that one concerning the two old-time chorus boys, who lost their tempers and engaged in a fierce quarrel.
> "Oh," shrieked the first exasperated pansy, "kiss my foot!"
> "See here!" snapped the other whoops m'dear, "we're fighting not romancing!"

Winchell liked to poke fun at male celebrities whose behavior he thought was unmanly. Winsor used Francis to defend Winchell's victims, including Spanish pianist José Iturbi. "Like many foreigners, he wears a bracelet for identification and can't understand why people snicker. Untrue publicity seldom bothers him, but he was slightly startled to read in the world's most famous column that he was planning a divorce. He has been a widower for six years."

Yet Winsor's boldest criticism of Winchell came only days after *Design for Living*'s premiere in Cleveland. Francis ran an item about Eugene Malin, a six-foot, two-hundred-pound entertainer and former female impersonator, who packed patrons into Manhattan and Hollywood nightclubs as "Jean" Malin, a proudly effeminate emcee.

He wrote: "Jean Malin, who Winchell described as the sort of person 'who wears a flower in his buttonhole because it won't stay in his hair'—may be the sensation of Hollywood with his new night club, but the person who took him to the snobbish Mayfair club lost his membership."

Utilizing Winchell's transparent code, Francis accused Cleveland's Mayfair Club of discriminating against homosexuals and punishing their hosts. Francis was demanding respect for "pansies" and "whoops m'dears," an extraordinary opinion for a newspaper columnist in 1933, when mainstream media wouldn't so much as write about those who practiced outré behavior, let alone defend them.

Local readers sometimes compared Francis to "the world's most famous columnist." They meant to be complimentary. Winsor was not pleased, and he said so under the Francis byline. "I am not trying to be a Cleveland Winchell!"

With his journalistic intentions clear and his newspaper debut successfully behind him, the columnist took a vacation at the end of July 1933. "That's all for two weeks." Before he was "off for the east," Winsor gave readers his latest hangover remedy: "A few nips of olive oil before you step out on the town will help no end to keep your head clear."

Where was he going? New York City. In a new 1932 Ford coupe, Winsor spent an entire Sunday crossing the length of a merciless Pennsylvania. "They would let you choke before breaking the blue law, claiming it's naughty to serve three-point-two on the Sabbath." On August 1, he reached Manhattan, "sweltering under unbelievable heat. The nightclubs are perspiring in darkness, but you will find the speakeasies frantic with gayety."

Speakeasies were not what drew Winsor to New York. He was headed for an address on Park Avenue to meet his fiancée and listen to his future mother-in-law's plans for their wedding. He was in love with a woman.

"Please bear with my incoherence"

Winsor and Miss Margaret Frueauff, an enchanting combination of Broadway pizzazz and inherited wealth, sat in the backseat of her mother's limousine and watched "squadrons of police" restrain the crowds outside the Music Box Theatre. Giddy adults cheered as faces familiar from newspaper and magazine articles arrived for the New York premiere of Irving Berlin and Moss Hart's new musical revue, *As Thousands Cheer.*

When the Frueauffs' chauffeur opened the limousine's passenger door, rubberneckers recognized the female occupant and shouted her stage name: "Margaret Perry." Begging for autographs, they swarmed like fruit flies around "a beautiful . . . tawny-haired . . . little actress," to use Winsor's description. "Little" was not a disparaging word. In person, Margaret stood several inches shorter than the columnist. In Manhattan society, however, she was quite a bit taller. Her father was the late Frank W. Frueauff, a utility millionaire and director of more than a hundred corporations before he died in 1922, leaving a fortune to Margaret's mother. Under her maiden name, Antoinette or "Tony" Perry, Mrs. Frueauff was a show business legend. (The American Theater Wing's Tony Awards for theater excellence are named in her honor.)

In 1929, she had directed *Strictly Dishonorable,* a romantic comedy combining "fairy tale and sex." At the time, her daughter was enrolled at a Manhattan finishing school: Miss Hewitt's. After lunch, on a December afternoon, the Frueauff limousine arrived unexpectedly at school, and Mrs. Frueauff "snatched" her daughter from a classroom. In the car, she informed Margaret that she had just dismissed the female star of *Strictly Dishonorable.* The press was told "mumps" or "chicken pox" had forced her to "withdraw" from the cast, but in fact the temperamental actress had slapped her leading man. Mrs. Frueauff had "something like six hours" to find a replacement or refund a full house of disgruntled ticket holders.

The show must go on, so Mrs. Frueauff told her daughter she would be replacing the star at that night's performance. Margaret had seen only "four rehearsals," so her mother reached into her "over-sized handbag" and drew out a script. While they were driven to the Avon Theater in Times Square, mother began drilling daughter with the lines the playwright had written for a sexually curious young woman from Mississippi. At the end of the first act, the male lead, a womanizing opera tenor, would remove Margaret's clothes while dressing her in a pair of his own silk pajamas. With her mother's coaching, Margaret memorized the lines, sweetened the drawl, perfected the striptease, and stunned Broadway with her debut. "Margaret," Winsor wrote, "literally became a star overnight."

She was sixteen years old.

Four years later, Winsor slipped "a cigar band" on her ring finger and asked her to marry him. She said she would, and although circumstantial evidence suggests Mrs. Frueauff may have had reservations, she accepted her daughter's choice. Mrs. Frueauff did not have a show in rehearsal during fall 1933, so she lavished her talent for dramatizing life's singular events on her daughter's wedding. The ceremony was scheduled for 4:30 P.M. on Saturday, September 30, in St. Thomas Church on 5th Avenue.

Then Mrs. Frueauff learned that Berlin, America's most popular and prolific songwriter ("God Bless America"), would open *As Thousands Cheer,* at 8:45 P.M. on the same night. The mother of the bride would not allow her daughter to be upstaged by Berlin, yet she did not care to compete with him for an audience in New York City. So Mrs. Frueauff postponed her own production for a week and moved it to another church with the same seating capacity (forty rows of pews) but a more opulent proscenium: the glittering glass mosaics of St. Bartholomew's Church on Park Avenue.

With her wedding postponed, Margaret, like most of Broadway's aristocracy, bought tickets for *As Thousands Cheer,* so that she and Winsor could attend the opening. At the Music Box, the crowd propelled the petite couple toward the theater's entrance. "Noel Francis" recorded the event for his readers in Cleveland, focusing on celebrity members of his own generation, the so-called younger set that newspaper publishers were anxiously trying to cultivate. He spotted actress Janet Gaynor surrounded by fans. Already the veteran of thirty-seven silent films and ten "talkies," Gaynor was twenty-six years old. A new organization promoting film, the Academy of Motion Picture Arts and Sciences, had recently handed her its first Best Actress award, in the form of a gold statuette that was not yet nicknamed "Oscar." Winsor didn't believe Gaynor deserved acting awards: "Her perpetual coyness, goodness and cunning little fits of temper practically drive me from the theater."

As he scoured the crowd for more items, Winsor displayed an eye for pelts. "Silver foxes" embraced Marlene Dietrich. Three years earlier, her portrayal of Lola-Lola, "an erotic and aggressive" cabaret singer in *The Blue Angel,* had shocked audiences at the film's premiere in Berlin. The future star, whose voice was considered the "incarnation of sex," was still struggling to launch a career in Hollywood. She was thirty-one.

Following Dietrich was Barbara Hutton Mdivani, who "drifted down the aisle . . . in ermine and diamonds." She had just inherited a Woolworth's five-and-dime-store fortune—$50 millions—and divorced her second husband, Russian prince Alexis Mdivani. Hutton was twenty-one.

Precisely at 8:45 P.M., Berlin's overture began. Winsor, who was one of more than a dozen newspaper columnists attending the premiere, searched nearby seats for familiar faces. Behind Barbara Hutton he spied Fred Astaire, who had recently abandoned the Broadway stage for Hollywood studios. He had just finished the first of five films with a twenty-two-year-old actress named Ginger Rogers, movies that would "embody the fantasy life of depression era America" and "redefine the entire notion of popular dance on the screen." Astaire, who was eventually called the twentieth century's "greatest song-and-dance man," was thirty-four.

Berlin measured the running time of *As Thousands Cheer* in seconds. House lights dimmed at 8:49.50, which was when Winsor saw a dim figure "swathed in chinchilla and dripping orchids" rush to a seat on the aisle.

Winsor knew the chinchilla. It belonged to Mrs. Libby Holman Reynolds, a woman with absolute rights to the title "torch singer." Winsor claimed "a freak tonsil" had created her "guttural, dusky voice." Others noted "unreliable pitch" and "a tendency to swallow whole phrases" but celebrated her skill at combining "toughness and vulnerability," the emotional essence of her bluesy repertoire. Reynolds was making her first public appearance since the birth of her son, Christopher, and the death of the boy's father, Z. Smith Reynolds. Like Barbara Hutton, Reynolds had been the heir to a family fortune: millions of tobacco dollars. He and Libby had lived on his estate in South Carolina. There, after a small dinner party in 1932, Reynolds was shot, fell into Libby's arms, and died. He was twenty-one.

More than a few people at the Music Box thought Libby had pulled the trigger. South Carolina prosecutors accused her of murder but eventually dropped charges because of insufficient evidence. Many friends had abandoned the singer, but not Winsor and Margaret. They were planning a honeymoon that included a week in Havana with Libby and her lover, Luisa d'Andelot Carpenter Jenney, the daughter of a du Pont, who was in the process of divorcing her husband, John Lord King Jenney, an executive in her mother's family's chemical company. Luisa Jenney, who owned at least a million dollars worth of Du Pont stock, was not shy about her sexuality. She often appeared publicly in men's suits and ties. She was twenty-six years old.

Despite Libby's exceptional companion and the murky circumstances surrounding the death of her husband, Francis consistently defended her: "Let's have the truth at last. . . . She lives quietly at Watch Hill [Rhode Island], with two very necessary guards for her son. Tanned to an ebony color, she seldom wears anything but white and is spectacularly beautiful in the evening." Winsor called her detractors "the people who love to wreck reputations." The widowed mother was twenty-nine.

At 8:50 P.M., what appeared to be a newspaper headline flashed above the Music Box proscenium:

MAN BITES DOG

At the same moment, stage curtains "plastered with magnified newsprint" rose and revealed a Park Avenue dining room where a testy husband watched his wife fuss over a Pekinese. The Peke bit the husband, who bit the dog in return.

Blackout.

Lights up on a newspaperman's desk equipped with a telephone, wicker basket, and an inkwell. An excited editor had just stopped the presses so he could publish the journalist's classic three-word definition of news: "Man Bites Dog." A chorus of nimble newsmen vilified the canine:

Not a great big manly he-dog,
A little she-dog—a bitch—which
Gives us a headline off the beaten track:
A bitch bit a man and the man bit the bitch right back.

Berlin and Hart, the show's sarcastic twenty-nine-year-old librettist, were satirizing American newspapers. One of Berlin's biographers, Laurence Bergreen, claimed the collaborators' "ultimate target" was that "prowling, oversimplifying, unpredictable fraternity known as the press"— Winsor and his colleagues. Contemporary drama critics didn't perceive the songs and dialogue as ridiculing the press. They found the format flattering. Berlin and Hart had "built their show in the image of an animated newspaper," Brooks Atkinson wrote in the *New York Times*. "It is lucid and simple and feverishly up to date." The *New Republic* praised the "journalistic design" because it wasn't "stuffy, pseudo-grand or pretentious, but witty, rich and alive."

Another headline flashed in the dark:

WOOLWORTH DECLARES REGULAR DIVIDEND—
BARBARA HUTTON TO WED PRINCE MDIVANI

Did the cast know Barbara Hutton was in the audience? Did her friends laugh nervously when they saw an actor impersonating a foppish, self-concerned Russian aristocrat, who boasted from the stage,

> My shoes and spats
> My opera hats,
> And my cravats
> Are made just for me.

Were they amused by an impoverished nobleman's confession that his interest in Hutton was his desire for her money because,

> My castle will need some restoring,
> Ceiling and flooring,
> Furniture, too.

Newspaper accounts don't answer those questions. They did describe "Miss Hutton's" song—"How's Chances"—as a "mellifluous" and "rhythmic ballad." The actress, wearing a costume that recalled newspaper photographs of the heiress, sang to the prince,

> How's chances,
> Say, how are the chances
> Of making you love me
> The way I love you?

Contrary to his New York newspaper colleagues, Winsor was offended by "How's Chances" and *As Thousands Cheer.* Francis said so in the *Cleveland News.* Barbara Hutton had watched "her marriage be brilliantly if cruelly satirized on the stage." Readers, who had not heard the lyric, had no idea what provoked Francis. Not surprisingly, a week before Winsor's own wedding, he objected to a song that mocked a wealthy woman's decision to marry a man of modest means, especially when the unmanly caricature's "way" of love was different than hers. Winsor conceded that the song "brilliantly" portrayed the Hutton-Mdivani marriage but was angry because he assumed Berlin and Hart were ridiculing Hutton's decision to marry a handsome homosexual. "How's Chances" was a stinging reminder of what some thought about Margaret marrying Winsor.

Excerpts from the version of the same song published in the form of sheet music during the 1930s dispel any doubts about the meaning of Berlin's ballad. Lyrics to be sung by a female voice include,

When I want to see the boys,
I know where to find the boys.
I don't go through a club or two;
I just find you and there are the boys. . . .
How many men must I fight with
To be in right with,
In right with you.

Conventional wisdom was that women who married homosexual men were "beards"—disguises for their husbands' embarrassing preference. The orthodox majority could not imagine a loving relationship between a man and a woman that included a mutual understanding of each other's sexual preferences. Margaret wasn't Winsor's beard. He never disguised his sexual preference. Two of his half-sisters, Martha Eaton Hickox and Anne Eaton Parker, remembered that he "sat us down and told us" he was homosexual. Nor did he hide his love for Margaret. Winsor was objecting to how Berlin and Hart had "cruelly" derided his own and others' unconventional marriages, their "very, very daring" designs for living with uncommon desire.

Cocktails following the performance would ease any discomfort the couple might be feeling. The final curtain at the Music Box descended at 11:07. Outside the theater, Mrs. Frueauff's chauffeur waited to drive them to 52nd Street between 5th and 6th Avenues, where several speakeasies violated the U.S. Constitution by serving beverage alcohol behind the sober stone and brick facades of former town houses. The most exclusive were 21 and Tony's, the latter "run as a sort of family party for celebrities. Every New York evening had to end at Tony's," which was exactly where Winsor and Margaret were headed.

By the time they arrived, two popular authors had commandeered a prominent table: Dashiell Hammett, novelist and screenwriter, and Dorothy Parker, poet and critic. They were older than Winsor and Margaret's close circle of friends. Hammett, the author of *The Maltese Falcon,* a detective story that had set a new standard of realism for the genre, was thirty-nine. Parker, known for a cruel wit, was reviewing books for the *New Yorker.* She was forty. Neither writer measured up to Winsor's standards. He dismissed Hammet as "the so-called Hemingway of mystery writers." And at *PARADE,* he wrote that *Death and Taxes,* a collection of Parker's poetry, was "a mere mass of jingles, written with all the earmarks of frenzied, careless haste."

Unlike Winsor, Hammet and Parker were openly critical of American politics and economic policy. Both eventually promoted Communism. At Tony's, Winsor slyly needled Parker about her radical views. She and her future husband, actor Alan Campbell, who had appeared in the Cleveland cast of *Design for Living,* had recently engaged in a cosmetic act of solidarity with exploited laborers. The couple visited a parlor in the slums of New York's Bowery where they had "bleeding hearts tattooed on their arms." On Saturday night, Winsor noted that the actor was "nursing . . . his tattoo" and felt "too ill to laugh" at Parker's scoffing humor.

As Winsor collected tidbits from more of Tony's patrons, Noel Francis observed, "the never-to-be-evaded columnists, jotting notes while people ambitious even for notoriety crane their necks and try to be loudly clever." Winsor did not see himself as a ubiquitous ear for his newspaper, a professional outsider paid to finagle his way inside an exclusive speakeasy and describe its illustrious clientele. When he rang the doorbell at Tony's, Winsor was welcomed as part of the "family" of "celebrities." He was Mrs. Antoinette Frueauff's future son-in-law! Winsor's sense of himself as a full-fledged member of café society gave him both access and a point of view that none of his Cleveland competitors could match. During the first week of October 1933, Francis entertained readers with anecdotes from private New York City parties while modestly neglecting to inform his audience that he and Margaret were the guests of honor.

They were entertained at 21, an elaborate speakeasy often called "Jack and Charley's" because Jack Kriendler and Charley Berns were the owners. The public rooms filled two floors of a large former residence, an illegal enterprise so profitable that the men had purchased a portion of the "glass collection from the King of Spain's palace in Castile, recently confiscated by the new Republican government." The proprietors used the crystal when "someone wants to give a little more elaborate dinner than usual." On one of those occasions, Winsor spotted "a debutante . . . wearing her baby teeth strung on a platinum chain."

Winsor's eye for unconventional female fashion was one of his most valuable assets. Newspaper publishers hoped about-town columnists would build readership among women, a key market for newspapers' retail advertisers, especially department stores, who could buy a full-page ad every day of the week and sometimes two on Sunday. His female competitor at the *Plain Dealer,* Eleanor Clarage, wrote about "the bright sophisticated things of the moment" that she found in the "style shops" and "tea rooms" along Euclid Avenue. Winsor described what women were wearing in the swankiest speakeasies of Manhattan: black satin "is the latest rage. It doesn't matter how you wear it or at what hour of the day"; blue artificial eyelashes "wink on the most expensive eyelids"; and women "of fashion are parting their hair diagonally."

Even Walter Winchell couldn't match Winsor's New York City access. The "baby teeth" Winsor saw at 21 would never have appeared in the "world's most famous column." The owners had banned Winchell from their establishment because his "only purpose . . . was to snoop around and eavesdrop in order to publish titillating tales of newsworthy clientele." They did not serve "tattletales." Yet they seated Winsor upstairs on 21's banquettes and served him the finest illegally imported Scotch. The owners didn't know about "Noel Francis." Their ignorance reassured Winsor's future mother-in-law.

Her uneasiness about Winsor's profession was evident in the press release she wrote and sent to New York City and Cleveland society editors announcing Margaret's engagement. The information Mrs. Frueauff provided about him was a classic example of how socially prominent mothers of the bride used newspaper society pages to enhance the stature of unconventional grooms and how the editors of those pages accepted omissions, inaccuracies, and exaggerations.

Mrs. Frueauff was "sensitive about publicity," according to Brock Pemberton, her friend and producer of *Strictly Dishonorable.* For years she had pursued a theatrical career and respectability, a difficult balancing act in the 1930s. The Frueauffs' social standing had been purchased with old, Western money. As a writer noted in *Variety,* Margaret's mother "came of a Denver Socialite family" and "was independently wealthy." She had married even more Western money, millions of dollars amassed by her husband, who was the only partner of Henry L. Doherty & Co., and a vice president of the Cities Service Company, a giant holding enterprise that owned more than two hundred natural gas utilities and oil firms. The Frueauffs lived in a "great house" at 1069 5th Avenue and maintained a second home in Newport, Rhode Island. The *New York Times* considered them "prominent socially." After her husband's death, Antoinette Frueauff sold the house on 5th Avenue and eventually moved to 510 Park Avenue, where she was living with her two daughters, Margaret and Elaine, at the time of the wedding.

"Noel Francis" might have smudged her family's reputation, so in her press release she didn't mention Winsor's nom de plume, nor did she use the terms "movie critic" or "about-town columnist." Instead, she opted for a notably vague phrase: "member of the editorial staff of the *Cleveland News.*" To increase his acceptability, Frueauff also took certain liberties with her future son-in-law's past. Her version of his family and schooling has become part of the historical record. Corrections are in order.

For example, Mrs. Frueauff's press release stated that Winsor's father was

Joseph O. Eaton. Not so. Eaton was Winsor's stepfather and a junior. The first Joseph Oriel Eaton was "a talented portrait artist of the Hudson River School," who painted Herman Melville and Abraham Lincoln while they were living. Eaton Senior's painting of Lincoln hung in the Eaton home. In 1910, Winsor's widowed mother, Edith Ide French, married Eaton Junior, a graduate of Williams College.

The columnist's father was Winsor Pitcher French, who died in 1908, a descendant of a distinguished American military family. Winsor was actually a II, but he never used the Roman numeral. His grandfather Brigadier General Winsor Brown French commanded the 77th New York Volunteer Regiment during the Civil War. In 1864, according to Evelyn Barrett Britten, General French "helped save the nation's capital from Southern forces in a bloody battle." General French was the great grandson of Joseph French, a lieutenant in the Army of George Washington. On his mother's side, General French was descended from Roger Williams, who founded Rhode Island.

Winsor's schooling was eventful, although you would never know it from reading Mrs. Frueauff's press release. She tried to make him look like a gentleman scholar: prestigious Episcopal prep school and small private college. She claimed he was "an alumnus of St. Paul's School, Concord, N.H., and attended Kenyon College, Gambier, O." Two newspapers embellished her facts. The *New York Times* and the *Cleveland Press* promoted him to "graduate of St. Paul's."

Not so. "As a young man," Winsor wrote, "I presented my family with certain problems and I was sent, over the maturing years, to a good many educational institutions." How many? Six and a private tutor.

1915: Winsor's stepfather moved his wife and six children from Montclair, New Jersey, to Cleveland, Ohio. Eaton, the president and a founder of a pioneering truck parts company, wanted to be closer to his customers. They rented a house in the Village of Cleveland Heights, a new streetcar suburb built on "Heathen Ridge" overlooking Cleveland and Lake Erie. Winsor was ten and enrolled in the fifth grade at Roxboro Elementary, a public school. It was the only "educational institution" that Winsor attended uneventfully.

1916–17: After a year, he transferred to University School, a private preparatory school for boys in Cleveland, where he acquired the fundamentals of pranking. "Most kids wore belted, Norfolk jackets," Winsor recalled, and in the dining room "it was considered very clever to bend back a few spoon handles, flip them over the belt of the guy in the next chair and then let him jingle his way out of the room." During sixth and seventh grades, he learned "to send a butter pat spiraling to the ceiling in such a manner as it would stick there." During the daily assembly, "Miss Patty Stair . . . a frail, timid looking little thing of no particular age . . . played the organ. Hardly a morning passed that pennies, pins, or some other metallic object weren't bounced off the silvered pipes with clear ringing tones that must have been terribly upsetting to the poor woman as she sat there, head bending over the keyboard, doing her best to bring a little musical culture to a lot of practical joking heathens. Once she was really upset, this when some unsung genius had been able to conceal in the organ a few white mice that scattered for freedom when Miss Stair uncovered the keys."

1918: When Winsor was thirteen, he contracted rheumatic fever. It damaged his heart and forced the removal of one of his kidneys. While recuperating, he was tutored at home by James Hawken, the founder of Hawken School, another private institution for boys in Cleveland.

1919: For the ninth grade, Winsor was sent to St. Paul's, the elite Episcopalian boarding school where "goodness outweighs knowledge." He resisted "goodness," so his mother was summoned for a conference with the head of the school, the Reverend Samuel Smith Drury. The rector's demeanor affected her. During their meeting, she called him "Rev. Dreary." Her faux pas did not help her son win a reprieve. As a result of Winsor's behavior, he wrote later, "I was fired from St. Paul's."

1920: For the tenth grade, the Eatons tried Winsor in another private boarding school, the Ridgefield Academy in Ridgefield, Connecticut. Before completing a year, the boy wrote, "I ran away to go on the stage. After four or five days on the loose, detectives brought me home."

1921–22: To discourage him from running away from the eleventh grade, the Eatons shipped their oldest son to Wyoming. At the Valley Ranch School near Cody in the Shoshone Valley, Winsor's classmates included three "more or less incorrigible" fifteen-year-old sons of Cleveland families: Orville "Bill" Prescott, who would become book editor of the *New York Times;* Walter Halle, who would become president of his family's department stores; and Jack Morgan, a "wild" son of Percy J. Morgan, owner of a large printing company, who would become a frequent "failure," according to a former in-law. Of the boys' train trip to Wyoming, Winsor wrote, "All of us had been sent West to get over something or other, and that no one was going to get over anything very quickly became abundantly clear before we were an hour out of Chicago. I was, at that historic moment, sitting in a drawing room with my companions and they were regarding me, I noticed, in a rather peculiar fashion. A plot, it was apparent, was in the works and I decided to withdraw. I was not successful and my eventual exit from the room was not at all the way I had planned it.

"First, they didn't think much of the clothes I was wearing, so using what you might call force they removed them—all of them! Next, in the very best Egyptian technique of swathing a mummy, they carefully encased me in rolls of the best grade toilet paper, brought aboard for just such an occasion. Finally, with a huge sign around my neck reading TUTANKHAMEN, they gently rolled me through the door into a car filled with chattering, female school teachers on their way to a convention somewhere.

"The Burlington people didn't appreciate it a bit."

After he reached Valley Ranch School, Winsor wrote, "for two winters I nearly froze to death." There was no escape, so he graduated.

1922: Winsor was driven to the campus in Gambier, Ohio, eighty miles south of Cleveland, where he entered Kenyon College as a freshman. He "chafed under the restrictions of a tiny village and very small college." Six weeks after he enrolled, his parents sailed for Europe. While they were at sea, he phoned his house and ordered the family chauffeur to pick him up and take him home. "My education was completed with two months at Kenyon which were enough."

His disorderly education endeared Winsor to his self-taught newspaper colleagues, but the same facts troubled the mother of his fiancée. Despite her discomfort with the sheer number of his alma maters, Mrs. Frueauff was exceptionally tolerant about his financial prospects.

During the summer of 1933, Cleveland newspaper publishers had cut reporters' pay to an average of about $30 a week. The exact amount of Winsor's salary is not known, but before the reductions, Sydney Andorn, a journeyman about-town columnist for the *Press,* earned $25 a week, plus $10 for expenses. At the *Cleveland Press,* veteran rewrite man and columnist Herman Fetzer earned $45 a week. The cutbacks drove Winsor and his colleagues to their favorite speakeasy—the Vermont Club, "Walter Murray's sunken garden. If you drop in any Sunday morning you will find a group of the boys talking over details over pretzels." It was Prohibition, so Francis neglected to mention what beverage was served with the pretzels. The columnist did not hand police written evidence to raid a friend's establishment.

"The gentlemen of the press" eventually invited *New York World Telegram* columnist Heywood Broun to visit Cleveland and "talk up the continually increasing possibility of a newspaper union." In the speakeasy's "back room," Winsor observed Broun "overflowing from his chair, tipped against the wall" as the Socialist praised the power of organized labor. Broun persuaded Winsor. On August 20, 1933, he joined the Cleveland Editorial Employees Association as a "charter member" and received "reporter's badge No. 6." His support of the nascent union, despite millionaire friends and an industrialist stepfather, earned the young man respect among the "hard-boiled" guys in the *News* city room. By mid-October, the Cleveland group had become the first chapter of the American Newspaper Guild.

Union membership did not immediately raise his salary, and on occasion he felt forced to plead for money. When the first payment was due on his new car, Winsor phoned his stepfather. Eaton was busy, so his secretary, Josephine Carroll, took the message: "Winsor called . . . . The car is being delivered today and it is necessary for him to make a payment of $47.00. . . . Winsor does not have $47.00 . . . or the money for the insurance [$11.40]. He wants you to send . . . a check." Mr. Eaton obliged. The Ford cost $522.60. Winsor and his stepfather split the total—six equal payments apiece, according to Carroll's accounting, which Eaton saved in a file labeled "WINSOR."

During his August vacation in New York City, Winsor ran out of cash, so he phoned his personal banker, the proprietor of the Vermont Club. "Francis" thanked him in a column. "More than one news gatherer is toasting Walter Murray . . . because when they run short on vacation he wires them that precious paper."

Winsor minimized his expenses by living at home. His stepfather monitored his accounts. For September and October 1932, months that Winsor was unemployed, Eaton paid his bills for groceries, drugs, pants, and use of the telephone, expenditures totaling $106.32. The amount did not include Winsor's speakeasy bills or the cost of filling the Ford's gas tank. His salary at the *News* eventually defrayed his expenses, but it would not support a wife from Park Avenue who was a Broadway star.

Mrs. Frueauff's friend Brock Pemberton explained how she could be nonchalant about Winsor's penury. "Money meant nothing to her. She was born with it, knew she'd always have it and treated it with contempt." In that "over-sized handbag" she routinely carried, Mrs. Frueauff "often had difficulty locating any money. 'I had a hundred dollars there this morning and now it's gone,' she'd say. No wonder, since she could never pass a derelict without slipping him a bill." One hundred dollars was more than twice the amount of Winsor's weekly salary. There was a second reason she didn't worry about her daughter and money. In February 1934, Margaret would be twenty-one years old and assume control of $675,000 from her late father's estate. She could afford a husband of limited means.

With a handful of press clippings that portrayed Winsor as a credible candidate for matrimony and the promise of Margaret's inheritance, the parties celebrating the attractive couple's imminent nuptials marched toward the altar. On the Wednesday night before the wedding, Pemberton and his wife entertained Margaret and Winsor at the exclusive Mayfair Yacht Club, New York City's "most elegant" café. "Practically the entire theatrical world and its fringes" were invited, according to "Noel Francis." Comedienne Ilka Chase "came trotting in wearing a hat that looked as if it might have been whipped up by a comic strip artist, but so does everyone else that makes any pretense to smartness." Actress Peggy Wood had "a terrific time carrying on a conversation without confusing it with her lines" in a new play she was rehearsing. The *New York World Telegram*'s Ward Morehouse, "fresh from the Alps," was "frantically trying to gather items for "Broadway after Dark," his about-town column.

Morehouse didn't mention that to amuse their guests the Pembertons had hired Dwight Fiske, a performer whose material was considered humorously and metaphorically pornographic. *Variety* called Fiske the "King Leer" of "double-entendre pianologists." Winsor described him as a "world-weary" entertainer who used the "approach sinister," a classic example of how he described subjects that other columnists thought were unacceptable in daily newspapers.

Winsor wrote about every sexual preference. Following his return from New York City in August, he told readers, "Broadway is holding its breath to see what the reaction will be to *The Green Bay Tree,* a new play planning to reach those shores in the early autumn—and that supposedly makes *The Captive* look like a bedtime story." *The Green Bay Tree* implicitly explored homosexual themes by showing how a wealthy middle-aged man, who claimed to have "adopted" a working-class "son," reacted when the young man decided "to marry a woman of his own age." *The Captive* was billed as "a serious depiction of the 'social problem' of lesbianism." In Cleveland, if you wanted to see nude women (painted or live), Winsor had the answer, as well as advice for those who liked to watch all-male revues and listen to entertainers like Fiske, whose song lyrics were risqué. Of the revues, he wrote: "Chuck Wilson, one of the few male toe dancers in captivity, is holding forth. . . . Jean Pearson . . . is bringing in six more of the boys . . . who like to wear wigs and talk in high voices."

So, to the ceremony at St. Bartholomew's Winsor brought an appreciation of blue humor, no college degree, a new Ford coupé, very little spending money, a union card, and an uncommon sexual preference. He also made Scheherazade look tongue-tied. He knew more than 1,001 stories to make Margaret laugh and had almost as many loyal friends to entertain her. From this group he selected fourteen of his most physically attractive male buddies, four of whom were openly homosexual, and asked them to escort guests and Margaret's ten wedding attendants down the aisles of the church. In appreciation of their services, Winsor's stepfather hosted the gallant entourage at the Hotel Pierre for cocktails and hot and cold hors d'oeuvres, Paupiette of Sole à la Pierre, Mignon of Beef aux Primeurs, trays of cheese, demitasse, cigars, cigarettes, two bottles of imported champagne for each usher, plus all the bootlegged Scotch, brandy, and cocktails they could drink. On the night before the wedding, seventeen men accepted Mr. Eaton's hospitality.

In the months since *PARADE* had folded, Joseph Bryan III had returned to Manhattan and was writing profiles for the *New Yorker*. His current assignment was a twenty-six-year-old actress named Katharine Hepburn, who had just finished filming *Little Women*.

Another former *PARADE* writer had returned to *TIME*. Under the pseudonym "Trevelyan Higgins," Alan R. Jackson had also written a play called *Mrs. Dana's Dinner Party*. Producers changed the title to *A Touching Proposal*, and critics said, "The title was the only decent thing about it." Jackson, who was six feet tall, was one of Libby Holman's earliest romantic interests.

When *PARADE*'s former art director, "the second-handsomest man in New York," Jerome Zerbe had applied for a job as a photographer for magazines published by Condé Nast (*Vanity Fair* and *Vogue*), he was rejected because he didn't know "the right people." To establish his social credentials, Zerbe had begun working on his first book, an album of photographs of the international "champagne set in key moments of abandon."

Edmund Coffin Stout Jr., Princeton's "outstanding athlete" was the pitcher for Briton Hadden's amateur baseball team who compiled "a 20-game losing streak."

Roger Davis, "the world's funniest man," in Winsor's opinion, had just completed the road tour of *Crazy Quilt*, a musical revue featuring vaudeville star Fanny Brice that was written, produced, and directed by Brice's husband, showman Billy Rose. Although Davis played only a small role, he served as the comedienne's "stooge," enhancing her performances by making her laugh right before she went on stage. Winsor claimed that Davis's "crisp observations" were often credited to Dorothy Parker. "They should never be compared. Unlike Miss Parker, Davis is never funny at anyone else's expense."

Musician Roger Stearns was in New York City to record "a medley of Noël Coward's tunes for the Gramophone Co.," and he had been engaged to present his own one-man show at a "Sunday Night Supper club in the Algonquin Hotel."

Paramount motion picture studios employed Forney Wyly to protect Gary Cooper "from his sometimes too ardent female admirers." Wyly was "one of the few persons who have actually met Greta Garbo. This historic incident took place in a New York speakeasy, and she spoke just four words to him. These were, 'How do you do?'"

Editors at *Town & Country* magazine chose "Cleveland's best known bachelor host," Leonard Hanna, as the perfect dinner companion for socially prominent women in an article headlined "To Eat and Not to Mate." Initially, Hanna's education was a model for Winsor's. They both attended University School in Cleveland and St. Paul's, but Hanna actually received a diploma from the "Reverend Dreary" before entering Yale.

One of Cleveland's finest polo players, Bernard "Bernie" Towell had been a "permanent fixture in almost every night haunt" until he married a "honey blonde." Now, Francis claimed, "he sits home evenings and holds yarn for his wife."

Paul Lennon, a Brown graduate, lived "most of the year" in Paris, spent summers in Sandwich, Massachusetts, and rented mansions in Palm Beach, for "the late season" in Florida. (The "late season" was the month of March.)

Benjamin D. Holt married well. His wife, Nancy, was the daughter of industrialist Charles S. Payson, old Maine money.

Completing what Zerbe called "Winsor's posse" were his brother-in-law, Daniel Dewey, who had married Winsor's oldest sister, Edith French; Winsor's twenty-three-year-old half-brother, Joseph O. Eaton III; and Stephen Brown, who eluded the author's research efforts.

On Saturday morning, in his room at the Ritz-Carlton, Winsor required "quarts of tomato juice and every other pickup I've ever heard." They were "utterly ineffective" in "repairing the results of a bachelor dinner." By mid-day Francis had wired a dispatch to editors at the *News*. "Your wedding morning is no moment to try to write a column, but it seems to turn out that I must and so please bear with my incoherence."

For the critical task of delivering Winsor to the church in a timely manner, Mrs. Frueauff chose a forty-year-old former newspaperman who had been married to an actress for nine years: Poet, playwright and Paramount Studios screenwriter John Van Alstyne Weaver was married to Peggy Wood, a popular musical comedy star. Weaver had recently published a collection of poems, *Trial Balance: A Sentimental Inventory,* that was dedicated to Winsor's patron Leonard Hanna, who frequently "played godfather to lean but gifted friends." As Weaver and Winsor were driven to St. Bartholomew's, the experienced groom tried to bolster the younger man's courage with stories of his own marriage ceremony in Bermuda. The effort failed. "On the way to my own wedding," Winsor confessed to "confused emotions."

At the church, usher Roger Davis tried to inject some humor into "a somewhat pretentious wedding." On the church steps, he "stunned the arriving guests by . . . loudly selling librettos. 'Buy a book on the opera,'" he cried, "'or you won't know what it is all about.'" When the distinguished actress Katherine Cornell arrived to be taken down the aisle, Davis offered his arm and "suddenly became a department store elevator operator— elaborately calling each floor's wares as he passed from pew to pew."

Waiting under a half dome of Byzantine splendor was Winsor's best man. He was neither a pal from *PARADE* or the theater nor was he the handsome young heir to a fortune. Rather, he was Winsor's sixty-year-old stepfather. A few minutes after four, the two men turned to face the rear of the church as a pipe organ filled the ceiling vaults with triumphant thunder.

From the gloomy depths of the narthex, Margaret broke with tradition and led her bridesmaids in a slow, measured, march toward Winsor, who was, by his own account, hung over. Past forty rows of pews, the bridal attendants approached in gowns and matching hats of "cornflower blue velvet." Helen Worden, society editor for the *New York World Telegram,* observed the women's entrance. "No . . . Broadway chorus," she wrote, could "have been better than the evenly matched blonde-haired attendants who followed Margaret down the aisle."

At about this time, Winsor recalled, his hands began shaking. Because he wasn't wearing his glasses, he couldn't see Margaret clearly until she entered the gilded apse. There he discovered that her tulle veil was almost "ten yards long." That Mrs. Frueauff had costumed her daughter as if she were appearing in a Broadway finale came as no surprise to Winsor. Margaret had been starring in her mother's productions "since she had been able to crawl. Her first role . . . was that of a centerpiece on the family dining room table. Happy as a lark, she sat suspended in a swing of flowers throughout a large, formal dinner."

Following her mother's parties came *Strictly Dishonorable,* a part in John Van Druten's *After All,* and a single film in Hollywood. Criticism of her film role was so devastating that Margaret "dyed her hair, stained her face and ran away to Mexico." From there she fled to Europe. "Eventually, however, Margaret came meekly home" and "retired from both screen and stage." Soon after her return, Winsor's sisters believe, their brother met Margaret at a party in Saratoga Springs. The courtship was not long. The ceremony at St. Bartholomew's was Margaret's first major public appearance following her unhappy trips to Hollywood, Mexico, and Europe.

An Episcopalian rector, The Very Reverend George Paull T. Sargent, officiated. Winsor remembered his "hands trembled so at the altar," the Reverend Sargent "had to apply the ring to the bride's finger."

Was Mrs. Frueauff's production successful? Worden believed she had set a theatrical standard to which New York society might aspire. "Take any big time matrimonial venture," Worden wrote, "the bride's family plunks out a huge sum of money on gowns, the church, the decorations and the music" ($18,000 in Margaret's case, according to the State of New York's Probate Court). "But the part the bridesmaids, best men and bride and groom are to play in the church is left to the hit-or-miss direction of relatives at last-minute dress rehearsals." Her recommendation? Engage "Broadway producers . . . for our best weddings."

Eventually, Winsor and his new wife were driven to the main ballroom of the Park Lane Hotel, where they took positions in the receiving line behind Mrs. Frueauff. Jerry Zerbe photographed the guests for *Society on*

Parade. (Both Zerbe and Winsor tried to perpetuate the memory of their deceased magazine in their subsequent careers. "The Night Parade" had been the standing headline over Winsor's about-town column at the *News.*) Zerbe hoped to give his book, scheduled for publication in the fall of 1935, social cachet by securing the services of Lucius Beebe, the *New York Herald Tribune* columnist, who had raved about Aileen Winslow's Sunday suppers. The photographer offered to put Beebe's name on the book's cover if he would write the introduction. Beebe agreed.

According to Walter Winchell, the queer-baiting columnist of the *New York Mirror,* Beebe would do anything Zerbe asked. Winchell had recently drawn attention to Beebe's affection for Zerbe by commenting that Beebe's column, filled as it was with constant references to Zerbe, should be headed not "This New York" but rather "Jerome Never Looked Lovelier."

Perhaps his romantic relationship with Zerbe led to Beebe's slightly risqué introduction to *Society on Parade.* He described Zerbe's art as "news pictures of a highly specialized sort, showing elegant or famous or witty people in brief instants of parade or pleasure, sometimes, as the phrase goes, in drink, sometimes, as tradition dictates, in bed."

Zerbe's photographs of Winsor, Margaret, and their reception guests were "in drink," and Winsor appears fully recovered from the ceremony. While the wedding party had set a high standard, so did the guests. "The Park Lane reception," Beebe wrote, "brought together as complete a cross-section of celebrities, social figures and the crowd from Tony's as any private evening of the year." Be that as it may, several of the women who appear in Zerbe's photographs had found husbands problematic.

Ilka Chase had been married briefly to actor Louis Calhern. After he left the comedienne, she told Winsor that she was going through her desk and "came upon some visiting cards engraved Mrs. Louis Calhern. Wrapping them up, she mailed them to actress Julia Hoyt, her successor for the moment, with the message, 'Darling, I hope these reach you in time.'"

Author Dorothy Parker attended the reception with actor Alan Campbell. She would marry and divorce him twice.

Who knows what Libby Holman Reynolds did or did not do to her first husband? She had a very specific idea what Mrs. French should do with hers. Libby loved Winsor, about that there was no question. She once gave him a photo of herself that was autographed, "Winsor, no one's love for you is as big as mine." As the reception came to a close, Margaret followed tradition and tossed her bouquet of white lilacs to her eight blonde bridesmaids. No one remembers who caught the flowers, but Luisa Carpenter remembered what Libby told her. "Instead of throwing the bouquet to the bridesmaids, Margaret should have tossed Winsor to the ushers."

"What price Repeal?"

On New Year's Eve at the Avalon, one of the "gilded gin palaces" lining Carnegie Avenue, the thump, thump, thump on the skin of a tom-tom announced a hymn to obsession: "Night and day you are the one / Only you beneath the moon and under the sun." Earlier in the year, Fred Astaire had chanted the lyric on Broadway before dancing up and down a grand staircase in *Gay Divorce*. The Avalon's owners had tried to capture the popular musical's elegant atmosphere by building a similar staircase from the dance floor to a raised platform where the orchestra was perspiring under spotlights.

The Avalon was the first Cleveland speakeasy to be renovated in anticipation of the repeal of the Eighteenth Amendment to the Constitution, which for thirteen years had prohibited the sale, manufacture, and transportation of intoxicating liquors—an effort to end the crime, poverty, and misery caused by drunken behavior. Since 1920 the nation had been divided between "dry" Americans, who supported "Prohibition," and "wet" Americans, who did not.

Winsor and his friends were outspoken "wets," and he welcomed the Avalon owners' investment in "extravagant" interiors as evidence that America's experiment in legislating public morality was about to end. Two enormous bars on the former speakeasy's ground floor—one "circular," the other "serpentine"—were now located on the first floor. Rising above the splendid furnishings were two levels of balconied dining rooms creating an intimate theater for staging an urban nightlife where alcohol lowered inhibitions.

Yet Winsor's coverage of the Avalon's opening also showed how public officials were unprepared for Repeal. On the night before Thanksgiving, the owners had "turned on the lights" for the first time. Twenty-four hours later, Cleveland cops had turned them off. Police removed "$3,500 of exceedingly good bottled stuff" and locked the speakeasy's doors.

The raiders' timing was odd. Three weeks earlier, Ohio residents had voted overwhelmingly to end Prohibition. They had joined thirty-five like-minded states, the number required to repeal the Eighteenth Amendment. The state was "wet" by popular vote, but legally "dry" until Ohio legislators enacted new liquor regulations, a task dawdling politicians had yet to complete. "Every other spot in town blazed brazenly away, entertaining the holiday throngs." On the following afternoon, police confounded Winsor. They returned the Avalon's bootlegged spirits, and "the doors opened again. Although everybody knows, no one will tell what it's all about."

Winsor's items about the Avalon illustrate how he used his about-town column at *PARADE* and the *News* to embarrass authorities charged with enforcing the Eighteenth Amendment. As for the ban on transporting intoxicating beverages, he told readers that illegal shipments arrived in Cleveland from Buffalo in weekly truck caravans that thundered down the highway unhindered by so much as a speeding ticket. When the long arm of the law finally intervened, bootleggers were out of reach. "Those airplanes that disturb your sleep these nights are more than apt to be bootleggers who have taken to the air in an attempt to fool the Buffalo police who are suddenly becoming conscious of the trucks that have been puffing merrily across the border." When the columnist had driven to Manhattan to visit Margaret, he had encountered "interminable lines of bootleggers' trucks" that thwarted his progress by clinging "stubbornly to the middle of the road" and "puffing through the darkness like tired old men."

In Cleveland, after the trucks were unloaded, bootleggers' agents went door to door downtown trying to sell their contraband. When the depression reduced sales, Winsor documented how peddlers abandoned subterfuge. "They now go brazenly down the corridors of office buildings, knock on doors and walk right in, without ever considering the possibility of your being a federal agent. Then, without so much as even asking your name or mentioning that they've been selling to all your best friends for years, they plunge into a solicitation, pulling, of course, the old gag of special prices."

To make sure readers didn't fall for the "old gag," Winsor told them how much to pay. "An escorted truck from . . . Montgomery, Ala., sent us 175 cases of Scotch in 26 ounce bottles and more brands than you could drink in a year priced at $75 the case." Because bootleggers were barred from buying space in newspapers, Winsor's items were essentially free advertisements that broke the law. On the occasion of another shipment, he actually published a price list: "Champagne can be had for $72 a case; Bacardi $40; Scotch, in imperial quarts, $80; sherry $6 a gallon; and imported gin, $50. Don't pay more."

Many newspaper reporters attended and wrote about private parties where liquor was served but never mentioned the drinking—to protect their hosts from embarrassment, or worse, a police raid. Not Winsor. On at least one occasion, he named the law-breaker (a member of Cleveland's prominent and powerful Hanna family) and how the host had amused guests with the threat of law enforcement. As you entered the house, "you were presented with a tag reading 'In case of a raid, my name is not ——.' Your name was in the blank so nobody had to bother with introductions. Then at midnight, a good hour to go home, the police came—that is, what looked very much like the police."

In New York City, Winsor discovered that the very behavior Prohibition was trying to prevent was the basis of a parlor game: "Blotto. It consists of a map of New York City with all the speakeasies on it. You start off by rolling dice, and then move your men accordingly. If you hit a speakeasy, you have to go in and take a drink. Sometimes you have to drink bottoms up; sometimes all the players have to drink bottoms up. Occasionally you bump into a lamppost on your way home and you have to pay a forfeit."

Private hosts were not the only persons to thumb their noses at the law. In Cleveland, "the town's oldest speakeasy, conveniently situated in the busiest business section, has never had a raid since the day it opened, which was simultaneous with the birth of Prohibition." It was equipped to feature aggressive drunken behavior in a sort of floorshow. The speakeasy's centerpiece was "a six-foot boxing ring. On stools in two of its corners, you'll find twelve ounce boxing gloves, and when customers get to the argumentative stage they are invited into the ring to battle it out."

Winsor wondered if police knew "how many downtown restaurants (not to mention drug stores, sandwich bars and cigarette counters) are gaily showing the real article across the table cloths." One afternoon, the columnist "ordered a glass of ginger ale" at a "refreshment stand in a downtown office building. 'With or without?' he was asked. 'With,' said he, dreaming vaguely of ice. And what he got was an orange blossom cocktail, strong enough to knock over a horse."

As support for repealing the Eighteenth Amendment gathered momentum, Cuyahoga County sheriff John M. Sulzmann, an official responsible for enforcing liquor laws, explained his policy one night at the New China Restaurant, a popular Cleveland nightclub. Winsor was in the audience. "In the midst of a gala-gala . . . the fabulous white-haired John" stepped into "the middle of the dance floor and there, in the full glory of the spotlights" said that "he would never, never enforce 'this most damnable, most infamous, most iniquitous law that has ever been put over on the American people! As long as I am sheriff I want you to enjoy yourselves as I did when I was a youth!'"

Given the sheriff's attitude, Winsor could risk breaking the law banning liquor ads without much fear of punishment, but he did avoid the hypocrisy of reporters who ordered drinks in their favorite speakeasies after spending a day writing stories that exposed and criticized corrupt officials who were not enforcing liquor laws. Compared to his colleagues, he was notably explicit in his published advice for finding illegal speakeasies or brewing your own liquor. He had only one reservation: "Please, for obvious reasons, stop telephoning for speakeasy addresses."

After flouting authority in his columns, it should be no surprise that Winsor and Margaret did not celebrate the first New Year's Eve following Repeal at the Hollenden, Statler, or Carter Hotel ballrooms, all of which were still obeying liquor laws. Instead, despite the Thanksgiving raid and rumors of bribes, the couple drank and dined at the Avalon. In a haze of blue-gray cigarette smoke, they watched women in floor-length gowns whirl about their tuxedoed partners on the circular dance floor.

Winsor searched the crowd for names to fill his column. He observed Leonard Hanna hosting a small dinner party and claimed to be "astonished" when he recognized the "slicked-down jet black hair" and impish grin of a slightly built, boyish-looking guest. It was "none other than Cole Porter." The man who would "single-handedly provide the words and music for thirty-three stage musicals" wasn't a household word in Cleveland, so Winsor educated his less sophisticated readers. "In case you are so remiss as not to know," Porter "was the composer of last season's most successful tune, 'Night and Day.'" Another man at Hanna's table was Monty Woolley, who had directed Astaire in *Gay Divorce*. Porter and Woolley had accepted Hanna's invitation to spend the New Year's weekend at Hilo, his 316-acre estate on Little Mountain Road east of Cleveland.

Since 1924, Hanna had been reassembling the stones, timbers, and tiles of historic "farm" buildings imported from England. They included a rambling, twelve-room gatehouse where Hanna lived, as well as pigeon crofts, pigsties, stables, covered bridges spanning creeks, a contemporary swimming pool with a bar in the bathhouse, and greenhouses to provide fresh flowers and vegetables throughout the year. When completed, Winsor wrote, "Every period of English architecture will be represented." Hilo was one of the most elaborate estates in the Midwest.

Before Margaret married Winsor, she had visited Cleveland to meet her fiancé's family and friends. Hanna entertained the couple at Hilo with one of his elaborate six- or seven-course meals. No record of the menu exists, but during the summer Hanna often served a cold cream-of-apple soup as a first course, followed by roast lamb or pork that had been raised on the estate.

For Hanna, Porter, and Woolley, New Year's Eve at the Avalon was a Yale reunion of sorts. Hanna and Porter were Class of 1913, Woolley was 1912. Porter told biographers he had sought Hanna's friendship after discovering the iron ore heir had the "largest allowance of any boy" in his class. As a sophomore, Hanna had appeared in *Cora,* a musical Porter composed for their fraternity, Delta Kappa Epsilon. At football games, Porter and Hanna wore "mink-lined stadium coats" while singing "Bull Dog" and "Bingo, Eli Yale," fight songs Porter wrote as an undergraduate.

All three Elis preferred males for sexual partners, according to their many biographers. In their mid-forties, Hanna and Woolley were bachelors. Porter had been married fourteen years but was in Cleveland without his wife. He frequently visited Hilo, where he had composed music for two of his shows on Hanna's piano. One of them was *Star Dust,* which was to star Peggy Wood, the wife of John Weaver, who had dedicated his book of poetry to Hanna. As his houseguest in November 1931, Porter had put the "finishing touches" on the show, which, according to Winsor, was "written around a girl in a broadcasting station." Those who had heard portions of the score told the columnist, "The music is marvelous—seductive waltzes in the Viennese manner. When the play goes into production, the enormous red-bearded Edgar (Monty) Woolley, who has been in Cleveland, will direct it."

Subsequently, Winsor wrote that *Star Dust* was to have its world premiere at the Hanna, but he was forced to correct that item when the theater's stage equipment proved to be "insufficient for the demands of a sitting, standing, running, diving, leaping production." He added, "The play will open in Boston shortly after Christmas." Three weeks later, he was forced to print another correction. Rehearsals had been "interrupted, despite the fact that its production date has already been announced."

Why *Star Dust,* which had a "string of wonderful songs," was never produced has puzzled the composer's biographers. Based on a comment of Porter's, biographers have written that the show was "abandoned because a large tobacco company, which was going to put up the money, backed out when an extra tax was levied on cigarettes." Subsequent items of Winsor's suggest that after the company pulled out, Hanna considered financing the show. Winsor was careful about the language he used. He reported a "rumor" that rehearsals "will soon be resumed and that the financial angel is a wealthy Clevelander." He didn't specifically mention Hanna, who guarded his privacy when it came to his money and his personal life. Hanna's efforts were unsuccessful, and Winsor eventually reported that *Star Dust* had been "withdrawn from production" and that Porter had "sailed for Europe, book, score and all with him." Nevertheless, *Star Dust* represents another example of Hanna's unrecorded patronage that reflected his wide-ranging artistic interests.

Two years later, Porter was working on still another new show when he was spotted at the Avalon. Hanna asked Winsor and Margaret to join their party, at which Porter played a private concert for "a privileged few," including "several of his new and still unpublished numbers." What did he play? Porter was working on *Anything Goes,* so one of the songs was "I Get a Kick Out of You," which he was recycling from *Star Dust.* Another was the show's title song, which captured the era's tolerance for what was once considered taboo behavior:

> The world has gone mad today
> And good's bad today,
> And black's white today
> And day's night today.

When Porter finished performing, Hanna proposed a change of venue. Margaret French and her four male escorts headed east on Euclid Avenue until Hanna's chauffeur stopped the car in front of a large house near East 86th Street. Except for a porch light, the building was dark and appeared deserted.

Hanna's party climbed the porch stairs and stepped into a pool of light. For a moment, their faces were reflected in a black glass mirror on a door, which quickly opened to admit the group and just as quickly closed behind them. In a small vestibule, another door swung aside and the shameless perfume of burning tobacco and iced gin welcomed the revelers to the Patent Leather, Cleveland's "snappiest" speakeasy.

The owners, "Bernie" Bernstein and "Rubber" Goldberger, did not require guests to remember a password or possess a card to gain entry. They had installed a one-way mirror in the door, so they could see if customers or cops were standing on the porch. In either case, Rubber would have been the perfect host. "No one can feel worse and show it less," Winsor wrote. Rubber's grin was "a fine example of perpetual motion," lubricated with "brandy and Benedictine."

Did Hanna's guests want to be seated in the upstairs dining room, which had recently been enlarged and redecorated? No, they wanted tables in the cocktail lounge where "huge black musical notes outlined with neon lights" hung on "silver walls." There they could watch the Patent Leather's entertainers: Harold Simpson, Annastean Haines, and Poisen Gardner. In Winsor's opinion, they were "one of the real highlights on the local horizon."

Simpson and Haines, the "bronze Helen of Troy," danced and sang to Gardner's "frantic" piano syncopation. A connoisseur of voices and vocal music, Winsor once criticized Simpson, a whispery crooner, for affecting the accent of "a phony British duke with an 'A' a mile broad." (His stage name was "Mistah" Simpson.) Instead, he told Simpson to "sing in his grand old manner." According to a second item, he followed the advice, an example of Winsor's clout. Part of his column's power was derived from the fact that he often introduced Cleveland performers to powerful friends who could help their careers. On this particular occasion, Margaret had been so impressed with the trio that she was trying to "interest a New York manager in booking them for Les Ambassadeurs in Paris," a nightclub that presented the finest African American performers.

At the Patent Leather, Winsor did not record the party's drink orders, but he was within days of launching a personal crusade: "Perhaps someone will remember that the Parisian Ritz bar built its fame on a foundation of fifty-cent champagne cocktails, instead of forcing their thirsty clients to buy a full bottle." In this particular category, the Patent Leather served one of Winsor's favorites: "Hot-house peaches—in a tall glass of champagne."

After an undocumented number of drinks, Porter and Woolley thought the speakeasy's entertainers needed new music and fresh direction, so they took command of the "tiny dance floor" and "staged a little floor show," which included Winsor, Margaret, and other members of the audience.

What happened following the Patent Leather's improvised revue is not entirely clear. Winsor wrote that "one gay little group engaged body-guards to escort them into the remote region of Bolivar Road," the site of Cleveland's Greektown. He did not name the participants, although he had recently published a guide to the neighborhood's nightspots in his column.

During "the commonplace hours of the day, Bolivar looks like nothing more than a busy commercial street with great trucks continually backing up and drawing away from the wholesale grocers' doors—but the moment it grows dark, and the lights go on, the place becomes fraught with excitement and mystery." Right before dawn, Winsor preferred the Venus, "where Nick Psaros stands behind his resplendent new bar. The later the hour the more amusing."

The "gay little group" that left the Patent Leather had not developed a sudden thirst for retsina. According to Winsor, "they were searching for reefers. Jaded Society has turned to Mari Juana cigarettes. After you have smoked three . . . nothing matters." Still later, about "seven in the morning," the party returned to Carnegie Avenue and joined customers "flocking into the Avalon . . . for a final nightcap—or should it be called good morning cap?"

In daylight, Winsor and Margaret reached their home in Cleveland Heights, where they were renting the last house on the north side of Delamere Drive, a quiet, dead-end street eight blocks east of the Eaton family home. Their shuttered and shingled saltbox had a wide front door that beckoned to passersby like an inn on Cape Cod. *News* society editor Polly Parsons remembered, "Winsor and his bride . . . entertained a constant stream of visitors." On New Year's Day, a familiar presence occupied the guest room: Mrs. Frueauff, Winsor's mother-in-law.

Clevelanders did not learn of her visit in Winsor's column. Competitors at the *Press* and the *Plain Dealer* broke the news. Twice in December, Antoinette Frueauff had boarded the New York Central Railroad's overnight train from Manhattan to Cleveland. The first time she visited, she watched her daughter in the dress rehearsal of *Criminal at Large,* a "zip-zowie, hair-raising mystery melodrama," at the Cleveland Play House. According to William F. McDermott, the *Plain Dealer*'s drama critic, Margaret was impersonating Isla, "an overwrought young lady addicted to conversation while walking in her sleep."

Mrs. Frueauff gave her daughter notes of advice and left before opening night. Isla was "not a big role," McDermott wrote after watching Margaret's performance, but "a trying one for a young actress, requiring some faculty for creating the semblance of intense emotion." Although Margaret was only twenty years old, in McDermott's opinion, she had achieved "the effect of a veteran trouper, substituting for wide experience an apparently native intuition."

On Mrs. Frueauff's second trip to Cleveland, she brought Margaret's sister, Elaine, and they spent the holidays on Delamere Drive. Not a word of their visit appeared in Winsor's columns, which was unusual. Many guests read about themselves in the *News*. Mr. and Mrs. Man Mountain Dean had dropped by during December. Dean was a forty-two-year-old professional wrestler famous for his "running broad jump." (He "hurls his opponent to the mat, then takes a running leap into the air and lands, rumble seat first, on his prostrate opponent.") Dean's wife, Doris, was his "secretary and manager." Winsor found the wrestler's weight (317 pounds) unremarkable. Instead, he told readers about Dean's diet. "For your private information," he "never smokes or drinks." For a nightcap, the wrestler preferred "a bottle of milk (!) and a marmalade sandwich."

Following the wrestler was one of Winsor's ushers: Forney Wyly. He unpacked his bags in the guest room and stayed "two weeks," spending "his evenings touring the nightclubs and his days sleeping." Forney found "it impossible to start a day without having a gin buck before breakfast."

During this same period, Margaret became newspaper column fodder. Whenever the probate court in New York authorized expenditures from her inheritance, the details appeared in the *New York Times* and Cleveland's

Press and *Plain Dealer.* In deference to its own movie critic, the *News* kept silent about Margaret's personal fortune. On December 2, the *Plain Dealer* reported that Margaret would receive an allowance of $2,225 a month until her twenty-first birthday, when she would assume full control of her father's legacy. While she was appearing in *Criminal at Large,* the *Press* reported that the court had approved her mother's "expense account . . . for the wedding," an amount totaling "$18,851.10." The following morning, curious neighbors could read in the *Plain Dealer* that Margaret's trousseau cost $7,480 and the "advance" for her honeymoon with Winsor was $1,000.

Margaret's publicity didn't hurt Play House ticket sales. In the 1930s, the seven days leading up to Christmas were considered "the worst theater week of the year," but *Criminal at Large* proved so popular that the Play House broke an eighteen-year tradition and performed on Christmas Day. In the first week of January, director Frederick McConnell asked the cast members if they would extend their contracts for a week. Margaret had already announced plans to visit New York City but agreed to delay her trip. Unaware that the actress had changed her travel plans, *New York Mirror* about-town columnist Paul Yawitz wrote that she was "back in New York alone."

The word "alone," which suggested his marriage was already in trouble, infuriated Winsor. Among New York City journalists, Yawitz had a reputation for homophobia. Two years earlier, he wrote a series of articles for the *New York Evening Graphic* on the "depravity" of Greenwich Village. His articles took "a scornful look at the gay clubs of MacDougal Street," which he called "the innermost stations of Greenwich Village's sex, pollution and human decay."

Francis quickly set the record straight. "In spite of Paul Yawitz's crack in the *Mirror* . . . she is still appearing at the Play House. And in spite of an announcement yesterday that after the close of *Criminal at Large* she would go to Manhattan to take part in a new Broadway production, let me inform you that Miss Perry's trip will be for the week-end only, with no Broadway production in sight."

While columnists gossiped about his marriage and his wife's money, Winsor shuttled between nightspots trying to foresee the future of legalized drinking. Earlier in the year, the State of Ohio had approved the sale of beer with an alcoholic content of 3.2 percent, but licenses for proprietors said "nothing about selling to minors." Although the permits prohibited retailers from selling "less than six bottles to carry away," Winsor found "more restaurants are selling beer at two bottles for 27 cents to carry away." Later that summer, he reported "beer garden proprietors" were accommodating customers' lust—and earning extra income—by renting "their private upstairs rooms." Speakeasy owners were also complaining to him, insisting they would be forced to continue their illegal operations because they could not afford to "fork out a tidy sum for licenses." Their chief concern was how to compete with hotels and restaurants that would be legally selling liquor by the glass. "When winter comes along, several of the small speakeasies will offer strippers in the burlesque manner."

Plans to attract customers with G-strings and bedrooms alarmed "drys," who believed saloons were hotbeds of sexual misbehavior. Furthermore, the prospect of Prohibition's repeal had reduced the cost of intoxication. "The prices for your favorite beverages are being slashed to pieces in a riot of competition. The coveted 'open sesame' for the most exclusive doors is a thing of the past and the swankiest speaks are peppering the town with applications for membership."

"Drys" were not the only readers alarmed by Winsor's items about ambitious speakeasies: Cleveland hotel owners were equally upset. Before Prohibition, customers had filled the voluminous chandeliered ballrooms at the Hollenden, Statler, and Carter Hotels. The Hollenden's manager told Winsor he was "afraid people may not care to drink in the Crystal Room. It's too public in the first place, too near the lobby in the second, and finally, authorities on the subject insist it will take us all more than a year to accustom ourselves to drinking any place except in a speakeasy or a hideout."

The continuing legal limbo created by the repeal of the Eighteenth Amendment and the absence of state liquor regulations caused problems for ethical bartenders. The Artists and Writers Club, one of Winsor's hangouts, found itself serving liquor without a license because the State couldn't issue one until the politicians wrote the rules. "Stricken by conscience," officers "locked the club's doors, not to reopen until the liquor question has been definitely settled." No such ethical dilemmas bothered speakeasy owners. "Murph's, and now I can print the address, so turn towards 2429 W. Superior and climb the stairs, has gone in for the most fantastic wallpaper these eyes have ever gazed on, a new load of sawdust to irritate your toes and, better yet, cheaper drinks." The only benefits Winsor saw in strict enforcement of new liquor laws were potential bargains. "If and when the government gets around to closing the speakeasies via the raiding method, instead of pouring the confiscated liquor in the gutter, they'll sell it to you cheaply at public auctions."

Finally, on Friday, January 19, 1934, Ohio announced the details of Repeal. To drive bootleggers out of business, "hard liquor would be sold in sealed packages at state run outlets." To close speakeasies, the State of Ohio legislated that "drinks by the glass" could only be sold with a license, which had four different price tags, depending on the establishment:

- For railroads, fifty dollars.
- For private clubs, one hundred dollars. (Speakeasies posing as "private clubs" would have to collect "dues" from their "members.")
- For hotels and restaurants, five hundred dollars.
- For nightclubs, exactly twice as much as their hotel rivals—one thousand dollars!

For the first time in fourteen years, the sale of liquor by the glass was legal in Cleveland. The *News* heralded the milestone with a front-page photograph of a woman sipping a cocktail. In his column, Winsor exposed a fraud. "That picture . . . was very cheering—only it happened to be coffee she was drinking." This was the first in a series of items in which Winsor disagreed with stories on his employer's front page or was amused by behavior reported as dangerous or unethical:

News front page: All night carousals went on as in the old days of Prohibition. The truth is Cleveland didn't handle its liquor well.
Winsor: The first weekend of legal drinking has been pleasantly survived with no serious results and virtually everybody happy.
News front page: While hotels and legitimate restaurants closed their bars at midnight, Saturday, observing the restriction against sale on the Sabbath, the nightclubs continued to serve liquor all through the night. Their patrons, driving home Sunday morning after hours of over-drinking, constituted a traffic menace.
Winsor: After midnight Saturday, when the hotels had to close up shop, the speakeasies did practically a New Year's Eve business—in fact some were crowded until after daylight.
News front page: Some [nightclubs] are planning to use a loophole of the law to win a license for the minimum fee. Fifteen nightspots have filed applications for the $1,000 nightclub permits. But three have decided to classify themselves as private clubs, and thereby obtain a license for $100.
Winsor: I'm very amused at some of the wide open nightclubs that have insisted they are running on a strictly membership basis when applying for a license.

When Cleveland police finally responded to newspaper pleas for aggressive enforcement, officers raided a large downtown speakeasy on Chester Avenue. The *News* applauded; Winsor was appalled: "Save your sympathy for the Backstage Club—because the law paid them an unhappy visit yesterday morning."

Bootleggers and speakeasy owners were some of Winsor's best sources. When it came time to write Prohibition's obituary, the columnist was most concerned how his law-breaking friends would survive. Instead of demanding enforcement of liquor laws, he criticized newspapers for not reporting crimes that threatened nightclub owners. "I wonder why no one has printed the fact that the Pink Elephant was robbed the other evening. The cash register was smashed and the musical instruments were stolen." As for customers' cars, he wrote: "Something ought to be done about the nightclubs' parking places around town. Almost every weekend some unfortunate somebody parts with something from his car—and not so long ago an automobile was towed away bodily from one of the swankier clubs, taken to a vacant lot and completely stripped." And what about the "pathetic little girl who can't be any more than 10 years old who is dragged around from nightclub to nightclub, to dance for the nickels and dimes people throw out on the floor? Can't anything be done about that?"

Raids, crime, and beggars were killing Cleveland's nightlife. "Quiet hardly describes the condition of most places." One by one, the "gilded gin palaces" on Carnegie humbly applied for licenses. Afraid of jeopardizing their applications in Columbus, former scofflaws acted like temperance ladies. "At the Avalon you can't buy anything stronger than beer—which also went for the Patent Leather the last time I happened that way. . . . Here and there, of course, you will stumble across self-conscious looking waiters who will bring you a shot of warm whisky in a teapot."

Two weeks after Ohio began issuing licenses, Winsor started counting casualties. He called them "Foldups of 1934." The "all star cast" included the Chez Paree, Belvedere, Blue Danube, Pink Elephant, and Broadway Billy's Ballyhoo.

Cleveland's nightlife literally lost some of its brilliance when "Broadway Billy" Rochester closed her Ballyhoo; one of her gold teeth was the setting for a large diamond. Her first neighborhood speakeasy established her unique style. "Dim lights, bead curtains . . . and elaborate dolls occupying most of the chairs. . . . What you were drinking is anyone's guess. Colorless it was, until Billy . . . let it take on the tints from strips of crepe paper she kept . . . in the kitchen closet." When Repeal became inevitable, Billy decided to pour good liquor and open a legitimate nightclub on Euclid Avenue with her savings: $6,000, according to Winsor. He publicized her decision, and she immediately had "reservations . . . stacked up to run three weeks." Then Billy learned a license would cost a thousand dollars. She didn't have that sort of money, so she closed the Ballyhoo and lost her savings.

Billy Rochester was one of the Prohibition characters that made Cleveland's nightlife unique. From "murky speakeasies and hideaways," Winsor wrote, "there emerged an entirely new group of exciting and sometimes valid personalities." In the first few weeks of Repeal, Billy and her Ballyhoo were replaced by the Gingham Club, which opened in the local branch of the Childs restaurant chain. Its license cost $500. Customers could listen to a piano and "sit or dance all evening for a five-cent cup of coffee."

The cost and restrictions of local liquor licenses and their impact on Cleveland's nightlife disappointed Winsor: "Prohibition went out like a lamb and Repeal followed her in like a meek, twin sister. The nightclubs . . . were all ready for gayety, but gayety there was not." One evening, he counted "fifty-two lonely looking people" in Playhouse Square. "The merrymakers were so frightened by the sound of their own whoopee that they had to give up and go home."

Winsor and Margaret were already plotting their escape from the dreary reality imposed by the new laws. The European honeymoon they had postponed in October was now scheduled to begin in late February, continue for at least seven or eight months, and include an extended residence in Paris. Like those of many writers who had come of age following World War I, Winsor's literary heroes included members of the Lost Generation, disillusioned Americans who stayed in France following the Armistice or moved there soon afterward. The most famous included novelists F. Scott Fitzgerald, John Dos Passos, and Ernest Hemingway, men whose experience was portrayed by characters in Hemingway's 1926 novel, *The Sun Also Rises*. Although most members of the Lost Generation were ten to twenty years older than Winsor, he identified with their disdain for conventional morality and traditional gender roles.

Winsor had confided to friends that he wanted to "write a world-shattering novel," a goal of "serious writing" he shared with several colleagues his own age. Among his groomsmen, Jackson had completed plays; Bryan was writing for national magazines, and Zerbe was photographing world-famous personalities for a book. All of those efforts rewarded their creators with more prestige than a local newspaper's about-town column.

Before launching *PARADE,* Winsor had tried to complete at least two novels. In the year Hemingway published *The Sun Also Rises,* Winsor asked his parents to finance a year abroad that would combine studying at Oxford University in England with "serious writing" in France. Although their son's request came only four years after his chauffeured exit from Kenyon College, they accepted his proposal, and he sailed for Liverpool in late April.

Winsor was a poor correspondent, but his stepfather saved letters and telegrams he wrote trying to manage a free-spending twenty-three-year-old on his first trip to Europe. Eaton was forced to track his stepson's whereabouts through notices of his bank withdrawals, which were frequent and large. "The letter of credit for $1500 was supposed to last you for six months," he wrote in July. "Apparently it has lasted less than three." Despite his concern, Eaton raised Winsor's allowance to "$75 per week until further notice" but issued a warning: "If you do not take advantage of the opportunity that has been given you, you certainly are the most foolish boy in the world." (Was Eaton penurious? Three years later, Zerbe "went off to Paris, on an allowance from his father of three hundred dollars a month," an amount equal to Winsor's and which Zerbe's biographer, Brendan Gill, thought "quite magnanimous.")

While the Eatons believed Winsor was studying at Oxford, he cabled them from Paris, where he had arrived without thanking his stepfather for increasing his allowance. "I have received no . . . indication that you appreciated the new arrangement," Eaton wrote. "On the contrary we received word that you are starting off on a trip to hide, which is a perfectly ridiculous thing to do and of which both Mother and I heartily disapprove. . . . Unless you can settle down . . . I am of the opinion that you had better arrange to come home."

Winsor was hiding in an attic room over a restaurant in Neuilly, a village on the outskirts of Paris. After bouts with a typewriter, he would saunter downstairs and take a seat at one of the tables in the garden, where his landlady, Madame Dumas, dressed "smartly in black" and wearing "diamond rings," would offer him "a bottle of wine and if business was brisk, champagne." The restaurant's cook was "Louise," and both women looked after Winsor as if he were "their own." Yet he ran out of money before he finished a satisfactory manuscript and was forced to sail home during the first week of October.

Less than six months after suggesting his stepson might be "the most foolish boy in the world," Eaton agreed to finance a second trip to Europe, this time for a "year of study" at the Sorbonne and a room in the heart of Paris at the Hotel Beaujolais, "a picturesque if somewhat shabby firetrap carved from a wing of the palace. The walls of my room . . . cut a plump, rococo cupid, obviously once part of an elaborate ceiling, right in half. I had his behind."

Again Winsor tried Eaton's patience: "I assume from your letter that you have about used up the express checks that you took with you," he wrote. "If $75.00 a week is not enough for necessary expenses with a moderate amount over for incidentals we certainly will have to increase it, but we are not disposed to allow a very great margin for entertaining at lunches at the Ritz."

The Ritz was the hotel where Winsor developed a taste for champagne cocktails served in the Men's Bar, an enterprise run by Georges, a "slight, blond and wiry" Frenchman. "There seemingly is nothing the man can't accomplish," Winsor wrote. The bar became his headquarters, and Georges served as an assistant. Later that summer, an unspecified illness forced Winsor into the American Hospital at Neuilly. After only four months, he returned to Cleveland and never attended classes at the Sorbonne. During both summers, he claimed to have completed novels and destroyed them: "They were all lousy." Marriage to Margaret offered him a third chance for some serious writing in Paris without financial worries. He had not abandoned the idea of a novel, but he was equally "excited about an idea he had for a play."

The opportunity to leave Cleveland became even more attractive as the wealthiest nightclub owners, who could afford thousand-dollar licenses, waged "war in earnest" with hotels over how new liquor laws would be enforced. "Nightclubs think the hotels should be forced to close their bars at midnight Saturday, but that they, the clubs, should be permitted to sell and sell and sell. Furthermore, they are going to carry the battle to Columbus."

"Silly" was the word Winsor used to describe the dispute. "The majority of places sell after the closing hour anyway. Last Saturday . . . most of the heavy drinkers started laying in a supply before midnight. At the Rainbow Room, for instance, I saw a tray holding twenty old-fashioned cocktails go to a table of four people!"

One weekend, Noel Francis counted three places where it was "practically impossible to crush through the doors, what with other guests leaving rather hastily, and need I add involuntarily. Business however was booming."

Yet after a month of legalized drinking, Winsor yearned for "a small intimate bar. Drinking, like most of the other pleasures in life, is a great deal more fun when practiced in secluded corners." He and Margaret still preferred the atmosphere of a speakeasy: the Patent Leather. On the night before Valentine's Day, they sipped champagne cocktails and listened to Harold Simpson, while Winsor scanned the cocktail lounge for items and spotted a popular fan dancer, Faith Bacon. She was appearing four times a day at the Palace Theater and experiencing Repeal's discomfort with sexually titillating performances. "Before she struts on stage," Winsor wrote, the entertainer was inspected by a representative from the "policewomen's bureau" to make sure "she wears more than a few feathers." She was at the Patent Leather "trying to forget how mean the police had just been to her."

While Winsor continued searching the room, a third item "dropped into the Patent Leather like a bolt from the blue." Forney Wyly was back. Unannounced! He asked if the French guest room was booked? No, the couple replied, but it would be permanently closed in two weeks, when they planned to put their furniture and wedding gifts in storage before visiting Florida and Cuba in late February and March. In April, they would sail to

Europe. If and when they returned in the fall, Winsor would not be visiting local nightclubs six days a week in pursuit of amusing items. He would be polishing a novel or play script. On February 1, he resigned from the *News*.

He did regret missing one noteworthy event on the smoke-and-music beat. While the Avalon was waiting for its license, the owners had searched for "an extraordinary orchestra" with which to inaugurate serving drinks legally. They hired an ensemble led by jazz violinist Joe Candulla. He was a veteran of a historic event. In Winsor's words, Candulla had appeared "on the Broadway stage with Mae West in a little epic called *Sex*."

Written by the stage and screen actress under the pseudonym Jane Mast, *Sex* was a popular comedy whose characters used raunchy language in a no-holds-barred pursuit of sexual pleasure. West, whose theatrical persona was a tough, female sexual predator, starred in her own production. Her play and two others, all of which dealt with sexual themes, were raided by police and closed in February 1927. Police had succumbed to demands from newspaper publisher William Randolph Hearst, who was using his two New York City newspapers, the *American* and the *Evening Journal*, to pressure state legislators to pass a statewide stage censorship law. Police arrested West and members of the cast. The actress was eventually convicted of "maintaining a public nuisance" and sentenced to ten days in jail. Two months later, New York's legislature "amended the public obscenity code to include a ban on any play depicting the subject of sex degeneracy, or sex perversion." The law was interpreted as "specifically banning the appearance of homosexual people or discussion of homosexual issues on the stage."

Winsor did not explain the significance of *Sex* to his readers, but those familiar with the "little epic's" history would understand that Candulla had participated in an event that led to historic legislation prohibiting discussion of unconventional sexuality including, specifically, homosexual behavior. With hindsight, Winsor's employment at the *News*, and his editor's tolerance of sly items about sexual behavior, suggests that despite catty verbs like "flutter" and derisive items about "bedroom slippers," Cleveland's newspapers were less homophobic than their New York City counterparts.

In mid-February, Winsor's resignation from the *News* became apparent when Harland Fend, a former publicity agent for movie studios, began reviewing films. Winsor's nom de plume, "Noel Francis," continued to appear above the about-town column. The editor had accepted Winsor's resignation, but kept Noel's byline. That same week, the Cleveland Newspaper Guild signed an agreement with local publishers calling for a "five-day, forty-hour week." Before leaving Cleveland, Winsor celebrated the victory with the guild's other founding members at the Vermont Club, where they could now drink legally.

On Friday, February 23, 1934, Margaret's twenty-first birthday, the couple was in New York City, where she officially took control of her inheritance and immediately invested a portion in a Broadway show: the Elsie Janis-Leonard Stillman revue *New Faces*. The cast included pianist Roger Stearns, one of Winsor's groomsmen.

While the show was still in rehearsal, Margaret and Winsor joined Libby Holman Reynolds and Luisa Carpenter in Palm Beach, Florida. Libby, after a bitter dispute with her late husband's suspicious family, had been awarded $750,000. Her son had inherited $6.25 million. For the moment, her "design for living" included Luisa. Winsor sent the *News* a postcard showing the former columnist "tanning" with his wife and Libby. His message contained an item for Fend: "Bicycle polo on the dance floor of the Colony Club is the newest diversion of the idling classes."

He did not mail another card until the couple had returned to New York City and attended a performance of *New Faces*. Now that the show was "a substantial hit on Broadway," he let Fend run another item: "It may interest you to know that Winsor French and his wife . . . own an imposing slice of the production." A more accurate item would have read, "Mrs. French purchased an imposing slice . . . ."

On Saturday night, April 7, 1934, Margaret and Winsor were driven to Pier 84 at the foot of West 46th Street where the SS *Europa* was docked. Porters hustled the couple's collection of trunks, luggage, and hand baggage aboard ship and stowed it in their stateroom, where a telegram from Winsor's stepfather waited. "LOVE AND GOOD VOYAGE MEDDLING FATHER." Outside their cabin, Winsor and Margaret sipped champagne with friends who had come to wish them bon voyage. For his book *Society on Parade,* Zerbe photographed Margaret, actress Judith Anderson, and Broadway producer Brock Pemberton and his wife, who had hosted an engagement party for the couple.

When cabin boys began hammering chimes and calling, "All ashore that's going ashore," guests descended the gangplank and waited on the pier to be showered with confetti thrown by passengers aglow with champagne. When crewmembers took positions to pull up the gangplank, one man reportedly broke from the crowd on the pier and scrambled up the gangplank. Who made "a last minute leap aboard the *Europa*"? Forney Wyly! Rather suddenly, he had decided "to sail for Europe with Winsor and Margaret French," according to Fend.

"Scarce" describes written accounts of Winsor's honeymoon. His stepfather did write Margaret to share "a great secret": Eaton, Winsor's mother, his brother Joe, and sister Peggy were planning a trip to Sweden and England in July and August. They would take their "Lincoln car, but not William," the Eatons' chauffeur. "Joe and Peggy will do the driving." The "meddling" father expected the honeymooners to "meet us in Sweden, but if that could not be arranged, we certainly would join you in London."

A second letter from Eaton asked Winsor to find a London hotel for the family: "I should like very much . . . a first class, low priced, convenient, attractive hotel, preferably small. Do you suppose you can spot such a place and see what kind of an arrangement you can make for a sitting room, two double rooms and one single room?" Winsor's sisters don't remember why, but sometime in June, the Eatons cancelled their trip. No one knows what happened to Wyly.

Winsor's published recollections of the honeymoon include a description of how he and Margaret departed from London. They were driven to Victoria Station, where they boarded a bright yellow coach on the Golden Arrow, a luxury train destined for Paris. Winsor remembered they were "rushed through the customs" and "ushered to large, upholstered arm chairs. Everything moves by clockwork, and in a few minutes . . . a polite voice comes over the train loudspeaker, casually mentioning the fact that the bar is open."

One night in Paris, the couple donned evening clothes and joined "the very top of the carriage trade" at Ciro's, a restaurant where "your path to a table [was] through an avenue of bowing lackeys." On another evening, they sipped cocktails on the sidewalk outside Fouqet's, then climbed upstairs to dine at an "open window, looking out over the chestnut trees and the Champs-Elysees." On a Saturday night they attended the Folies Bergère, where the "songs are fairly tuneless" and the comic sketches "interminable." Parisians enjoyed the "vast ballroom scenes hung with chandeliers of Nubians clutching crystal swags—slowly revolving until the nude ladies have been brought once again into the blazing light." For Winsor and Margaret, the spectacle was "an endurance test. The curtains go up at 8:30, fall at 12:30; the heat is almost unendurable and the air is blue with smoke." Late on a Sunday morning, the couple recovered with a breakfast at the Armenonville, "a gilt and crystal restaurant" nestled in a forest. Through windows the couple watched as "people riding horseback" dismounted for a drink served at "tables under the trees. . . . Brightly colored paper lanterns used for galas fluttered overhead in the breeze." After breakfast Winsor and Margaret strolled through the public gardens, joining other couples who "walked along arm in arm, every now and then stopping to kiss in the perfectly candid, unashamed manner of the French."

When they needed "theater seats, a hired car or whatever," the couple sought the assistance of Georges at the Men's Bar in the Ritz Hotel. He kept track of café society, including Cole Porter and Howard Sturges, who received "their mail at the Ritz Bar." Winsor recalled "the fabulous era" when Sturges lived at the Ritz, "maintaining one suite for himself, another for his lion." Georges, "utterly unconcerned, used to take the lion for his morning and evening walks until the beast became too big, not to mention dangerous, and had to be given to the zoo."

Winsor also recalled a singular evening when he and Margaret had visited the hotel. Georges did not seat them in the Men's Bar. Winsor remembered "a happy little sign on the door reading, 'Women and Dogs Not Allowed.'" Across the corridor, in "a small paneled room," the couple joined two titled friends: the Baron Nicolas Louis Alexandre de Gunzburg, thirty years old, a "pencil slim," somber son of a wealthy Russian banking family who had been ennobled by a czar. In 1934, the baron was dabbling in movie production, but he would eventually become the senior fashion editor at *Vogue* magazine. His companion, Fulco Santostefano della Cerda, Duke of Verdura, was thirty-six years old, an "intelligent, charismatic, cultured, sexually ambiguous" Sicilian nobleman and probably the twentieth century's "best jewelry designer." A protégé of Coco Chanel, the duke had created a necklace of pink topaz for Barbara Hutton.

While sipping an undocumented number of fifty-cent champagne cocktails, the duke "snatched" the hat off Margaret's head, which, Winsor remembered, she "had just bought at considerable expense." Verdura's designs reflected "erudition, taste, fantasy"—none of which he saw in her chapeau. So he "sent for a pair of scissors and re-made it, there and then amidst the backgammon players."

No one blamed the duke, but not too many weeks later, Margaret returned to the United States alone. Winsor's younger sisters remember receiving a sad letter from their brother in France, telling his family that he and Margaret were separating. At the end of June, Eaton wired Winsor $250. In late August, Winsor arrived in Cleveland without a novel, a play script, a wife, or money. Eaton rented Winsor his former bedroom for $15 a week while he looked for work.

Louis Seltzer, editor of the *Cleveland Press,* one of America's oldest "workingmen's" newspapers in the Scripps League, offered Winsor an about-town column. He was an odd choice for a newspaper designed to represent the interests of Cleveland's laboring class. Established in 1878 by Edward Willis Scripps as the *Penny Press,* it was an alternative to the "radical, Socialist, Wobbly and anarchist publications"—many written in the native languages of European immigrants—that proliferated in American cities during the late nineteenth century. Scripps modeled the *Penny Press* after the *Detroit News,* started by two of his brothers in 1873. Scripps would eventually publish similar papers in Toledo and Columbus, Ohio, as well as St. Louis, Missouri; Pittsburgh, Pennsylvania; and San Francisco, California. Their "pro-labor, anti-monopolistic" editorial policies advocated a "concern for the economic well-being . . . of the laboring class—and expressly opposing the rich," a group that included some of Winsor's best friends and sources.

Seltzer understood, however, that Winsor might satisfy working men and women's curiosity about the social lives of wealthy people, like his patron Leonard Hanna, his favorite hostess Aileen Winslow, and his estranged wife, Margaret Perry. In the Scripps tradition, Seltzer used the *Press* to crusade for reforms that "appealed to the masses of the working class." Winsor's opposition to Prohibition liquor laws, flouting of authority, promotion of bars that served cheap drinks, and his early membership in the local chapter of the Newspaper Guild enhanced the working-class image the *Press* sought to maintain. Although the assignment would require him to visit local night-clubs six times a week, he accepted the offer and resumed his newspaper career on October 5. Winsor did not like what he saw and launched what would become a lifelong campaign to resuscitate the city's nightlife.

"By midnight the other evening, Playhouse Square was almost entirely deserted," he wrote. "Empty taxis cruised up and down—watching for fares that never appeared. There was no one on East Ninth Street except an occasional panhandler lurking in a doorway."

Lunchtime wasn't any better. "As a city, we are too tea room conscious and the average diner-out with a limited income usually finds himself in a little pink and white room, eating such dainties as almond rarebits."

Thursday nights were anemic. "By universal consent" they had once been "maid's night out." Young couples who were "bewildered and lost in a kitchen took to the town. Now . . . brides have learned to cook or dollars are harder to find—in any event the restaurants and cabarets no longer do the thriving business they used to."

Sunday nights? "Once again Martinis are being poured into teacups, waiters eye every newcomer suspiciously and the prices are soaring to the heavens. But if it is not too much to ask—what price Repeal? Of course there are those places that faithfully tread the straight and narrow. It's something of a shock to see a party come rushing in, sink into chairs, give their orders and then gasp with agony as the waiter sadly shakes his head."

Finally, prudes were in charge of hiring entertainers. The manager of a nightclub in the penthouse of the Lake Shore Hotel thought Dwight Fiske, who had entertained Winsor and Margaret at the Pembertons' party in New York City, was "too risqué" for local audiences. Winsor was dismayed that "King Leer" could sing about a virgin sturgeon and a lecherous octopus in New York, Paris, and London, but not in Cleveland.

During his absence, Winsor thought, Repeal had been slowly strangling Cleveland's nightlife, an assessment with which contemporary historians agree. A nation that had tolerated—even celebrated—illegal and unconventional behavior had suddenly legislated limits. New liquor laws made drinking legal but sought to control all sorts of behavior besides drunkenness.

In the first week of November, Winsor traveled to New York City, where his mood improved. At Manhattan's Ritz Hotel he was the luncheon guest of Lucius Beebe and Jerry Zerbe. Polly Parsons, the society editor at the *News,* called Winsor "the Beebe of Cleveland" but confessed, "Both probably resent the comparison. Fact is they are very much alike." They didn't dress alike. Beebe, whose nickname was "Luscious Lucius," wore silk top hats, evening capes, and showy jewelry, plus he spent an inherited fortune on elaborate meals, like the one Winsor described. "A small army of waiters bow you to a choice table—the wine is chilled to the correct and exact temperature—the food, of course, might easily have been served to Nero without anyone being beheaded—and the brandy and cigars that follow must be par excellence. Between the nodding and introductions to the continual passing parade, gossip, epigrams and rumors flow as freely as the champagne."

Between courses, Winsor's hosts showed him the proof of *Society on Parade.* "Jerry Zerbe's album, which hits the stands on Dec. 1, will contain photographs of everyone from the Grand Duchess Marie," Russian royalty, who survived the assassination of her uncle, Emperor Nicholas II, "to Conde Nast," the wealthy publisher of *Vogue* and *Vanity Fair* magazines. "The whole thing is to be ushered into prominence at an enormous cocktail party given by Mr. Beebe (who wrote the foreword) in the Madison Hotel, and the vague idea is to set back every fashionable pocketbook three dollars." Winsor did not tell readers that the book included pictures of his wedding and the bon voyage party aboard the *Europa.* The timing was painful. Just days after his lunch at the Ritz, Margaret filed for divorce in Nevada. In deference to its new columnist, the *Press* announced the nature of her complaint discreetly. "Dispatches from Reno indicate the divorce action will be based on charges of mental cruelty. Mr. French was in New York today."

A week later, the *News* published an item about Margaret and her mother that gave Winsor an opportunity to tell Clevelanders that despite what they might read elsewhere, Margaret and her mother were still taking his phone calls. "CORRECTING, if I may be so bold, another columnist. Mr. Noel Francis [Harland Fend] . . . had occasion to remark last week . . . that Margaret Perry, after crossing the wide Atlantic with the highly publicized Gertrude Stein, had persuaded her mother to produce Miss Stein's next opera." Winsor quoted his soon to be ex-wife's response. "Margaret has just wired, 'Having walked out on the cellophane asylum of "Four Saints" what do you think? Never laid eyes on the woman anyway.'" His about-to-be ex-mother-in-law, Mrs. Frueauff, also backed his account. Fend's report was "erroneous, absolutely erroneous; sorry, terribly sorry, devastatingly sorry." In mid-December, Margaret's mother traveled to Reno to attend her daughter's hearing. Her divorce became final on December 17, 1934.

In ten days, Winsor would be thirty years old. He was restless and looking for a change.

"The men wear anything they please"

LOS ANGELES

Friday, May 17, 1935, 6:30 p.m.

When Winsor was invited to a cocktail party former film actor William Haines was hosting with comedienne Carole Lombard, the columnist distinctly remembered that he was "asked for 5 P.M." For his debut in Hollywood society, however, the columnist decided to make a fashionably late entrance with two of his Cleveland friends, Jerry Zerbe, veteran of *PARADE* and St. Bartholomew's, and Benedict "Benny" Crowell Jr., an unemployed Cleveland gossip columnist. All three hoped stories or photographs of Hollywood's celebrities would boost their young careers.

At 6:30 P.M. the men arrived at Haines's house overlooking Sunset Boulevard, sauntered up the shallow flight of brick stairs, and rapped on a white paneled door with a hefty knocker of solid brass. The details caught Winsor's eye. Haines had recently opened an interior design studio with his longtime companion, Jimmy Shields. They had turned their stucco Spanish hacienda into an English manor with colonial New Orleans trim and painted the entire collage white. Winsor thought the result looked "exactly like a birdhouse," a classic example of the "maddest" residential architecture he had ever seen. In Southern California, he wrote, "houses in the most inconceivable taste sprawl all over the place."

Disdain colored Winsor's first reportage from Hollywood, a scheduled six-week series that *Press* editor Louis Seltzer promoted on the newspaper's front page as "a new kind of reporting." Seltzer promised readers, "Winsor French has entrée to the places where the Garbos, the Gables, the Bennetts gather not as sought-after celebrities but as human beings having fun."

For his "new kind of reporting," Winsor presented himself to celebrities as a "writer" who only reported what he observed, not a journalist "taking an interview. Who am I to ask a lady if she sleeps in pajamas or a nightgown, if she starts the day off with stewed apricots and ends it with stewed playmates?"

The first "celebrities" Winsor described without interviewing them were Haines and Lombard, and the "place" was the formal drawing room Haines had decorated. The walls were painted cool green, the moldings were gilded, and the room was empty. Haines and Lombard had invited two hundred and fifty guests, but at 6:30 P.M., Winsor "was almost the first person to appear." He was embarrassed and tried to explain to readers: "Los Angeles . . . stretches something like a hundred miles . . . which may have something to do with the fact people never are on time. Guests invited to dine at eight usually arrive by ten."

The dearth of guests allowed Winsor to chat with his host, whom he had met when Haines appeared in Cleveland to promote his films. The two men also had a number of mutual friends: Zerbe had drawn a pencil sketch of Haines on a previous trip to Hollywood, and Winsor's witty groomsman Roger Davis was part of a "dynamic circle" of Haines's male friends, an exclusive fraternity that was helping Winsor gain entrée to Hollywood's private parties.

By 7:00 P.M. another newcomer to California made an entrance: Dorothy Parker. She had moved to Hollywood to write movie scripts, and Winsor detected a change in her demeanor: "Her wit has lost its deadly barb." She sat "quietly in the background, never rising to annihilate some unfortunate with one devastating remark." Winsor tried to fill her vacuum. After actress Adrienne Ames made an entrance, he observed her "staring through old friends." She seemed "only able to remember columnists and the press." With the arrival of Louella Parsons, a gossip columnist for the *Los Angeles Herald Examiner,* whose syndicated work appeared in six hundred daily newspapers, Winsor noted that Miss Ames's "sullen mouth spread into a smile and she became a radiant, if temporary beauty."

Then Haines introduced Winsor to Lombard. Dressed entirely in black, the actress wore "an enormous picture hat and the most gigantic sapphires I have seen. . . . It was something of a shock. She is far more beautiful off than on the screen, and easily the most casual and outspoken woman in Hollywood."

The *most* casual and outspoken woman in Hollywood? How could Winsor know? He had been there four days! In May 1935, only one of the twenty-six-year-old woman's completed films, *Twentieth Century,* hinted at her comic genius. She had yet to perfect the sassy, fast-talking blonde who appeared in a half-dozen classic screwball comedies. She was about to begin an important film career, yet Winsor thought she was already the "most casual and outspoken woman in Hollywood."

One possible explanation can be found in Lombard's relationship with her cohost, William Haines. Studio executives had recently killed his film career. The thirty-five-year-old actor had appeared successfully in more than twenty silent films and an equal number of talkies. Winsor reviewed one of his last films, *Fast Life.* "If you don't get a kick out of William Haines piloting his boat in a race, with the police after him, his girl beside him, and Cliff Edwards lying alongside the engine, stopping a leaking gas pipe in the same manner the little Dutch boy saved the dike in Dutch legend; then you have become very, very blasé."

Haines was one of MGM's most popular leading men until an incident in 1932. According to his biographer, "Haines picked up a sailor in Pershing Square in Los Angeles and took him to the YMCA where he had a room. The house detective and Los Angeles Vice Squad burst in and arrested and handcuffed both men. MGM boss Louis B. Mayer told Billy Haines that he had to choose his lifestyle or his career." Haines chose his lifestyle, so "Mayer terminated his contract and ensured that he could not work in the film industry again."

By hosting a party with Haines in the house shared with Shields, Lombard was thumbing her nose at Mayer and his homophobic accomplices who had refused to employ the film star. She had already hired Haines and Shields to decorate her own house. Winsor's use of "casual" might be translated as "unconcerned about homosexuals" and "outspoken" as "bold in their defense." Was Winsor applauding Lombard's courage for standing by Haines? One cannot be sure, but "Billy's house," according to his biographer, "was the scene of many important gatherings" of prominent Hollywood personalities who practiced, approved, or were tolerant of unconventional sexuality.

Half an hour after Winsor swooned over Lombard, Haines's drawing room was a "milling sea of celebrities." Neither Garbo nor Gable was present, as Seltzer had promised, but there was a Bennett: Joan. Haines's biographer insists that the drawing room "was for those guests not intimate enough to penetrate deeper into the house." Haines must have enjoyed Winsor and his companions' company, because three hours later, the columnist was among "sixty-five of the original two hundred and fifty guests" invited to step down a flight of "four low black marble steps" and into "Bill's white dining room" with its "raspberry satin draperies." Dinner was served. "Tables groaned under platters—two or three kinds of soup, chicken, hot and cold meats, salads and great bowls of vegetables. At eleven o'clock the party trekked back upstairs. People left, more arrived."

Some time after midnight, Winsor left the party "to see Rufus."

That he left the party and that the reason was "Rufus" were not items printed in one of Winsor's columns or correspondence. Throughout 1935, he noted in a bold script where he'd been and whom he'd seen on the lined pages of a brown leather datebook, the first of a series in which he recorded his frenetic daily rounds, glimpses of his unpublished life.

According to Winsor's columns, Rufus was "a young Detroit socialite and one of the nation's better known playboys," whose last name was Caulkins. He was "being groomed" by Paramount "to replace Randolph Scott who is now under contract to R-K-O," but according to Winsor's datebook, when he reached Rufus, his friend was "asleep."

So what was Winsor to do? According to his datebook, "*back* again" to the Haines/Lombard party where he lost track of time. "At one or two o'clock supper was served and my head began to spin and my courage to wane— but still determined to see it out I plunged into another scotch and soda. The fun was about to begin. With Orry-Kelly [Warner Brothers' designer] whipping up the costumes, a floorshow was staged to end all floorshows. Scrap baskets with roses growing from them became headdresses; bedspreads, window curtains and sheets were twisted into creations." Lloyd Pantages, a local newspaper columnist, "danced a Bolero and Peggy Fears a tango. Someone else, executing a high kick, loosened a cluster of crystals from a priceless chandelier. Haines, the perfect host, knocked off a few more. Broad daylight filtered through the Venetian blinds and a Hollywood party finally broke up and departed for the Brown Derby for breakfast."

In his datebook, Winsor wrote, "Home at about 6," eleven and a half hours after his entrance. In his newspaper column, he exaggerated. He wrote that Hollywood "cocktail parties commence around 5:30 P.M. and keep right on going until morning. Leaving Bill Haines' the other day, I suddenly discovered I had been there fourteen hours."

Winsor's description of the Haines/Lombard marathon had honored Seltzer's promise to *Press* readers. The newspaper was carrying exclusive coverage of celebrities "as human beings having fun." Winsor catered to America's obsession with movie celebrity, intensified by the new "talkies." He believed his ability to satisfy that curiosity could help him achieve his ambition: national syndication of his newspaper column.

With that goal in mind, on an overcast May morning in Cleveland, Winsor had piled his suitcases with Zerbe's and Crowell's in the trunk of his new tan Ford and headed west. A week later, the trio approached Los Angeles at night through acres of orange groves. Winsor wrinkled his nose. He did not like the "sickly, heavy odor."

He and his buddies were "badly in need of fortification after endless hours of holding a car at 75." They expected to find relief at "Fulco's," a house in Hollywood rented by the Duke of Verdura. Since he had taken a pair of scissors to the expensive chapeau of Winsor's ex-wife, the duke had designed a gold, "curb-link bracelet watch" for Greta Garbo, the notoriously reclusive

Swedish film star. The duke had offered Winsor and his party a place to sleep until they rented an apartment of their own. By the time Winsor and his pals finally found Fulco's, it was midnight, but "Allen, Peggy Fears" and "Bert" were waiting for them.

"Allen" was Allen Vincent. He and Fears were stage actors trying to revive film careers in 1935. "Bert" was Bert Young, one of Cleveland's "cut-ups," according to Winsor, who spent "most of his time and all of his energy trying to discover ways and means of getting rich quickly." One scheme included "a hundred pounds of beeswax" that Young had salvaged and repackaged as "'Stach-stick: To take the muss out of mustache' . . . [and] make points at the tip." Items from Winsor's columns of 1933 and 1934 also record Crowell and Young's voyage around the world as deckhands aboard a freighter.

Later that same morning, after only a few hours sleep, Winsor and his traveling companions lunched at the Vendome, a "fabulous restaurant" where they paid a "fabulous check." The appalled columnist observed people dining "in their studio makeup." Women wore "pajamas," and men "anything they please—white flannel trousers, shorts and even the good old fashioned plus fours." The Vendome was "littered with telephones, continually being carried from table to table by the waiters." That same evening, Winsor dined with Vincent and visited the Tango and Trocadero nightclubs. Of this experience, he wrote, "People don't talk, they shout."

On Wednesday night, he dined again with Vincent, a thirty-two-year-old Dartmouth graduate under contract to Paramount. A few weeks before Winsor arrived in Hollywood, the studio had loaned Vincent to Warner Bros. for a supporting role in the *Return of Peter Grimm,* starring Lionel Barrymore, a member of the famous family of temperamental stage and screen actors. It was the first movie role Vincent had been offered in two years.

In the past, he had been frequently cast as "second lead," roles which had not earned unanimous critical acclaim. Of Vincent's performance in *Broadway Bad,* one critic wrote, "very good as the weak husband . . . but as he is never cast in any other type of part, by this time being weak must be almost second nature."

The critic's name? Winsor French, and he had more to say on the subject. Reviewing *I Have Lived,* he criticized Vincent's studio. "It is about time he was given an opportunity to play some other part than the nauseating social lion, who is continually spouting that women of experience could never make anything but impossible wives."

Finally, Winsor ridiculed Vincent's love scenes with the leading lady in *Daring Daughters:* "He never tries to kiss her."

Was he slyly exposing Vincent's sexual preference? The question will remain unanswered, but his datebook recorded still another "dinner with

Allen" on Thursday night. Friday was the Haines/Lombard party. On Saturday, Winsor arose in time to revisit the "Troc + Frolics Inn." "Troc" stands for "Trocadero" and the Frolics was the notorious Beverly Hills Café, not an inn. Located on Beverly Boulevard, the café presented a floorshow that consisted entirely of female impersonators. "The boys make their entrance . . . wearing tarnished evening gowns two or three years old," Winsor wrote. "All of them have artificial eyelashes and scarlet finger nails." Some "lean wistfully against the piano and try to sing seriously in the Libby Holman manner. Personally I always wonder what the principals look like in the daylight. Perhaps like other woodland folk they emerge only after dark."

Following the floorshow? Winsor wrote in his datebook, "Allen's (Spent the night)." Winsor and Vincent's romance proves that for the actor, Winsor's company numbed the sting of his needling commentary. Years later Vincent wrote, "I wildly enjoyed every one of those times I saw him." Not everyone in Hollywood was so forgiving. Two years of frequently scathing reviews of movies, film actresses, and actors had made enemies. Winsor wrote: "It was a tragic mistake ever to believe that Clark Gable was fitted for serious parts." And, he declared, Ginger Rogers "was never born to be an emotional actress." His language echoed that of his friend Noel Busch, Briton Hadden's cousin and *TIME*'s film critic in the late 1920s, who called Hollywood movies "insipid," "vulgar," and "interminable." Busch had allegedly "insulted" an actress by describing her as "a pretty little blonde girl with an affected way of showing her teeth."

The mouth of Alice White, a thirty-one-year-old silent film star trying to sustain a career in talking movies, received similar treatment from Winsor. He described her as one of those "cute blondes" whose "bee-stung lips were definitely a thing of the past." Although he did not mention her physical appearance, he criticized one of her films, *Employee's Entrance,* a purported exposé of philandering department store executives and their innocent prey—beautiful female sales clerks.

"If *Employee's Entrance* presents even so much as a blurred outline of backstage life in a department store," Winsor wrote, "then I worked in a morgue for two years." He was referring to 1922 and 1923, when the Halle Brothers Co. employed him in their store at Playhouse Square. In addition to dismissing the film, he wrote a single sentence about White in a supporting role: She "makes an attempt to come back to public favor, but as far as I am concerned she might have saved the effort."

Her thirty-five-year-old press agent, Sidney "Sy" Bartlett, who eventually became a prolific screenwriter and film producer, objected in writing: "I have just finished reading the national reviews on Miss Alice White's performance in *Employee's Entrance.* You stand absolutely alone in what you would defensively call your 'honest opinion.' Your opinion, in itself, as 'even your best friends' might not tell you, is very unimportant."

Unimportant? If so, why was Bartlett complaining about one sentence? Winsor was the most powerful critic in Cleveland, a major market for movies. His readers bought tickets. Theater managers remembered *Design for Living*'s sold-out houses. The tone of Bartlett's letter suggests its author was trying to intimidate an outspoken critic. Contemporary newspaper accounts claim Bartlett was also romantically involved with his client and would marry her within the year.

"If you could lose your inhibitions long enough," Bartlett suggested.

Had Winsor been any less inhibited in print, he might have been fired. He ridiculed movie censors. After they cut the song "I Like A Man Who Takes His Time" from Mae West's movie *She Done Him Wrong,* he pointed out, "You can buy a record of it in any music store."

He applauded friendly satire of homosexuals. In *Private Jones,* Winsor singled out supporting actor Walter Catlett, who played an "effeminate" YMCA worker and was "very funny about it."

And he warned readers when studios neutered scripts. Before the release of *These Three,* an adaptation of Lillian Hellman's play *The Children's Hour,* Winsor pointed out that the schoolgirl's invention of a lesbian relationship between two women had been changed to a "romantic triangle" between the women and a male. The "too, too purple passages have been given to Joel McCrea instead of a young woman which changes the connotation—if you get what I mean."

Perhaps Winsor's reputation for candor rattled Bartlett. In any case, he decided to belittle Winsor's department store experience: "In your spare hours away from the silks and ribbons counter." Winsor sold china.

Bartlett continued: "I believe that you were an ambitious young man and . . . developed and qualified yourself as a member of the Fourth Estate, who, by chance, finds himself with an ax in his hands. Your ax, by the way, is as dull as your intellect. I read your review twice and you were neither fish nor fowl."

By suggesting that Winsor was ambiguous and fond of soft fabrics, was Bartlett insinuating the critic was effeminate? If the agent thought he could silence Winsor by questioning his masculinity, he had picked the wrong man. Eight months after receiving Bartlett's letter, Winsor ran another item about his client: "I have always resented the appearance of Miss Alice White on any screen fairly vehemently. Her ridiculous overplaying and utter insistence of forever being coy have completely ruined the few pictures I have been forced to watch her work in."

If Bartlett thought his letter's innuendo would embarrass Winsor, he was wrong on that count, too. The columnist published the press agent's screed verbatim, including Bartlett's demand: "Tell me exactly what develops and breeds a caustic, drooling, third-string critic."

What motivated Winsor's movie criticism? Unlike his Cleveland newspaper colleagues, he took movies seriously. In March 1933, the Canadian operators of the Allen Theatre invited all the local critics to attend a private screening of the controversial German picture *Mädchen in Uniform.* Compare Winsor's review with the competition.

The *Plain Dealer:* No review.

The *Press:* It's about a girl's school with a principal who is a strict disciplinarian and a teacher who is more sympathetic. It's an admirably made story, but no one is killed, and its strongest appeal is in being touching. Incidentally, there is no man in the cast.

Winsor at the *News:* The action is laid entirely in a German school for daughters of army officers. To it comes a young and exceedingly sensitive girl whose mother is dead and in it she finds the first affection and understanding she has ever known—from one of the instructors.

Winsor used the dash shamelessly.

> But living under the unbearably strict discipline of the school she becomes more and more unhappy in her troubled adolescence. The few moments a day she is able to spend with her teacher only serve to upset her more and she can neither explain nor understand her moments of happiness or unhappiness.
>
> During a school party following a play, she drinks a little too much punch, becomes flushed with excitement, her nerves snap and shrieking her secrets to the entire school, she faints. When she is isolated and forbidden even to speak to her teacher, she cannot understand what horrible thing she has done and half in a trance climbs the long stairway to the top of the welled hall and attempts suicide.
>
> There is not a man in the large cast—and the story has been beautifully acted by an amazing group of women. . . . Certainly the theme . . . will meet with censor trouble, and although I hate to say it, I am afraid that the fine integrity of the play will drift over the audience's head.

It whizzed past the numbskulls at the *Press* and *Plain Dealer.* Winsor did not drop the subject. When he heard that Allen was "afraid to screen *Maedchen* because Hitler's enemies might grow violent," he called their position "silly. . . . If anything *Maedchen* is anti-Nazi propaganda."

When Allen finally abandoned *Mädchen,* Winsor began lobbying the Hanna Theatre to book the film. He succeeded. A week before its premiere, the columnist reported that the initial screenings were "practically a sell-out. . . . So rush in your order immediately." He helped generate a "terrific demand for tickets," which led the Hanna to show *Mädchen* continuously, rather than once a night, then for two weeks rather than one. Winsor maintained his support. "If you have not already seen it, I most certainly advise that you do. Not only is it one of the most unusual pictures ever produced, but the portrayals by Hertha Thiele and Dorothea Wieck are quite the most beautiful that have been seen in a long, long time."

Yet film historian Gretchen Elsner-Sommer claims it was not until a reconstructed print was released in the early 1970s and shown at women's film festivals that *Mädchen*'s "subversive anti-Fascist, anti-patriarchal themes . . . [as] the first truly radical Lesbian film" finally received the recognition they deserved.

Not so. In 1933, a male movie critic understood *Mädchen*'s themes and wrote about them using the vocabulary permitted in general-circulation newspapers.

Thus Winsor had arrived in California with high expectations for film, a reputation for intelligent, candid criticism, but low regard for the people who made movies in Hollywood. "In discussing the recent Fox-Twentieth Century merger with friends," studio head Sam Goldwyn "delivered himself of the divine remark, 'I think we have the mucus of a great organization.'"

Hollywood conversation? "Inane and stupid."

Hollywood lives? "Simply an enormous display of exhibitionism."

Behavior at movie premieres? "At the first drop of the curtain everyone rushes for the foyer, spotlight and waiting photographers. Only studio cameramen, incidentally, are admitted. The little boys and girls of the cinema world have learned only too well the horrors of the un-retouched picture." Outside the theater, "tedious autograph seekers with their pathetic little collections of glossy prints they hope to have signed before the evening was over stood on the sidewalk like vultures waiting to leap."

After less than a week in California, Winsor was gleefully predicting Hollywood's demise: "Take any and all bets, and at any odds, that the motion picture business will clear out of California. Metro Goldwyn Mayer already has purchased tracts of land in New Jersey and all the new contracts, both for players and authors, include clauses to the effect they are still binding in the event of an exodus. . . . Sooner or later the sequined celluloid babies will have to desert their swimming pools and trek east." (While MGM did consider moving its studios to New Jersey in the early 1930s, if any readers took Winsor's gambling advice, they lost money.)

While his columns exuded East Coast hauteur, his datebook was a cheery record of "cocktails with Allen," "Lunch with Allen," and a night spent in a rustic motel: "Keen Camp with Allen." Privately, Winsor was enjoying himself and California.

After he, Zerbe, and Crowell settled into a rented apartment, they began returning Hollywood's hospitality. Both Winsor's "new kind of reporting" and Zerbe's "candid shots of socialites and entertainers," which he had pioneered at *PARADE,* required picking up the tab at "gilded restaurants where celebrities gather to see, be seen and scribble autographs" as well as the "Troc," "the most expensive night club in the world." In Hollywood Winsor had no intention of partying within the "limits" of his pocketbook. He slipped the headwaiter a ten-dollar bill so he could be "conspicuously seated" at a "spotlight" table on the edge of the dance floor where he could observe celebrities without craning his neck. "Carole Lombard in floating white chiffon waltzes by . . . and stops at the table for a moment." When Marlene Dietrich danced past, he heard her singing "in a guttural exciting voice."

The *Press* reimbursed some of his expenses, but when Winsor noted in his datebook, "Car broke down," he also added, "wired Len for money." His salary did not cover repairing a Ford *and* dining at the Troc. He relied on his millionaire groomsman to subsidize "new reporting" at the *Press.* (Winsor was not the only local newsman to benefit from Hanna's largesse. He also gave monthly checks to Cleveland newspaper artist Augustus "Gus" Peck. To preserve his own anonymity, Hanna used Winsor's sister Margaret "Peggy" Eaton as his confidential go-between.)

Hanna's financial support helped insulate Winsor from the fear of losing his job for being too "outrageous" and allowed him to entertain his sources as their social equal. Ironically, Hanna was financing his family's competition. His cousins, headed by publisher Daniel R. Hanna Jr., had recently merged their *News* with the *Plain Dealer* to become major stockholders in the Forest City Publishing Company, relentless rivals of the *Press.*

During Winsor's third week in California, his sneering tone softened slightly. "Hollywood with its ridiculous trimmings and clap trap can massacre a sense of proportion quicker than any other city in the world. Even at this point I can't discover any good reason why restaurants shouldn't be built in the shape of derby hats . . . or why persons shouldn't go about behaving like freaks on a side-show holiday."

Winsor used the word "freaks" several days before he met Mr. and Mrs. Errol Flynn wearing skimpy swimwear at a Sunday afternoon "tea" on June 16, 1935, the day Hollywood seduced him.

Twenty-four-year-old Flynn, the notorious movie swashbuckler, had recently married film actress Lili Damita, who was twenty-nine or thirty-two, depending on which birthdate she was using. Winsor found them "sprawling in the hot afternoon sun" next to an "Olympian-sized" swimming pool that had been carved out of a hillside overlooking Sunset Boulevard. Backdrop for the pool was an Italian villa "covered with a great wisteria vine." The villa's owner, film director George Cukor, was in the water, lounging on a "sun-drenched rubber mattress," as well as the villa's interior designer, Billy Haines, "imitating [Johnny] Weismuller," the Olympic swimming champion MGM hired to play *Tarzan*.

A houseboy offered Winsor tea, sandwiches, hot buttered scones, or ice-cold sliced watermelon from a silver tray. He declined tea after spotting another young man making the rounds with "a portable bar laden with stronger beverages."

Cukor abandoned his mattress to show Winsor two of the villa's more interesting rooms. Haines had created an "enormous" oval lounge reserved for the movie director's intimate friends. He covered the walls with "beige steer hide, bound in copper." Speakers hidden beneath the leather whispered Bach's harpsichord music. "Large, half moon couches" curved in front of French doors that opened on the garden. The room's "only decoration" was a "great Japanese fig tree with glistening leaves." Nearby, in Cukor's library, Winsor was surprised. "It was actually a library, its walls lined from floor to ceiling with first editions that would make any collector green with envy. [Winsor collected first editions.] There are no uncut volumes . . . and none Cukor hasn't read."

The literary interests of the man who had directed Katharine Hepburn in *Little Women* and begun filming *Romeo and Juliet* threatened Winsor's stereotype of the "inane and stupid" Hollywood filmmaker. "Gasping" in admiration, Winsor returned to the pool where the Flynns were "talking shop." He listened, watched, and pronounced them "the best looking couple in Hollywood."

Cukor's swimming parties, like Haines's dinners, were a refuge for Hollywood's sexual nonconformists. They appear to have taught Winsor to be more tolerant of unconventional female behavior. When Shakespearean actress Rosamond Pinchot arrived "looking like something engraved on an old Greek coin," he noted that she was wearing "slacks." That was new vocabulary for Winsor. "Pajamas" was the word he'd been using. In Cleveland, he had pitied females who wore pants in public, calling them "victims" of the "fad" begun by Greta Garbo and Marlene Dietrich, who had been photographed in trousers. In the 1930s, some thought women in pants were advertising the fact that they were lesbians or sexual rebels. Oddly, nonconformist Winsor, who promoted *Mädchen in Uniform*, seemed to share their opinion. He had begged the Carter Hotel's management to "restrain women from dancing with each other" in their rooftop nightclub.

If one were to list which of Hollywood's attractions seduced Winsor, there would be at least ten. Numbers one and two were Cukor's "first editions" and Pinchot's slacks. Three was the Flynns' tanned flesh.

In the early evening of the day that seduced Winsor, he left Cukor's villa, driving west toward Venice beach, where the Ocean Park Fun House stood at the foot of an amusement pier in the Pacific Ocean. There he—literally and metaphorically—fell head over heels for "celluloid land."

His new friend Carole Lombard had asked two hundred "actors and actresses, stars, starlets and directors" to an "intimate little party" at the Fun House. When "Fieldsie" (Marion Fields, the comedienne's "large, blond and beautiful companion-secretary") had phoned to invite Winsor, she told him to wear "old clothes" and be prepared to "run through huge barrels and shoot down slides." Lombard's choice of party site troubled Winsor. He was a poor swimmer, so he asked Fieldsie what would happen if he fell in the ocean. She replied that Lombard had "engaged the services of two ambulances, and insured herself against the possibility of any accidents." He accepted.

When he arrived at the pier, he found ropes were restraining "hundreds of curious" onlookers. With stars "wearing everything from shorts to tea gowns," he "plowed through the mobs" and into an entrance tent where guests were met by "a gentleman with a microphone who gaily announced their names to the waiting hostess." The actress, Winsor learned, "will go to any end and spend a fortune to satisfy her love for practical jokes."

Inside the Fun House, he negotiated "sliding and rising and falling floors which were generously peppered with holes for . . . sudden blasts of air to bewilder and harass feminine arrivals." Eventually he reached a small stage "facing an audience of shouting, delighted guests who had all survived the same experience, then down a gang plank to meet Lombard who was waiting to fortify your spirits with everything from ginger ale to what have you."

Sipping a glass of "what have you," Winsor watched "guests make their confused entrances. . . . Marlene Dietrich and Hedda Hopper arrived in shorts to be greeted by groans . . . Norma Talmadge, because she was in a skirt, sneaked through a side entrance, but Constance Collier, also in a skirt, gave an involuntary performance that would have done justice to Sally Rand." (The latter was a notorious stripper.)

After midnight, Lombard served supper: "Fried chicken, hot dogs and steaming coffee—or if you wanted it—more of anything you had been drinking all evening." Impromptu entertainment included a "cabaret with Bill Haines and Dick Arlen, Lloyd Pantages, George Cukor and dozens of others all behaving in the manner of gay 90's chorus boys." (In the week following Lombard's party, Winsor and Zerbe managed to "crawl out of bed before dawn" and "whip themselves into evening clothes," so they might appear as "dress extras"—"gay and happy" nightclub patrons in a Walter Wanger film, *Every Night at Eight*. At the studio, Winsor and Zerbe were joined by Pantages and five more of his friends, a group that included Jimmy Shields, Billy Haines's companion. Hollywood's most handsome and outré males filled the movies' crowd scenes.)

Several days after Lombard's "fantastic and spectacular" party, Winsor was scheduled to begin driving toward Cleveland, his six-week assignment concluded. Instead, he wired Seltzer and asked for a month-long extension. His columns were selling papers, so Seltzer agreed. What Winsor didn't tell his editor was that he also needed more time to finish a movie scenario he was trying to sell one of the studios. Screenwriters' salaries were enormous.

"Samuel Goldwyn will pay Jane Murfin, the writer, a tidy $100,000 a year to keep her from becoming homesick for R-K-O." According to Winsor, Murfin had ninety colleagues at MGM, and each of those authors had a "private office and access to a secretary." The hours were flexible, too. "One highly paid gentleman with a weakness for a typewriter told me it is fairly good policy to show up at the studio at least for the first few weeks."

Winsor did not believe the studios were getting their money's worth, especially for the dialogue in Warner Bros.' *Oil for the Lamps of China*. "During one emotional moment," actress Josephine Hutchinson was "forced to mutter something to [Pat] O'Brien about their being and remaining together. 'Together,' he replies. 'Yes,' says Miss Hutchinson, 'and remember, it rhymes with forever.' I don't know how you care for that, but I cared so little I was out of the theater as fast as my feet could carry me."

Although Winsor didn't save drafts of his scenario, the subject was murder. Earlier he had visited the Los Angeles morgue to view a corpse and do research on a "murder story." He wrote during the day and partied at night. After one session, he wrote in his datebook "to Carole Lombard's for a drink," then he returned to his apartment "until Jerry brought in Cary Grant, Frank Horn and Betty Furness."

Winsor's datebook substantiates Zerbe's boast that he and Grant were lovers during the summer of 1935. The photographer told biographer Brendan Gill that he and "Cary Grant were so often to be seen in each other's company that Grant's studio felt compelled to cook up a synthetic newspaper romance." Gill, who described Zerbe as "strikingly handsome and flirtatious," wrote that the photographer and Grant "were obliged to honor the prevailing Hollywood taboos and at the same time generate favorable publicity in movie magazines and among Grant's doting fan clubs. To that end, Grant was reported in the press to be enjoying an impassioned affair with the starlet Betty Furness. Night after night, he took the good-natured Furness out to dinner and returned her to her apartment promptly at ten o'clock, after which Zerbe and he and assorted companions went out on the town."

Winsor and Allen Vincent appeared to have honored the same "taboos." Their restaurant and nightclub dates were often in the company of actress Alice Terry and her friend Muriel Ames. Terry, "once one of the greatest stars in silent pictures," had successfully made the transition to "talkies." She was shorter than Winsor, standing five feet, three inches high. "Blond and still lovely," Winsor thought, the actress had "hurdled the years with magnificent ease." She was thirty-three years old. For Terry and Winsor, there was never a hint of romance. For fourteen years, she had been married to film director Rex Ingram, who had successfully cast her in a number of his films. During the summer of 1935, Ingram, who had converted to Islam, was in North Africa writing a novel, and Terry was living alone in their Hollywood home "exactly as she pleases."

Toward the end of June, Cole and Linda Porter suddenly arrived in the Port of Long Beach after sailing the world. During the months-long cruise, the composer and playwright Moss Hart had written a new musical: *Jubilee*. The men decided to stop in Hollywood, on this, the Porters' first visit to California, to audition talent for their new production.

When Linda Porter learned of Winsor's presence, she invited him to hear her husband play "his new music" at their suite in a Beverly Hills hotel. That same evening Winsor invited the couple to attend one of Hollywood's most controversial nightspots, the Angelus Temple, where a theatrical preacher, Aimee Semple McPherson, was "saving souls" in person and over the radio. Linda declined; Porter accepted.

From seats in the temple balcony's front row, the two skeptics watched the "magnificently corseted" Sister Aimee in a "white velvet dress and a short cape lined in red velvet" as she manipulated the emotions of a packed auditorium. "Her hair is bleached to the last extremity, long flowing sleeves fall away from her arms and beautiful hands, a diamond cross hangs from her neck." She invited people to baptism "in a manner that would make you believe they were going to be taken to Coney Island for an evening of giddy nonsense." Although Winsor was not "moved to repentance," he "liked the way she carried on about Biblical characters— exactly as if she had just lunched with . . . them."

Throughout Winsor's stay in Hollywood, his columns were consistently dry-eyed, but during the week that he wrote about McPherson, his datebook recorded, "Crying jag." In his first published column after noting his uncontrollable tears, he confided to readers, "This city can give even a lad on the water wagon jitters." Had liquor caused the "crying jag"? Five days before leaving Cleveland for Hollywood, Winsor noted in his datebook, "Home drunk and Mother marvelous about it." Periodically, he worried about his drinking.

The columnist interrupted his ten-week cocktail party on a Friday night, remained dry on Saturday, but by Sunday afternoon was sipping liquor at dinner with Zerbe, Grant, and Furness, then finishing the night at the Clover Club with Allen Vincent, who had recently finished work on *The Return of Peter Grimm*. According to Winsor, Vincent had "turned in such a swell performance he is more in demand than any young actor in Hollywood." "His agents already are being deluged with offers." Winsor was not averse to overstatement on behalf of a companion.

The following evening Winsor dined again with Vincent at his apartment. Despite his praise of Vincent, he recorded a "row with Allen" in his datebook. Their argument was interrupted by the telephone: A friend reported that Rufus Caulkins had been discovered at the bottom of a hundred-foot cliff. Winsor had not talked to Caulkins since mid-June, when the two men had hosted a farewell lunch for the Duke of Verdura, who was returning to New York. In what amounted to an obituary, Winsor tried to set the record straight about his friend, who was in his midthirties when he died.

Wire service stories identified Caulkins as a "Hollywood apartment house owner." Winsor described him as "one of the most famous of the international playboys."

The Associated Press recorded that the deceased was the "son of Edward B. Caulkins, president of the Detroit Steel Casting Company." Winsor wrote that the Caulkins family was "excessively wealthy." For ten years, the scion had "spent his life covering the plush lined resorts of the world and giving parties that in their way made history. Suddenly last winter, however, Rufus became bored with 'first night' society. At one time he was engaged to marry Ruth Kresge of the ten-cent store millions—and another time it was rumored he would marry Ruth's sister, Kitty, as soon as she received her divorce from Count Carle Wyjk."

The *New York Times* reported "Caulkins had been in Hollywood since January, studying dramatics." Winsor added, "Although none of his friends suspected it, he had a certain and definite ability. RKO seriously considered him as a possible star for westerns." Caulkins had spent spare time "riding horseback" on the beach. "Last week Ernest Lubitsch watched him play several scenes in the Paramount Theater and there were rumors he was about to be given a spectacular contract. So ended a career that might easily have been brilliant."

Although his datebook contained an earlier note, "Rufus phoned drunk," Winsor didn't speculate in print about whether or not his friend's death was an accident or suicide and whether alcohol might have played a role. Winsor saw Caulkins's pursuit of an acting career as a sign of maturity: "The playboy era, like that of the flappers, has had its day. Million-dollar dinners with diamond bracelets for favors are a thing of the past." Winsor's seemingly carefree fraternity of single, slender, handsome, hard-drinking, cigarette-smoking, articulate, and amusing night people had lost a brother.

Just days later, the columnist announced his departure for Cleveland at week's end, "leaving unhappily a village I expected to laugh at." A "round of parties" commenced "immediately," including what Winsor called an "amazing evening" at the home of his frequent escort, actress Alice Terry.

She had returned his many dinner dates with a late-night buffet supper that included "Hawaiian singers strolling between the tables" and entertainment by invited guests, who included Allen Vincent. One of Winsor's favorite mimics, Dick Cromwell, impersonated Greta Garbo, Joan Crawford, and Katharine Hepburn; another guest sang; but, according to an entry in his datebook, Winsor performed the finale: "I did a strip." On his last night in Hollywood, the columnist joined the "enormous display of exhibitionism" he had once ridiculed.

Twenty-four hours later Winsor, Zerbe, and Crowell were driving toward Cleveland with an unfinished screenplay and two quarts of Scotch that comedienne Patsy Kelly had given them to ease their descent into reality. The liquor didn't dispel Winsor's cranky mood. "In Hollywood," he wrote from the road, "everyone looked like a movie star and sported a healthy, tanned body." Through Nevada, Utah, Wyoming, and Nebraska, he rediscovered humanity's "indifferent ugliness."

Upon his arrival in Cleveland, a reporter interviewed the columnist as if he were a movie star. Seltzer ran the article on the front page. "A very tan, dapper young man . . . blew into the *Press* office today, and such of his erstwhile acquaintances as were able to recognize the man hiding behind the sunburn soon realized that Winsor French was back." In the city room, he discovered that the headline over his column had been changed from "Let's Face It" to "Winsor French." He was a *Press* celebrity.

His newspaper colleagues assumed that Winsor was independently wealthy. At the *News,* Polly Parsons wrote that the about-town columnist had "descended" into the newspaper business "from proud parlors. He was born with a silver spoon in his mouth." At the *Press,* he was identified as the "chronicler of the hard-core rich," a representative of the "rich and talented younger set in Cleveland." The reality was more complex.

Based on Winsor's use of "excessively wealthy" to describe the family of the late Rufus Caulkins, the Eatons might be called "carefully wealthy," especially in their financial arrangements with their celebrity son. When Winsor returned home from Hollywood, he could not afford to share an apartment with friends. Instead, he resumed boarding at his parents' residence in Cleveland Heights with two younger brothers and three younger sisters. His stepfather charged $20 a week: "$15.00 for room and board and $5.00 on indebtedness." The latter was the unpaid balance of the $250 Winsor had borrowed from Eaton when he ran out of money in Paris. His stepfather was flexible. He wrote Winsor, "The $15.00 should be paid regularly each Saturday or Sunday even if the $5.00 payment is deferred at times."

"Room and board" included the services of paid caretakers, chauffeurs, cooks, and chambermaids who attended family members at homes the Eatons maintained in Cleveland Heights and Williamstown, Massachusetts. Winsor availed himself of their services. In an exchange of telegrams dated October 1935, Eaton made sure his stepson understood his responsibilities when he wanted to entertain friends at the family's summerhouse in Massachusetts.

Winsor: WOULD LIKE TO GO TO WILLIAMSTOWN THIS WEEKEND . . . COULD YOU PLEASE WIRE ME CARE OF LEN HANNA 277 PARK AVE HOW TO REACH CARE TAKER SO I CAN NOTIFY HIM WHEN WE ARE ARRIVING.

Eaton: CARETAKER ARTHUR SCHUMAKER . . . WIRE ME HOW MANY AND DAY OF ARRIVAL AND I SHALL SEND SCHUMAKER INSTRUCTIONS.

Winsor: ABOUT FIVE OF US AND EXPECT TO ARRIVE . . . AT ABOUT SEVEN SATURDAY EVENING.

Eaton: FRIEDA CAN EITHER COOK OR DO WAITING AND CHAMBER WORK BUT CANNOT DO BOTH . . . YOU WILL HAVE TO ARRANGE FOR SOMEONE AND ALSO ADVISE FRIEDA WHAT FOOD AND OTHER PROVISIONS TO BUY FOR OVER SUNDAY . . . IF YOU WANT DINNER SATURDAY NIGHT ADVISE HER WHAT TIME OR ELSE HAVE HER PREPARE IT AFTER YOU ARRIVE.

Winsor eventually cancelled the weekend incurring no expenses. On another occasion, he and a brother spent a week in Williamstown. Eaton's invoice records Winsor's expenses.

2 cases of beer $2.80 ea.	$5.60
Cigarettes for August	5.60

1 quart bottle Scotch	3.37
1 bottle Gin	1.50
Telephone calls	1.90
½ Katherine's salary	27.50
½ of Groceries $94.59	47.29
½ of Gas and Electric Light Bills	8.08
	$100.84

Winsor objected, insisting his brother smoked half the cigarettes. Eaton reduced the bill by $2.80; Winsor took a year to pay the debt, in five- and ten-dollar installments. His newspaper salary barely covered the cost of living at home, and Hanna didn't subsidize him when he was boarding with his parents.

The Hollywood bon vivant endured his straitened circumstances in a city whose nightlife offered little relief. "Darkened shop windows stared stupidly into the street, now and then a cruising taxi turned into the avenue and a slightly tipsy gentleman staggered into a hotel." The city, he wrote, "needed a stick of dynamite to blast it into action."

In December, however, he received a phone call from Margaret Moore, who identified herself as secretary to Cole and Linda Porter. Linda Porter wanted to know Winsor's schedule for next year. For the first six months of 1936, the Porters were leasing the Hollywood home owned by movie actor Richard Barthelmess. Reclining on a hillside in Brentwood, California, the estate included a swimming pool, tennis courts, and an unfurnished guesthouse. Linda Porter invited Winsor and one of his friends to spend March and April in the guesthouse, if he were available. He accepted the invitation, pending his editor's approval. He told Seltzer the Barthelmess estate would be a perfect outpost for the "new kind of reporting." His editor agreed, and Winsor gleefully began preparations for spending two months in Hollywood.

Winsor believed his "new kind of reporting" required him to appear to be a member of the "rich and talented younger set." To reinforce the image, he needed a suitable housemate. Zerbe was qualified, but busy in Manhattan where he had signed a contract with El Morocco. His photographs of celebrities lounging on the nightclub's zebra-striped banquettes were quickly becoming treasured souvenirs of café society. The chronically unemployed Crowell did not have the social cachet required for the assignment. Instead Winsor chose another groomsman, one of Porter's favorite pianists, Roger Stearns.

Like the composer, Stearns was a Yale graduate who had met Porter in 1925, when the pianist was appearing in *Out o' Luck,* a varsity revue directed by Monty Woolley, to which Porter had contributed three songs. As a student, Stearns had supported himself by playing piano at Manhattan soirees thrown by wealthy hostesses. After graduation, he worked during the day as an intern for an architectural firm in New York City. At night he continued playing piano and auditioned for parts in Broadway shows. He won a major role in *Garrick Gaieties,* a Theatre Guild production in which Winsor saw him share the stage with two young comediennes: Imogene Coca and Rosalind Russell. Stearns's theatrical and musical credentials made him especially well qualified to cohost parities where Winsor could observe their Hollywood guests at play.

Maintaining a guesthouse on the Porters' temporary estate was more expensive than sharing the rent of a well-appointed apartment, so Winsor pooled resources with Stearns and leased furnishings, including a grand piano. Arrangements required several phone calls to Los Angeles. Eaton's weekly rent did not include use of the phone. During the four weeks before Winsor's departure, Eaton billed his stepson $36.89 for long-distance calls.

The columnist also decided that the "new kind of reporting" required a new kind of car. At a chic Hollywood restaurant, he would be embarrassed to hand a sun-tanned valet keys to a four-year-old coupe. Winsor bought an automobile suitable for Los Angeles sunshine rather than Cleveland snow: A 1936 Ford Phaeton, a four-door, canvas-topped convertible that guzzled air through a dazzling chrome-plated grill, which included a discreet hole for the handle of an engine crank.

Because maintaining the guesthouse was going to deplete Winsor's cash flow, he thought he might have to miss a car payment. To avoid repossession, he registered the convertible in his mother's name: Edith Ide Eaton. At the same time, he worried about what might happen if a bullying state trooper pulled him to the side of the road. According to his driver's license, his last name was "French." The car's title was registered to an "Eaton." To make sure that he wasn't arrested for stealing a car, Winsor sought a confidential agent to complete a deception. He asked his stepfather's secretary, Josephine Carroll, to create an official looking letter on Eaton Manufacturing Company stationery. She typed, "Winsor B. French . . . has every right to be driving this car" and signed the statement, "Secretary to Mrs. Eaton." The title was a fib, but Winsor assumed the letter and his glib tongue would solve any problems he might encounter on the road to California.

With Carroll's letter, Winsor and Stearns drove west without incident and arrived in Beverly Hills three days before their guesthouse was ready. In front of the swank Beverly Wilshire Hotel, Winsor entrusted his Phaeton to a uniformed doorman while he and Stearns stepped inside the lobby. Winsor had not reserved a room. The Beverly Wilshire was full.

So he telephoned the Porters' secretary and begged for help. "A heaven-sent genius," Winsor wrote. At thirty-one years of age, Winsor had yet to develop do-it-yourself skills. They would remain dormant. "The only way to travel comfortably is to let someone else do the worrying, and it always manages to work."

Delegating anxiety succeeded in Hollywood. Within a week, the columnist had bought a dog and was reporting a sunny and pampered domestic life at the Porters' guesthouse. Linda was "the most charming and brilliant hostess." After the rented furniture was delivered, Winsor took inventory only to discover that Linda Porter had preceded him. She had anticipated his critical needs: "Liquor, . . . postage stamps," and "a typed list of the private telephone numbers of Hollywood's biggest stars." What Winsor did not tell his readers was that he and Roger supplemented Linda's ministrations with those of Placid Mallillin, a manservant they were paying $65 a week to perform various chamber, waiting, and cooking chores, the sort of service Winsor had enjoyed at home.

After a week in the guesthouse, Winsor described an "average day" as "commencing at 7:30 A.M. when Brunhilde, a young dachshund completely bereft of both manners and consideration, leaps on my bed demanding breakfast. The day, and with my having no say in the matter whatsoever, has begun."

On this particular "average day," Winsor and Roger hosted their first luncheon guest: "lean and lanky Clifton Webb, looking better than he ever has before." Webb was one of the stars in *As Thousands Cheer*, specifically, the song and dance man who had played Prince Mdvani, who was always with "the boys" when Barbara Hutton wanted to find him. He was probably in his early forties (various accounts list the year of his birth 1889, 1891, and 1894) and devoted to his mother, Mabelle Parmalee Hollenbeck, who called her son "Little Webb" for his entire life. Of Mrs. Webb, Winsor wrote, she "can be a great comfort when she wants to." Using their luncheon as the centerpiece for a column, Winsor pooh-poohed the actor's mental energy. "Conversation over the luncheon table" was "lazy and trivial. Roger Stearns . . . fusses around (without too much success) with a candid camera."

Winsor was feeling superior. On the Barthelmess estate, he and Mallillin were the only men actually working. Stearns had "calmly refused three job offers since his arrival," MGM was "giving Cole Porter a pleasant vacation with pay. Six of his twenty-five contracted weeks have slipped by and he is still waiting for an assignment." Yet, Webb's subsidized indolence eclipsed the others'. After *As Thousands Cheer* closed, MGM had reportedly offered Webb $3,000 a week if he would come to Hollywood to star in a film about a dancer. "After hanging around Hollywood for a year," the actor had "finally persuaded MGM to release him . . . just $100,000 to the good, and without having done a day's work." Webb was waiting for "the lease on his 90-rooms-but-still-a-home mansion to expire" and "concentrating on tennis during the day, Miss Dietrich as the dinner hour approaches."

Poor Winsor! After listening to Webb's and Stearns's prattle, the wretched scribe had to sit at a rented desk, sip some of Linda Porter's Scotch, and try to make a column out of a very lazy afternoon. At sundown, he and Stearns roused themselves to attend a cocktail party in another Hollywood mansion, one "that rambles over the most fashionable frontage in Bel Air." After a dinner of hors d'oeuvres and hard liquor, the men returned "home for a quiet evening. . . . Crickets chirped in the patio and Brunhilde, hiding behind a curtain, gaily devoured a patent leather pump."

Less than twenty-four hours later, the guesthouse was the setting for a buffet dinner. "A touch timidly," Winsor wrote, "we did our first inviting." The dinner guests were column items: Actress "Margaret Sullavan created a moment of wonder when she strolled through the front door followed by Henry Fonda. Miss Sullavan, for benefit of the forgetful, was once upon a time, Mrs. Fonda. Then there was Betty Furness, who has gone oh so domestic and sat quietly in a corner knitting a sweater for Cesar Romero." She no longer covered for Cary Grant and Zerbe. As for Allen Vincent, on Winsor's second trip to Hollywood he mentioned the actor only once. "I bumped into Douglas Fairbanks, Jr., quietly eating lunch at the Beverly Hills Brown Derby with Allen Vincent—going on at great length about everything from a pet monkey that died to his producing plans." Despite Winsor's item about Vincent receiving a "deluge of offers" following his appearance in *The Return of Peter Grimm,* he had not been offered another film role. With his career at a standstill, there was no news Winsor could use to promote his friend's career.

Two days after the dinner party, Winsor suddenly discovered a problem with his convertible, made more difficult by the fact that it was registered in his mother's name. He immediately wrote Josephine Carroll: "I must have new license plates before the first of April and don't know how to go about it out here. I wonder if you could possibly do a little research work for me? Should I have new plates airmailed to me from Cleveland—or buy them here—and how please do I go about it. I'm sorry to be such an idiot and will be very grateful if you can help me out." In a personal aside to her, Winsor wrote, "Hollywood is history and I would like to stay here forever—far from the madding creditors."

A day after writing this letter, the telephone rang at the guesthouse. Gerald Haxton, secretary to W. Somerset Maugham, the English novelist, playwright, and master of the short story, was on the line. He invited Winsor for cocktails in the hotel suite Haxton was sharing with Maugham. Winsor accepted his friends' offer of hospitality.

In 1925, when Winsor was in Paris frequenting the Men's Bar at the Ritz Hotel rather than lectures at the Sorbonne, he met Haxton, a thirty-three-year-old American expatriate, who introduced him to Maugham. The following year, when Winsor was working for *TIME,* he saw the two men again when they visited Cleveland for the world premiere at the Ohio Theatre of Maugham's play *The Constant Wife.* Winsor attended several parties where Haxton and Maugham were present and recalled the author giving "all his hosts autographed copies of his novels." Then in the late summer of 1934, after Winsor and his wife agreed to separate and Margaret returned to the United States, Haxton invited Winsor to lunch at Maugham's Villa Mauresque, a twenty-acre estate on the French Cap Ferrat, a tiny, lush peninsula in the Mediterranean Sea between Nice and Monte Carlo.

Winsor noted none of these previous encounters with Maugham and Haxton in his item, nor that Maugham employed and traveled with a male secretary. Yet he had told readers about "Fieldsie," Carole Lombard's secretary, and Margaret Moore, Cole and Linda Porter's secretary. By omitting any mention of a male secretary Winsor protected his friends. Haxton was Maugham's companion and lover. Winsor made sure his published account of their tête-à-tête would not provide information for gossips. His item was a classic example of his "new kind of reporting." In Maugham's case, it was also fawning. Years later Winsor confessed that he was "dazzled" by the author's fame, his "opulent" Villa Mauresque, and his "dashing secretary." He began his item by calling Maugham "almost my favorite person." While sipping his liquor, the columnist eavesdropped on his phone calls.

"During an attempt to consume two cocktails, if you care for statistics, the telephone rang exactly 11 times." Winsor revealed the contents of two calls: "There was a gentleman of the fourth estate who among other things wanted to know to what Maugham attributed his success. I tried not to listen as he faltered an answer. Still another gentleman of the fourth estate wanted to know if he were of the opinion that style didn't matter a damn. The answer to that classic, if you care, was that while a man should be perfectly dressed what he was wearing should be unnoticeable." Thus the newspaper columnist portrayed himself as the celebrity author's sympathetic pal, not a lowbrow newspaperman asking dumb questions. Winsor did reveal one interesting fact. Maugham's next stop was Alcatraz, the federal maximum-security prison on an island in San Francisco Bay, part of a "pilgrimage" to "penal colonies" based on "pure curiosity."

On the following night, Clifton Webb returned Winsor and Stearns's hospitality. The actor had "whipped up a little evening" for his friends and seven other guests. Winsor identified five: Cole and Linda Porter, Oliver Messel, Dick Cromwell, and Marlene Dietrich. Messel was a thirty-two-year-old British theatrical designer hired by film director George Cukor to design the costumes and settings for his *Romeo and Juliet*. Cromwell, the mimic who had entertained at Alice Terry's farewell party for Winsor, had added a new female movie star to his repertoire: Marlene Dietrich. Until he arrived at Webb's mansion, Cromwell was not aware that the actress would be attending the soiree. The comedian discovered her as Winsor did, "dressed in the crisp white habit of a nurse and scurrying about the Webb mansion. The costume was in effect because since early morning, she had been preparing a Russian meal the like of which I have never tasted anywhere."

Her menu? "Vodka, fresh caviar in feathery little rolls, Borscht with sour cream, boeuf stroganoff and eventually a dessert called kasha guriev, which actually was fruit pudding—and ambrosial. Miss Dietrich not only prepared and cooked the entire meal, but served it herself, darting between the places with incredible grace and blushing over compliments."

Winsor was entranced: "Half the belles in Hollywood . . . pose for the cameras . . . in front of a magnificent prop roast of beef. Not Marlene, however. She is a really good cook; although where she learned the Russian secrets none of us knew nor could find out. Later in the evening she changed from her robe de cuisine into something that was pure cloth of gold and Mr. Cromwell went through his bag of tricks."

According to Winsor, the subject was skeptical about her provocative sidelong glances.

"Do I really do that with my eyes?" asked the astonished Miss Dietrich. So someone told her, if she didn't she should, with the result the lady borrowed the floor and there was a half hour of breathless glamour as she sang all her old tunes in a matchless fashion.

As the evening wore on it became more and more hysterical. Oliver Messel did his famous monolog—it's not for children—of a gay evening in a Venetian hotel. This must be heard in a darkened room while Oliver goes not too quietly mad in another room. . . . The man should make a short of it for private release.

As a night cap, Cole Porter played all his new compositions, and one, designed for men who go down to the sea in ships, is a honey. "Rolling Home," it's called, and if the cinema boys ever can find a story for Porter to go to work on it should sweep the nation. . . . Then all too suddenly, it was nearly 3 o'clock and guests began sending

for their cars. White fog was drifting down from the mountainside—
veils of it misting the full moon. The most memorable evening I ever
had in this patchwork village had ended.

The morning mail brought Winsor back to reality. A letter from Carroll:
"I shall be glad to obtain the license plates for you," she wrote, "but the
enclosed letter may change matters somewhat."

Her enclosure was signed by his stepfather: "I notice that your car is
in Mother's name. . . . I do not like this arrangement as Mother would be
responsible for any accident that you got into and you probably do not
carry any liability insurance. Even if you do, I do not want the car in Mother's name, nor do I want her obligated for payments on it. Please send me
full particulars. I shall take steps to have the obligations of the ownership
of the car switched from Mother to you."

Despite her employer's displeasure, she was still willing to help Winsor. "I obtained the necessary information . . . and a license application
has been made out and is ready for your Mother's signature. The fee is
$10.25—if you will send me a check for that amount I shall get the plates
and air mail them on to you so that you will be able to drive after April 1st
. . . The title can be switched at that time."

Why would Josephine Carroll risk her employer's wrath by rescuing his
devious stepson? Winsor provided vicarious warmth. "Your column has
been most interesting every night," she wrote. "I envy your basking in the
sun while we are suffering such dreary weather. We have snow again and
it is beastly cold."

In replying to his stepfather, the columnist tried to defend himself:
"Enclosed is a check for the plates. I am insured for fire, theft and liability.
However, it certainly doesn't make any difference and although Mother is
in no way responsible for the payments—unless I were killed."

"Killed"?

Winsor never chose words casually. Instead of selecting the slightly less
melodramatic—"unless I died"—he chose a verb that evoked the image of
a fatal traffic accident or a violent assault. His vocabulary under fire con-
firms that criticism peeved him. To complete the sentence, Winsor wrote
that if he were "killed," his Mother "could turn the car back."

He wrote as if he were a war correspondent, risking his life to file
columns from Hollywood, yet anxious to relieve any petty concerns of
Eaton's: "Please have it in my name if it would make you feel any more
comfortable."

Without pausing to indent for a new paragraph, he continued: "I also just discovered that I completely forgot to file an income tax report, but as I have been able to claim enough exemptions, traveling et cetera, and have nothing to pay, perhaps they won't bother to try and fine me."

Furthermore, if his stepfather thought he was luxuriating on a Hollywood estate, Winsor added, "Our house is about the size of a pea."

"No more now," he concluded, "as I have to go to lunch."

For six more weeks, Winsor risked getting "killed" over cocktails, lunches, drinks, dinners, and nightcaps. In between columns and parties, he worked on a movie script. His tutors were two professional writers: George Oppenheimer, a playwright, and Sam Hoffenstein, a prolific writer of screenplays, dialogue, and light verse.

When you're away, I'm restless, lonely,
Wretched, bored, dejected; only
Here's the rub, my darling dear,
I feel the same when you are here.

Winsor also spent many evenings listening to Linda Porter. She told him how thoroughly she detested Southern California's climate and hard-drinking movie people, with their "scatological and obscene" babble. Sadly, she admitted that Cole enjoyed Hollywood. (If Winsor's reportage from 1930s Hollywood had been accessible in 2004, screenwriters for *De-Lovely,* which attempted to dramatize the Porters' unconventional marriage, might have written a less sensational account of Linda's miserable summer in Southern California.)

After Linda retired to her bedroom, Winsor often spent the rest of the night listening to Porter's newest compositions. About 10 P.M. he would begin writing a song. In 1936, he was working on the score for *Born to Dance,* including a song and dance number for Eleanor Powell, which had a repetitious refrain: "Rap-tap, rap-tap, rap-tap-tap, rap-a-tap-tap."

When Porter liked what he'd written, Winsor remembered that it was the composer's "unfortunate habit" to "drift" toward the guesthouse and find Stearns, so "they could sit down to the piano together and spin his latest brainchild into an endless duet. On one occasion, I listened to 'Rap Tap on Wood' for not less than six hours."

April 30 caught the columnist by surprise. "Sudden departure from the one place you want to live and die in is not only tragic, but torture." One more party, Porter and Linda's "gala" farewell for Winsor, then Brunhilde, Stearns, and he piled into the car and "left the opulent orange groves behind us." (Please note his use of the adjective "opulent." Less than a year earlier, those same orange groves offended him with their "sickly, heavy odor.")

The return trip was largely uneventful, except in Omaha, where Winsor violated the local dress code. "The mercury soared to 100 while the Nebraskan farmers, stripped to the waist, plowed their fields and planted their corn. I tried to follow suit, but an Omaha officer of the law had different ideas about suitable clothing—hence on to the mighty Mississippi and dressed as if for opera."

The *Press* announced Winsor's homecoming on page 1 in an article written by the "radio editor," Norman Siegel. "Mr. Pepys of Hollywood," Siegel wrote, had reappeared in the city room with "a walnut tan, a dachshund he calls 'Brunhilde' and . . . a new head of hair." The radio editor thought Winsor was sporting a crew cut, but he was corrected. "It merely fell out," Winsor explained, during a bout with the flu. "Contrary to all other indications I have not been wintering in San Quentin."

Yet the two months he spent in the Porters' guesthouse with Stearns and Mallillin convinced Winsor that he could manage his own household. By mid-June, he had moved to the Lakeside Flats—a mildly disreputable neighborhood of bachelors, bohemians, and panhandlers at the intersection of East 9th Street and Lakeside Avenue. Inexpensive rooms and small apartments in dilapidated three- and four-story buildings perched on the edge of the bluff overlooking Lake Erie.

Winsor was feeling flush. The success of his column had increased his remuneration. One apartment was not enough, so he rented two, side by side on the second floor of a building at 1232 East 9th Street, which he called "Sin Shanty." He set up housekeeping with Brunhilde, his dachshund, and Naomi, a maid. Polly Parsons described Brunhilde as "morose," Naomi as "dusky."

He was also optimistic about the future. "Before leaving Hollywood," according to Siegel, Winsor "completed a movie script which he reports is being considered for early production."

"You've never heard such music"

Wednesday, June 10, 1936, 6 p.m.

In the Statler Hotel's cocktail lounge, a sort of "field office" Winsor used on the smoke-and-music beat, the columnist was sharing a banquette with Cleveland's Republican aristocracy: two iron ore millionaires, Elton Hoyt II, and Leonard Hanna—fierce business competitors, hard-drinking, brotherly Republicans, and members of Cleveland's most exclusive private men's club: The Tavern. Its refusal to obey liquor laws while hosting Yale alumni in 1918 had led Cole Porter to celebrate the men with a song:

> Cleveland—praise the Lord and sing Hosanna
> Cleveland—it's the home of Hoyt and Hanna.

During the summer of 1936, however, downtown Cleveland was also the home of the Republican Party's quadrennial convention, at which it hoped to select a candidate who could depose President Franklin D. Roosevelt in November's election. Before attending the convention's keynote session in Public Auditorium, Hanna's party had stopped at the Statler for a drink. Hoyt brought his wife; Hanna escorted his female interior designer; and Winsor partnered Kay Halle, a friend of the Roosevelt family and an outspoken Democrat. Cleveland newspapers frequently ran Halle's dispatches from London, where she had become close friends with the family of another prominent politician—Winston Churchill. Several about-town columnists—but not Winsor—had published rumors that Halle would marry Winston's son, Randolph. To emphasize her own blond good looks, Winsor noted, Miss Halle was wearing the "maddest hat of the year—a sort of straw halo that gets all mixed up with black veil."

The three couples were seated near an upright piano, where Stearns was playing Porter, Berlin, and Gershwin. The Statler had engaged Winsor's Hollywood housemate for the week the Republicans were in Cleveland.

To fortify themselves for the evening's speeches, the group had ordered a round of mint juleps. "The boys serve them in a great cup of ice, and, I might add, they are very, very beautiful. If you don't like the mint concoction try a planter's punch." Winsor described their party as "very gay, too, until someone asked Roger Stearns please to play 'Happy Days Are Here Again,' and Roger almost did." Winsor was appalled by the song's mindless optimism and blamed former Republican president Herbert Hoover for the Depression's intractable unemployment.

"Give yourself a lesson in human values and walk down to the city dump and study the village that has sprung up there. Hundreds of homeless and unemployed men have built themselves tiny houses from old sheets of tin and wooden boxes and live in peaceful, if not lavish, contentment. . . . If you are curious, and willing to pay a little something, you can go inside many of the houses. If you misbehave, however, or do anything to disturb the peace their mayor will ask you to leave what they call Hoover City."

Hanna's friends did not visit the village. Residents had been evicted in April when construction began on the Great Lakes Exposition, planned for later in the summer. Instead, the party was chauffeured to Public Auditorium, where Winsor found Aileen Winslow, doyenne of his favorite salon, "sitting big as life in the front row of the press box." Broadway producer Brock Pemberton, who had hosted Winsor and Margaret's engagement party, was present "to shout for Mr. Landon," the governor of Kansas, whose first name was Alfred and nickname "Alf." Another of Winsor's well-connected groomsmen, Alan Jackson, had a seat near the speaker's platform and "caught a terrific sunburn from the photographer's flash bulbs." Winsor had recently used his column to help his friend find a job: "A tip to editors looking for an A-one man—Alan Jackson has left the staff of *TIME, Fortune* and *Architectural Forum*—after practically giving the latter a new lease on life."

Although Winsor frequently socialized with Hanna's Republican friends, in his datebook he labeled them "stuffed shirts." He was attending the convention because Hanna had asked him for help. His patron was hosting a post-keynote party for out-of-town Republican leaders who could help the iron ore industry and had asked Winsor to lead his guests on a tour of Cleveland's black nightspots. Unlike Hoover City's shanties, bustling black-owned nightclubs and restaurants were defying hard times. Although the Depression had left Cleveland's "better known nightclubs . . . screaming for oxygen," Winsor noted, "local emulations of Harlem are packing them in and laughing at trouble." No Caucasian knew the turf better than Winsor. He was the only local newspaper about-town columnist whose definition of "town" included black entertainment districts.

In the early 1930s, the number of African Americans living in the United States was thought to be about 12 million, a figure Winsor used. The 1930 U.S. Census claimed 8 percent of Cleveland's population was black, roughly 80,000 persons. Most were comparatively recent residents, part of the large migration of blacks that occurred when the onset of World War I curtailed immigration from Europe and Southern blacks filled the need for laborers in the nation's wartime economy. In Cleveland, the majority of new black residents settled "in an area bounded on the north by Carnegie Avenue, on the south and west by the Cuyahoga River, and the east by Fifty-fifth Street—the nucleus of what would become the post-World War I black ghetto."

White racial attitudes changed as the number of African American city residents grew and had a direct impact on the city's nightlife. Owners of downtown theaters initiated policies requiring blacks to sit in the back rows of their auditoriums. The combination of segregated seating and the increased numbers of African Americans had generated markets large enough for black entrepreneurs to open neighborhood "restaurants, bars, theaters, skating rinks and dance halls," which Winsor scoured for column items.

His reportage wasn't colorblind. He made sure readers knew if a nightclub's performers and audience were (in alphabetical order) "black," "brown," "colored," "dark," "Negro," "sepia," or "tan," and peppered his recommendations for African American nightspots with a cautionary phrase: "if you like that sort of thing." Some readers didn't understand Winsor's vocabulary. "I think it would be splendid if in listing places to go you mentioned just what sort of place each one is. Someone told me *PARADE* was the very best source of information, but in looking for a nightclub and using you as a guide I found myself in three barbecues before I finally landed at the Club Madrid. It was most annoying." (Winsor's thesaurus of racial synonyms shows how much more willing newspapers were to identify someone's skin color than they were to describe an unconventional sexual preference.)

Winsor focused on three entertainment districts. The first was Scovill Avenue, home for two popular burlesque houses. Near the intersection of East 14th Street, the Main Theater presented the Harlem Steppers, with its "cast of thirty," and "gave away groceries and vegetables to lucky ticket holders." At East 55th Street he enjoyed performers at the Nite Owl, a "black and tan nightclub," where he watched one "rough, rough" show and warned readers, "You'll have to hurry to beat the censors." Nearby, on what he called the "dark stretches of E. 55th Street," Winsor favored two black-owned nightclubs: The Subway, where "Clara Smith hangs out the blues and Harold Thomas is still tap dancing at a sixty-mile-per-hour rate," and the Sunset, where the bouncer was "Jim Williams, an ex-pug who used to take it on the chin with style, is now taking care of all complaints," and Floyd Walker, "who brushes your coat[,] is an undertaker." In the "cellars and purlieus" lining Cedar Avenue, Winsor urged readers who appreciated jazz to visit the Musicians' Club and The Rhythm at East 86th Street, or the Gardenia at East 89th.

In a white-owned, metropolitan daily newspaper published during the first half of the twentieth century, the content and frequency of Winsor's columns about African American nightlife were atypical, according to historians of American media who have researched coverage of minorities: "One study of news about blacks in the Philadelphia press between 1908 and 1932 found that coverage of African Americans constituted only two percent of the papers' news space, and between 50 to 75 percent of that coverage was devoted to black crime. Another study of coverage of blacks in seventeen major papers around the nation in 1928 and 1929 found that 47 percent of the news concerned antisocial behavior; the coverage emphasized the bizarre and pathological in black life."

Oswald Garrison Villard, a regular contributor to the *Nation* and the *New York Evening News,* a self-proclaimed "radical . . . on the Negro question," in 1930 wrote that African Americans believed that the "only Negro . . . who can reach the first page of the great dailies is the Negro criminal; if there is occasional recognition of a great Negro musician or scientist, it is usually with surpassing condescension, as one admires a leading horse or a trained seal."

Filling the void in several northern, urban African American communities were "race weeklies," black-owned newspapers that focused on "black society, sports, and business, as well as crime." In Cleveland, two struggling weeklies, the *Call* and the *Post,* had merged in 1927 to form the *Cleveland Call & Post.* Yet in the 1930s, editions averaged a mere four pages and had only three hundred paid subscribers.

While Winsor's columns did not appear on the front page of the *News* or the *Press* or reverse the ratio of black to white news in either publication, by 1936 his coverage was neither condescending nor did it focus on crime or antisocial or pathological behavior. He favored items on food and entertainers. Of the Brown Skin Burlesque Garden, he wrote about "tables where you can sit and eat if orchestra seats bore you." And Manuel's: "Go late, order waffles—and throw a couple of quarters to the soft-shoe dancers."

That said, he was not always an enlightened commentator.

The first written evidence of Winsor's interest in African American performers is dated 1927, when he was twenty-two years old and working for *TIME* in New York City. In a letter to his stepfather, he asked for $15,000 so he could invest in a London production of Dubose Heyward's *Porgy,* the play on which George Gershwin, several years later, would base his opera *Porgy and Bess*. "I am waiting until I can find out the figures, pay roll, publicity, theatre rentals, transportation, etc. It isn't any wild dream; the play is doing jammed houses here every night, with special matinees to take care of the turn away. England loves that sort of thing, theatres rent for much less than they do here, ticket prices are higher," and, Winsor added with a chilling acceptance of racial exploitation, "the pay roll, because the cast is made up entirely of Negroes, is very small." His stepfather was unmoved. "I am sorry to hear that you have gone 'black.'" Although *Porgy* eventually reached London without Eaton's money, his disapproval suggests Winsor did not reach maturity in a household headed by a civil rights advocate.

Five years later, when Winsor launched *PARADE*, he adopted several *TIME* practices, but not its format for reporting about black Americans. While he was on the editorial staff, *TIME*'s National Affairs section carried several departments, identified by all capital letters, including "NEGROES," "WOMEN," and "RADICALS." Before Winsor left, Hadden substituted "RACES" for "NEGROES," and the new department ran items about Jews and Irish Americans.

PARADE didn't segregate its news. In his "Book" column, Winsor reviewed *Brown America* by Edwin R. Embree, who headed the Rosenwald Fund, the third-largest philanthropic foundation in the United States in the 1930s. Its founder, Julius Rosenwald, chairman of the board of Sears, Roebuck and Company, was passionately committed to improving educational opportunities for African Americans. Embree wrote *Brown America* in part to recruit other philanthropists to the foundation's cause and build support among the general public. Winsor called the book the "most scholarly, authentic" analysis ever published about "the Negro problem" and praised its unusual "bibliography of the best Negro books, either by them or of them."

Winsor continued:

Since the beginning of American history, the Negro has been fought over, maligned and over-praised. Yet despite the chaos he has caused in our civilization, the bloodshed and the hatreds, he has gone on his serene and seemingly devil-may-care way, content for the greater part to let the white man solve his problems. Certain members of the Negro race have risen miraculously above their inheritances and achieved almost impossible goals when one considers the odds against them. The great bulk of their population, however, has crowded together in city slums . . . leading sluggish, lazy lives, breeding far more criminals than poets.

This generalization reeks of condescension. The callous assumptions with which Winsor perpetuated in print the most malign racial slurs—"let[ting] the white man solve his problems" and "leading sluggish, lazy lives"— proves the profound ignorance and intolerance in white journalists. Winsor was reiterating the classic media stereotypes that divided African Americans into "savages" and "Sambos."

American media historian Carolyn Martindale defined the "savage" as "those qualities that white Americans have attributed to and feared in black Americans: violence, an absence of restraint, sexual prowess and potency, physical strength and ability." Sambos were the "ignorant, lazy, carefree, good-humored blacks like those portrayed in minstrel shows—a childlike, singing, dancing, take-no-thought-for-tomorrow creature who is a permanent child."

Yet less than three months after publishing his book review, Winsor was promoting the Gilpin Players, "a group of Negro actors under the direction of Mr. and Mrs. R. W. Jelliffe, who have their own theatre, the Karamu, at 3807 Central Avenue." In a poor, predominantly black neighborhood, Rowena and Russell Jelliffe, two white social workers, had organized a "playhouse settlement" committed to interracial theater. Winsor attended and praised their productions and urged his readers to write the Jelliffes "and request that your name be placed on their mailing list for forthcoming announcements." His advice to rely on the U.S. mail acknowledges that neither he nor any other white journalist considered Gilpin Players' productions worthy of space in a major daily newspaper. Then a week later, Winsor announced the Hanna Theatre had booked "Ethel Waters in *Rhapsody in Black,* a Negro revue that could not stand the gaff in New York but is making good money on the road."

Winsor's decision that his white readers might be interested in the Gilpin Players' mailing list and Waters's revue may have been influenced by the fact that both had majority approval. White social workers were responsible for the local black theater; Waters had already become "the first black singer to receive top billing at a 'white' theater," attributed by some to her "strongly Anglicized enunciation" as opposed to some blues singers' more emotional styles, which Waters criticized for their "unladylike shouts and growls."

Contemporary media historians dismiss the sort of stories Winsor wrote about African American entertainers as perpetuating the "Sambo" stereotype. Martindale correctly insists that "news media are supposed to be or expected to be representing reality, the way the world actually is, not a fictional account"; to prove her point, she cites "communication scholars Clint Wilson and Félix Gutiérrez," who maintain entertainment is "make believe," but news is "real." The men's glib definitions deny the reality of the lives and achievements of black entertainers, artists, and entrepreneurs, which Winsor documented on Cleveland's smoke-and-music beat.

The columnist's growing enthusiasm for black nightlife occurred during a period that social historians have called the Negro Vogue, a period of intense national curiosity about African American entertainers, during the last years of Prohibition. Circumstantial evidence suggests Winsor may have been influenced by Leonard Hanna, who supported the Jelliffes financially and whose family's theater had booked Waters. Winsor and Hanna may also have been familiar with Cleveland's black-owned nightclubs because historically, according to George Chauncey in *Gay New York,* many were safe havens for same-sex couples.

For many reasons, in January 1932 Winsor decided to publish his first review of a black nightclub act in a black neighborhood. "Look in at the Sunset on East 55th Street, just beyond Central Avenue. . . . The crowd is very mixed and you see all manner of strange types. But the chief performer is the maître d'hôtel, a colored gentleman whose name is Mistah Simpson." This is Winsor's first written account of Harold Simpson, whose career he would promote for years.

"Sitting on a chair, strumming a ukulele," Winsor wrote, Simpson "starts crooning very softly. Gradually he works his voice up and up until he finally throws back his head and lets forth a series of primeval screams, and then he does what is called 'coming to town,' which consists of singing in a very staccato, guttural manner, at the same time doing frantic tap steps without leaving his chair."

A few weeks after Simpson's review appeared in *PARADE,* Bessie Brown, Cleveland's finest blues singer, invited Winsor for lunch at her apartment on Carnegie Avenue. While Hanna helped introduce him to African American performers acceptable to white theater owners, Brown showed him the reality of one black performer. She had found a white audience by accident and gave him an interview that produced an unusual profile by 1930s journalistic standards, which included a glossary of "Woodland Avenue English," the patois of local African Americans. Several terms reinforced the "savage" stereotype:

Dinker—salesman of policy game slips
Glasso—intoxicated, but still walking
Stick—razor used as a weapon

Many contemporary white journalists, who had never lunched with African American musicians, accepted as fact that they led lives of "illicit drinking in speakeasies and nightclubs, promiscuous women, erotic dancing, and related vices assumed to involve bootleggers and mobsters." Brown's story was less salacious. Unlike her white interviewer, the singer never took "a drink except a very occasional glass of wine, and never smoke[d] at all." In her apartment's dining room, she served Winsor a "marvelous" shrimp and chicken gumbo with cornbread, but when he praised her cooking, she demurred, claiming her "pastry was as heavy as lead." In the late afternoons, Brown liked to play contract bridge before her nightly appearance at the Club Madrid, Phil Selznick's downtown nightclub, which had not "come into its own," Winsor wrote, until the owner engaged Brown.

Winsor did think the singer's color preferences confirmed a stereotype: "She has the inherent love of color so typical of her race, and her clothes are always vivid red, red and black, purple, or orchid. She must always have hat, shoes and bag to match, and when she walks with her thoroughbred Borzoi, Galli, she wears beige and white to match him."

She was candid about her personal life. After her father died, Brown was raised by her grandparents, and she married when she was fifteen. After giving birth to a daughter, Helen, she divorced her husband. Her daughter went on to Ohio State University, graduated, earned a master's degree, and was teaching school in Mississippi when Winsor interviewed her mother.

One aspect of her singing career confirmed conventional wisdom: It began in speakeasies. In Cleveland, the first was a "gin parlor on Woodland Avenue," then the Royal Inn on 55th Street, which had become the Sunset Club where Simpson performed. "There Bessie found her first white audiences. They drifted in by mistake, heard her deep, rhythmic chant, and came back again and again."

Of the article's many revelations, the most important was Winsor's description of how white audiences preferred black performers who embodied their preconceived notions of African Americans: "White intellectuals of the twenties evinced a fascination with 'primitives,' that led them to Taos and Harlem," according to social critic and journalism historian David P. Peeler. Brown's audiences confirmed Peeler's observation. Members complained to Winsor that "her nightclub work lacks the primitive rhythm of her race and that she emulates, to her disadvantage, white artists." They didn't give her credit for creating her own unique style of blues singing, in an era of American music that composer and historian Virgil Thomson called "our finest period in the creation and singing of blues." Brown combined "the plaintive, tragic spirituals her grandmother had taught her" with classical training she received during high school, an achievement that didn't fit the white stereotype.

Readers' letters prove Winsor's profile was pioneering journalism. "It took 'intestinal fortitude' to print that article on Bessie Brown," one wrote, "because I would be willing to bet that half the city of Cleveland will jump on your neck, although Bessie is a fine woman and Cleveland ought to be proud of her." Another criticized: "Bessie Brown, a colored night-club singer!" Another wrote, "Why don't you give your next issue over to Bill Robinson, the colored tap-dancer?"

When Republicans finally arrived in Cleveland for their convention, they were not interested in visiting a white-owned nightclub or hearing the refined blues of Bessie Brown. To satisfy convention-goers' curiosity and hunger, Winsor's tour focused on Cleveland's restaurants and nightclubs in black entertainment districts. The first stop was the Vaudeville and Comedy Club, an all-night barbecue that had recently opened in the Majestic Hotel on Cedar Avenue. Every day, between 5:00 and 9:00 P.M., Louise Brooks, who "knew all the great tricks and arts of Creole cooking," personally prepared the dishes. Her spare ribs were legendary, but Winsor preferred her "shrimp gumbo" for supper or "Virginia ham in generous slices with walnut waffles" in the wee hours of a Sunday morning. Her cooking had been so profitable in 1933 that the former showgirl had "dug deeply into her pocketbook and pulled out $750 to buy herself a new fur coat."

Winsor had first seen Brooks on the stage of the Cleveland Theatre, where she made her debut as "the original 'Topsy' in Stetson's version of the old tear-wringer, *Uncle Tom's Cabin.* Later she became the first half of Brooks and Moss, a dancing and singing team that used to regale the audiences in the old Priscilla Theater." Brooks and Moss toured Europe and played New York, where Brooks was "unable to venture up Fifth Avenue without being stopped by the inevitable autograph hounds." In the mid-1920s she returned to her hometown, opened her first restaurant, and assumed a new role: "Mammy" Louise Brooks, Cleveland's preeminent Creole cook and restaurant owner. Republicans wolfed down her food. During Hanna's "gay dinner," Mammy Louise "ran entirely out of spare ribs to barbecue." With her kitchen devastated, Winsor resumed his tour of "late spots."

The "fastest show" was staged by the Cedar Gardens, which featured national stars. During the convention, torch singer Baby Hines was the headliner, "dancing now as well as sighing those lullabies." She was the first wife of jazz pianist Earl "Fatha" Hines. Performing on the same stage were the three Esquires. "These boys," Winsor wrote, "come very close to reaching a new high in tap dancing and if their hearts hold out I wouldn't be surprised to see them smiling over the footlights of a Manhattan theater—and I don't mean in Harlem either."

While weaker members of the Republican delegation returned to their hotels, Hanna and Winsor continued east on Cedar Avenue to the Turf Club, "a smoky little chamber that was always jammed to the doors."

In the basement, Rose Murphy, "sitting on a stack of telephone books," played a piano "that sounded as if it hadn't seen a tuner in a decade. To her thronged all the musicians in town" as well as Hanna's Republicans. "In a tiny, flute like voice," she sang as she "tortured the chipped ivories." Patrons were stunned by "her inimitable technique of suddenly removing both hands from the keyboard and continuing the rhythm, tune and all, with her feet." Waving dollar bills, enchanted Republicans "detained Rose Murphy at the . . . piano until 6 A.M."

The tour wasn't over yet. On Cedar Avenue "they reached the Heat Wave's front lawn at an hour when everyone should be in bed" and "caught" Mistah Simpson "relaxing or trying to." He was still crooning ballads while conventioneers sipped a breakfast of alcohol.

In broad daylight, Winsor finally made his way to the *Press* city room to write a column for the afternoon edition that documented the night Republicans toured Cleveland's black nightspots. Given the number and quality of professional African American actors and musicians publicized in 1936, it is shocking to learn that as late as 1940 the Play House cast a white actress in a black role. About the comedy *Here Today,* Winsor wrote, "Evelyn Chevillat makes a satisfactory colored maid although I think the moment has arrived when the theater might well dispense with black face makeup and come forward with reality." Winsor's columns did not dismantle racial barriers in the city's elite cultural institutions, a fact that did not persuade him to change course.

From the *Press* offices, Winsor could walk to his new home in Lakeside Flats, which he described as a "small but select artists' colony at the foot of East Ninth Street overlooking the Stadium." He had occupied his back-to-back apartments on East 9th Street for less than a week. After spending the entire night on Cedar Avenue, he would try to sleep until mid-afternoon, ignoring Brunhilde and the clanking streetcars. If the columnist was hungover when he awoke, he had already found a place for repairing the damage: a neighborhood bar called "Fleet's Inn." It catered to a male clientele of lonely Great Lakes sailors and landlubbers who liked "rough and ready honky-tonk." In 1936, "immaculately clean little freighters from Holland, Norway and Denmark tied up" at Cleveland's "crowded docks." At the Fleet's Inn, the owner exchanged foreign currency for American dollars, and "the grateful lads with three-word English vocabularies repaid her with foreign bottlings that put the back bar on a par with any in the country." Winsor sometimes felt his throat would "be slashed at any moment, while you are actually as safe as if you were in your own drawing room. I hope."

His new neighbors were column fodder. On the sidewalk outside his apartment, he spotted "two very inebriated bums . . . eating strawberry ice cream cones" and "gypsy fortune tellers . . . looking colorful as the devil. But I have yet to see a customer crossing a palm with silver."

At night, crowds were drawn to other attractions. One was Jean's Funny House. People came "to be terrified by the too realistic photographs of terrific accidents and war scenes in the window." Jean's was full of slot machines, including some for boys studying anatomy: "Youngsters with pennies in their hands drop in to buy practical jokes and stay to look at a few of the burlesque opticons." A more respectable neighbor was Charlie Rohr's restaurant, which had employed a friend of Winsor's, the "young, literally starving artist," Gus Peck, to paint a set of murals for the back room, "an intrepid caveman eating the first oyster." Peck received "free meals and all the drink he wanted, which was considerable. As far as Rohr was concerned it was well worth it. People used to crowd the tables, waiting for Gus to fall off the scaffolding, but he never did."

Winsor, his friends, and celebrity houseguests quickly established themselves as unique members of the sidewalk spectacle. During the day, the columnist appeared in bold summer sport coats and was dubbed "the lad in plaid." A male friend, who had purchased a few rag rugs at a department store's clearance sale, had them made into a coat with a hood. "You can see him strolling down East Ninth (between seven and eight), gaily swinging a bamboo sword cane—debonair, resplendent and a touch startling." When aspiring actress Peggy Fears stayed at Sin Shanty, she took "brisk little walks, usually wearing slacks, a knee length silver fox coat and a diamond or so about the size of compact mirrors. Outsized diamonds were seldom seen in the vicinity . . . and Peggy of the wistful brown eyes used to cause the young men who were up and about town to stop in their tracks."

The artwork in Winsor's apartment became a local legend. His walls displayed a framed collection of photographs of stage and screen stars. Polly Parsons interviewed him in his apartment and was surprised to find that some well-known females had autographed their pictures "fervently." Actress Kay Francis wrote, "Looking right at you and I still say I love you." In Winsor's opinion, the artwork that caught the spirit of the Lakeside Flats were murals Cleveland artist Dorothy Rutka painted inside the apartment of three bachelor friends. Her subject: "people without any clothes on peeking through windows at people who have," an apt metaphor for Winsor's neighbors.

There was little time for the columnist to enjoy his apartment. The first weekend after the Republicans decamped, Cole Porter arrived from California and demanded his own tour of Cedar Avenue. On Saturday night, he "managed to find time to hang over Rose Murphy's piano as well as look in on Mammy Louise and Baby Hines."

On Sunday afternoon, Porter entertained his tour guide at a private party. With Roger Stearns accompanying local singer Ned Parrish, a "socially prominent tenor with a sob in his throat," the composer "ran through the score" of *Born to Dance,* his first MGM musical. The songs included two Porter classics, "Easy to Love" and "I've Got You under My Skin." In Winsor's opinion, they would put "the quietus on 'Night and Day.'"

During Porter's weekend in Cleveland, Winsor found his friend to be "entirely sold on anything and everything that has to do with Hollywood." Before leaving, he invited Winsor, Hanna, and Stearns to escape Cleveland's winter by joining him in Hollywood. The composer was considering the purchase of the Barthelmess estate, despite his wife's loathing of the weather and the local residents.

After Porter departed, Winsor turned his editorial attentions to the Great Lakes Exposition, an ambitious attempt to lure free-spending tourists to 135 acres from West 3rd Street to East 20th Street on the shores of Lake Erie. In Winsor's words, it was "incredible to pass a dump one day and the next to find it a garden complete with rolling lawns and flowering shrubs." Grass and flowers were fine, but he worried that sponsors who had collectively contributed $1.5 million to build the exposition were neutering the human exhibits. Financial backers were "staid" and "proper" local Republicans, who didn't know "what it means to be gay."

Winsor's first contretemps concerned the naked human body. He expressed his disappointment when officials forced Zorine, a nudist, to abandon her project, which was horticultural in nature. She proposed "a modern Garden of Eden . . . with spots for segregated sun bathing, an open forum for the presentation of health lectures and pageantry depicting the evolution of clothes." Unfortunately, exposition officials had declared "no nudists may camp along the lake front next summer."

His second fight was over gigolos. An "unpredictable" twenty-one-year-old acquaintance of Winsor's, Ted Peckham, proposed anchoring a "bar barge" in the exhibition's lagoon, where the "accent will be on swank," he told reporters. "There'll be dancing, with personable young men available at a fee. 'Something,'" he explained, "'to give the women the idea they're doing something wild—they'll love it.'"

While majoring in English at Western Reserve University, Peckham, still another part-time newspaperman, had supported himself by writing a "society column," acting in summer stock at the Hanna Theatre, and renting out bicycles from a storefront in Shaker Square. Upon graduation he moved to Manhattan to pursue a career as an actor or a journalist. After numerous rejections in both fields, he used his experience with bicycles to launch a business renting young men for women who wanted a male companion for an evening on the town. He called it the "Guide Escort Service" and charged "five dollars for an early evening" [6:00 until 10:00 P.M.], and "five more dollars every two hours thereafter. Of course, the lady pays all expenses." As escorts he preferred men like himself: tall blondes with college degrees who had yet to reach their twenty-eighth birthdays—"the flower of American manhood."

When officials rejected his proposal for a "bar barge," Peckham offered to provide his service from a "French" casino that was under construction in the exposition's "Streets of the World," two hundred cafés and bazaars "vaguely reminiscent of the countries they represented." Although Peckham loathed the term "gigolos," that was what Winsor called the escorts, explaining that they would "ask lonely ladies to dance." Providing handsome men would only be fair, since the casino's operators had already hired a chorus line of "some 24 women, imported from the four corners of the country." During the evening, they would strut along an outdoor "cat walk" at the casino, "this a brilliantly illuminated promenade around the roof where girls, and clad in the scantiest of costumes, will parade and parade."

Then, on the day before the exposition opened, Winsor was dismayed to learn that the same officials who had banned nudists had barred gigolos. "The sudden decision," Winsor wrote, "is just a bit staggering. Professional dancers, so called, have been flourishing for years in the deluxe restaurants of every great European city. In Rome, London, Paris, or any other place you care to think of, it is not only considered perfectly correct for a lovely lady to go to tea, dinner or supper dancing and pay for her partner, but even the most puritanical and corseted dowagers don't even lift an eyebrow."

Despite his disappointment, Winsor spent opening day covering as much exhibition ground as possible. At the foot of East 9th Street, only a block from his apartments, he shouted for a "chair," one of the rickshaws drawn by a local collegian. He thought nothing was better than the "plutocratic sensation of riding around in a rickshaw." He recommended "the corn-on-the-cob bars, . . . the water ballet during the afternoon in the Marine theater, . . . speedboats at dusk, and cocktails on the Horticultural terraces, especially when the fashion show swings into action." He told readers to avoid "barkers that pull you into unfinished side shows" and bemoaned "the early hour the lights go out in the Streets of the World." Stringent liquor laws inhibited exhibition nightlife.

Winsor thought the "gayest spots" were the Alpine Tavern, where local restaurateur "Herman Pirchner miraculously contrives to carry some 36 steins of beer at one time," and the French Casino, sans gigolos. "The Casino . . . definitely has the snappiest floor show that has come to town since my

orders were to be home by midnight—or else. Long before closing on Saturday more than 6,000 people had helped to consume 200 cases of beer and
watch callipygian beauties strut their stuff." (Callipygian? "Having shapely
buttocks.") The best time to attend the exposition was at night, when the
"grounds, flooded with real and artificial moonlight, are staggering."

By the time the turnstiles closed in September, officials had counted 4
million people, whose ticket sales generated income that employed 11,000
workers in a depressed economy. Directors debated whether or not they
should raze their $1.9 million investment or reopen the grounds for the
summer of 1937. Another season would require new money to "winterize,
refurbish and improve the layout."

Winsor did not explicitly take sides in the debate, but he told readers
that for the first time in his life Cleveland had enjoyed "a giddy honky-tonk
summer. The town has accustomed itself to eating out of doors . . . and plying the Exposition midway until all hours." One unexpected development
troubled him: the lakeshore nightclubs had emptied uptown sidewalks.
Playhouse Square was dead during the summer. In September, the Carter
Hotel had opened a new nightclub, the Petite Café. After watching customers frequent the new establishment, Winsor thought Prospect Avenue was
"beginning to look happier."

The columnist could smell winter approaching: "Burning leaves, ripen-
ing apples" and "heavy coats . . . coming out of mothballs." Without the
exposition, he pursued thrills by "slumming . . . on the fringes of Kingsbury
Run." He found the Cocoanut Grove, "the newest nightclub on the Harlem
front" at East 83rd Street and Kinsman Avenue. The club was "small, rowdy,
and sometimes very, very gay," but Winsor warned readers, "lock, double
lock and padlock your car. The neighborhood toughies have reduced strip-
ping to a fine art."

As the end of the year approached, two of Winsor's editorial projects had
not materialized. "Early production" of the movie script he had boasted
about in May never occurred. The reason why is a mystery. At the same
time, he did not receive an offer to syndicate his about-town column; if he
wasn't on assignment in Hollywood or New York City, Winsor could not
generate the sort of items about national celebrities that would convince
newspaper editors outside of Cleveland that their readers would enjoy his
columns. To build a larger audience, he began emphasizing theatrical news
in the fall of 1936, which did include well-known stage and film stars. His
decision could be considered to have posed a challenge to George Davis,
the veteran drama critic at the *Press,* of whom Winsor had a low opinion
and who was one of Seltzer's favorite writers. Winsor avoided a direct confrontation by limiting himself to out-of-town shows, an increasing necessity

because Cleveland was no longer considered for premieres of important plays like *Design for Living.*

Winsor was particularly annoyed that the Theatre Guild—the New York City theatrical society founded in 1919, which initially produced noncommercial work by American and foreign playwrights—had chosen Pittsburgh for the pre-Broadway tryouts of *And Stars Remain,* its first production for the 1936–37 season. The show's male star was that overpaid Hollywood idler, Winsor's friend Clifton Webb. It would be his first appearance in a show where he didn't sing or dance. In pursuit of the sort of column items that might justify national distribution of his column, Winsor was forced to drive to Pittsburgh in his cloth-covered Phaeton as "a cold gray rain washed the rusty countryside." At the William Penn Hotel, he found Webb in a suite of rooms "buried in mussed newspapers, surrounded by baskets of fruit and putting away a banquet as if he hadn't a care in the world."

That night on stage, Webb played "a wise-cracking, cocktail drinking gentleman whose passion for down cushions and reclining on the nearest available sofa keeps him from getting to the point with his co-star Helen Gahagan—and the point being he is in love with her and far from the superficial epigrammatist he pretends to be." The columnist was impressed with the actor's portrayal and combined his "new kind of reporting" with drama criticism. "If . . . you have thought of Mr. Webb as merely a highly polished and debonair dancer, which he is of course, you have only half understood him. Seldom have I seen a more finished and absolutely right performance."

Following the show, the actor invited Winsor back to his hotel suite, where Webb "combined a midnight supper with a post mortem, dissecting the play, fault for fault, with all the calm of a surgeon. This reporter finally going to bed, convinced the critics will rave and be satisfied to leave a pair of the world's most famous dancing shoes forever in a closet," a remarkably accurate prediction of Webb's future. *And Stars Remain* failed to thrive in New York City, but Webb began a notable career as the "urbane master of drawing room comedy" on both stage and screen.

Winsor returned to Cleveland and left almost immediately for Boston to continue his pursuit of more glamorous names to populate his columns. Porter had invited him to a dress rehearsal of his newest musical, *Red, Hot and Blue,* and Randolph Churchill had asked him to drop by his sister Sarah's show at a "vaudeville palace" in the same city. In 1936, their father, Winston, was still unemployed.

At a midweek matinee, Winsor saw Sarah Churchill run out on stage "wearing a costume of ostrich plumes." She "does a brief and uninspired turn on her toes while the chorus of dancing beauties . . . indulges in some of

the most cruel and ironic face twisting I have ever seen." After the final curtain, he went backstage, introduced himself as a friend of the star's brother,
and asked the doorman "to find out if Miss Churchill could give me a few
minutes of her valuable time. The doorman relayed the message to her maid,
who in turn relayed the message to her secretary, and eventually I was asked
to wait a few minutes. After 45 of them had passed, I discovered she had
completely forgotten my existence and gone in search of a podiatrist."

Cole Porter's welcome was warmer. The columnist found him "in the
first row of the orchestra . . . shouting last minute suggestions as the unut-
terably weary troupers strut their stuff over and over again. Ethel Merman
saves her voice, Jimmy Durante his mad clowning . . . technicians fuss
with the lights and the orchestra struggles with its cues. New changes go
in and out at the drop of a hat and at 1 A.M. the company is still stymied
in the middle of the first act. The confusion and bewilderment is so great
one wonders how there ever can be a show—much less an opening on the
following night." On the following day Winsor parked himself in the lobby
of the "austere Boston Ritz" and counted "dozens of the faithful Porter
followers" pouring into the hotel. Later, Hanna hosted "a gala dinner" for
Porter's fans, rushing to the theater "just in time to see the curtain rise."

Howard Lindsay and Russel Crouse's book was driven by

a deliciously scatter-brained group of individuals who upset the
nation with a mad search . . . for a young woman who accidentally
was pushed on a hot waffle iron at the tender age of 4—and presumably still carries the brand. It makes little or no sense—but manages
to supply Merman and Durante with every opportunity to display
their wares and pokes fun at everything from the present administration and prison reform to the Junior League.

At exactly five minutes of 12 the wildly enthusiastic audience
finally permitted the curtain to fall for the last time and then once
again the mad scramble for the street and taxis. Then the post mortem, with all the visiting firemen as well as almost the entire cast
crowding into Len Hanna's rooms for cold chicken and champagne.

In the morning, Winsor and Hanna left Boston for New York City, headed
for Hanna's town house at 255 Park Avenue, where they began several days
of their "exceptionally strenuous" social lives. Before a pre-theater dinner,
Hanna poured cocktails in his very sleek drawing room. The walls were
painted black, the floor was covered with white carpeting, and the windows
were covered with leather draperies. "White pigskin!" Winsor claimed.

Following a little Scotch and soda, the men were driven to 21, where anonymous jewels were column fodder. Women wore "everything in their hair from rubies the size of a hen's egg to clusters of orchids caught with a huge diamond clip." Hanna's chauffeur waited outside the former speak-easy until the men emerged with only minutes to spare before the curtain rose at the Empire Theater, where John Gielgud was playing *Hamlet.* Winsor was overwhelmed. While Gielgud, Lillian Gish as Ophelia, and Judith Anderson as Gertrude were "living their too brief lives before your eyes you are left breathless and weak with excitement."

After the show, the driver dropped Winsor and Hanna at El Morocco, where Hanna commandeered what Winsor called a large spotlight table and claimed it was "no longer the fashion to notice anyone else. It was ten minutes before most of the people in our party realized Helen Hayes had drawn up a chair." Winsor hadn't seen the actress: "The vision of Norma Talmadge re-doing her face had been occupying my attention." Jerry Zerbe dropped by their table. He was supporting himself by photographing celebrities and publishing the results in various magazines. He gave Winsor two self-serving column items: Zerbe had leased his apartment to Gielgud and insisted "the rooms echo with soliloquies." The photographer had thrown a cocktail party for Princess Brinda Kapurthala of India, who "arrived carrying an unset diamond, ruby and emerald in her clenched fist." The princess told Zerbe "to take his choice. Just like that he decided on about five carats of emerald which are now being set into a headlight for his dress shirts."

Winsor's frenetic pace did not allow much time for introspection, but this particular round of premieres and parties, with its items about diamond hair clips and emerald shirt studs, unsettled him. The no-holds-barred tactics of his less well-connected colleagues embarrassed him. Newspaper "photographers and reporters were in everybody's hair" on the night *Hamlet* opened, and he was forced to struggle through a "solid mass of curious people." Yet "curious people" were exactly whom he was paid to satisfy with his column. After a lunch with one of his best show-business friends, he was also uncertain about the value of his own journalistic technique. "A reporter goes forth in search of chatter—supposedly commencing over a quiet luncheon table with Libby Holman—only Miss Holman had apparently decided it was her day to lunch with all the unattached males in Manhattan." Her own and her escorts' conversation yielded one line of copy: "There was . . . a great deal of chatter about nothing at all."

Despite Winsor's misgivings, a few weeks later he was back in Manhattan for the New York opening of *Red, Hot and Blue.* On the same trip he saw *Sweet River,* an adaptation of Harriet Beecher Stowe's *Uncle Tom's*

Cabin, written by George Abbot, who would become the twentieth century's preeminent producer of American musical shows. Winsor noted, "The
cast has both white and colored players, and here, I think, Mr. Abbot was
in error. The white Margaret Mullen playing of Eliza lacked both reality
and sincerity and I am quite sure there are dozens of young women out of
jobs in Harlem who could have filled the bill to perfection."

As for Porter's newest musical, Winsor judged it to be a "much better
show" than the version he had seen in Boston. All of the costumes had been
replaced. "Silver foxes and sable trail all over the place and when Miss Merman appears as a bride she is wearing a gown made entirely of ermine."
She had "romped through her numbers and was cheered until I thought the
chandeliers would fall. . . . Jimmy Durante once more picked up the town
and put it in his pocket."

Winsor's column recorded that Linda Porter was "was too ill to be at
hand," an observation that the composer's many biographers have quoted
verbatim and interpreted as the beginning of the couple's disaffection. He
did not elaborate on the significance of her absence. Good friends' marital
difficulties were not subjects for his "new kind of reporting." In her absence,
Porter asked Hanna to join him in the first row of the balcony. The men
avoided any published innuendo about unconventional sexuality by escort-
ing two well-known movie actresses: Mary Pickford and Merle Oberon.
After the final curtain, "the velvet and white ties," according to Winsor,
partied at "the Morocco where Cole was all over the place, grinning like
Mickey Mouse over the compliments. At four o'clock in the morning a few
of us gathered around Len Hanna's bar with Cole, waiting for the reviews.
Once again the critics proved to be consistently inconsistent. Some of them
raved, some of them panned, but at least none of them were indifferent,
and all of them admitted it was staggeringly beautiful." Once again, Winsor
expressed discomfort with the "silly fanfare and chi-chi of a first night."

He returned to Lakeside Flats and Sin Shanty just long enough to celebrate his thirty-second birthday and give a tour of Cedar Avenue nightclubs
to a "tall, dark and good-looking" classical musician, Nicolas Nabokov,
whose *First Symphonic Suite, La Vie de Polichenelle,* was to receive its world
premiere by the Cleveland Orchestra. Winsor met Nabokov at the home
of Sam and Blanche Halle, where Nabokov was a houseguest and "a floor
show all in himself," entertaining guests with his "biting and acid" impersonations of celebrities.

"A geyser of enthusiasm and violent opinion," the thirty-three-year-old
Russian aristocrat's grandfather was justice minister to Czar Alexander II.
His cousin Vladimir Nabokov would eventually write *Lolita,* among other
critically acclaimed works of literature. Winsor introduced the composer

to singer Baby Hines at the Cedar Gardens and pianist Rose Murphy at the Turf Club, where "spare ribs littered the tables, blue notes crowded the atmosphere, and Rose, resplendent at her new grand piano, all but wore her fingers to the bone before the man ran out of requests." After Nabokov left town, Winsor expedited his own departure, packed his car, and headed for "the land of the eyebrowless film stars and nutburger stands." He began his third trip to Hollywood by driving southeast, toward the nation's capital in a caravan of "three cars with a baggage trailer" that carried "20 pieces of luggage."

Winsor and Stearns were each driving an automobile, but the columnist didn't identify the third motorist. It was Hanna. The caravan's itinerary included the National Theater in Washington, D.C., to revisit Gielgud, who was touring with *Hamlet,* then on to Raleigh, Charleston, and a long weekend at Melrose, one of the Hanna family's plantations in Thomasville, Georgia, where some of Cleveland's oldest money avoided snow. Winsor treated ice-cold readers to a rare glimpse of plantation lifestyle. Curious newspapermen, especially gossip columnists, were not welcome in Thomasville.

"Across the lawn comes the sound of dice and backgammon. . . . Beyond the players a covey of dove has just come fluttering to earth. Thousands of bees trouble the roses and everywhere there are red and white camellia bushes—pale green crepe myrtle trees imported from Japan—massive live oaks and forests of white dogwood just about to burst into bloom. A stone's throw away is an enormous swimming pool under glass—above it decks for sunbathing. Down the road is a little theater called The Show Boat where tonight our host is showing us *Beloved Enemy.*" The film starred Merle Oberon, the woman on Porter's arm at *Red, Hot and Blue*'s New York opening; note that Winsor's host remained anonymous. As for Melrose, Winsor once again bemoaned the lack of intellectual content in his friends' activities: "Life is simply too easy for any serious concentration."

From Hanna's plantation, the caravan proceeded southwest through Mississippi. Winsor, whose knowledge of how blacks lived in the South was derived almost entirely from stage shows and movies, was curious about the setting for Heyward's play *Porgy,* which had piqued his curiosity in the late 1920s. In Charleston, South Carolina, he "poked [his] nose into Catfish Row and went in search of fish cries by the old market." Along the highway somewhere between "Sopchoppy and Biloxi," Winsor saw his first chain gang, a singular practice of Southern justice he had learned about in Warner Bros. movies. "Chain gangs," he wrote his Northern audience, "sleep along the roadside in their black and white striped uniforms in the hot, noonday sun. They are all colored—look entirely unconcerned—and as far as I could see had nothing whatsoever to do except continue lying there in the sun. . . . At first the sight of the men lolling against the road bank was terribly depressing, but later they seemed to blend into the landscape and become too familiar to be upsetting." After writing how quickly he had become accustomed to the sight of black men in chains, a guilty conscience caused him to change subjects in the middle of a sentence. He was shocked "at the really appalling fact that [he] was actually able to stare at chain gangs as calmly as if they had been fan dancers."

In New Orleans, Winsor went "slumming" on the city's waterfront, reportedly "the most dangerous in the world." He wrote, "So far, though, I have only discovered houses that are collector's items, bars that are certainly colorful enough but as safe as a country churchyard. New Orleans' vices are no less tawdry than Akron's." Their search for decadence thwarted, Winsor, Stearns, and Hanna left Louisiana "with clean noses" and hurried west to the glittering nightlife of Hollywood.

At the Barthelmess estate, they found Cole Porter, but not Linda. She was at her apartment in Paris. Linda had told Winsor that her respiratory illness would prevent her from joining them in Hollywood. Once again, she "was too ill to be at hand." Linda's absence meant Winsor had to work harder. Without a "brilliant" hostess to throw a party announcing his return to Hollywood, and lacking her current list of private phone numbers, he was forced to reintroduce himself and learn the numbers from someone else.

He made a reservation for lunch at the Vendome, the restaurant "owned by Billy Wilkerson, the diminutive and alert publisher of the *Hollywood Reporter.*" Winsor explained that "players who have been on location or out-of-town practically rush there from the station to gather up a collection of the perpetually changing telephone numbers and let it be generally known they are back on the scene."

Well, Winsor was back and needed numbers, so he allowed the Vendome's car jockey to park his Phaeton and plunged through the "autograph collectors," who had gathered "to watch the film stars arrive in their sleek and exceedingly impressive motors." The restaurant's interior was "an asylum packed with waving, chattering women, producers, visiting firemen, any celebrity you can think of—and, of course, a generous sprinkling of properly awed tourists." Winsor called them "trippers" and claimed they were "led to the far end of the room and firmly seated at tables where, with a little luck, they may occasionally catch a quick view of Gloria Swanson eating in the far distance." Wilkerson displayed his most famous guests "in booths just inside the door" where "pages" carried "telephones from table to table. Contracts are signed over coffee and stars are suddenly created over a soufflé." The Vendome's décor was "simple," the food "good, but hardly extraordinary," and "the service is no cause for swooning. Yet, if the maitre d'hotel calls you by name it means you are on the way up on the Hollywood social ladder."

After he was seen at the Vendome, Winsor began receiving the sort of invitations that produced column items. He attended a party where Billy Haines had "decided it would be cunning to litter the rooms with no less than 750 stuffed doves, a stripped eucalyptus tree strung with 1000 gardenias, and a nude lady in white marble who was clutching a dozen purple orchids." Jewels continued to generate items. At a reception, he observed "Princess Sigvard Bernadotte . . . wearing an emerald and ruby necklace presented to Gustav of Sweden by Queen Victoria." Her Royal Highness "suddenly decided it was too heavy and calmly checked it in the ladies retreat."

Despite a few amusing anecdotes, Winsor's third trip to Hollywood did not produce events like Carole Lombard's bash at the Ocean Park Fun House or Clifton Webb's soiree catered by Marlene Dietrich. Instead, the columnist encountered get-togethers "where everyone beat little drums" or played guessing games and dominoes. The latter was "such a fad there isn't a set to be had in town." For someone drawn to rowdy bars, chain gangs, and dangerous waterfronts, dominoes were bound to be disappointing. Winsor puzzled in print why Hollywood residents "insist on calling this town wild." Another disappointment was that his movie script, completed two years earlier, was still "awaiting production."

The columnist reported that Porter "had reached another gilt-edged conclusion" with MGM. "As soon as he completes a rather extensive tour of India he will report in Hollywood again to write scores for a brace of musicals." The news seemed to set Porter and his wife on irreconcilable paths. She had recently told Winsor she was "considering delivering an ultimatum" to her husband: "Choose between films and his marriage."

Then, a week before he was scheduled to leave for Cleveland, Linda arrived in Santa Barbara, a hundred miles north of Hollywood. There she entertained friends who were not film industry boors, as well as her husband. After dinner, her guests competed in a "spelling bee." How was Winsor going to become a nationally syndicated columnist if his most newsworthy friends, the ones whose privacy he protected, were going to entertain themselves with spelling contests? He worried that the "new kind of reporting" was a waste of his time and talent.

"I may have been a little harsh"

At an oak desk smudged with ink, Winsor chattered to himself as he fed a sheet of crisp paper into the top of his cast-iron typewriter. He tucked the paper's edge into a shallow crease behind a hard rubber roller and twisted its knob clockwise until the buff-colored sheet arose behind a thin silk ribbon impregnated with carbon black. Human hands, not electricity, powered his typewriter. When he punched a key, it struck the ribbon, imprinting a letter on the paper, the first of more than a thousand tiny jabs in a piece of criticism.

Earlier in the year, before the theater season began, Winsor had asked Louis Seltzer to change his assignment from about-town columnist to drama critic. The editor did not immediately grant this request. Seltzer did not share his doubts about the value of his "new kind of reporting." It set the *Press* apart from the competition. The *News* and the *Plain Dealer* had drama critics, but they didn't have Winsor's celebrity anecdotes. Yet Winsor was adamant; he wanted off the smoke-and-music beat. Documenting local nightlife would not satisfy his ambition.

Winsor's parents introduced him to the theater when he was ten years old. On Saturday afternoons, the Eatons took him and Zerbe to the Hippodrome Theater on Euclid Avenue, the most profitable vaudeville house in the United States, where they saw Vaclav Nijinsky in *The Specter of the Rose* (Winsor got the dancer's autograph) and Maude Adams in *Peter Pan* "flying miraculously through the air on taut, gleaming wire." Zerbe tried to duplicate her feat "from the top of Winsor's toboggan slide with the aid of an umbrella and with disastrous results."

Another one of Winsor's childhood neighbors, Mary Louise Brown Curtiss, remembered that she and her playmates staged shows in a neighbor's third floor, charging "three safety-pins" for admission. She recalled Winsor's entertaining "impersonations," in which he appeared with "a long black stocking tucked around a girl's hat for hair."

As boys, Winsor and Zerbe were both cast in Cleveland Play House productions. Zerbe appeared in the repertory company's first theater, a remodeled church on East 73rd Street. "On that occasion" Winsor wrote, Zerbe's costume was a "loin cloth and a nose ring." After graduating from high school, Winsor played a devil in a "spectacular" production of Christopher Marlowe's *The Tragical History of Dr. Faustus.*

During this same period, he sought advice about a theatrical career from a successful actress, Katherine Wick Kelly, a member of the Play House repertory company. "Always the eager champion of youth," she "would labor long and hard, recklessly spending her own energy in an effort to fan small flames into fine fires." Winsor's talent was barely flammable, but "time after time," she "lifted me from deep ruts of despair and into the clear again."

Even before joining Stuart Walker's Stock Company, Winsor had tried writing plays. In 1927, following his brief employment at *TIME,* he submitted a résumé for a play to the Theatre Guild. The guild would premier work by Eugene O'Neill and produce *Porgy and Bess,* george Gershwin's adaptation of Dubose Heyward's play. Winsor told his stepfather that guild directors thought his idea "had GREAT chances," but there is no evidence that he developed the play beyond a proposal. He understood firsthand the difficulties of both the actor's and the playwright's roles in an art form that had a unique power to illuminate the human experience. For Winsor, drama criticism offered a more serious purpose for his writing skill than an about-town column and greater potential for building a national reputation.

Eventually, Seltzer proposed a compromise that combined criticism with the about-town column. Winsor could review theater, but after analyzing a performance, the editor wanted to see at least four or five local or national items. He accepted the offer; at the end of each critique, he wrote "addenda" that revealed his unique local perspective as well as his continuing and superior access to contemporary celebrities.

On opening nights in Cleveland theaters, the new drama critic for the *Press* appeared to be an anachronism. Although he observed "hardly anyone in evening clothes," Winsor refused to abandon the swank costume of his youth. According to Polly Parsons, "with his dinner coat," he wore "red bedroom slippers." Reporters were still obsessed with his footwear. Parsons committed the same faux pas as the *Plain Dealer*'s Glenn Pullen had four years earlier. They weren't bedroom slippers, but red velvet evening pumps—ones Brunhilde hadn't mutilated. After a performance, often near midnight, Winsor would arrive in the *Press* city room in tailored black silk, loosen his bow tie, unbutton the collar of his starched white dress shirt and begin typing his name, date, and page number on the upper left-hand corner of a sheet of paper.

Witnesses insist that Winsor "chattered" while he typed. Those who sat close to him heard him tell his typewriter what to print at the same time he hit the keys. When he was a stroke or two away from the right margin, a silvery bell inside the typewriter would caution him with a tiny "ding." To begin the next line on the opposite side of the paper, he grabbed a chrome-plated lever with his right hand and shoved the roller to the left. Two things happened when he stroked his typewriter. The paper rolled up with a ratcheting sound, and the roller thumped the left-hand margin, where Winsor would resume typing. Thus each line of his audible monologue was punctuated with dings, ratchets, and thumps.

By several accounts, Winsor sometimes accused his typewriter of mangling his sentences, which forced him to rip the paper from the machine's grip, crumple it with both hands, and throw the wad in the direction of his wastepaper basket, where it plopped on the floor. Watching and listening to Winsor bully his typewriter with a deep baritone growl, accompanied by the usual percussion, plus the occasional rip, crumple, and plop, was a city room spectacle that entertained his colleagues. He no longer raised eyebrows. Winsor's stories, early union membership, and extraordinary capacity for liquor had earned tolerance from the "tough guys." By 1937, the wall of the Vermont Club reserved for portraits of famous persons included his photo.

On this particular December night, the critic was lecturing his typewriter about movie actress Joan Bennett's appearance at the Hanna Theatre. She had played the leading role in a revival of George S. Kaufman and Edna Ferber's *Stage Door.* "A young girl," Winsor wrote, is "determined to become a successful actress. Eventually . . . she is awakened in the middle of the night by a film executive, no less, who believes in her ability to such a degree that he throws up his weekly stipend and sends her back to bed with promises of a leading role on Broadway. Understandably moved, the young neophyte suddenly imagines herself to be in a similar position to the young Victoria" and requests a room of her own.

"Miss Helen Hayes," Winsor told his typewriter, "played this same scene on the same stage no longer than a week ago, and played it, if I am too bold, with rather more dignity and assurance." Poor Joan Bennett. He was about to compare her with an actress he adored. After a recent visit to Hayes's dressing room on Broadway, he wrote, "She is one of the most simple and consequently fascinating people I know. On stage she can be anything from a kitchen slavey to an empress—and always vital, alive and magnificently human."

Ding. Ratchet. Thump.

"Joan Bennett, as one might well imagine, is extremely easy on the eyes, but as an actress she seems unfortunately lacking in either poise or assurance. She is strident, uneasy and her voice is both monotonous and colorless."

Ding. Ratchet. Thump.

Winsor's specific concern about her vocal assets was a legacy of his internship in Walker's acting troupe, where the voice was considered an actor's most important tool. How performers used their voices on stage, in film, or on the floor of a nightclub played a much greater role in his appraisals than in those of his newspaper colleagues: Harry Richman "is still singing through his nose." Frances Stevens "has a vocal range of six notes. (Typesetter, it's o.k. if you spell it 'sex.')"

On the occasion of Bennett's performance, Arthur Spaeth, drama critic for the *News,* did not mention her voice but wrote that "the art she acquired in the films serves her well in keeping within bounds a character that might easily become maudlinly sentimental in unsure hands."

William F. McDermott, drama critic at the *Plain Dealer,* did critique her voice: "Her technique is not flexible enough to articulate the depth and variety of feeling that is implied in the role. She misses the minor notes, the plaintive quality, the immediacy of feeling by which tone and inflection are made to seem the inevitable expression of varying shades of emotion." McDermott's language was kinder, but he agreed with his colleague at the *Press.*

In her suite at the Statler Hotel, Bennett initially suffered Winsor's review of *Stage Door* silently, but he had more comparisons to make. On the day after his critique, he was substituting for the *Press* movie critic. Coincidentally, or maybe not, he reviewed RKO's film version of *Stage Door.* "Completed weeks ago, its release date has been held back to permit the stage version to run its course."

Bennett's role in the film was played by Katharine Hepburn. In Winsor's opinion, she gave "the most compelling and distinguished performance of her career." He could not resist reminding readers, "Personally, I didn't care for Miss Bennett's performance (although I may have been a little harsh)."

Someone must have complained about the fairness of the coverage, because Seltzer assigned a reporter to interview Bennett, who used the opportunity to respond to Winsor's criticism: "The modern actress almost has to appear in public to counteract wild impressions created by candid cameramen and imaginative writers. Writers are like actors," she said. "Their performances vary. Few are consistently good."

Touché.

Winsor might have agreed with her. He had recently criticized Sheilah Graham, the syndicated Hollywood correspondent for the North American Newspaper Alliance, because she acted as if film stars were her "personal property . . . a cynosure for the penetrating eyes of the Fourth Estate." Yet two days after the *Press* printed Bennett's interview, the following addendum appeared in Winsor's column: "The Carl Hannas tossed a cocktail party for Joan Bennett in their Hanna Building penthouse yesterday afternoon. Incidentally, so they tell me, Miss Bennett insisted on her own private elevator at the Statler all week—and reported operators who were careless enough to pause for other passengers. It must be wonderful to be a film star."

Ding. Ratchet. Thump.

After reading that item, Bennett called Western Union and dictated a reply, which, Winsor claimed, "was delivered to my desk at about 2:15 A.M. Sunday morning in the form of a telegram." Before quoting from the document, he provided readers with context. "Suddenly, for one reason or another, I suddenly find myself in the midst of a feud with Miss Joan Bennett. It has always been my opinion that a critic was paid to give honestly his honest impressions of such works as it becomes his business to cover. Apparently, I have been in error." The repetition of "suddenly" in Winsor's first sentence and "honestly" and "honest" in the second sentence suggests he was typing so hastily and redundantly that he forgot to rip, crumple, and plop.

"In the wake of my discussions concerning the Hanna Theater's recent relations with the play *Stage Door*, there followed all sorts of tales that I was being personal, had been determined to put Miss Bennett in her place—et cetera. One or two gentlemen, so I understand, have even offered to punch my nose. Nothing could be less personal than my feelings for Miss Bennett."

Ding. Ratchet. Thump.

He went on:

> I have never met her, but I believe her to be very nice. As a matter of cold fact I am indebted to certain members of Miss Bennett's family for some of my happiest memories of Hollywood. I did, however, think her performance in *Stage Door* was unfortunate—and said so—I am sorry now if it was taken personally.
>
> It also seems to me that actors and actresses are seldom given access to speak their own minds. They simply have to take their reviews on the chin, good or bad, and let it go at that. Consequently I am more than happy to herewith print Miss Bennett's opinion of me.
>
> Says Miss Bennett in part . . . "Congratulations on being full of more misinformation than any columnist I know of. You bet it's great to be a movie star. Probably if you were you wouldn't be so sour on life in general and sink to the petty maliciousness that fills your stupid column. And something besides viciousness might slip through

your microscopic brain. Chalk me up to the host of enemies you already have. Joan Bennett."

In dinner jacket and red velvet evening shoes, Winsor typed, "I am framing the telegram for a permanent reminder that a lovely and glamorous lady once left me standing corrected, humble and with head bowed."

By publishing her letter, he had played one of journalism's trump cards: allowing persons to discredit themselves, a practice sometimes called "kill 'em with their own quotes." Miss Bennett's language destroyed her carefully nurtured public image of a modest, sweet-natured film star. Yet he admitted to publishing her telegram "in part." He did omit two crucial words: Her salutation. The telegram did not begin "Dear Mr. French" or "Dear Winsor." It began "Dear Queenie."

Winsor's editing of Joan Bennett's message illustrates the limits with which he felt comfortable revealing his own sexuality or another's homophobia in print. By refusing to quote her well-known slang term for homosexual, the casual reader wouldn't understand why she thought he was malicious, vicious, and "sour on life." While wealthy and powerful friends surrounded him, their presence did not shield him from snubs and slurs. Bennett and Sidney Bartlett, Alice White's lover and sneering press agent, prove intolerance was constantly present, if not always overt. For Winsor, Bennett's telegram became a prized memento. Visitors to his apartment could read her screed, complete with salutation. He hung the framed document on the same wall that held the photographs he collected from friendlier celebrities.

So Winsor's admission that supporters of Joan Bennett thought he was "determined to put her in her place" begs a question. Did he use his column to harass homophobes? A few years earlier, he had relentlessly ragged his queer-baiting competitor Walter Winchell. A close reading of columns Winsor had written a few months before reviewing *Stage Door* suggests a similar motive drove his coverage of notable entertainment personality Billy Rose. He was the impresario hired by the Great Lakes Exposition to lure millions of paying visitors during its second summer on Lake Erie's shore. Rose proposed to stage a water pageant in Lake Erie starring three Olympic swimming champions: Johnny Weissmuller; Eleanor Holm Jarrett, who performed under her maiden name, Eleanor Holm; and Aileen Riggin. To support the stars, Rose hoped to recruit a chorus of local singers and dancers—who weren't afraid of water.

Throughout April and May, Riggin was responsible for training chorus members. Cleveland was "not a swimming town," she recalled later. "It wasn't easy to find that many people . . . that could all keep time with their arms, and synchronize swimming with a ballet for thirty or more girls, maybe fifteen or sixteen boys. And there was no pool to practice in big enough for that many girls." Instead, Rose rented the ballroom in a downtown hotel. "We would walk around doing the stroke," Riggin said, "trying to keep in time with the music that they were going to play in the show."

While his cast rehearsed, Rose pursued newspaper publicity that would generate interest in his show. When members of the Building Service Employees Union struck the Lake Shore Hotel, where Holm and Riggin were staying, Rose invited newspaper reporters and photographers to their apartment to watch Holm dust and sweep her suite. She told the press, "I'm a lousy housekeeper," a statement so newsworthy it appeared on page 1 of the *Press.*

Rose charmed Cleveland newsmen, with one sarcastic exception: Winsor French. While still writing his about-town column, he belittled the show almost daily without ever mentioning the publicity hound's name. He began by suggesting that the anonymous producer was lying about the male star he had promised: "If Johnny Weissmuller is actually going to display his tricks in . . . Aquacade this summer—where is he?" Just days later, Weissmuller arrived at Cleveland's Union Station "roaring" for Winsor's "blood because I have questioned, from time to time, the probability of his ever reaching the Aquacade stages." Winsor didn't apologize for doubting Rose's word.

After lunching with the sixth and most popular film actor to play Tarzan, the monosyllabic jungle hero created by author Edgar Rice Burroughs, Winsor patronized Weissmuller. The Ape Man "did nothing wilder than drink my iced tea and imitate a seal (somewhat to the astonishment of the other patrons)." As for Holm and Riggin, he didn't mention them before the show's opening. Instead, he praised another female star: a sleek, bewhiskered seal. "At the moment this fascinating and celebrated lady is being kept in the ladies' washroom in the stadium, but any moment now will be ready to snap for herrings."

For items about seals, Winsor practiced a venerable journalistic technique. He didn't rely on Rose's press agent; he cultivated sources in the cast, including Aquacade chorus boys. For the glamorous privilege of wearing a phosphorescent swimming cap and performing in "dirty" and "cold" Lake Erie, where the ice had to be removed for the early rehearsals, the young men were "paid a streetcar pass." Several were guests of Winsor's at Sin Shanty. "I visited your Ninth Street apartment one day with Ray Twardy, one of the comedy divers," John Silvey wrote him. "Roger Stearns, the pianist at the Statler, was visiting you at the time." He had hoped to spend the summer at the exposition, playing at his own nightclub on a barge in Lake Erie. Despite Winsor's promotion of Stearns's plan, he did not receive an attractive offer from Rose.

Winsor did plug tickets for opening night: "The demand for tables . . . is so great that a special telephone bureau has been installed for reservations. If you want one call Cherry 0802." Then he made phoning sound futile. "You will be lucky if the number isn't busy."

At the dress rehearsal, Winsor didn't mention Rose but identified John Murray Anderson as "putting the Aquacade boys and girls through their paces—and having his troubles. Squatting beside the most tuneless piano mortal ears have ever listened to, and shouting directions through a microphone, his greatest difficulty seemed to be in eliminating the backstage gaiety. Once someone appeared, stopped the proceedings and calmly announced the stage had drifted out of place and couldn't be fixed for 15 minutes. Everyone yawned and sat down to wait and I had visions of the whole thing suddenly taking off for Cedar Point."

Compare Winsor's description with the story written opening night by *Press* movie critic Charles Schneider: "The stage, at Mr. Rose's will, moves off toward Canada for a distance and then halts while the army of performers swim, dive, clown, dance, sing and make pretty patterns against water, sky and scenic backdrop. The thing is positively colossal—and the word is not used facetiously. If I hadn't seen it myself, I wouldn't believe it."

That's the sort of press coverage Rose desired and expected. In fact, Schneider's praise mirrored the public's approval, which generated millions of dollars worth of ticket sales at ten, twenty-five, and fifty cents each. Why wouldn't Winsor acknowledge Rose's achievement? It was not a philosophical objection to spectacle. He loved the circus. He did criticize another impresario, Florenz Ziegfeld, for his willingness "to throw a fortune into sequins, plaster elephants, and miles and miles and miles of coq feathers," but he did not object to musical revues whose only goal was entertainment, a category that would include Aquacade.

Polly Parsons, who interviewed Winsor in the 1930s, explained his truculence. He had "one outstanding characteristic beyond his sophistication," she wrote. "It's his loyalty to friends—upon whom he bestows the divine right of kings. They can do no wrong." Fanny Brice, the forty-six-year-old vaudeville comedienne who had been married to Billy Rose for eight years, was Winsor's friend. Her backstage confidante was Roger Davis, one of Winsor's groomsmen. Brice had appeared with both Davis and Roger Stearns in *Crazy Quilt,* which Winsor described as "Billy Rose's not so vaguely risqué revue." During that show and others, Rose complained that his wife was "up to her ass in nances," a derogatory term for homosexuals that did not endear him to Davis or Stearns, who were both Winsor's friends, thus, by Parsons's definition, blameless.

While Rose was in Cleveland, his wife was performing on Broadway with Davis. During rehearsals, Rose later confessed that "he fell in love with Eleanor the first time he saw her dive into the water at Aquacade." From that moment, the impresario, who was thirty-eight years old, and his star, who was twenty-four, were "almost constant companions." Herbert Goldman, Brice's biographer, wrote, "When a friend told Fanny she had seen Billy going into Eleanor's room in Cleveland's Lakeshore Hotel, Fanny phoned, told Eleanor she was 'Mrs. Rose looking for Mr. Rose,' and promptly hung up the receiver." Within two years, Rose and Holm would divorce their spouses and marry each other, but during Aquacade their behavior was flagrantly adulterous.

With the benefit of contemporary context, Winsor's items about Aquacade seem to reflect his contempt for Rose's extramarital activity and the showman's blatant homophobia, which had directly affected three of his friends. One cannot dismiss the possibility that a similar attitude colored his opinion of Joan Bennett.

No one reading Winsor's movie or drama criticism ever doubted that he held strong opinions. On the subject of theater, he expressed disgust with authors' "careless play writing" and disdained the "wholesale slaughter" plays received from newspaper critics who "didn't know what it was all about." Experience as both frustrated performer and playwright meant Winsor thought he knew what theater was all about. Like his "new kind of reporting," he wrote as an insider, not an arms-length newspaper critic. His stated goal at the *Press* was to revive his hometown's "fast fading interest in the theater" by increasing the number and improving the quality of shows touring Cleveland. His concern was not new. At *PARADE,* Winsor observed, "Each year shows a noticeable decrease in the number of good plays we get; more and more in sheer desperation the theatre-going public is drifting toward movies and vaudeville." He continued to promote Cleveland for world premieres and was still nursing a grudge against the Theatre Guild for having chosen Pittsburgh rather than Cleveland for try-outs of Clifton Webb's *And Stars Remain.* A year later, Winsor scolded the society when it cancelled a *Madam Bovary* booking in the Hanna Theatre and sent the show to Chicago: "Once again," the guild "sold us down the river. The Hanna must be black with despair. It is more than a little discouraging to have one production after another back down. What Chicago has that Cleveland hasn't, probably, is a million or so looser dollars, but, nonetheless, it would be pleasant to see a little activity around town."

Because there were so few new productions in Cleveland, Winsor wrote some of his most illuminating reviews about shows in New York. He had no use for that city's drama critics: "Nightly they march sullenly to their seats, sit there as if bored to extinction and then retire to tear each and every new production . . . to pieces. At this point it is just a little confusing to discover what they expect—or what their standards are."

Some of the columns that clearly illustrate Winsor's standards, as well as his differences with New York City's critics, were written in December 1939, when he was in Manhattan to review Cole Porter's newest musical, *Du Barry Was a Lady,* and a half-dozen Broadway shows. In a week's worth of columns, he combined criticism with the "new kind of reporting." He began his reportage with dinner at the Colony, "the world's most deluxe and expensive restaurant. If you don't know . . . the headwaiter," Winsor wrote, "you might just as well cross it off your list. With polite austerity he always leads the unfamiliar faces to obscure corner tables where they neither can see nor be seen."

The Colony's maître d' recognized Winsor's hosts, Cole and Linda Porter. This was the first time in fifteen months that the Porters had appeared in one of Winsor's columns. In October 1937, while horseback riding, the composer's "nervy" mount "shied at some bushes, reared, and fell back upon Cole," who was "unable to disengage his feet from the stirrups." As the horse struggled to stand, it fell back twice upon the composer and crushed both his legs. After doctors examined him, they recommended amputating both limbs.

Linda was in Paris when she received news of the accident and the recommendation to amputate. She and her husband weren't speaking to each other. Citing Winsor as his source, Porter biographer Brendan Gill wrote that by "the autumn of 1937," Linda "would almost certainly have left" her husband. Nevertheless, by phone from Paris, she assumed her wifely responsibilities and insisted that no decision be made about her husband's legs until she returned to New York City. "Although still angry," another biographer, George Eells, wrote that "she rushed to Cole's side . . . [and] told their mutual friend, Winsor French, 'It's too heartbreaking, you don't desert a sinking ship.'" The composer was forty-six years old and proud of his trim body and boyish looks. Appreciating his vanity, his wife in consultation with his mother (Kate Porter, née Kate Cole) decided amputation would maim and humiliate the man they loved, so both told doctors to save his legs. An excruciating series of operations began immediately.

The dinner at the Colony marked the first time Winsor had written about Porter since the accident. His legs were in braces and he was in "constant pain." In his column, Winsor did not reveal that Porter's chauffeur and Ray Kelly, his "tall, broad-shouldered" paid companion, carried him into the restaurant. The gentlemen set him at his table in the section reserved for celebrities. The trio ordered "snacks." At 8:00 P.M. they were due at the 46th Street Theater for *Du Barry*'s debut.

On opening nights, according to biographer David Grafton, "the Porters and their guests always arrived on time, sweeping in on a wave of chatter, perfume, furs, and jewels to their seats in the middle of the second row." With his "party of friends," Cole laughed and applauded his productions "as if he hadn't the slightest doubt of their success." At intermission, he would tell friends "in a tone of honest admiration, 'Good isn't it?'" For *Du Barry* Winsor sat with Porter, making no effort to appear like an objective critic by keeping an arm's distance from the composer. He was not an ingrate. Could he give his readers a fair appraisal of a Porter show after having been the composer's guest at the Colony?

In his review of *Du Barry,* he began by identifying Porter's collaborators: Herbert Fields and B. G. De Sylva. They had supplied an "appropriately disrespectful book," Winsor wrote. "Ethel Merman and Bert Lahr are the principal clowns. The plot, if you can describe it as such," was "concerned with the towel dispenser in the gentleman's room of a fashionable night-club who wins a sweepstakes prize, accidentally drinks a 'Mickey Finn' intended for a rival suitor of Miss Ethel Merman's charms and goes into a dream sequence wherein he imagines himself to be Louis XIV. Miss Merman, of course, emerges as Du Barry." The two "chase and run away from one another through Raoul Pene Du Bois' setting that would make Versailles look like a fumbled housing project." Winsor conceded that Fields and De Sylva had "put words into the players' mouths and placed them in positions that never can be described in print. Mr. Lahr's great moment, for instance, is a scene requiring a court physician to remove an arrow which has been shot with perfect marksmanship into his expansive derriere by the idiotic Dauphin. . . . There is no way of retelling this nonsense with a vestige of decency."

Winsor's opinion about one particular song, "But in the Morning, No!" permits comparison with his professional colleagues. The number was a duet between Merman and Lahr. In what is essentially a quiz, Louis XIV and Madame Du Barry inquire about each other's sexual experience, skills, and preferences. Their answers are naked double entendres. Du Barry asks the King about his "poker" skills: "Can you fill an inside straight?"

He wants to know about her "politics": "Do you like third parties, dear?"

Winsor described the song as a "risqué little number" that "revives the most slumbering imaginations." Brooks Atkinson of the *New York Times* called the lyrics "slatternly." The *New Yorker* sneered, "Dirt without wit." Porter biographer Eells maintained that the duet "offended more reviewers than any other song Cole ever wrote."

As for Atkinson, "slatternly" was just the beginning of his diatribe. "Mr. Porter's ideas are a little skimpy this time," he groused, "and never more microscopic than in 'But in the Morning, No.' The authors have struck a dead level of Broadway obscenity that does not yield much mirth."

Porter and his collaborators had written *Du Barry* for Ethel Merman, a "big and brassy" twenty-nine-year-old musical comedy star. One cultural historian described her "vocal sound" as "godawful. When she was belting, which was most of the time, it was raucous, strident, abrasive, brassy, nasal, open and just plain loud." Merman didn't apologize. "I don't bother about style, but I do bother about making people understand the lyrics I sing," which meant the audience understood every one of Porter's double entendres.

She remembered that on opening night her duet with Lahr provoked "outright hostility" and "the comedy scenes didn't play well." On the same evening Winsor claimed the audience was so amused "people practically rolled out of the balcony." He not only disagreed with the critics, but the female star, too. *Du Barry* was a "completely mad and exceedingly bawdy evening." Winsor was not alone in his opinion. One other respected newspaper critic, Burns Mantle of the *Daily News,* thought the show was "coarse . . . but enjoyable." Compared to all the other reviews, however, Winsor's critique reads as if written by a shill. He predicted *Du Barry* would be "the first really smash . . . hit of the season" and subsequently promoted a recording of "But in the Morning, No!"

Surprisingly, his judgment was confirmed by the second night's audience. "Ignoring the negative reviews," Merman remembered, they "laughed and applauded . . . lustily." The cast "played to 98 standees on Saturday night," according to Eells, "outgrossed any other show in town during its second week, and eventually racked up a run of 408 performances." Winsor had a greater appreciation for vulgarity than Atkinson or the *New Yorker,* and a keener understanding of the public's mood in the last month of the 1930s.

Opening night's hostile audience did not curtail the Porters' festivities. Their party ended the night at 21, the former speakeasy. In his column, Winsor insisted that the Colony, *Du Barry,* and 21 had been "too much of a merry-go-round for an Ohio boy accustomed to a bowl of onion soup at the Vermont Club or a wild evening at the [Hotel] Cleveland."

Baloney! Winsor spent his life searching for fast, brilliant, jangling merry-go-rounds. The world was his amusement park, and Manhattan was the Fun House. Later in the week, his ex-wife invited him to her birthday party. She also invited her second ex-husband, actor Burgess Meredith, whom she had divorced after two years of marriage. Winsor and Meredith had more in common than Miss Perry. The actor was born in Cleveland, where he had worked as both a department store clerk and a newspaper reporter. They traded stories and made a date to see William Saroyan's *The Time of Your Life.*

In a "dingy, waterfront saloon . . . shrouded in an aura of gin and beer

fumes," Winsor and Meredith encountered Saroyan's "bewildered" characters "seeking . . . some integrity to help them continue the business of living." Their "wonderful" conversation was "steeped in alcohol." The cast was
"concise, understanding and always gives the impression they believe infinitely in the things they are saying." That the playwright had not supplied a
plot was of "minor importance." *The Time of Your Life,* Winsor wrote, "tears
your heart out." Burgess Meredith cried throughout the evening. "I know,"
he wrote, "because I was sitting next to him." He respected his seatmate,
"an extremely fine actor." Meredith was "so excited that he kept shouting,
'My God! Where did they find these people?' and it finally reached the point
where I thought the management would turn us into the streets."

Following Saroyan's barroom, Winsor visited a neurotic girl in a sanitar-
ium, a "sordid laundry," and "tenement lodgings," the settings for Sidney
Kingsley's *The World We Make.* Loaded with what Winsor called "inevita-
bilities," the woman falls in love with a man and "pours infinite energy
into the business of trying to make him happy and in the process begins
to find herself and to drown her fears. Then the war comes, from every
miserable window drifts the ceaseless sound of radios announcing terror
and catastrophe. Fear, hatred and panic race over the face of the earth;
they are the very emotions that drove her to illness in the beginning and
they commence to do it again." Winsor described the characters as "valid,
honest people . . . struggling as best they can to live in a world that at best
has little to offer them—and they all come accurately to life."

Both Saroyan and Kingsley had brought "depth and power, understanding and beauty to the theater," Winsor wrote, "yet the critical writers,
whose opinions mean so much to the box office, pass over them lightly
and give more serious attention to such pleasant events as *The Man Who
Came to Dinner.* Far be it from me to snub comedy, but if the theater is to
endure we must have our serious prophets, too, and if they are to endure,
their audiences must find them out."

Winsor did not snub *The Man Who Came to Dinner,* "the most outrageous,
annihilating and devastating play Moss Hart and George S. Kaufman have
written." Monty Woolley was playing Sheridan Whiteside, a drama critic
with a "flashing wit" and "sophisticated charm that could turn impishly vulgar." Whiteside was a parody not of Winsor but of another drama critic,
Alexander Woollcott, of the former *New York World,* who was known as a
"master of the insult . . . a repressed homosexual who never found a mate."
While Winsor acknowledged that the playwrights had not given Woolley
"so much as one banal phrase to read," the fifty-one-year-old actor was "on
stage throughout the entire play and though he brings down fire and brim-
stone on the heads of innocents, you will never be able to hate him."

And Winsor certainly couldn't hate Woolley; they'd been friends for at least ten years. "The theater has few actors who have worked harder, laughed off more disappointments or been more deserving of encouragement—outrageous as the bellowing bearded beaver is." Winsor and Woolley shared the same birthplace, Saratoga Springs, New York, but, more important, the actor was one of Hanna's and Porter's closest friends from their years at Yale, where they "shared a love of gossip, café society, costume parties, practical jokes and pranks, drinks and cigarettes, handsome young men, and, above all, anything to do with the theater." Woolley's wit, Yale diploma, and sexual preference made him a frequent houseguest at Hanna's Hilo Farm. (In response to a request from Kaufman and Hart, Porter wrote a song for a Noël Coward–type character to sing in *The Man Who Came to Dinner*, called "What Am I to Do?" In a spoof of Coward's style, the composer listed the author as "Noël Porter.")

After a week of splendid theater and fewer than two years as the *Press's* drama critic, Winsor returned to Cleveland determined to resume the "new kind of reporting," this time on a luxury ocean liner. During their dinner at the Colony, Linda and Cole Porter had invited him to join them for a two-month cruise to the South Seas aboard a Swedish American ocean liner, the MS *Kungsholm*. Porter planned to devote his days aboard ship to writing a new musical for Ethel Merman, *Panama Hattie*. He thought a nightclub singer's efforts to thwart spies bent on blowing up the Panama Canal might make a good story. The idea of a sea-going studio was a reprise of the Porters' 1935 voyage, which had produced the "complete score and book" for *Jubilee*.

Linda enjoyed Winsor's company. To make the voyage more attractive to him, she was trying to shanghai two of his best friends and former groomsmen: Roger Stearns and Leonard Hanna. Stearns could play the music Porter composed aboard ship. While Porter, Stearns, and Winsor worked, Hanna could sleep. In bed he wore "a black bandage over his eyes to prolong the darkness," Winsor wrote, and Hanna "intensely disliked being spoken to until after he had has coffee." Another friend remembered that he "seldom arose before noon, and often not until evening."

Porter was also recruiting William Powell, a veteran of the first "working" cruise. A "Yalie and great friend of Len Hanna's," "Little Bill Powell" supported himself by writing travel articles and publicizing clients. To promote the products of the Johnson Wax Company, for example, he had persuaded his friend Helen Morgan "to slide a bit" whenever she "slithered onto the piano" at a nightclub where she was singing. Then she would ecstatically moan, "Oooh, that Johnson's Wax!" Powell's antics made Porter laugh.

In Cleveland, Winsor had little trouble persuading Louis Seltzer that *Press* readers would prefer details of the Porters' escapades at sea rather than his own critical efforts to build an audience for serious theater. While packing his steamer trunks, Winsor fired a barrage of snide year-end farewells.

He promoted the Christmas pageant at the Roxy Burlesque: "Renee, wearing no more than the law demands, brings in the reindeers, holly, mistletoe and what have you, to the evident delight of the high kicking ladies of chorus."

He infuriated fans of Nelson Eddy: "As an actor he would be a good pastry cook."

He walked out on Laurel and Hardy: "A little pie throwing, so I thought, would be very much in order. But before a third of the footage had flashed across the screen I realized that either I or the two comedians had changed, and sadly went on my way."

When John Barrymore appeared inebriated on the Hanna stage, Winsor was horrified: "In my sentimental memory he is the greatest actor I have ever seen and now, in actuality, he turns up as a middle-aged mountebank, apparently delighted over the opportunity of turning intoxication into a commercial commodity."

Finally, he castigated the Statler Hotel for closing his field office, in what reads like an obituary for the intimate nightlife Winsor treasured:

> The other afternoon . . . I looked into the old bar where Roger Stearns used to serve as host, struck a few matches and found the place just exactly as it always was. The little piano is still there, the tables are stacked neatly in a corner and the giddy murals still stare down from the shadowed walls—none the worse for the passing years. It would be nice if the Statler would suddenly remember this was the most attractive and successful cocktail lounge in town and open it again. Roger Stearns was the most affable and gifted musician who ever has played here during the cocktail sessions and hardly a day passed when people weren't turned away at the doors. Now all that is changed. The bars, for the most part, are all huge, smoky and noisy rooms. The entertainers, inevitably, are tasteless strollers who go about shouting "South of the Border" into the ears of "coke high" drinking debutantes and glamour seems to be a thing of the past.

Cleveland bored Winsor. The year 1939 was "one of the most depressing, unwanted years in all history." He left town while the temperature was eight degrees below zero and headed for New York City's docks.

"Nights are . . . a Bacchanalian rout"

NEW YORK CITY, NEW YORK

Saturday, January 20, 1940, Midnight

"Shivering, apprehensive passengers struggling with their luggage" and shouting "a thousand stupid questions" milled about Winsor and his "over-burdened" porter as they tried to reach the gangplank and climb aboard the MS *Kungsholm,* a great, white, Swedish American ocean liner tied to a pier in the black Hudson River. In an hour, she was scheduled to set sail for the South Seas.

Winsor observed that the "bon voyage orchids" pinned to women's mink coats had "drooped" in subzero temperatures. "Friends who had come down to the pier to say goodbye stood first on one foot, then the other, obviously wondering how soon they could politely escape."

Arctic air prevented the festivities that had made steamship departures such romantic occasions for Winsor in the past. "Music played, multi-colored paper streamers were tossed from deck to pier and from every stateroom came the invigorating sound of popping wine corks. Amid all this wonderful confusion the ship would gently ease away from its berth and start drifting down the river. Behind you was the fantasy of the Manhattan skyline, a glittering background embroidered on black velvet. Ahead was the dark, open Atlantic and for a moment you were suspended between the two . . . [as you] took a turn around the deck to watch your familiar world disappear."

Winsor was not about to take a turn around the deck of the *Kungsholm:* "It was much too cold." Through a porthole, he watched "the sailors pull the covered gangplank back onto the ship," while he "stood midst the cluttered luggage and boxes" in his stateroom. As in the past, the Manhattan skyline retreated, but in 1940 Winsor's eye was drawn to "Liberty," who "held her torch high and then . . . disappeared." Next came Staten Island and "the vast deserted liners that have been sent into tragic exile by the war."

Adolf Hitler's conquest of Europe and the English and French declarations of war prevented the *Kungsholm* from safely entering the "dark, open

Atlantic," where German U-boats threatened sea lanes. Nazi bullies had even generated items in Winsor's smoke-and-music beat column. In 1933, he described how friends had been harassed in Berlin's nightclubs. "The Swastikas go from table to table selling postcards, and you don't dare to refuse to buy them. And after you have invested you discover they are gaily decorated with portraits of Bismarck, Wagner and Hitler! Is that conceit?"

Nazi arrogance quickly degenerated into virulent anti-Semitism. Winsor documented local protests: "Because Jewish books are being burned in Germany," Korner and Wood, a popular Cleveland bookstore, had made its inventory of Jewish authors "even more conspicuous by stacking them around an artificial bonfire." In London, he wrote, "the famous Duke of York Theater is being turned into a home solely for the plays of ousted Jews." After wire reports from China described Japanese atrocities, Winsor asked readers to "feel sorry for Toshio Fujii . . . who runs the Sukiyaki restaurant on Euclid at East 96th Street. Born in the Hawaiian Islands and an American citizen, he has never been to Japan." Yet news reports were "wrecking his business. Which is all very silly. If you aren't bothered with prejudice of that nature and find exotic dishes fascinating—go try Toshio's shrimps in batter."

That Winsor and his friends were trying to escape the "dark and terrible things" that were "wrong with civilization" was not a secret. According to a front-page article in the *Press* announcing the voyage, Swedish American officials "intended to show war-afrighted would-be travelers that there is still peace on earth and good fun for men, women and children . . . in the South Seas." Perhaps, but the *Kungsholm*'s owners were not taking chances. They had painted large Swedish flags on both sides of the ship to proclaim her neutrality, in case her silhouette appeared in the crosshairs of a belligerent's periscope. "The highways of the seas," Winsor wrote, "have nearly all been eliminated and every day the far-off places to which it is possible for the restless to travel become fewer and fewer." The *Kungsholm*'s journey, her first to Hawaii, Samoa, Tahiti, and the Galapagos Islands, was "an experiment. If it is successful it may open up entirely new horizons" for the cruise company.

On board, Winsor finished unpacking and left his stateroom to avoid the "shattering . . . letdown for departing voyagers who eventually found themselves, deserted and alone in smoke-filled cabins, surrounded on all sides by half-emptied glasses and overflowing ashtrays." He made "a grand tour" of the cruise ship, beginning in the Porters' cabin. Linda was pleased that he had joined her entourage. The day before the *Kungsholm* sailed, she wrote a friend, photographer Jean Howard, "We are off on our cruise tomorrow morning . . . Len Hanna, Bill Powell, Roger Stearns, Winsor French, . . . and I: Doesn't that sound nice."

The couple's cabin was "crowded to the ceiling with trunks, special radios, bookcases, liquors of every description and a completely incredible collection of paraphernalia." The columnist noted that Porter was not unpacking his own gear. That chore was reserved for a "bewildered valet," Paul Sylvain.

To enhance the creative process, "two unpredictable gentlemen" named Howard Lindsay and Russel Crouse, who had collaborated with Porter on *Anything Goes,* had sent the composer a package "with a note explaining they wanted to give him something he would be unable to buy on the boat."

"Well," Winsor wrote, "they succeeded." When Porter unwrapped their gift, he discovered "a huge statue of a very modern, nude lady—executed in brown plaster. It now stands majestically in a corner, waiting for Cole to dress her in appropriate clothes bought at various ports of call on the voyage." Her wardrobe would provide ideas for *Panama Hattie*'s costume designer. "Leaving Mr. Porter to contemplate his confusion and treasure," Winsor headed for one of the cruise ship's "numerous bars."

To his snowbound readers in Cleveland, Winsor pronounced the *Kungsholm* "perfect." In addition to the bars, there were "two swimming pools, one indoor and the other out, Finnish and Turkish baths and no end of places to hide away from the inevitable bores and life-of-the-party-types that always pop up on a long trip." As the *Kungsholm* sailed south along the frigid New Jersey shoreline, heading toward Havana, Cuba, Winsor returned to his room and wrote, "In a few more days the open air restaurant will be in use—not to mention the pool—and we will all have readjusted ourselves to a new and, as far as I am concerned, very welcome life." He had been told that the owners of the *Kungsholm* would host cocktail parties "until they have entertained every passenger on the boat. Considering every nook and cranny is occupied by escapists that's a very large order."

Reality occasionally appeared on the horizon. "Every now and then we also sight other ships in the distance and everyone remembers the state of affairs the world is in and rushes to the rail to look for belligerent flags." *Kungsholm* officials tried to ease passenger anxieties by making sure European hostilities "slipped into the background. The ship's paper carries only brief little bulletins."

Winsor's dispatches prove valuable sources of information. They document the lifestyle of the Porters and their friends and also how the composer sought musical inspiration. Until now, Porter's many biographers have described the voyage superficially or erroneously. In *Red, Hot, and Rich* David Grafton placed Lindsay and Crouse's gift on the wrong trip ["aboard the *Franconia*"] and described it as "a large, ugly statue of a woman with a bulging figure." Grafton's source claims that Porter "ordered the grotesque

statue dressed in native garb for each port-of-call." In fact, it was a manne-
quin for costumes that Ethel Merman and female cast members would wear
in *Panama Hattie*. Because of the figure's dark brown color, Porter named
her *Dorothy Lamour,* because she resembled the sensuous, twenty-six-year-
old nightclub singer and movie actress of French Louisianan descent, who
had worn a sarong in *Jungle Princess,* a garment she would make famous in
numerous films. (Winsor described Lamour in *Chad Hanna* as "a perfectly
appalling actress.")

Winsor recorded details of steamship travel that would change drastically during his lifetime, providing a source of cultural history at the same
time as he gave insights into his own lifelong—and worldwide—pursuit
of racial, ethnic, religious, class, and sexual tolerance. In his columns he
decided not "to say anything about populations, the mean temperatures or
how much sugar is grown annually in Cuba." Instead, readers would learn
about "the things I have personally found colorful."

Fortunately for Winsor's readers, after only two days at sea, the *Kungsholm* approached the western hemisphere's capital of commercial cocktail
parties—Havana—and the air became hot and muggy: "My first visit to
Havana in five years is going to be a very moist one." In a natural harbor,
amid "magnificent yachts . . . trim American destroyers and frail little sailing
boats apparently moored for the night," a perspiring Winsor was forced to
fill out a "landing card" before he could disembark and find an empty barstool at Sloppy Joe's, where the "daiquiris were the best in the world." Official documents flummoxed him. "I always manage to do everything wrong
with brilliant consistency." So, he handed the card to another member of the
party: Linda Porter's traveling secretary. After she completed the document,
he was ferried ashore, where he found "most" of Havana's residents looked
"as if they had been dressed for the finale of a musical comedy."

Winsor allowed the Porters to arrange his social life. Jeanne Murray,
a young passenger aboard the *Kungsholm,* thought Linda "mothered" her
male companions. The Porter party hurried to Sloppy Joe's for those superb
daiquiris, where Winsor admired the "lanky, dark-skinned natives," who
tried to sell him "fantastic strings of beads and . . . alligator belts." Then,
under "a tremendous Brazilian lily tree" on the "cool patio" of the Prado 86
Club, he drank "still more daiquiris and . . . ate quantities of olives treated
in garlic" while watching "swanky, gay Cuban playboys . . . gather for cocktails." Next, to the Café de la Paris in Cathedral Square, where their party
sat "on a terrace, serenaded by street singers" while eating "pink, Morro
crabs." At Pasade, an "all-girl rhumba orchestra" consisting of ten sisters
"flirted" with the shore party.

Their fifth nightspot, a native "rhumba shack" called Uncle Sam's, located down a "narrow, dark street," captivated Winsor and provided Porter with rhythmic inspiration for *Panama Hattie*.

> The night we were there we were the only white people in the room— excluding the proprietor who served us rum we drank at the risk of forever wrecking our digestions. The room itself looked like something designed by Metro-Goldwyn-Mayer for Clark Gable to wander into and discover Joan Crawford glamorously going to the dogs against the upright piano. The clientele consisted of a half dozen or so very black Cubans and an equally black orchestra in straw hats. In the beginning there was very little action and then Cole Porter ordered drinks for the house and things began to happen.
>
> Delighted people rushed in from the street, tossed off a beer in record time and then went into a dance. There were rhumbas, conga chains and every conceivable rhythm you can imagine. The men smoked cigars, the women cigarettes, they swayed in tempo with their eyes closed and then they suddenly became hysterical, disjointed contortionists. If the boys and girls didn't have their hearts in their work, then they were all magnificent fakers.

Nothing else in Havana matched Uncle Sam's. They taxied to the "conventional" yacht club: "No interest there." The Sans Souci, where "croupiers stood waiting behind empty roulette tables," looked "dull and expensive," so Winsor and his friends returned to the *Kungsholm* aboard the "last tender . . . crowded with people who had gone too many times to the flowing bowl." While they were enjoying Havana's nightlife, "the stars had disappeared, clouds were gathering and it looked like rough weather ahead."

Winsor was prescient. Two days later, the *Kungsholm* was "still pitching," and the dining room was "mysteriously empty. Fortunately, rough weather doesn't phase me, although it is a bit difficult writing when your typewriter is skidding all over the room." During the stormy interlude, Winsor described why he found Havana so attractive. "The natives are tolerant as only Latins are and consequently Havana is all things to all people. Whatever your diversions, you can find them without much trouble."

Helping readers find diversions was one of Winsor's journalistic missions. For those who sought places to satisfy lust of one sort or another, he provided directions in what would eventually become a discreet international directory. While his colleagues often warned readers away from bars filled with rough trade, he often provided addresses for disreputable neighborhoods or nightspots he had personally inspected and found safe in Cleveland. Of the Crystal Slipper, he wrote, "You get a girl to dance with for your dime." And at Schultze's Cafe, "The crowd is as mixed as a Philadelphia pepper pot and as the yawning point approaches everyone becomes very friendly and intimate."

What made Havana's honky-tonks safer than those in other cities was an official policy that discouraged the sort of publicity that could damage reputations or kill a career, such as the articles that appeared in Los Angeles newspapers after actor Billy Haines and a sailor were arrested in a room at the YMCA. The publicity gave intolerant film studio executives an excuse to cancel Haines's contract. In Havana, "the government's desire to cater to the tourists is so boundless that if you suddenly find yourself in uncomfortably warm water the police are not only on your side, but your case will be heard in a closed tribunal." Daiquiris, swanky playboys, and rhumba shacks chaperoned by permissive police may be what led Porter to hope, "Heaven must be awfully like Havana."

The storm prevented the *Kungsholm* from landing at Vera Cruz, so the ship's officials rerouted the ship toward the northeast coast of Panama and the San Blas islands, where Winsor encountered aborigines for the first and last time in his life. "None of them is more than 4 feet tall. Except when ships anchor nearby or when they go to the mainland, nudity is the order of the day." He had no desire to be aboriginal. "Three months of it," he wrote, "and you would be screaming for traffic jams, Shirley Temple movies and all the other things."

From the San Blas Islands to Acapulco, the columnist left a trail of warnings for those who might follow in his wake:

Colón: "Crowded with opportunists eager for American dollars and not too particular how they get them."

Panama City: "You drink rum swizzles at Kelly's Ritz, watch dog races at a track. One moment you feel you are in the Argentine and the next in Akron, Ohio."

Acapulco: "Everyone we came in contact with was sullen and disagreeable."

Winsor's attitude improved in Guatemala, where, he claimed, "the national pastime is the marimba."

Antigua: "We were served cocktails of native rum that went down like water but had all the power of a marching army."

Guatemala City: He was "shocked" by "a funeral procession, the mourners following the casket on foot, their arms filled with calla lilies and keeping time to the literally gay rhythm of a marimba that goes along with the little group."

From Guatemala, the *Kungsholm* spent nine hot, sunny days at sea before reaching the Hawaiian Islands. "The freshwater showers and baths had been turned off," so Winsor was "perpetually sticky." He wrote, "You live in shorts and eat all your meals out of doors."

Relief came in Honolulu, the first port of call where friends of the Porters took charge of the group's social life on shore. One of the composer's richest and most frequently married friends sent her children to greet the *Kungsholm*. She was Margaret Emerson McKim Vanderbilt Baker Amory, the one and only heiress of her father, Isaac Edward Emerson, who patented the formula for Bromo Seltzer. Her children were Alfred Gwynne Vanderbilt Jr. and Gloria Baker Topping. Her son's father was Alfred G. Vanderbilt, who was the richest young man in America until he drowned with the *Lusitania* in 1915. Having recently married Henry J. Topping Jr., a tin millionaire, Gloria made her society debut in 1938 wearing a $50,000 dress. She was reported to have "more suitors than her mother had husbands."

While Margaret Amory's children approached the *Kungsholm* on a Vanderbilt "fishing boat," Winsor watched "slender bronzed Polynesian youths" who "bobbed about on the sea in outrigger canoes, diving for coins." When the members of the Porters' party finally landed, they immediately began a series of prearranged parties.

Of cocktails at Lester McCoy's "famous" house, Winsor wrote: "Tiny little Japanese maids with orchids in their hair and wearing kimonos pattered gracefully about through the soft shadows, bringing people drinks."

He described dinner at architect Albert Ely Ives's house: "You dine looking into a cool, indirectly lit patio, roofed with tropical vines loaded with great purple blossoms that kept shedding their petals throughout the evening." The menu: "Grapefruit and fresh litchi nut cocktail, chicken pot pie, fresh green peas and a heavenly mixed green salad."

To his surprise, Honolulu retired early. Shortly after midnight, the party retired to the Royal Hawaiian Hotel, where Winsor shared a nightcap with Cole Porter in his suite. "There he was sitting on his balcony, or lanai, if you want to be Hawaiian about it, entirely surrounded by plates of sandwiches and insisting fresh milk was a far better drink than Scotch." The disappointed columnist returned to his room.

He felt remorse for having finagled a swank assignment that allowed him to avoid winter in Cleveland and its increasingly restrictive nightlife: "I feel infinitely sorry for all of the people who would have liked to be in my position, but couldn't." He also wanted readers to know that he encountered certain hardships while being entertained by wealthy Hawaiians. After a luau in Margaret Emerson's home (Mrs. McKim Vanderbilt Baker Amory was using her maiden name), Winsor filed the following dispatch:

The native orchestra: "Inevitable."

The pig roast: "Supposed to be ceremonial but one that nonetheless received very little of my attention."

Poi: "Looks and tastes exactly like an exceedingly revolting library paste."

Squid, raw octopus, raw salmon, taro wrapped in ti leaves, chicken wrapped in taro, and the roast pig: "I tried them all and then reluctantly gave up, but everyone around me not only went to town but sent back for more and more."

The hula: When Aggie Auld, a thirty-five-year-old dancer and songwriter ("Hula Lolo") began inviting guests to join her in Hawaii's traditional dance, Winsor "retreated to comfortable shadows" to avoid being asked and "waited until it was over." Afterward, he and an anonymous friend "dug out a hamburgers place and had a little feast of our own. I hope Mrs. Emerson never finds out. The next day I discovered a really well done luau costs the cool sum of $15 per person, excluding drinks and entertainment! Furthermore, they don't even give you a spoon! The whole thing must be eaten with your fingers."

On his third and final day in Hawaii, Winsor's attitude improved after he was served a "Kuhio," a concoction of "gin, vanilla ice cream and fresh coconut water (NOT milk), mixed in equal proportions and shaken until ice cold." At least one helped him say "goodby to the islands."

As the *Kungsholm* sailed across the equator toward Samoa, Winsor sat at his typewriter "clad only in a Turkish towel, water pouring off my body like rain. They tell you not to drink iced drinks (and everyone does), they tell you never to sleep entirely nude." The relentless heat had frazzled everyone's nerves. "Yesterday I was among the furious, bellowing passengers who insisted they would leave the ship if something wasn't done about the blue-stockinged old women who had gone screaming to the captain that shorts were an obscenity! This morning, however . . . shorts are in evidence and no one has been thrown in the brig."

The *Kungsholm* passengers were not entirely self-absorbed. The plight of European refugees had finally penetrated the owners' news blackout. Passengers

organized a tombola (lotteries are forbidden in Sweden and we are on Swedish soil), the profits to go for aid to Finland. Cole Porter, surrounded by 10 lovely young women wearing Swedish costumes, will draw the lucky numbers from a huge Guatemalan basket. So far we have raised more than $3000 and if the crew and staff had been permitted to participate the sum would have been much larger. The crew, all on its own . . . has collected about $1500 for Finland. The spirit is very moving and a little shaming when one considers the vast fortunes represented on the ship.

On the day following the tombola, the *Kungsholm* reached American Samoa and anchored off Pago Pago, a village that had intrigued Winsor ever since he saw *Rain,* a dramatic adaptation by playwright John Coulter of a W. Somerset Maugham short story about a bold prostitute's encounter with moral hypocrites, the subject of an exceptional interview Winsor had written in 1936. Four years earlier, he had not admitted to several meetings with the author and his secretary. Now he mentioned "lunching with Maugham in his villa on the Riviera," where he had asked him about *Rain.* "He told me Sadie Thompson was an entirely fictitious character conceived while he was stranded at Pago-Pago between boats and nearly driven mad by the rain." Contradicting the author, the *Kungsholm*'s agent claimed that Sadie "lived, was actually arrested and charged with prostitution and that Maugham's failure to change her name very nearly resulted in a dangerous libel suit."

After Winsor disembarked from the *Kungsholm,* a sudden downpour reminded him of the play and sent him searching for the village's only hotel. "Called the Sadie Thompson Inn, it is upstairs above a sort of general store and I am sure it must have served as the model for the stage setting in the original production." In the tiny community of Americans, Winsor sensed "intolerance . . . perpetual gossip and nerves driven to the ragged edge of collapse by the unbelievable humidity."

On their second day in Pago Pago, Linda Porter took charge and arranged a native feast for her traveling companions and a few of their friends in a tiny outpost far from the dreary village. Her noteworthy picnic is a glimpse of how she orchestrated her husband's social life. She hired a large bus to transport her guests through the jungle. "Samoan singers squatting on the floor" of the vehicle entertained during the entire ride through the jungle. The view outside the bus caught Winsor's eye. "Women with unbelievable figures, nude to the waist, stand under waterfalls, red hibiscus flowers over their ears and the tall, bronzed Samoan men sit cross-legged in their houses. The serenity is almost frightening."

During the ride, Winsor was reminded of Maugham's Reverend Davidson and his religious colleagues: "On the way we passed any number of persons, shamelessly bathing themselves in the community bath—a sort of shower contraption—and you could only think of the missionaries who have taught them nakedness is a sin and encumbered their beautiful bodies with hideous Mother Hubbards and badly cut, shapeless trousers."

Just as "the sun vanished behind the horizon and the entire sky went molten gold," the bus pulled to a stop at a cluster of grass houses. As the travelers emerged from the bus, they were greeted by a portable bar, fully stocked and fully staffed. Linda Porter had decided a "native" feast would taste better with alcohol and had arranged with the *Kungsholm* to provide that beverage. "We had cocktails first that had been sent ahead and somewhat astonished the dark, curious and polite people who stood smiling at us, and then we went into one of the grass houses to sit cross-legged on mats and eat."

The menu included more "taro and roast pig" but also

native crab and lobster and tiny roast doves—all washed down with green coconut water. Young boys and girls wearing lava-lavas (Polynesian loin cloths or skirts) stood behind us, forever passing great bowls of water to wash our hands in and explaining the somewhat exotic dishes. Our plates, so to speak, were huge banana leaves tied in basket shape and we ate, of course, with our fingers. The matting walls of the house that came down when it rains were all up so that we could look out at the calm Pacific, and all around us, but out of sight, people were singing in the shadows.

Because her husband sought musical and choreographic ideas for *Panama Hattie,* Linda arranged for native performers following dinner. To Winsor, they presented "strange, almost Balinese patterns danced to the rhythmic beating of drums and hand clapping and punctuated every now and then with shrill screams from the dancers. They wore, all of them, the most beautiful, colorful costumes imaginable—augmented with tremendous, farouche feather headdresses and necklaces of wild boars' teeth. The men wore lava-lavas, the women were uncovered to the waist, they were of all ages and they looked as if they had been carved from gleaming, red marble."

On the long return drive through the jungle, Winsor wrote, "the moon shone brilliantly on the dense tangles—washed by the extremely heavy dew. When we passed through the villages, young couples were walking nude through the shadows—singing to each other. " Back aboard the *Kungsholm,* "The moon was so bright, you could read by it, the air was light and fresh, the rains hadn't started to fall yet and the only sounds disturbing the silence were the echoes of singing voices coming across the water. It was impossible, in the presence of such peace, to realize all of civilization is being menaced by wars and unrest and violence and hatred."

Winsor sustained his illusion until "the little pilot boat led [the cruise ship] out of the still harbor into the dark Pacific," where the crew of the *Kungsholm* was preparing to weigh anchor and head for British Samoa, a disappointing port. Apia was "governed by the missions with an iron, intolerant and uninteresting hand. At once you sense regimentation, needless laws and discipline that is both unnecessary and unattractive. It was Sunday and so the shops had to be closed, the native dancers we wanted to see were not allowed to dance and dismal looking people robbed of their pride and dignity and ancient heritage went about on bicycles in dreadful looking clothes."

The next stop was Tahiti, the southernmost port on the *Kungsholm*'s itinerary. "Surrounded by French tolerance, you . . . do exactly as you please and no one cares. Furthermore, living is so inexpensive it is ridiculous. Wonderfully appointed beach houses can be rented for as little as $40 a month. Chinese cooks can be had for $15 a month, native servants for $6."

In Papeete, Winsor found "bars and honky-tonks where everyone gathers to exchange gossip," yet by March 1940, most were "strangely deserted." Frenchmen had "all been mobilized and at night the island is blacked out and much of the natural gaiety suspended." For Winsor, the "long sinister shadows" of war had finally invaded the South Seas.

For the Porters' party, however, there was still one more elaborate luncheon, hosted by Carrie and Eastham Guild. (Carrie Guild would earn mild notoriety for tasting a cocktail invented by restaurateur Victor "Trader Vic" Bergeron. After a single sip, she announced, "Mai tai," which means "out of this world" in Tahitian.) Every room in the Guilds' residence was a separate, small house "surrounded by great verandas where you can escape the heat." Facing the ocean and a "black, sun-baked beach," the estate included a "private yacht landing, magnificent gardens, a perfectly equipped carpentry shop and every other conceivable comfort." Eighteen servants waited on the Guilds, but according to Winsor, the cost was "next to nothing." He was envious. "Don't tell me we time-clock punchers aren't a pack of idiots."

Luncheon was served on a small patio. "Bamboo leaves hung on strings above our heads to keep the sun out and while we ate, lovely Tahitian girls danced slowly to native music." The meal "consisted of raw, fresh tuna that had been soaked for hours in lime juice and coconut milk, suckling pig, taro, breadfruit and any number of strange, sweetish exotic fruits, all washed down with an ice cold, very light white wine."

From the Guilds' residence, the party was driven back to the pier in Papeete, where new passengers were struggling with their luggage and French custom officials. Before boarding the *Kungsholm,* Winsor and his traveling companions supplemented their shipboard diet. They bought "ordinary canned goods to eat on the rest of the voyage." Winsor claimed, "It was the most wonderful investment I have ever had anything to do with."

Once aboard ship, he noted "the inevitable souls who had misjudged their thirst . . . barely knew where they were." For that matter, Jeanne Murray, the passenger who had observed Linda's "motherly" manner, thought, "the Porter party drank quite heavily." During the voyage, Porter wrote "Make It another Old Fashioned, Please," in which *Panama Hattie* tries abstinence:

> For when you lay off liquor
> You feel so much slicker,
> Well, that is, most of the time.

When the *Kungsholm*'s crew finally lifted the anchor off Papeete, Winsor's "heart dropped. Passengers who had been left behind came out in launches, a member of the crew, feeling apparently the same way I did, jumped overboard and started to make for shore. They got him, though, and now the poor devil has had his romantic wings clipped and is in disgrace."

Since leaving New York, Winsor had counted eleven members of the crew who had "deserted at various ports . . . or else were left behind because of illness. We have picked up four stowaways who have all been signed on as crew—a lucky break for them, considering it is a prison offense." Later that night, as the *Kungsholm* sailed from Tahiti, a passenger died. The first death aboard the ship did not interrupt the cocktail parties, according to Winsor:

> Our existence is like living in a very whoopee hotel. In the beginning the parties were stiff little seated cocktail pourings, but things have changed and the nights are assuming the proportions of a Bacchanalian rout. Now the cruise directors and staff don't have to worry their heads about thinking up entertainments—the passengers have taken matters into their own hands and things are becoming more and more elaborate. Grass huts go up on the decks for cocktail parties of 50 or more. There are breakfasts and dinners and dances going on all over the ship and the bartenders, I should think, must be ready to drop from exhaustion.

He observed that while "more conventional passengers" watched movies or a concert, "smaller groups play backgammon for extremely high stakes in the bar. Printed invitations for this or that, each a little trickier than the last, are pushed under stateroom doors every morning and then the day commences. Martinis . . . have replaced sherry at the swimming pool in the morning. If you want to sleep on deck you can do so with perfect confidence no one will disturb you either at 2 A.M. or 11 A.M. So life is pretty ideal."

Perhaps, but Porter biographer George Eells maintains Linda Porter was uneasy. She believed both she and her husband "suffered from rootlessness since the closing of their Paris house. She had looked at places in California and found nothing. She had investigated Long Island but uncovered no house that suited her. Newport had been considered and rejected. But during the cruise," Winsor "suggested Williamstown, Massachusetts, and Linda was intrigued." Her husband opposed the location as "impractical," but Linda made Winsor promise to take her house hunting in Williamstown when they finally landed in the United States.

Life as a vagabond wasn't troubling Winsor. "The only menacing cloud on the horizon is the realization our escape from clothes and telephones and life's duller details is rapidly drawing to a close." Before the voyage was over, however, Cole Porter upstaged everyone with a dance in honor of "Dorothy Lamour, the tall bronze lady sent to him as a sailing present by Howard Lindsay and Russel Crouse."

At Apia, Porter had wired Tahiti and ordered, "hundreds of palm fronds, bunches of bananas, any number of coconuts, breadfruit, pineapples and mangoes" to be put on board in Papeete. "They were all used to turn an entire deck into a lush mysterious jungle."

Winsor described the bash: "Everyone came in lava-lavas, straw skirts or any kind of colorful costume they had, mats were strewn around the floor for people who didn't want to dance and the orchestra played everything from Hawaiian chants to the hottest new tunes. Every now and then it rained, a soft, warm rain that dripped gently from the palms and only added to the beauty. Actually, I never have been to a more beautiful or luxurious looking gala and it was all brought to a climax by a new ballad Cole wrote especially for the occasion." The song was "So Long, Samoa," and Winsor was convinced it was "destined for the hit parade, if he ever releases it." (It was not released. Porter rewrote the song in 1949 as "Farewell, Amanda" for the Katharine Hepburn–Spencer Tracy film *Adam's Rib.*) And the party went on all night: "About an hour before dawn, we were out of the rains, the skies cleared and we had a blanket of stars over us and a full moon. Everybody must have been exhausted, but the orchestra kept playing, people had breakfast and the signal for gaiety on a large scale was given."

After Lamour's debut, the *Kungsholm* turned toward the Galapagos Islands, "the most savage, unfriendly country" Winsor had "ever seen. Insolent pelicans stared at us stupidly . . . and miniature penguins, too bored to even look at us, turned their backs as we passed."

At Balboa, on the western entrance to the Panama Canal, Hanna, Stearns, and Winsor left the ship. The Porters and Bill Powell stayed aboard until New York. Six months later, *Panama Hattie,* a show full of "brass fortissimo," opened on Broadway and ran for five hundred performances. For Winsor, however, there was one more adventure before he returned to Lakeside Flats. After watching "old and new friends steam away" on the *Kungsholm,* he joined Hanna and Stearns aboard a Pan American plane destined for Guatemala City. The flight was not direct; there were twenty-minute stops in the capitals of Panama, Costa Rica, Nicaragua, Honduras, and El Salvador. Winsor was "somewhat hesitant about taking the trip" and confessed he wasn't "air-minded," but when the men finally set down in Guatemala City, the columnist was ecstatic. "We had flown 1100 miles over five countries in perfect comfort. We were served a delicious luncheon at an altitude of 12,000 feet. The service was flawless."

After touring Mayan ruins, the men flew on to Mexico City and then Los Angeles, from where they took the train to Cleveland. At Sin Shanty, Winsor discovered that gangster Al Capone's nemesis, the legendary Eliot Ness, who had accepted the job of Cleveland's safety director, was renting a third-floor apartment, and a new restaurant had opened in the neighborhood. Of the latter, he wrote: "The Wheel Inn . . . serves enough red wine to float a ship and then, on Sunday, serves a hangover breakfast. The only one in town."

In June, Winsor kept his promise and took Linda house hunting in Williamstown. According to Eells, who interviewed Winsor, none "of the places shown them by the local real estate agent that morning . . . seemed suitable. They decided to go to lunch and then look at one other possibility— Buxton Hill. As they drove up the long, winding drive to . . . the handsome fieldstone house . . . a rainbow suddenly appeared. Linda . . . decided it was a good-luck omen" and rented the 200-acre estate.

In August, Winsor traveled again to Massachusetts to review summer theaters. In Williamstown, he found the Porters ensconced in their new retreat and Hanna "relaxing" on the terrace. In Stockbridge, Winsor visited Benny Crowell, one of his Hollywood traveling companions, who was "holding down an apartment with a cat, typewriter and pile of manuscripts from here to there." By mid-1940, his closest male confidantes had deserted Cleveland.

While Crowell was in Stockbridge, Zerbe, Stearns, and Hanna were in New York City. The photographer was still peddling celebrity photographs at El Morocco, and the pianist was talking to Porter and Hanna about opening his own club in Manhattan, an idea he had discussed aboard the *Kungsholm* with them, both potential financial backers. Hanna could be found in his Park Avenue town house as often as at his estate in Mentor, Ohio, or the family plantation in Thomasville, Georgia.

Winsor was reviewing movies again because there were not enough Cleveland theatrical productions to keep him occupied. The Hanna Theatre, where Noël Coward once staged the world premiere of *Design for Living,* had booked what Winsor called a "hesitant" season. Saroyan's *The Time of Your Life,* scheduled to open on New Year's Eve, was "the only really important play, barring a miracle, Cleveland is to see all season." The drama critic found himself attending a two-year-old production of *The Little Foxes,* starring Talluah Bankhead: "At this point any comment on Lillian Hellman's biting and vituperative melodrama would be on the superfluous side."

Although Winsor had no interest in being superfluous, he loved Bankhead. "She has a well-developed loathing for stupidity. I know, because there have been those moments, sometimes at my own expense, when I have seen the Bankhead temper in action, and it is far more magnificent and arresting than any dramatic situation Lillian Hellman ever dreamed of. At the moment her particular idol is President Roosevelt and she can tear apart a Willkie booster in nothing flat—leaving her poor, bewildered victim wondering what happened to him." As an example, Winsor reported that when she "scrawled her name in the Hanna Theater's guest book recently, she wrote after it, 'Vote for Roosevelt.' The Carl Hannas won't like that. They're voting for Willkie."

After Roosevelt decided to run for an unprecedented third term, Winsor's Republican friends had begun calling the president a "dictator." Willkie agreed: "This campaign of mine is a crusade . . . to preserve American democracy." Presidential politics played a cameo role in the Hanna season's second production. After the theater was dark for two weeks, Katharine Hepburn arrived in the touring company of Phillip Barry's *Philadelphia Story.* During the play's run, an unabashed Willkie booster "sent 30 telegrams to Miss Hepburn, furious because of the Roosevelt ad in her program and announcing she would play to empty houses the rest of the week." Her "polished" and "fully developed" performance trumped politics. "*The Philadelphia Story* played to better than $23,000—and that, my friends, is money." As for her own choice of presidential candidate, when Miss Hepburn signed the Hanna's guest book, she added, "Tallulah's right."

In the midst of the Hanna's "hesitant" theatrical season, Winsor was forced to drive to Pittsburgh for the press preview of Charlie Chaplin's *The Great Dictator,* "an extremely disturbing film." At the preview, "a vast audience gathered together to roar first with laughter at the cinematic shadow of the world's greatest clown—and, then, eventually, to walk silently from the theater, wondering whether they had just watched a side-splitting comedy, complete with all the old Chaplin tricks, or a tragedy of almost

A. E. M. Bergener, the managing editor at the *News* who gave Winsor his first newspaper job, was reportedly the model for Walter Burns in Ben Hecht and Charles Mac-Arthur's play *The Front Page*. The plot is driven by Burns's attempt to hide an escaped convict in a desk, so he can scoop competitors with stories of how his news-paper captured the man before turning him over to police. In Cleveland, Bergener kept a fugi-tive embezzler in hiding before turning him over to police, so the *News* could scoop its rivals and publish his "exclusive" confessions. Courtesy Cleveland State Univer-sity *Cleveland Press* Col-lection

Aileen Winslow's local celebrity was enhanced by her friendship with Wal-lis Warfield Simpson, the twentieth century's most publicized courtesan. Her "design for living" included a divorced husband, a London car dealer, and Edward, Prince of Wales, who was crowned King Edward VIII in 1936. When his decision to marry her was opposed by the Church of England because she was a divorcée, Edward abdicated the throne, was demoted to duke, and was exiled to a villa in France, where Winslow (left) was a frequent guest (*Cleveland Press,* 13 Apr. 1937). © 1931 *PARADE* Maga-zine. All rights reserved.

Jerome Zerbe was one of the first photographers to take candid shots of what he called "fashionable" people, chiefly socialites and entertainers, a "type of photography," according to the *New York Times* (23 Aug. 1988), "adopted decades later by the paparazzi" and one of the "elements on which café society thrived" in the 1930s. In 1937, Zerbe became photograph editor of *Bachelor,* a monthly magazine for single men, and published a self-portrait in the first issue. An essay by Louis Bish in the same issue, titled "What Is a Bachelor?" illustrates how the word "bachelor" had an ambiguous meaning in the 1930s. The author maintained that an unmarried man's preference for "lavender" underwear was not evidence of "a persistent thymus [lack of maturity] or a touch of Oscar Wilde," the era's most famous homosexual. Courtesy Cleveland Public Library Periodicals Collection, *Bachelor* magazine

Before Jerome Zerbe joined *PARADE,* he was a popular local portrait artist; he had begun developing this talent at age thirteen when he enrolled in Saturday morning classes at the Cleveland School of Art. Zerbe perfected his technique by sketching childhood friends like Winsor, shown here. Note Zerbe's elaborate monogram, below the sketch. Courtesy Joseph Dewey

A 1932 photograph showing Barbara Hutton and her husband, Prince Alexis Mdivani, validates the published version of "How's Chances," the ballad Irving Berlin wrote about the couple for *As Thousands Cheer*. An actress playing Hutton complained she always found Mdivani surrounded by boys. The prince was from the Russian Republic of Georgia, but Winsor scoffed at his presumptions: Mdivanis "are not princes but merely Russian gentlemen" (*News,* 28 Nov. 1932). Hutton was one of America's richest women in the 1930s, and Mdivani was the second of seven men she married. Newspaper writers assumed her many husbands were evidence that money could not buy happiness, so they often referred to her in headlines as the "Poor Little Rich Girl." Credit: © Hutton-Deutsch Collection/CORBIS

From the wedding reception in New York City, Winsor and Margaret French took a train
to Niagara Falls, where they spent the night with film actor Franchot Tone's parents in an
"enormous Victorian mansion" (*News,* 11 Oct. 1933). In the morning, the couple posed for
a photographer before taking the train to Chicago, where they spent a week at the World's
Fair. According to Winsor's daily dispatches, they watched a "haggard creature" roll "poi-
sonous vipers into little balls" and put them in his mouth and stood in line for hours "to see
Chicago's premature babies sleeping in their tiny glass houses" (*News,* 16–18 Oct. 1933). At
night, they frequented nightclubs on the fairgrounds, where Winsor bribed waiters to bring
bottles of hard liquor to their table. Courtesy Martha Eaton Hickox

Winsor's first passport, issued when he was twenty-two years old, documents his ambition. He listed his occupation as "author." To realize that goal, Winsor persuaded his stepfather to finance an extended stay in Europe. Joseph Eaton booked passage aboard the SS *Caronia,* "a one class ship, slow, inexpensive," and, Winsor recalled, "obedient to the winds and waves as she bounced about like a frantic cork." During a storm on the "first night out, a rivet that had been carelessly left along the ceiling molding of my cabin bounced out of its little nest, ricocheted around the room and finally hit me square in the head. Naturally, I thought the ship was falling to pieces. I rushed to the purser's office with the rivet in my hands as an offering of proof, and very nearly created a panic." Thus began a lifetime of shipboard stories. Courtesy Martha Eaton Hickox

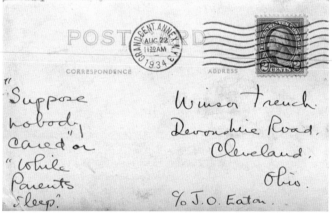

"Suppose nobody cared" or "While Parents sleep."

Winsor French.
Devonshire Road,
Cleveland,
Ohio.
% J. O. Eaton.

In August 1934, while his marriage was unraveling in France, Winsor's bachelor friends sent him a postcard reminding him of the masculine camaraderie that awaited his return. On the back of the card, the anonymous sender wrote a plaintive note about the life of homosexuals. He proposed two titles for the tableau: "Suppose nobody cared" and "While parents sleep." Atop the horse, photographer Jerry Zerbe; pressing his temple to the horse's thigh, actor Monty Woolley; seated in the carriage (from left), jewelry designer Fulco de Verdura and Cleveland industrialist Leonard Hanna; standing at rear (from left), an unidentified man and violinist Nathan Milstein. Courtesy Martha Eaton Hickox

In addition to dismissing Winsor's film criticism with vague suggestions about his sexuality, Sidney "Sy" Bartlett's campaign to restore Alice White's movie career included using newspaper publicity to generate interest about the romantic relationship he was having with his client. Coincidentally, here the couple was photographed dancing at the Club New Yorker, a Hollywood nightclub featuring Jean Malin, one of the best-known homosexual entertainers during New York City's "pansy craze" (Chauncey, *Gay New York,* 314–20). Courtesy Cleveland Public Library Photography Collection

At Carole Lombard's party at the Venice Beach Pier (*Press,* 20 June 1935), Winsor insisted that "everyone commenced to remove as much skin from their shins and elbows as possible" in various contraptions, including the barrel roll, pictured here with (from left) film stars Peggy Fears, Billy Haines, and Marlene Dietrich. Courtesy Cleveland Public Library Photography Collection

In June 1935 the Republican Party held its national convention in Cleveland. Supporters of Kansas governor Alf Landon, the eventual nominee, booked the Hollenden Hotel as their headquarters. During the day convention-goers attended business sessions in Public Hall or marched down Superior Avenue (shown here). At night they satisfied their curiosity about African Americans by filling the clubs lining Cedar Avenue and East 55th Street. In the 18 June 1936 *Press*, Winsor gave one delegation an insider's tour, concluding, "The staid and proper Republicans . . . are doing their best to show the town what it means to be gay." Courtesy Cleveland Public Library Photography Collection

Overleaf: In 1935 artist Jim Herron mapped the city's nightlife for the *Press*, placing Winsor and artist Gus Peck in the middle of the black entertainment district on Cedar Avenue heading toward Val's, where jazz pianist Art Tatum played. Herron misspelled the musician's name, and his drawing displayed local newspapers' schizophrenic coverage of race in the 1930s. Black nightclubs popular with white patrons were depicted, but none of more than fifty tiny caricatures of the city's nighthawks was African American, although Tatum, Bessie Brown, Rose Murphy, and "Mammy" Louise Brooks were celebrities. The map skirted liquor laws by showing Rubber Goldberger, owner of the illegal Patent Leather speakeasy, dancing above an anonymous building on Euclid Avenue and slyly placed Winsor's competitors (Eleanor Clarage and Glenn Pullen of the *Plain Dealer*) at the margins of Cleveland's nightlife. Courtesy Martha Eaton Hickox

Before Bessie Brown was "able to walk," Winsor wrote, "she had a full, clear soprano" (*PARADE,* 17 Mar. 1932, 16–19). She began her professional career as a "male impersonator" in one of the acts on a small vaudeville circuit in Chicago. By the time *PARADE*'s Charles Tudor drew her caricature, she was working during the day at "the Mme. Walker beauty shop" and at night singing at the Sixty Club, an east-side speakeasy. Officials of the Brunswick recording company heard her sing and offered her a contract, Winsor wrote, which made her "Cleveland's most famous and best-selling blues singer" (*Press,* 29 May, 2 June 1964).

In April 1937, "Mammy" Louise Brooks pondered a photograph of Father Divine, founder of the Peace Mission Movement, who had been accused of "keeping a harem" of female followers. Brooks claimed to have been one of his "wives" in the late 1920s. In May 1933, she was running the Creole Club. Courtesy Cleveland State University *Press* Collection

In October 1933, Winsor heard Art Tatum playing at the Apex Club, a tiny speakeasy "where some sort of complex kept him in a small back room." As Winsor wrote in his 17 June 1933 *News* entry, "Few people know that . . . the pianist rage of the moment is blind." Artist Jim Herron redeemed his misspelling of Tatum's name with this splendid portrait of him in 1954, when he was leading a noted jazz trio. Courtesy Cleveland State University *Press* Collection

Before Rose Murphy had graduated to a grand piano at the Turf Club, she held court at Val's, a "ramshackle joint" in an alley at 8610 Cedar Avenue (*Press,* 4, 25 Sept. 1954). Owners could not afford a liquor license but had an attraction stronger than booze: Rose Murphy and her friends. Winsor's advice: "Take your own liquor and appease your hunger with pigs' feet and beans" (*Press,* 9 Jan. 1936). Courtesy Cleveland Public Library Photography Collection

His birth certificate read "Dorwyn Rennels Herron" (*Press,* 28 Apr. 1935), but the *Press* artist called himself "Jim" at Shaw High School in East Cleveland, which he left before completing his senior year (*Plain Dealer,* 24 Nov. 1983). Herron joined the newspaper in 1927 and specialized in caricatures of theater people. A fixture of opening nights at the Play House and the Hanna Theatre, Herron's drawings appeared the following afternoon with the drama critic's review. "Tall, quiet and red-haired," the artist was photographed in 1947 painting *Ann's Wagon.* Courtesy Cleveland State University *Press* Collection

Vain about his need to wear glasses, Winsor removed them whenever a camera appeared. Here, they're in his right hand, with a lit cigarette, 1934. Courtesy Cleveland Public Library Photography Collection

To educate new readers about how stories were produced, the *Press* photographed a portion of the city room showing men at the rewrite desk taking facts over the phone from reporters in the field, then writing stories, which were sent to the city desk for the city editor's review. If he approved, the article was forwarded to the horseshoe-shaped copy desk, where the "watchdogs of reportorial clarity and public morals" sat in judgment on every single word and gave the story a headline (Julian Krawcheck, *Press*, 28 Sept. 1972). When the process was complete, the man inside the horseshoe curled the copy paper into a loose roll and placed it in a metal carrier, where it was sucked into the composing room by a vacuum tube. There, men retyped the stories in trays of metal molds, which would eventually hold the hot lead that would form the individual type with which the story would be printed. Newspaper headlines on the copy desk at the *Press* suggest this photograph was taken in the early 1940s, when Cleveland mayor Frank J. Lausche was elected governor of Ohio. During World War II, the *Press* city room was still largely a fraternity; the only woman present was the switchboard operator. (Note the cuspidor at the bottom of the picture.) Courtesy Cleveland State University *Press* Collection

Stage and film actress Joan Bennett enjoyed a cigarette as she and her cocker spaniel posed for newspaper photographers in her suite at the Statler Hotel, where she stayed while appearing in *Stage Door* at the Hanna Theatre. Winsor panned her performances; she could not have been surprised by his critique, if she had read any of his reviews of her films. In *From Arizona to Broadway,* Winsor wrote, she was "not very convincing, but for that matter she seldom is" (*News,* 1 Sept. 1933). About *Vogues of 1938,* he wrote, "All the sables in creation couldn't make an actress out of Joan Bennett" (*Press,* 6 Oct. 1937). One of her publicity photographs did not hang on Winsor's wall of celebrities, but a copy of her angry telegram did. Courtesy Cleveland Public Library Photography Collection and Anne Eaton Parker

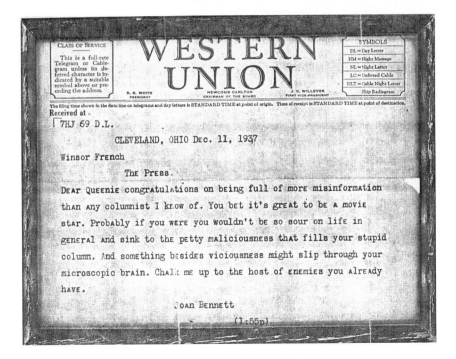

WESTERN UNION

The filing time shown in the date line on telegrams and day letters is STANDARD TIME at point of origin. Time of receipt is STANDARD TIME at point of destination.

Received at -

7HJ 69 D.L.

CLEVELAND, OHIO DEC. 11, 1937

Winsor French

The Press.

DEAR QUEENIE congratulations on being full of more misinformation than any columnist I know of. You bet it's great to be a movie star. Probably if you were you wouldn't be so sour on life in general and sink to the petty maliciousness that fills your stupid column. And something besides viciousness might slip through your microscopic brain. Chalk me up to the host of enemies you already have.

Joan Bennett

(1:55p)

The Aquacade's chorus consisted of forty-eight young Clevelanders who could sing, dance, dive, and swim. Called "aquagals" and "aquaguys," they rehearsed their kaleidoscopic patterns flat on their backs in a gymnasium at the Allerton Hotel before plunging into Lake Erie's fifty-degree water in mid-May, "so cold," aquaguy Kevin Leigh wrote Winsor, "we darn near gave it up" (Kevin Leigh to WF, 24 Feb. 1959). The stage was 185 feet wide with an orchestra at either end. The Aquacade's patriotic finale filled the space, but Leigh remembered that "the final curtain [was] a water spout that drenched all the people at the first few tables." Courtesy, Cleveland Public Library Photography Collection

Cole Porter staged a lavish debut for Dorothy Lamour, a plaster statue that was the bon voyage gift from the producers of *Panama Hattie,* the show Porter wrote during his voyage aboard the MS *Kungsholm.* In front of the palm fronds he had brought aboard the ship in Tahiti, the ship's photographer took a picture of Porter (far left) with his wife, Linda, and their gay entourage (from left): pianist Roger Stearns, Winsor, publicist William Powell, and Leonard Hanna. (Note the cane on the mat to the right of Cole Porter.) Unidentified passengers sit behind the group; Dorothy Lamour, the plaster statue and guest of honor, was camera shy. Courtesy Joseph Dewey

While Roger Stearns played the piano at his 1-2-3 Club in Manhattan during the 1940s, Winsor (right) worked the crowd, which often included comic actress Bea Lillie (center) and Leonard Hanna, one of the club's financial backers recruited by Cole Porter. At 1-2-3, Winsor renewed a friendship with Lillie, who, he claimed, answered her own phone "irritating her friends by imitating a Cockney maid and informing them Miss Lillie is out" (*News,* 14 June 1943). Courtesy Martha Eaton Hickox

As a young man Winsor's stepfather, Joseph Oriel Eaton, wrote a tennis column for the *Cincinnati Enquirer,* for which he earned five to ten dollars a week, a rate that led him to pursue a career in business and eventually found the Eaton Corporation, a pioneer manufacturer of auto parts, although the founder never learned to operate an automobile. Eaton, like his stepson, pursued "good food, good wine, and good companions," founding the Racqueteers, a group of Cleveland industrialists whose uniform was "crimson blazers with an emblem of crossed tennis racquets and martini glasses" (James Wood, *The Tavern,* 121). Courtesy Ann Halle Little

During 1947 and 1948, Shondor Birns was seldom at the Alhambra Lounge. He spent six months supposedly performing forced farm labor at the Cleveland Workhouse. And, according to an undated *Press* article, "another six months in the County Jail for contempt of court in an attempted jury fix" (Cleveland State University *Press* Archive). While he stayed in the Workhouse, he was often seen at Gruber's, having dinner in the company of police. Here he's leaving Cleveland Police chief Frank Story's office in May 1953, after being told he would "be arrested on sight on [the] streets of Cleveland unless he's en route to consult his attorneys." Courtesy Cleveland State University *Press* Collection

Winsor's praise for Gruber's restaurant, which appeared as news stories—though they read like paid advertisements—stretched journalistic ethics even though they often promoted worthwhile charitable causes. Gruber's chef Joseph F. Bortoff exploited Winsor's power to influence opinion by creating an entree for Winsor, who christened it "Crabmeat a la Joseph." The *Press* photographed Winsor at Gruber's entrance in 1954. Courtesy Martha Eaton Hickox

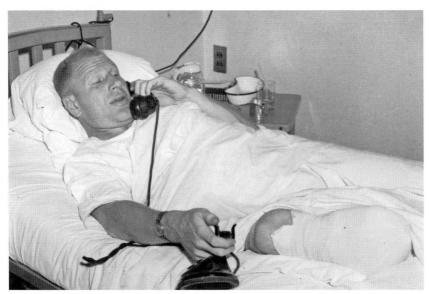

Winsor, who was having trouble with his own legs, was fascinated with how Bill Veeck, the owner of the Cleveland Indians, accommodated a prosthetic limb. On the first day of 1947, the columnist reported that Veeck hoped he could discard crutches for a prosthetic device in two weeks. "Measurements for the artificial leg were to be made today," Winsor wrote, "and the manufacturers have promised Bill that he will have it within two weeks. When the leg arrives Veeck will celebrate by staging a dance for his friends—and himself. Bill likes to 'cut a rug' with the best of them" (*Press,* 1 Jan. 1947). The dance was a mistake. Veeck didn't give his leg time to heal and by late June had returned to the Cleveland Clinic for a second operation. He invited news photographers to his bedside so fans could see he was managing the team by phone. Courtesy Cleveland Public Library Photography Collection

In April 1939, Franklin A. "Whitey" Lewis (right) had left radio station WGAR and rejoined the *Press* as a sports columnist and editor. Here he's pictured with Cleveland Indians third baseman Ken Keltner. The *Press* never published the photograph, but it remained in the newspaper's morgue. Across the back of the photo, someone wrote, "Ken Keltner and Lewis go for each other," the sort of homophobic comment provoked by evidence of men expressing affection. Courtesy Cleveland State University *Press* Collection

Winsor used his newspaper celebrity to raise money for the Cleveland Area Heart Society in the early 1950s, chairing four Valentine's Day Heart Fund dinners that each raised $10,000 to $12,000. At the 1954 dinner, Winsor (third from left) was photographed with (from left) Bernard Towell, an unidentified woman, and pianist Roger Stearns (right). *Courtesy Martha Eaton Hickox*

The Roxy, Cleveland's only surviving burlesque house in the 1950s, anchored the cluttered south side of Short Vincent, across the street (called the "Gaza Strip" by local residents) from Mushy Wexler's Theatrical Grille and the Weinberger family's Kornman's Back Room. "The apogee of Short Vincent was reached in the postwar decade," according to Cleveland historian John Vacha, "when a group of bon vivants known as the Jolly Set made it their stamping ground under the suzerainty of Winsor French" (*Showtime in Cleveland,* 177). Courtesy Cleveland State University *Press* Archive

Winsor described *Press* artist Bill Roberts as a "gentleman" who enjoyed "deflating inflated egos" (French, *Curtain Call,* 52). In a mural completed during the early 1950s, Roberts applied his technique to selected members of the Jolly Set and residents of Short Vincent, whose behavior begged for caricature. Winsor appears wearing glasses at the painting's midpoint. To his right are Cleveland Indians manager Hank Greenberg, a bartender and *Press* sports editor, and columnist Franklin "Whitey" Lewis. Courtesy Cleveland State University *Press* Collection

The man Winsor called "Tommy" was Thomas Jefferson McGinty (at the microphone) whose nickname was "Black Jack" among members of the Cleveland gambling syndicate (Lacey, *Little Man*, 97–99). McGinty prospered as a bootlegger until Prohibition was repealed, when he became the host at the Mounds Club, a swank local "carpet joint" offering dinner, dancing, a floorshow, and illegal gambling located discreetly in a separate part of the roadhouse. Winsor recommended reservations: "Tables are at a premium—usually crowded with the socially prominent," including women wearing "broadtail and Russian sables . . . between skirmishes at the gaming tables" (*News*, 22 Aug. 1933; *Press*, 18 Sept. 1954). Eventually McGinty invested his profits in casinos: the Desert Inn in Las Vegas, Nevada, and the Nacional in Havana, Cuba. He was photographed in January 1951 as he began testimony during a hearing investigating organized crime. Courtesy Cleveland State University *Press* Collection

Anxiety, as this is being written, is in the air. Everywhere in town, people are glued to television sets, listening to radios and hoping that the Indians pull out of their sickening collapse.

Seems to me, though, things haven't come quite up to the fever pitch of 1948 when Willie Veeck was in the driver's seat and casting discretion to the winds.

Could be, of course, that the 1948 super-charged hullabaloo was brought about in part by the unhappy fact the Indians hadn't snatched the pennant in 28 years and that when they snatched it the lid blew right off the town as never before.

Right away Veeck, who had hardly ever been lacking in imagination, sat down and really began imagining a few tricks.

It belongs to history now. The play-off game in Boston, the party afterwards in the Kenmore Hotel that no two people were ever able to describe in similar colors (and no wonder!), the train ride home and then the really uninhibited madness.

Kissin' Kids

All manner of phenomena developed and not the least of them was the violent outburst of kissing among major league baseball players. That is, among the Indians and the Boston Braves. In the other clubs, one imagines, knives were sharpened.

In the wigwam, though, it was a perpetual game of post office and to the violent annoyance of the sports writers, notably Whitey Lewis, who all but promised public execution to the next photographer who tried to sell him another necking shot. The boys stopped kissing and started playing ball.

Headquarters for the celebrations, meanwhile, were set up in Hotel Hollenden with Veeck at the helm and there was bedlam for the next many hours.

Not a stone, as they say, was left unturned. For the first time in major league history special attention was devoted to the wives of the baseball writers.

Ladies' Day

Telegrams were sent out to all of them inviting them to the festivities, headquarters were set up for them in the Hollenden, entertainments of a fairly elaborate nature were pushed into action. To say that the ladies responded is putting it mildly.

As far as that goes, all over town everyone

Love Those Champs!

left, Gene Bearden busses Jim Hegan. Center, Mel Harder hugs Bearden (Catcher F Murray waits turn for a squeeze). Finally, Steve Gromek embraces Lou Boudreau.

The 1948 World Series was a hug! as these pictures surely will testify.

PRESS OCT 2 '54

was in what you might call a responsive frame of mind.

The Hollenden ballroom was the scene of a 24-hour-a-day floor show that set a new high for all time in released inhibitions. Every act in town was drafted into service and willingly obliged.

The pay was fine, so was the food and drink. That wonderful little hoofer, the late Willie Shore, presided as master of ceremonies.

Gene Sheldon, the pantomimist, was on hand as well, and as always, getting his fingers caught in the strings of his guitar. Bob Hope showed up, so did Abbott and Costello.

Veeck and Burgundy

Meanwhile the orchestras alternated while the local brass, visiting firemen and inevitable freeloaders washed down mountains of groceries with champagne, sparkling burgundy (Veeck was always a burgundy man), gin, Scotch, whisky, beer and everything else that comes packaged in bottles.

It was quite a party and when it was over the ball club picked up the tab. And about that, it will be remembered, there was considerable discussion at a later date.

But THE party hadn't even begun. And this one didn't take place in Cleveland at all, but on the train ride back from Boston after the Indians had deposited the Braves on a cold, Boston shelf.

At that hysterical moment Willie began expanding all over again and instructed Marsh

Samuel and Spud Goldstein to buy up al champagne and sparkling burgundy availal the Kenmore Hotel.

There was quite a lot of it, I might add, a sparked one of the most spectacular journe rail in history.

Floor Show Unnecessary

There was no floor show, to be sure. Johnny Berardino nicely filled the gap w prolonged impression of Charles Laughto Capt. Bligh of the Bounty.

As he delivered his lines the grateful aud in the dining car kept shouting, "Look out other wave on the way!" So there was—a of champagne!

And so it went through the night, all e with a parade through the sleeping cars marchers beating on kitchen pans, waiters' and anything else available.

There was another parade in the mornii bona fide one through the streets of a gra wildly excited city. This one the conqu heroes weren't ready for.

Neither were two reporters, Lyall Smith John Carmichael of the Detroit Free Press the Chicago Daily News. Both were eage catch a train standing in the depot.

They never made it. Along with everyone they were swept up by the cheering multit hurried into cars and paraded up Euclid. there ended the notable 1948 series.

The dog-eared clipping from Winsor's personal effects suggests the importance he attached to the article he wrote in 1954 about the 1948 World Series that included the "necking shots" he claimed had offended *Press* sports editor Franklin "Whitey" Lewis. That Winsor felt free to tease Lewis about the photographs in print and publish the pictures to prove his point illustrates his own confidence in openly discussing male affection and his newspaper's willingness to tolerate criticism of its own skittishness about the subject. Courtesy Martha Eaton Hickox

In the 1950s, Winsor illustrated columns with his own photographs. At a party hosted by
Margaret and Francis Sherwin in September 1951, the columnist shot Mrs. Frank Taplin, the
former Margaret (Peggy) Eaton Sichel, one of his half-sisters, seated behind a piano with
his favorite disc jockey, Henry Pildner, a pianist he had promoted since his *News* pieces of
28 January and 1 May 1933, when his musical talent was being "wasted" playing at Euclid
Beach Park. Courtesy Margaret Eaton Hickox

To celebrate Winsor's fifty-fifth birthday, his friends rented the Roxy Burlesque, hired Short Vincent's premier restaurateurs to provide food and drink, and paid the theater's headliners to entertain their guests. Two Santa Clauses carried Winsor to a throne on the stage where Bill "Smoochie" Gordon entertained the columnist and the crowd. Courtesy Martha Eaton Hickox

Behind Leonard Hanna's residence at Hilo, a "timbered and gabled bathhouse" in Winsor's words, was equipped with a bar and "plenty of pastel rubber bathing suits" for women (*Press,* 12 Jan. 1938). Trees and shrubbery surrounding the pool created a private playground where Hanna's friends and guests indulged themselves. For Winsor, that once included a mud facial. Courtesy Joseph Dewey

Part of Winsor's legend was that he was the only local newspaper reporter to arrive at work in a chauffeured Rolls-Royce (Milt Widder, *Press,* 30 Oct. 1969). After the columnist's death, Sam Hill, who drove and cared for Winsor's cars, added an ironic coda. "Mr. French finally got tired of the Rolls and bought a Cadillac. Someone stole it so he had to buy another" (Dick McLaughlin, *Press,* 9 Mar. 1973). As for Hill's own car, he paid off the loan with a gift from Winsor: a handful of travelers' checks the columnist hadn't spent on a trip to London. Hill served Winsor for thirteen years and called him "the best friend I ever had." Courtesy Cleveland State University *Press* Collection

Late every afternoon for many years, Winsor visited his mother, Edith Ide French Eaton, at the family home on Devonshire Road in Cleveland Heights, then in later years at her apartment atop Cedar Hill. From Europe, he tried to write his mother daily. Winsor treasured, and perhaps inherited, his mother's "high spirit" and "sense of humor that could never be defeated" (*Press,* 25 Jan. 1960). Ann Halle photographed Mrs. Eaton in 1938. Courtesy Ann Halle Little

When Winsor's mother disposed of the family home on Devonshire Road, she presented her son with a large carton of memorabilia. He recalled: "Out of that dusty old box came tumbling all the lost, half-remembered years. Stacks of letters, neatly tied with ribbon; photographs by the score—photographic records of first trips abroad and one of two fantastic winters spent on a ranch school in Wyoming. There were autograph albums, old valentines, a piece of my own wedding cake in a soiled, white monogrammed box and even baby pictures. Those really did me in, though if they are of me, I can easily see I was a remarkably handsome infant" (*Press,* 21 June 1952). Courtesy Martha Eaton Hickox

Left: Winsor's European junkets aboard the *Queen Mary* provoked an envious cartoon from *Press* artist Jim Herron. Above: While his colleagues toiled in Cleveland, Winsor held court on a deck chair with Mrs. Walter Halle and Mrs. Francis Sherwin (center), the former Margaret Murphy Halle. She was the first woman to whom Winsor proposed marriage. She accepted and told her mother, Mrs. Samuel Halle, who sent her to her bedroom, Mag told the author years later, "and told me not to come down until I had phoned Winsor and called it off. 'The marriage won't work,' Mother said." With regret, Margaret did as she was told but remained fast friends with Winsor. Courtesy Martha Eaton Hickox

When Winsor finally abandoned downtown Cleveland, he leased an apartment on Van Aken Boulevard near Shaker Square. For the first time, he encountered a kitchen, which he immediately decorated with a print by Edgar Degas in space that would soon be spattered with grease. By his own account, he was a reluctant cook. As for the chef's helper, Winsor claimed to have taught his pug, Kim, "to sit quietly at the edge of my stove." The columnist wrote in a *Press* column, "If I push the wrong button, Kim will commence to singe and let me know about it" (undated clipping). More often he hired the Weinbergers or the Grubers to cater his sit-down dinners. (Note the lit cigarette in an ashtray on the counter.) Courtesy Martha Eaton Hickox

Winsor, family, and friends chartered the *Thendara* for their bargain tour of the Greek Isles. Nightly cocktail parties included guests like author John Steinbeck, shown with Mag Sherwin and Winsor. A *Thendara* crewmember and Winsor pose with a phallic shard. Courtesy Martha Eaton Hickox

Grecian proportions. It is also a little difficult to find yourself roaring with laughter at the spectacle of a wistful, pathetic little Jew running away from storm troopers. Or to find custard pies and various other slapstick devices involved with brutality and totalitarianism."

After returning to Cleveland, Winsor was cheered when Roosevelt defeated Willkie and the Cleveland Play House staged George Oppenheimer's *Here Today*, a "gay and frothy caricature . . . about people who rapidly are retreating into the shadows. The principal figure is an unsuccessful author with a taste for the bottle," a description that Winsor sometimes applied to himself. While in Hollywood four years earlier, he had asked and received Oppenheimer's advice on writing screenplays, a fact that might have colored what read as a very defensive critique.

Of the play's characters, Winsor wrote,

You have met their prototypes time and time again in drawing rooms, bar rooms, street cars or what have you. They talk a great deal and say very little . . . yet they happened once, and fools though they may have been, you can't help laughing at them. And, mind you, with them. In this November of 1940, it is a little difficult to realize that once upon a time the *Normandie* used to sail from Manhattan on a regular schedule, and hardly ever without a bright young man at the bar. . . . Perhaps we have forgotten how gracefully or heavily he rode his hangovers.

Cleveland newspaper critics panned *Here Today*. The *Plain Dealer*'s William McDermott called it "weightless . . . irresponsible gayety . . . aggressively inconsequential." At the *News,* Arthur Spaeth called the production a "dusting off party" and an "uninspired creaking relic of the unexhilarating theatrical past."

Winsor would have none of it. He took their comments personally and used a second column to defend himself and the playwright. "At the time George Oppenheimer pounded it out there was, so to speak, a fashion for a group of people commonly referred to as the 'bright young set.'" (In Cleveland, Winsor had been declared a "pace-and-style setter" of that "bright young set" by no less an arbiter than Polly Parsons.) "In those days," Winsor continued, "people who arrived at dinner parties less than two hours late were hardly considered housebroken. Crashing parties, even house parties, was the order of the day.

"I think *Here Today* has gained in weight. Surely it was never intended as anything but a featherweight comedy. Mr. Oppenheimer merely tried to put down on paper an impression of his great and good friend Dorothy Parker, during that era when Miss Parker's bon mots and pointed darts were stinging the innocent all over the land."

Miss Parker, Winsor added, had

more than once expressed her opinion of such tragedies as the war in Spain and she is no longer shedding epigrams in the back room of Tony's.

Yet all the careless banter that goes on in *Here Today* used to be as commonplace as rain, not so long ago either, and its characters, I believe, are absolutely typical of their era. Now George Oppenheimer may not be the most superior craftsman in his guild and certainly he is no minor Sheridan, yet I still insist, horrible as it may seem, that the "scotch and soda set" he has described belongs as much to a period in history as the frivolous mannered in *The School for Scandal.*

This may be true, but the cruel fact was that six weeks before his thirty-sixth birthday, two drama critics had called Winsor, along with his circle, an "irresponsible relic."

Finally, *The Time of Your Life* arrived at the Hanna, and Winsor applauded Saroyan's discussion of life in a San Francisco waterfront pub.

He has written a vastly entertaining and arresting play about an absolutely valid cross-section of people. There is the wise and under-standing bartender who never sends anyone away from his door hungry; the colored boy almost at the point of starvation who wants to dance for his supper; the mad prospector who fell in love with a midget 37 inches tall; the unhappily married woman; the over-dressed slummers and all the usual types who seek out obscure bars to find escape from loneliness, unhappiness and defeat.

In this reporter's opinion it is one of the important plays of our time. Mr. Saroyan has managed to capture the elusive quality of futil-ity that has overcome so many people today, and held it up for close and brilliant inspection. Actually he presents no problems; neither does he offer any solutions. He is simply writing about a group of lonely, bewildered and sometimes frightened people seeking escape and anesthesia in drink and once in it, as so often happens, they fre-quently find the talent for self-expression and honesty. It may not be a very pretty picture, but few bars are, come three o'clock in the morn-ing, and more and more people these days are finding themselves in them and behaving just exactly the way Mr. Saroyan's characters do.

Critics who found the play "aimless and without meaning," Winsor wrote, were those "that have never been around people who sometimes

drink too much—or lost, stranded souls who can find no meaning or purpose for their living. Saroyan understands them though, and he brings
them to life with almost terrifying accuracy."

After finishing his review, the columnist walked around his neighborhood in Lakeside Flats, observing the New Year's Eve revelry. "The honky-
tonks defied description. The line leading into the Roxy marquee reached
for a block. Sailors, civilians, men, women and the bright young things
were overflowing into the street from Gallaghers. And everywhere you
went there were laughing drunks, crying drunks and fighting drunks, and
all of them delighted to say goodbye to the tired year."

And while he was on the subject of drunks, he told how "the Hanna Theater survived a tragedy New Year's Eve when an inebriated gent sitting in
the first row of the balcony suddenly became nauseated, causing the management to return the revenue on 32 seats below—at $3.30 a portion!"

Before one more lackluster theatrical season opened at the Hanna in
front of an audience that couldn't hold its liquor, Winsor asked his stepfather to consider keeping the family summer residence in Williamstown
open all year. He offered to pay utility and food bills; Eaton accepted the
arrangement. Then Benny Crowell agreed to give up his apartment in
Stockbridge and rent a room in the Eaton household. The columnist emptied his two apartments in Sin Shanty, shipped his furniture and collection
of celebrity photographs to Williamstown, and announced his resignation
from the *Press*. His last column appeared on September 12, 1941. "I am
about to lock up my desk again. At intervals there will be letters hurried
into the mails from Manhattan, Boston or wherever the theatrical limelight
happens to be focusing its rays. I will also try to pass on the Manhattan
chit-chat and capture in some small way the general New York scene."

What Winsor did not tell his readers was that Carmel Snow, editor of
Harper's Bazaar, had asked him to write a monthly about-town column
and review plays. The columnist had finally achieved national circulation
for his "new kind of reporting." Yet Benny's rent money, fees for monthly
freelance articles, and an occasional piece in the *Press* would not support
his lifestyle. He was still looking for a job as he prepared to leave Cleveland. Before he could board the train for Williamstown, however, he had
one last task to complete: Bidding his colleagues and readers farewell.

"I will not be here when the critics, society reporters and photographers
are on hand to cover the performances both on stage and in the audience
at the opening of the Hanna. It will seem strange indeed not to beat Bill
McDermott or Arthur Spaeth to the taxis after the last curtain.

"I find it a difficult and unhappy job to sign off. But there it is and this
is goodby."

"Our own design for living"

WILLIAMSTOWN, MASSACHUSETTS

Tuesday, December 2, 1941, Mid-afternoon

"Dear Father, Len and I were alone for Thanksgiving." A homesick Winsor was writing his landlord about the experimental household he was trying to establish. It would allow him to maintain close ties with his family and live openly with his male companions. "I had a cocktail party for Len. Mrs. Crowell came . . . with Benny—and B is living here now—trying out our scheme and I hope it works as he is both company and financial help."

Winsor's income included payments for his columns that were appearing in *Harper's Bazaar,* but without his byline, a decision by his editor, Carmel Snow, which can't have pleased him. Snow, according to Winsor, was "seeing a great deal" of journalist Janet Flanner, who would eventually write a "Paris Letter" for the *New Yorker* over the byline "Genet." What did Flanner see in Snow? Winsor described "his boss" as having "ice blue hair" and a "cynical smile." To supplement fees from *Harper's Bazaar,* Winsor had been in New York City and Washington, D.C, searching for a job. The effort had been unsuccessful. He was feeling pinched. "A lovely little note . . . arrived yesterday from the Collector of Internal Revenue reminding me I owe my last payment."

To the cocktail party for Hanna, Winsor had also invited his ex-wife. "Margaret Perry stopped off . . . on her way to Boston—and I am so glad she did. It was really the first time I have seen her since our divorce except in nightclubs, etc., and whatever sentimental feelings I may have had in the past are gone. . . . She is sweet and generous and has all sorts of good qualities—but My God how boring she is really, and I put her on the train for Boston . . . with the most wonderful sense of relief that we aren't married any longer."

He confirmed plans to meet his parents in New York City for the weekend. "I'll see you and Mother on Friday—lots and lots of love—devotedly, Winsor." Friday was the fifth of December 1941. He was still in Manhattan on

Sunday, December 7, when the first news dispatches from Hawaii reported Japanese airplanes had bombed the U.S. Navy base at Pearl Harbor.

Four days later, Winsor returned to Williamstown and wrote Anne Eaton, his youngest sister, describing his confusion in the first few days following the attack.

> Everyone's reason seems to have been unseated. . . . I went to the Red Cross today and signed up for Civil Defense—also offering myself to the State Guard with the understanding I would go wherever they might send me. And next week I am starting a course in safety-first instruction, first aid and God knows what else. But what I really want to do, as soon as things settle down to a state where a man can find useful work, is to get into the intelligence. But I imagine if I went to Washington right now I would be thrown out on my face.

In New York, the fifty-three-year-old Hanna volunteered as an American Red Cross field worker and "asked for duty in England." Within sixty days, he was in London as a zone director, finding and staffing clubs where troops could rest. Zerbe enlisted in the U.S. Navy. His assignment: photographer. Roger Stearns was playing piano in a Manhattan nightclub.

Winsor and Benny Crowell continued to search for wartime assignments. Winsor sympathized with students at Williams College who abandoned degrees to enter the armed services. "I wish something could be done so the youth of the nation could be trained for service while IN college—and that the older men could go first. It seems so terrible—the sacrifice of the healthy young when there are so many people around, such as I, who could go so easily and with so little loss to anyone."

In a separate letter, he reassured his stepfather that all was well in Williamstown: "Having Benny here is working out beautifully—and you have no idea what a comfort it is to go to bed at night and know someone within shouting distance is on hand. It also saves money—although this month will be pretty steep as I have bought [Christmas] trees, decorations, etc."

Winsor's frugal landlord replied with a proposition for increasing his stepson's income. "I am wondering what sort of financial arrangement you have with Benny. I think it should be a fixed amount per week or month and that it should cover one-half of your estimated out-of-pocket expenses plus a charge covering a portion of the expense that I am put to in maintaining and keeping the house open which, of course, would be so much to the good for you as I have no intentions of making any fixed charges, but there is no reason why that should be donated to Benny."

Eaton's file does not contain an answer from Winsor. He had a legitimate excuse for not writing: he had drunk unpasteurized milk and had run a persistently high temperature. A doctor diagnosed undulant fever. For months Winsor felt too weak to write. While he was recovering, Eaton had another, more patriotic proposition. President Roosevelt was urging Americans to plant victory gardens that would reduce food shortages on the home front. "I have had in mind . . . to use our twenty-five available acres at Williamstown next summer to grow something useful. There is an official known as County Agent with headquarters, I think, in Pittsfield who represents the Massachusetts Department of Agriculture who can advise people on such matters as this. Also they arrange for free fertilizer and all kinds of things. . . . If you can get hold of him he could look the place over and advise us on the most useful and practical crops we could grow."

Eaton must have missed Winsor's columns from Beverly Hills and Havana. To imagine his stepson managing a twenty-five-acre farm is to overlook the fact that he needed Linda Porter's secretary to find him a bed in Beverly Hills and to fill out his landing cards aboard the *Kungsholm,* to say nothing of the role Eaton's own secretary played in keeping Winsor's cars licensed. Given his policy of delegating "the worrying" to others, it should come as no surprise that Eaton's file does not contain a document indicating his stepson ever found—or even searched for—the elusive county agent.

Winsor had excuses.

Dreary skies: "There have only been two days of sunshine in the three weeks I have been back. In fact the weather is exactly like Cleveland."
Loneliness: He was depressed "watching all my friends go away." After less than three months as a tenant, some sort of personal crisis had caused Crowell to leave. Furthermore, Carmel Snow had decided *Harper's Bazaar* did not need an about-town columnist during wartime. "Believe me I feel isolated and useless," Winsor wrote his sister Anne. "I wonder how I am going to go through this war—cut off from everything, doing nothing of any value except writing (and that, God knows, is equivocal)."

Winsor sought male friends at Williams College and found "a lean, lanky guy" named Kellogg Smith, who was an undergraduate when one of his fraternity brothers invited Winsor to their house on campus. "We soon became friends," Smith recalled. When visiting New York City, Winsor occasionally invited Smith and his girlfriend to accompany him. "We used to see a lot of him. Winsor was a demon entertainer." Two of their host's destinations were the editorial offices of the *New Yorker,* where he was submitting fiction pieces, and the 1-2-3, one of the city's newest and "most attractive and pleasant" supper clubs on West 54th Street.

The 1-2-3 was Cole Porter's idea. He craved "a nice little hangout" of his own and asked his favorite pianist, Roger Stearns, if he would leave his current employment and consider running the place. Stearns thought Porter's idea about a supper club was "swell" but asked him, "What about money—doesn't it cost money to open a club?" Porter said it did and quickly recruited four notable gold-standard investors: Dwight Deere Wiman, a prolific theatrical producer (Porter's *Gay Divorce,* Richard Rodgers and Lorenz Hart's *On Your Toes*) and Yale graduate, who left his maternal family's agricultural implements firm for the theater; Mary Conover Mellon, the first wife of the philanthropist and art collector, whose husband was the nation's eighth-wealthiest man, according to *Fortune* magazine; J. J. Hill II, grandson, namesake, and heir to a great family railroad fortune; and Porter's perennial Cleveland patron Leonard Hanna. To ensure a return on their investment, the backers insisted Stearns play the piano every night the club was open.

Why would two musical theater giants and three of the wealthiest people in America prefer Stearns's music to all others', especially in New York City, capital of the nation's nightlife? His style was described as "suave," but Winsor thought what really distinguished his friend from the competition was his "remarkable memory," which allowed him to develop an intimate musical relationship with his regular patrons and made any club in which he performed "one of those places where friends gather" to avoid "the loathsome privacy of their own home." It was Stearns's ability to turn a commercial enterprise into a nightly party of best friends that helps explain why American nightlife of the 1930s and 1940s was such an important part of the nation's social life and why metropolitan daily newspaper editors asked writers like Winsor to devote themselves to documenting their cities' nightly events.

Winsor and Cleveland played a key role in Stearns's career; Stearns insisted that he began developing his intimate approach to café entertainment during the winter of 1935 in the piano lounge just inside the Euclid Avenue entrance of Cleveland's Statler Hotel. "Being a bar pianist is lonesome work," Stearns explained. "Nine times a day one chains oneself to the piano for a full half-hour, and, with luck, one is not spoken to. But when a familiar and welcome face appears, it is so pleasant to be able to play the favorite tune, which is a way of saying, 'Ah, how nice it is to see you, and we'll talk later.'" Stearns took those favorite tunes and turned them into "umbilical chords."

When Stearns saw Porter enter 1-2-3, he played an esoteric version of "Rosalie," one of five or six versions the composer had written for the MGM film of the same name. The studio eventually had selected another version and Stearns claimed that whenever Porter heard the music, he would come to the piano and say, "That is charming—what is it?" and would be delighted to learn it was one of his compositions.

For Winsor, Stearns had assembled—with "great difficulty"—"a dossier" of five of the columnist's favorite pieces. "There is only one drawback. When he enters with his party, I always go through the five. But as the last dulcet note is dying away, he will just have finished giving the waiter the order and will turn and call to me 'Hey, kid, where's my music?'"

Winsor's reaction was atypical. Monty Woolley's "umbilical chord" was "Small Hotel," which he sang in the original cast of Rodgers and Hart's *On Your Toes*. The actor used the popular tune to draw attention to himself. He would "stand at the entrance until his music came, then make a courtly bow and go to his table, stopping at the piano just long enough to say in stentorian tones, 'Now, my boy, I would like a bit of Vincent Youmans in two flats— I believe you call it B flat.'" For most patrons, "umbilical chords" recalled pleasant memories, establishing a nostalgic mood that made an evening with Stearns enjoyable, even during the early days of World War II when newspaper headlines had a sobering effect on public behavior. According to a contemporary account in the *New Yorker*, when Winsor and his guests from Williamstown dined at the 1-2-3, they found Stearns playing the piano and other patrons playing quiet games of "gin rummy."

Card games at the 1-2-3 were not what Eaton had in mind for making Winsor useful to the war effort. His stepfather added dairy products to the proposed victory garden in Williamstown:

> You had better have Louis look over the old tool house and see if it is big enough to house a cow in bad weather and also what repairs would have to be made as to the roof, etc. [Louis was a handyman Eaton employed.]
>
> It is also a possibility that we might arrange with Monahan to use one of the sheds in the back corner of his place. I have in mind particularly the one that was used for a teahouse. You had better have Louis and perhaps Betty make some inquiries as to the cost of a good cow that has just come in. [Betty cooked and cleaned for the Eatons.]

"I prefer Guernsey," Eaton added, "or a Guernsey with a slight mixture of something else." His file does not contain a written reply from Winsor regarding the Guernsey, but his sister Anne got an earful. "I hope I can persuade Father NOT to buy a cow. Mercy! If you have one that is going to live alone, it has to be one that was raised alone and not in a herd. Otherwise they go berserk. They need constant attention, 365 days of the year, and MUST have it. And I personally will always have a milk bill because after my experience I flatly refuse to drink raw milk, use raw butter or any part of them. . . . And I wonder if the damn things save money."

Winsor had an excuse for not writing his stepfather about the cow or, for that matter, finishing more short stories. Eaton had put him in charge of readying the Williamstown house for a wedding reception. Anne planned to be married there in May, before her fiancé, Whitney Dodge, was shipped overseas. News of Anne's wedding had prompted Linda Porter to invite Winsor to Buxton Hill. "Linda gave me her wedding present to you yesterday and what to do with it? It is a three-strand necklace of very old, very beautiful hand carved, blue Chinese beads, with white, Egyptian beads spacing them. I hope to God you like it—because at the same time she brought out a short, choker necklace, also very old and also very beautiful, but I thought this was more your type."

More tedious chores than selecting jewelry filled Winsor's days. "My, the details. What with the gardening and the painting and the things everyone promises they will do and then fail to do, I don't seem to ever get any more time to write." He did have time to tease Anne. "I'm going to take Whitney out and liquor him up and introduce him to low characters." Whatever bachelor parties Winsor arranged did not postpone the wedding. Following the ceremony, Anne moved to her husband's home in Burlington, Vermont.

A few days after the event, Winsor received another letter from Eaton, who had taken farm and dairy planning into his own hands. "I have written to the State Agricultural Department to find out why their state agent cannot be found." Winsor was delighted to read that his stepfather had also heard "very discouraging news about cows and certainly I shall do nothing until I return to Williamstown."

He arrived in June and shortly thereafter rented a cow named "Amy," much to Winsor's chagrin. After a month, he decided the animal was starving for sex. "Deprived of bulls," Amy had "taken to escaping from her pasture and going in search of them. On the first escapade she ate her way through miles of asparagus fern and even left her card at the kitchen door after gracefully managing the walk and those dreadful stone steps down the hill."

Winsor was writing his sister in Vermont during a lull in another visit by his mother and stepfather. "The family got back last night—mother exhausted and father in somewhat of a state (understandably) as they had lost MY zipper bag complete with among other things, FOUR bottles of liquor!!! Father is only here until tomorrow night, but long enough to make things hum. Mercy! Chickens are being slaughtered—raspberries picked and the deep freeze inventoried."

But Winsor's real reason for writing Anne was that he missed her. "You owe me a letter. You just squat and squat there and by the time you come back I'll probably be so old and senile I won't recognize you. You are a self-ish slut to desert me this way." His affectionate scolding produced an invitation to Burlington. He quickly accepted for himself and Benny Crowell.

The whereabouts of his former tenant had already provoked an angry outburst from Winsor. "The cat, so to speak, is out of the bag about Benny as Mother asked me if I had stopped to see him; so I thought what the hell and whose business is it anyway and gave forth with both barrels."

Winsor's sisters insist that he adored his mother, and she returned his love without conditions. For him to fire verbal shots at her—with "both barrels"—suggests an extraordinary confrontation. Why would Benny's departure from the Eaton household infuriate Winsor? He did provide a hint in a letter he wrote Anne following the men's visit to Burlington. "I loved seeing you and even if you were left in a state of utter and complete exhaustion it was all my idea of fun. And I am sure we lifted Benny out of a rut of despair and gave him the comforting assurance he still had friends left."

Whatever the cause of Crowell's distress, Winsor had lost the company—and the added income—of his good friend. In Vermont, he regained that companionship for a splendid weekend. "Burlington was such fun and we all get along so beautifully we should have our own design for living." Winsor's and Crowell's lives, like those of Coward characters, were "diametrically opposed to ordinary social conventions." Like the men in *Design for Living,* they were trying "to find our own solution for our own peculiar moral problems."

In the summer of 1942, Winsor's solution was to be Anne's neighbor. He proposed purchasing property next door. "Perhaps, if I can get that house, come peace and decency and such things as dreaming again, we can all plant trumpet vines and lima beans together in our little back patch of ground." Yet for Winsor, there was the perennial problem of money. For a down payment on his design for living, he considered approaching a brother. "I wonder if the rich Mr. Ted French would dig into his jeans and come up with enough thousands to help me clinch the deal. Dear God—the pain and degradation of not having a million dollars."

If Winsor had been able to buy the house, he believed Anne and her husband would have to make one critical addition to their household. "Do, please, get yourselves a maid." Anne did not encourage her brother's fantasies. "It would have never worked out. He was so critical."

For several reasons, Winsor did not enjoy the return to Williamstown. "The trip back from your haven, if I may say so, was a nightmare. The damned bus only stopped once for creature comforts, not at all for lunch and it was crowded with swaying, smelly standees the entire way."

Theoretically, he could have avoided the indignities of wartime travel by driving a car to Vermont. Before leaving for London, Hanna had given Winsor his tiny Crosley, but even if he could have produced enough gas rationing coupons to fill its tank, he did not trust the automobile. Each time he drove the Crosley, he complained, "EVERYTHING BREAKS. The other evening, for instance, Sturge and I were pushing it." "Sturge" was Howard Sturges, a wealthy, hard-drinking bon vivant and regular member of Cole Porter's entourage. "When I ran to jump in, my leg gave out. I slipped and the damn thing ran over me."

Adding psychological pain to Winsor's bruised leg were the editors of the New Yorker. They had repeatedly rejected his submissions of short fiction. To "earn some money," he had turned to nonfiction articles and taken interviews and notes for "two free lance profiles" he hoped to sell to other magazines. During that same period, he observed a session of a short story class offered at Williams College. "Very amusing," he wrote his sister. The instructor had read the efforts of three students. Winsor thought two were "quite good," but his was a minority view. "Dear sweet God the criticism! I wouldn't ever toss a paragraph to those vultures for comment. Youth is too searching, too afraid of clichés, too demanding in its integrity, too, too, too everything." Ten years earlier, certain authors whose work was reviewed in PARADE might have said the same thing about Winsor. According to him, Daphne du Maurier's "characters are merely names, lifeless puppets. . . . Her dialogue consists of loose, careless sentences, strung along a page." Edwin Arlington Robinson's "verse seems only a faltering echo of fine music . . . a tired man attempting to warm his stiffening fingers over coals that have lost their warmth."

Several weeks passed, and Winsor suddenly complained to his stepfather that he was "absolutely stymied" as a writer because he had "lost all the notes" for his nonfiction profiles and couldn't complete them. The New Yorker's rejection slips, his negative reaction to student criticism, and the "lost notes" mark a turning point in Winsor's sense of his own skills. He lost confidence in his ability to do "serious writing." There would be no more talk about writing a novel, short stories, or screenplays. He would occasionally mention his desire to complete a play script, but there is no evidence that he actually put words on paper. While his personal correspondence and journalistic reportage do not contain an explicit reason for his diminished ambition, his book reviews for PARADE offer a plausible explanation.

Winsor couldn't satisfy the high standards he set for authors. The former about-town columnist loathed fiction that had "no more literary merit than a cheap newspaper sob story."

What did he expect from a writer? He championed brevity, praising dialogue "bitten off in short staccato sentences that are never overdrawn or sentimental." He expected writers to "eliminate every unnecessary word," leaving only those that "like the stroke of an artist's brush" supplied a "highlight, lacking which, the novel would be poorer." English author Evelyn Waugh had "a genius for knowing just how much detail and what sort to use," but it was American novelist William Faulkner who "with one line can burn a brilliant and unforgettable picture on the mind."

A "good" book needed "suspense, wit, tragedy"; those "that neither contradict nor assert very much" were boring. He cited English author Vita Sackville-West as one who could "handle a quiet, intensely difficult theme" and "intermingle the past and the present so adroitly that the transitions are almost imperceptible." Content shouldn't be "cloyingly sentimental" or "abnormally morbid and ugly," but he praised those who wrote about "complete depravity and degenerates without being offensive." In this genre, Faulkner was Winsor's model. "His brain may concern itself with laboratory analysis of every vice and mental deformity, but he deserves the attention of every literate person." To this end, he gave his three teenage sisters, Margaret, Martha, and Anne, copies of Faulkner's novels and made sure they read them.

The author and book that best reveal Winsor's literary taste and ambition are Virginia Woolf and *The Waves*, published in 1931. The *New York Herald Tribune* reviewer called it "a novel for novelists, mainly interesting as an experiment." For Winsor, it was "unquestionably the great book of 1931."

That year Woolf was a forty-nine-year-old Englishwoman who had been married for twenty years, but who had fallen in love with another married English author—Sackville-West. She was Woolf's model for *Orlando*, which she called an "autobiography." The author and Winsor shared an interest in gender relations. "In every human being a vacillation from one sex to the other takes place," Woolf wrote in *Orlando*. "Often it is only the clothes that keep the male or female likeness."

Winsor was discreet. He called *Orlando* "brilliant" and "enigmatical," perhaps the "biography of a well-known contemporary who had allegedly posed for its illustrations." Yet other critics argued that the book dealt with a "bleak abnormality"—the two women's mutual sexual attraction. "Whatever it was, is not our question," Winsor wrote. "She is the outstanding figure in contemporary letters."

He compared her to English male authors: John Galsworthy "may weaken and topple from the high level of his Forsyte book"; Hugh Walpole "may become quaint"; Somerset Maugham could "write a potboiler and vacation in the Orient on his royalties"; James Joyce "may, in his *Work in Progress,* give up English as we have come to understand it and go in for an utterly meaningless jargon—but never Virginia Woolf. Her integrity is inspiring." As for her female competitors, Willa Cather "draws beautifully delicate laceworks of simple gentle folks"; Edna St. Vincent Millay "writes nostalgic, whining lyrics on love"; Vita Sackville-West "excels in panorama" and "close character drawing"; Rebecca West, like Woolf, "is concerned with conflicts and the stream of consciousness. But none of them has her [Woolf's] broad sweep or genius."

A realist, Winsor expected *The Waves* to have a "small audience. A prose that is almost blank verse, situations that are not sensational, everyday people meeting everyday crises simply, living as life *is* lived, not as in a cinematic thriller, is perhaps not exciting enough a dish for our jaded age. But there is nothing lukewarm about Mrs. Woolf or *The Waves.* The book is as deep or as shallow as its reader."

He didn't paraphrase his better-known newspaper and magazine colleagues. The *New York Times* called *The Waves* "clear, bright, burnished, at once marvelously accurate and subtly connotative." The *Saturday Review* published a condescending critique: "To have a room of one's own was once recommended by Mrs. Woolf as a method whereby gentlewomen could write good novels, but *The Waves* suggests that this chamber music, this closet fiction, is executed behind too firmly closed windows. . . . The book is dull. The peculiar form adopted by Mrs. Woolf exacts much attention and gives too small a reward." The critic who sounded similar notes to Winsor's was Rebecca West in the *New York Herald Tribune.* "Mrs. Woolf's new form is absolutely valid, . . . and in this form Virginia Woolf comes to a curious and secret flowering."

While one cannot know exactly why Winsor was disappointed with his own writing, it is not hard to imagine that a man who recognized and applauded Woolf's genius, who appreciated and promoted the work of Faulkner, and who expected high technical perfection from every author he read might find his own prose fell short of his literary standards.

In Williamstown, the weather intensified Winsor's self-doubt. Although it was August, the temperature was so cold, he wrote Anne, "that I am confident my manhood has been lost for all time. The mercury has tumbled to 30 something and personally I think it is a visitation to punish us for planting so many tomatoes."

For the next several months, Winsor continued to search for work. As shortages increased during wartime, Eaton's thoughtful secretary supplied him with necessities. "Dear Miss Carroll," he wrote on stationery from the Waldorf-Astoria Hotel, "Thanks for the soap—which is getting scarce here." At Buxton Hill, Linda Porter kept track of his plight. In a letter to a friend, she wrote, "Winsor French still hasn't a job, poor soul!"

In November, another of his sisters, Peggy Eaton Sichel, helped organize him in Williamstown. He wrote their father, "Peg and I are getting things accomplished and trying to push life towards a system. Yesterday was pig day and the deep freeze is now overflowing with sausages, loins, chops and God knows what else." With the larder full, he wrote, "I must now settle down and pay some bills. Though with what I wouldn't know." Despite his finances, he told Eaton "that a maid of sorts would be a help" in managing the household. "Please give my love to mother and all the family—and don't forget us here on what I sometimes feel is Tobacco Road."

Winsor's civil defense responsibilities included "a lonesome watch" in the attic of an old house near the Porters' estate in Williamstown, where he listened with earphones for sounds picked up over the Atlantic Ocean by a huge, horn-shaped electronic receiver. He told brother-in-law Charles "Char" Hickox that he had once "heard a droning that he felt surely must be the whole Luftwaffe" and promptly called for help. "A military detachment rushed to his aid to find that bees were swarming in the horn," Hickox recalled.

To a brother stationed in Europe, Winsor—a master at breaking liquor laws—recalled sending "pints of Scotch carefully concealed in loaves of bread. Illegal, of course, but they always got through. I also used to send him nylons to boost his stock with his girl friends (which needed no boosting), but only one in an envelope. Pairs never made it."

Winsor's virtual silence throughout 1944 panicked Cleveland friends, who feared for his life. Eventually someone found him. On its front page, the *Press* reported his reply to rumors that he was dead: "I'm not. I haven't even a hangover."

Meanwhile, his closest friends had found roles to play in the war effort. During the relentless German aerial bombardment of London, Hanna had "established one hundred clubs" for troops stationed throughout England. After allied troops successfully landed in France and began to rout German armies, Winsor's patron had "applied for a new assignment in Europe, but a 'crippling illness' forced him to return to the United States." In 1944, Stearns took a temporary leave from the 1-2-3 and toured European military bases in *The Barretts of Wimpole Street,* starring Katherine Cornell. On Thanksgiving night, he recalled, the company "did an hour-long radio show exclusively for the Fifth Army, which was freezing it out along the Po" River in northern Italy. "The high spot of the hour was Miss Cornell reading Elizabeth Barrett

Browning's *Sonnet from the Portuguese* beginning 'How Do I Love Thee?' A moment before she went on she murmured, 'Roger, we have to have a little soft music behind me, but nothing too highbrow.' So I at once settle on 'All the Things You Are,'" which became their "umbilical chord" whenever the actress entered 1-2-3 following the tour's conclusion.

During this same period, and despite relentless poor-mouthing, Winsor decided to abandon Cleveland and make his permanent residence in Williamstown. He purchased a six-room, colonial-style frame house on an acre of land neighboring his family's residence. Then, inexplicably, on October 1, 1945, after both Germany and Japan had surrendered, his photograph appeared on the front page of the *Press* with an article by editor Louis Seltzer. "Mr. French's volatile personality has been missing from the Cleveland scene," he announced. "His return will brighten Cleveland's own white way." What the editor expected from Winsor—and promised readers—was "brittle comment and bright chatter about local and national personalities"—six days a week.

Brittle comment and bright chatter: Was that to be Winsor's legacy as a writer?

"Solid gold from wrist to elbow"

CLEVELAND, OHIO

Monday, October 1, 1945, 11 a.m.

Winsor's first published column following his sudden decision to resume his writing career as a Cleveland newspaper columnist was devoid of "bright chatter." His mood was reflected in a short note he gave Seltzer, who had asked him for a couple of paragraphs he could use to introduce the columnist to new *Press* readers. "I was born in Saratoga Springs, N.Y. Christmas Eve, 1904. I am one of eight living children . . . have been married and divorced." He drastically abridged an account of his formal education and work history and explained why he hadn't fought in the war. "Because of a bad heart I am not able to do any violent exercising." Winsor completed his self-portrait with two plaintive sentences: "I would rather live in Hollywood than any other city in the world. Ambitions: (1) to write a good play and (2) never to have to go to another nightclub."

Seltzer did not include Winsor's last lines in his announcement. The *Press* promoted Cleveland. Its editor would not boast about a columnist who longed to live elsewhere, nor would he mention his unfulfilled ambitions. Seltzer believed being a fine newspaper columnist was a worthy calling for any writer. Furthermore, he had not demanded that Winsor cover the city's nightclubs. He could write about whatever he wanted. On his return to Cleveland what he wanted readers to know was that he didn't like what he saw. "Through the grime of a Pullman window the other morning at the East Cleveland Station, misted in a gray drizzle, my first impression was 'here is where I came in.' Nothing had changed."

Over the weekend, he revisited favorite places and found he was wrong. The world war had changed Cleveland. Avant-garde artists and their bohemian friends had abandoned Lakeside Flats. Thirsty, young, and sometimes lonely sailors no longer crowded Fleet's Inn, and on the sidewalk around the corner from Winsor's apartment in Sin Shanty the gypsy fortune-tellers had decamped. "A long life and the pursuit of happiness was their eternal promise," but the war had proved "that no one ever again need consider the crystal gazers very seriously."

Winsor missed the days when "you could walk right into a liquor store and buy a bottle of Scotch, or even 12 of them without the slightest trouble." Wartime rationing meant customers often bought liquor under the counter or tried to "waylay servicemen," who were exempt from rationing, to do their shopping "in the eternal manner of youngsters trying to crash a movie."

His favorite "cellars and purlieus," where he had discovered Art Tatum and taken curious Republicans, were closed. New occupants were not as friendly. "You were just as safe in a Cedar Avenue rib joint as a country churchyard and on brisk October evenings the fragrance of Mammy Louise's barbecue pit was something to remember." Cleveland's finest Creole cook had moved to Chicago.

"What has happened, please, to the quiet back rooms and the beery cellars where two chairs were the divine right of every customer? The little rooms where the affairs of any world, no matter how disordered, could be swept clean in an hour's conversation. . . . Everywhere the tables are reserved well in advance and the bill for a simple little dinner would stagger Croesus."

Winsor did not enjoy the music he heard while eating—"Jerome Kern knew more about melody than the rising tide of Tin Pan Alley zootsuiters"—but he did see one hopeful sign in postwar Cleveland's nightlife: "Gone are the stretches of empty dining rooms that used to line my beat. The carpets used to roll up well before midnight. Euclid Avenue became a dismal, dim waste bordered by darkened windows and [on] E. 9th Street cars clanked along their way—empty throughout the night. But no longer. People would almost seem to be homeless. Come 2 A.M. and the streets are still crowded with the excitement of noon. And me, I feel a little like a visitor, hesitant in a foreign land, unsure of everything, brother, except that changes have been made."

The smoke-and-music beat bored Winsor, and he was appalled by the poverty of women widowed during the war: "The bereft and desperate [are] selling shoelaces or patented potato peelers." If widows were selling shoelaces in Cleveland, he wondered how women were coping in London and Paris following the most devastating war in modern history. He thought his readers would be more interested in knowing how the "average European" was adjusting to peace, if not prosperity, so he asked Seltzer if he could spend six weeks in Europe, where he would look up "old friends" and report on how they were recovering. Seltzer decided Winsor would be a unique foreign correspondent and sent him on what would become a legendary trip in Cleveland newspaper history.

Berths on trans-Atlantic steamships were scarce, so the columnist booked passage on a battered U.S. Army troop ship, the SS *John E. Ericsson* with money he borrowed from Len Hanna. Ironically, the *Ericsson* was the MS *Kungsholm,* rechristened, an eerie relic from Winsor's "careless days" as a member of Cole and Linda Porter's entourage on their cruise to the South Seas. Since then "initials carved into the railings" reminded him "that not so long ago she carried vast, human cargoes into the terrifying unknown."

U.S. Army regulations that prohibited the use of liquor for "beverage purposes" were still in force, but, the child of Prohibition noted, "Bottles could be bought (bootlegged) the first couple of days out (Hiram Walker Imperial, $10), but the ship is dry now." Winsor was "riding the wagon" and sharing "a room with six bunks." He advised readers not to follow his example: "If you are going as cattle, go that way. In other words, ask for a room with 20 bunks rather than six or eight. It is more impersonal and you don't have to be polite to the bores."

On the dock at Southampton Winsor was "breathless, excited" because it had been twelve years since his last visit to England. He established head-quarters in a suite at his favorite London hotel—the Berkeley: "In less than five minutes a maid and valet appeared offering to take over the unpacking. Hot on their heels came the floor waiter with ice, soda and Scotch. Next a boy with the evening papers," notably fine service in a city where sandbags were "still piled in the cloisters" of Westminster Abbey and at Buckingham Palace the horse guards were still in "battle dress." Winsor urged restoration of "the brilliant coats" and those "skin-tight white pants."

While the maid and valet stowed Winsor's belongings, he set out to take the pulse of London's postwar nightlife and diagnose the city's physical and emotional health. Within twenty-four hours, he wired Cleveland, "The visitor in London can find practically everything his or her little heart desires," which contradicted the overwhelming number of newspaper stories that described the miserable lives of the war's survivors.

Why was the experience of Winsor's friends so different? "I can count on one hand the people I have met who don't frankly admit they are up to their ears in the black market . . . desperately hoping there will be a little more meat and less bread in their sausages." A few days later, in the embrace of an overstuffed leather armchair at Boodle's, an exclusive private club, Winsor noted, "Everyone is tired, bored and a little hungry. The peace is worse than the war. During the war, everyone will tell you, the spirit was much higher. There was a reason for every sacrifice, going without things and pulling in the belts. Now they want something better even if it is only a little better."

Winsor thought reviving London's nightlife could cure the public's depression. In his opinion, a wartime curfew needlessly drained the energy from London's once lively theatrical scene. To get audiences home before curfew, producers were forced to raise their curtains at 6:30 P.M. "Most people arrive in a glow from cocktails consumed far too rapidly. By the time the second act begins the glow is gone and pangs of hunger set in. The evening drags on and anywhere between nine-thirty and ten the crowds pour into the streets again, rushing to find a taxi and then a restaurant where they can still get dinner. By that time the sharp edge of your appetite is gone and so are most of the even slightly interesting items on the menus, and it all seems so totally unnecessary."

Although Winsor did write about shortages other reporters ignored. For a new Sadler's Wells production of *The Sleeping Beauty,* Oliver Messel, who had amused Winsor at a Hollywood dinner party hosted by Clifton Webb and Marlene Dietrich, told him the company's dancers were "only permitted two pairs of shoes, one brown, one white." Messel's costume shop had "resorted to hand painting anything they can lay their hands on as there are no dyes either." Yet his friend had "created as beautiful a production as I have ever seen."

Orry-Kelly, who had costumed the spontaneous midnight revue at the marathon Hollywood party hosted by Billy Haines, faced similar shortages for a film production. "All the available costume jewelry, such as it is, is made of wood. . . . White rayon hangings, after being used for backdrops, went into dance dresses."

Winsor noted one sign of confidence: "More sleek, highly polished Rolls Royces in one block than you could count in Manhattan in a week." Nevertheless, the recovery was moving too slowly. After two weeks, Winsor boarded the Golden Arrow for Paris, "one of the few luxury trains . . . still maintaining prewar standards in Europe today. . . . You could have lunch, either at your seat, on the boat crossing the Channel or during the last lap of the journey from Calais to Paris. Sensing turbot in an ersatz cream sauce, boiled potatoes and over-cooked string beans, I settled for the French cooking. I was right to wait until late afternoon for lunch. It was still turbot, boiled potatoes and string beans, but it was cooked with what you might call more imagination, and there were bottles of red and white wine on the tables to wash things down with."

Wine brightened Winsor's outlook. He described the scene framed by the train window: "Trees, clipped so many times for firewood they resemble brooms, edge the roadsides, and along the roads go peasants on bicycles . . . wearing clothes faded by countless washings until they have become the same incredible color of blue as the sky above them." At the Gare du Nord, he "ran" from the train to a taxi that puttered "up the Champs Elysees, crowded with Jeeps, cyclists and hundreds of GI's walking their girls under the chestnut trees. . . . It was a warm, whispering spring night without a cloud in the sky. I was in Paris."

In his room at the St. Regis Hotel, the columnist found crude signs of wartime occupation. "A German soldier carved his name into the desk, the shelves are papered with old German newspapers and if the valet or the maids find it difficult to understand your French they at once commence talking German." But Winsor spent little time in his hotel room; he headed straight for the Ritz to find Georges. "When I walked in for the first time in 12 years, he greeted me as if I had never been out of the place, calmly saying, 'How do you do, Mr. French, haven't you lost a little weight?'"

The war had lowered barriers at the Ritz. Women and dogs had gained entrance to the Men's Bar. At noon, it was "crowded with Americans and English, stopping in for a drink after picking up their mail and all wanting Georges for something, addresses for nylons or where perfume can be bought without giving up a bottle." On one of his first visits, Winsor met friend and fellow journalist Randolph Churchill. The "blonde Hyacinthus" was living "very simply in a suite at the Ritz." The envious columnist noted that Churchill drove "everywhere in a snappy little car. He proves, without a question of a doubt, that journalism can pay off importantly."

In Winsor's slightly less expensive version of newspaper work, he used local bars as offices. At the Scribe, he eavesdropped on the *New Yorker*'s Janet Flanner. "Prematurely white, scorning makeup, she almost always walks with an umbrella and looks and is as forceful a woman as you will meet in a long, long time. Frequently in the later afternoon she holds forth in the Scribe, surrounded by the best brains in Paris." At the Ascot, Winsor listened to American GIs. "They sit on their bar stools, grousing over the price of drinks and wondering how long it will be before they can get back to Main Street and unlimited cokes with ice in the glass. On the other hand, I haven't seen half a dozen drunken GI's since my arrival. . . . The men are beautifully behaved and their manners and above all their smile, if you want to read between the lines, charms a great deal more than the birds from the trees."

After spending the night collecting items in bars, Winsor would return to the St. Regis in the predawn darkness and summon the hotel's elevator for a trip to his room.

You step into an air-cooled birdcage and drift perilously heavenwards. Once there, you get out . . . as quickly as possible, and it descends with the speed of a falling sparrow. The French operate on the theory that an elevator is intended only to take passengers upward; that it is foolish to ride down when you can walk. When you descend, however, it is usually on your hands and knees—and not because the liquor has been flowing either. The French, when it comes to money, are an extremely careful people, and one of the quaintest economies is leaving their stairways and corridors plunged in eternal darkness. This national trait is emphasized by a current shortage of coal, which makes power conservation a necessity. There is, if you can find it, an automatic button on each landing that turns on the lights for a few brief seconds. But, unless you move with the speed of an antelope, you find yourself again plunged in darkness and suspended, so to speak, in mid-air. And that is what happened to me.

On this singular evening Winsor described, the elevator

failed to stop at my floor, and I was carried several flights beyond. There was nothing to do then but struggle with the lighting system— a problem that involved a considerable amount of groping around in pitch-black darkness with a rapidly failing cigarette lighter. A little of that, as anyone who has tried it can tell you, goes a long way, and eventually I decided to try and make it on my own. Unfortunately, my legs are none too certain even in broad daylight.

There I was, minding my own unhappy business, when I suddenly tripped and plunged headlong into what, for a terrible moment of eternity, seemed a bottomless abyss. Eventually, I revived, and to enter the department of anti-climax, that was all there was to it beyond a broken shoulder and a face that hereafter is going to resemble a some-what clumsy Heidelberg duelist. On the other hand it also served to introduce me again to the American Hospital in Neuilly.

For more than a week, Winsor "picked out" his columns "with one fin-ger" on a typewriter in his hospital room. "I myself feel rather as if I were seeing an extremely dull movie for the second time." One afternoon of his convalescence, he returned to the restaurant in Neuilly where he had spent the summer of 1926 writing novels. Madame Dumas and Louise "were still there, but old women now." Madame Dumas was wearing "a faded green shawl and I noticed the diamond rings . . . were gone. Yet she offered me coffee in the garden . . . and there we sat, dismally trying to recapture yes-terday. It was a mistake. There are certain roads it is foolish to travel over twice and that, for me, was one of them."

When released from the hospital, Winsor needed a haircut, an event that generated his first published interview with an "average" man. "This morning my barber told me that he has needed a pair of shoes for months, but simply has been unable to afford them. It is all he can do to buy food. Last week, for instance, his and his wife's ration coupons permitted them to buy one can of Irish stew! Potatoes are scarce and frightfully expensive. The bread is getting blacker daily and is strictly rationed. Coffee, milk and cream do not exist and such things as strawberries and cherries, although they are in season, are way beyond the workingman's means. The same is true of vegetables." He concluded the item with a political note: "A great many people are turning to communism with a sort of despair—the same way you are apt to rush to a new doctor when the old family retainer appears to have exhausted his bag of tricks."

Winsor decided the warm, sunlit beaches of the French Riviera would help heal his own torn face and broken shoulder, so "at least once every day" for two weeks, he visited a travel bureau to "apply in advance" for accommodations. On each visit he was told, "There is nothing at all." Desperate, he began "talking to a man who knows a man, etc." and bought his ticket on the black market. He wanted a berth or roomette for the overnight trip, but "sleepings, as they are called, are reserved for royalty."

Winsor's black-marketer told him to "arrive at the station an hour in advance" of his departure. "The train is obviously never there and so you stand, nearly dying of fatigue and heat, amid the multitude. Then finally, you rush to find your place and naturally discover it has been sold to at least three other people. By the time the problem has been ironed out, you are on your way, tearing at breakneck speed through the lovely countryside."

Luggage? "It is a very simple matter to check it straight through to your destination, but simplicity and the French are natural enemies and the result is that everyone travels with virtually all of his worldly goods kept, whenever possible, in full sight. Consequently, suitcases, bulging parcels, umbrellas and even small trunks overflow from the baggage racks into the narrow corridor outside the compartments, making it something of a feat to move from one car to another."

To dine, Winsor was forced to negotiate the crowded corridors. "A waiter from the diner goes through, ringing a hand bell and everyone rushes to form in line. The queue stretches miles, lasts for hours and the better part of wisdom is to be among the first. There is no power on earth strong enough to make a Frenchman hurry at meals, and everything, from soup to fruit, is served in courses, usually adding up to at least seven. The long line, meanwhile, sweats it out late into the night."

On returning to his compartment, Winsor prepared to spend the night with four traveling companions.

A gentleman who apparently existed on a diet of garlic; a middle-aged couple who ate peaches, cherries and hard-boiled eggs all the way from Paris to Marseilles, and another individual so passionately addicted to drafts that he insisted on keeping our window, the compartment door and the corridor window open all night. I shivered in a seersucker suit, was bathed in cinders every time we passed through a tunnel, and prayed for liberation. At one point the engine gave up with a sigh and we waited for hours in the quiet darkness for another one to be brought up—which, of course, meant traveling at an even more desperate speed to make up the lost time. We lurched around corners and a hatbox came tumbling down on my head. The man next to me snored endlessly and, at one point or another, a poodle wandered into the compartment and settled down comfortably on my feet. Everything passes, however, and at ten-forty-five the next morning, right on the dot, we pulled into Cannes.

Accompanied by a porter pushing a two-wheeled wooden cart piled with his luggage, the columnist headed "straight to the Carlton Hotel, a room overlooking the sea and a bath that looked more beautiful than anything I ever have seen." Refreshed, he headed for the beach, and a series of columns that would startle *Press* editors and Cleveland readers. "During the Petain government all the men had to wear tops to their suits and any woman lying on the beach with her legs pointing in any direction other than the sea was fined. Now people, relaxed again, are as nearly naked as possible." Men's swimsuits, he noted, were "far from brief . . . merely a suggestion."

As for food shortages, at 7:00 P.M., Winsor joined "the fashionable folk" on "the terraces of the Carlton bar to eat quantities of olives stuffed with anchovy and drink martinis, champagne or a mixture of fresh cranberry juice and champagne, served ice cold." He was shocked when the Duke of Windsor "threaded his way between the tables, coatless, wearing an Hawaiian shirt. The times and customs, my friends, have changed."

After a few days in Cannes, he boarded a bus for Nice. "Holding the accelerator to the floor," the driver careened through the countryside. "Now and then, as in a flash of sudden, midnight lightning, you . . . catch a glimpse of a feathery green olive grove. For the most part, however, it is only a blur seen through the swaying bodies clinging desperately to the seats or hanging onto whatever there is within grasp—an indignant woman dressed to the nines, or a peasant with a breath you could hang your clothes on. Then, at long, long last, Nice."

Winsor did not describe how he eventually reached Monte Carlo, where he booked a hotel room facing the water with its own balcony "designed so that you can sun bathe . . . in the altogether without giving anyone cause to raise an eyebrow." After tanning his cuts and bruises, he pampered his palate: "Melon, a clear soup as only the French can do it, lobster, chicken and so on, right down the line to raspberries in heavy cream." After describing this remarkable meal, he expressed his surprise at uncovering a decadent secret of postwar France: "The papers are filled with news of strikes and shortages at home, bread rationing in England and the general despair throughout the world. But not here."

In the gambling salons of Monte Carlo's casino, Winsor observed, "Women's arms are solid gold from wrist to elbow. Rings are enormous and earrings seem to have vanished entirely. Now they wear absolutely tremendous jeweled clips in their ears, jeweled birds or feathers in their hair. It is not 1946 at all—it is 1929, gone completely mad." During the day, the columnist saw women enter Cartier's to have their gold bracelets assayed, "hoping they will weigh enough to permit them to buy something newer, gaudier and more impressive."

Press editors questioned Winsor's accuracy. "I am in no position to talk about general conditions throughout Europe," he responded. "Millions of people are starving. The problem of the misplaced persons is tragic and all but insoluble. There is no coal to speak of. And such countries as Germany, Poland, Hungary, Austria and others far too numerous to mention have been rendered wastelands. However, the fact remains that I am a reporter, here for the express purpose of surveying the scene. Make no mistake. Life all along the Côte d'Azur is pure luxury, gilt-edged and with everyone trying either to out-dress or under-dress everyone else."

The opulence troubled him. "I reached the conclusion I had better get moving while I still had car fare—not to mention what is known as a sense of proportion. I did find it extremely easy to entertain more than a few lethal thoughts about some of the enameled ladies pub-crawling their jeweled path from one bar to another." Determined not to spend another sleepless night in a crowded compartment, Winsor indulged in the black-market luxuries he had criticized. The columnist informed the hotel porter he "would be packed and ready to leave at such and such an hour, that his was the problem of finding me a berth, mine of paying for it. My French is a disgrace, but that is a language we both understood and within an hour I was fully equipped with all the documents necessary for traveling in comfort on a Pullman. What they cost is a secret that will die with me."

On the station platform, he watched as "crumpled bundles of francs were exchanged through the open windows for plums, apricots and ripe figs. Porters by the dozen shouted horrible invectives at the bewildered people who had just over-tipped them." In the "mild twilight," the train left the station, Winsor went to dinner and eventually retired to his expensive sleeping accommodations, where he discovered "a large portion of my magnificently paneled compartment had been taken over by a young

Frenchman. Waving gloved hands at me (the French, and very sensibly, always travel in gloves), he explained he had given his own place to a lady as far as Marseilles and did I mind? I didn't, and for the next hour I listened to his hysterical hatred of the present government, of the difficulties in getting a decent price for his farm produce, and then finally to the fact he had become so bored by his wife he had decided to take a trip to Paris, visit his tailor and buy some new clothes."

When the men reached Marseilles, they "drank watery beer together in the station buffet" and parted. Winsor decided "to go to bed, still amazed because no one had come along to claim his right to the other berth. In the middle of the night, however, the lights suddenly flashed on and in walked a beardless but otherwise flawless European version of Man Mountain Dean," the 317-pound wrestler Winsor and his ex-wife had entertained in their Cleveland Heights home.

Unlike Winsor, his traveling companion had a restful night: "Grunting and groaning, he climbed up into the upper and immediately fell into a beautiful sleep, punctuated by orchestral snoring. Sleep, under such conditions, was difficult, but I finally managed it and when I awakened the opulent gentleman already was engaged in the process of shaving, a ritual so complicated that when he had completed it we were in Paris. Consequently, unshaven, unwashed and uncombed—in fact all but unbuttoned—I descended from the train. In flight, however, I stopped to pick up a label that had fallen from the man's suitcase. It read, 'Raimu.'" Winsor had spent the night with a famous French film actor (Jules Auguste Muraire).

After checking into his hotel, he hurried to the Men's Bar at the Ritz, where he picked up his mail from Georges and ordered a champagne cocktail. "They float huge, fresh peaches in champagne," a recipe that brought back memories of Rubber Goldberger's speakeasy. Winsor watched patrons "prodding the peaches with forks then swooning over them after they have finished the wine."

His mail contained a letter from Roger Stearns and an invitation from Gilbert Miller, a theatrical producer. Stearns had sent a newspaper clipping listing modestly priced Paris restaurants. "It must have been written by someone in a delirium," Winsor responded. "Last night I had the cheapest dinner I have sat down to since my arrival in France. It cost, without tip, exactly 300 francs and consisted of a small portion of fish, potatoes, a slab of cheese, a cup of absolutely terrifying coffee and a glass of white wine not fit to drink."

Fortunately, Miller's invitation was for dinner. Winsor "went right through the caviar, Dover sole and cold chicken without a qualm." When the bill arrived, Miller had "to put the bite on his wife. Frankly, I wasn't worrying. The man is here to shop for an airplane. I don't imagine the wolf has managed to move into his living room quite yet." Winsor's host was also buying books in Paris, but returning to the United States by plane. The producer complained that postwar shipping was both expensive and unreliable, so Winsor offered to carry his books aboard ship on the voyage home. He also found time to attend *L'Homme a Chapeau Ronde,* a new French film, starring Raimu. Winsor thought the man he shared a room-ette with gave "a really superb performance as a bungling, disenchanted failure who plots some very slick revenge indeed, but can never bring it off and succeeds only in completing his own ruin."

On Bastille Day, the columnist visited "the little bals and dancings" to see the "rapidly-disappearing remnants of the Apaches—feverishly waltzing to broken-down pianos. The men never remove whatever they happen to be wearing on their heads, and inevitably they have the dead stub of a cigarette or cigar stuck in the corners of their mouths. The women, for the most part, look as if they could stay several rounds with Joe Louis. Fights are frequent and contagious. The drink is frightful but obviously compulsory."

Another afternoon, Winsor was invited to call upon the world's "most expensive and sought after interior decorator," Lady Mendl, the former stage actress Elsie de Wolfe and a close friend of Linda Porter's. At an apartment on Avenue d'Idena, "West," Lady Mendl's companion-secretary, greeted Winsor. "She must have a first name, but I have never heard anyone use it." She escorted him to a "huge elaborate corner" of the apartment— a "bathroom," according to Winsor—where the "ancient and diminutive" Lady Mendl received guests. "Although she admits to 76, there are those who tell you the figure is closer to 90." (Actually, she was eighty.) Lady Mendl "keeps her hair a very soft blue, wears it in tight, Grecian curls and always with tiny flowers, both artificial and real."

She spoke English with "a broad, unaffected American accent. Her voice, in excitement, is hard and rasping and she talks almost as much with her hands, usually ending up with a sharp, sudden thrust of her fingers into your ribs."

The "apostle of elegance" offered Winsor a seat on a banquette that ran "around the walls" of the bathroom. Furnishings included "a crystal bar, huge tables groaning under hundreds of perfume bottles, a desk, tele-phones and a sunken tub large enough to keep trained seals in. The tele-phone rings continually." In the space of an hour, he logged calls from Noël Coward and the Prince of Monaco.

Seated on a banquette near the columnist was Mercedes D'Acosta, who Winsor identified as a "playwright and Garbo's great friend." Miss D'Acosta, he wrote, "always wears tailored suits. Her jet black hair is cut short as a man's, she doesn't look unlike the young John Barrymore, and to say that her entrances and exits attract a certain amount of attention is putting it mildly."

According to contemporary biographers, Greta Garbo, the beautiful Swedish film star, famous for wanting "to be alone," and D'Acosta were lovers. Biographers of Lady Mendl claim she was Miss D'Acosta's lesbian "tutor." For thirty years before she married Lord Mendl, Elsie de Wolfe had lived openly with theatrical agent Elizabeth Marbury, whose clients included Elsie and Oscar Wilde. In 1946, however, the significance of those facts was unprintable in a daily newspaper, so Winsor approached the subject obliquely.

He also noted that Miss D'Acosta was negotiating with film director Alexander Korda about "a possible production of her new play—a biblical, extremely simple and moving story of Mary. It is for Garbo, if the great star can be persuaded to return to the cameras." D'Acosta planned to fly to New York to meet with Korda. In Manhattan she also hoped to sell sixty Spanish mantillas she had inherited from her sister. D'Acosta complained that postwar shipping was both expensive and unreliable, so Winsor, the perfect guest, offered to carry her mantillas aboard ship on his voyage home.

The conversation at Lady's Mendl's was so outré it produced two columns for Winsor. He noted how she spent "most of the day" in bed "to preserve her health." Lady Mendl was "so frail she looks as if a mild, spring breeze would blow her into eternity, but she has the energy and determination of a mule." To prove his point, he described how the woman led Winsor on a tour of her apartment "preceded by West, opening and shutting windows."

"Right at the moment her great pride is the baroque dining room . . . with gleaming turbaned Nubians supporting marble tables, the antique mirrored walls and a completely incredible clock she bought from the Rothschild collection that is a gold coach and four. When you wind it the horses gallop across the table." The room that stunned Winsor was Lady Mendl's bedroom. "Her comforter, thank you very much, is a little bagatelle consisting of uncurled, white ostrich feathers. Just how much warmth it gives on a cold, wintry night I wouldn't know—but believe me it adds more than a fabulous touch to a series of rooms that look as if they had been designed at least for Marie Antoinette."

Yet what Winsor envied most was how Lady Mendl negotiated the streets of Paris. "She is driven about in a Rolls. Walking very much tires her. It does me, too, but, not being an international institution, I have to wear my shoe leather thin." The visit with Lady Mendl essentially concluded his reportage on the "average European" recovering from World War II. As he

prepared to depart Paris for Rotterdam, where he would board a ship for
New York City, the columnist who told his editor he hoped "never to have
to go to another nightclub" could not resist comparing Parisian nightspots
with Cleveland's. The French version had "something to offer beyond the
annihilating check at the end of the evening."

About the Casanova, he wrote that

> you lounge in plushy comfort in soft, mysterious candlelight. The
> smooth, stringed orchestra plays the kind of music best described as
> soothing, and the champagne every Parisian club insists you order in
> lieu of a cover charge, will be served to you in solid silver goblets.
> Furthermore if you are the kid who doesn't give a damn about the
> cost, an almost insultingly polite waiter will be charmed to bring you
> large portions of smoked salmon or caviar bedded in ice. Well kids,
> where in Cleveland, O., are you going to find that kind of atmos-
> phere? Or, for that matter, the endless, noisy little swing joints Paris
> has to offer, or the countless sidewalk cafes where you can sit for
> hours over a glass of beer and watch the most fascinating floor show
> in the world. Simply people passing by . . . . One of the things I
> love most about the French is their determination not to do anything
> indoors that can be done out.

Winsor continued, "I may be much too close to the picture to know what
I am talking about, but as far as I am concerned the French recuperation
seems just about complete. Even the bereft and desperate have a certain
flare about them. Instead of selling shoe laces or patented potato peelers,
they carry trays of flowers."

A final column described his hotel room before he left for Rotterdam.
Miller's books filled one corner, and D'Acosta's suitcases full of mantillas
were "everywhere, towering to the ceiling." Then Marlene Dietrich phoned
and asked him to carry one more "very small" package on board. "She
described it in that voice of hers," and Winsor was seduced. He agreed to
carry the item before he saw the package. When it arrived, he insisted the
package was "bigger than I am." (In New York City, he learned the package
carried Miss Dietrich's dirty laundry. She didn't trust Parisian cleaners.)
Together with his own "odds and ends," he left for Rotterdam. "It is all
over, as the saying goes, except for the shouting."

Winsor's 1946 columns quickly became a legend of Cleveland journalism
that found its way into the 1987 edition of *The Encyclopedia of Cleveland
History:* "Sent to Europe to report on the condition of the average European in 1946, he cabled back a series of interviews with such representa-

tives of the downtrodden as Noël Coward, Beatrice Lillie, and Somerset Maugham," a myth that was subsequently enshrined on the plaque commemorating Winsor's posthumous election to the Cleveland Press Club's Journalism Hall of Fame.

Yet Winsor never interviewed anyone in the conventional sense of asking someone a series of questions. He described his social encounters. In 1946, he had none of those with Coward, Lillie, or Maugham. His columns were filled with "brittle comment" and "bright chatter" about postwar Europe. His eye for detail captured images that characterized post–World War II life in London and Paris, including the tasteless spectacle of the idle rich indulging themselves on the Riviera: "With the exception of the celebrated *Times*," all newspapers "are four page tabloids." Shoes are "repaired with metal discs . . . if you close your eyes you have the impression an army of tap dancers is marching by—and at breakneck speed."

Seltzer recognized the value of Winsor's unusual travel reportage. His 1946 trip was the first of his almost yearly junkets to Europe, which established him as one of the most prolific and popular travel writers in an American daily newspaper.

"Blow off a little steam"

Sunday, October 3, 1948, 8:30 p.m.

In the bowels of the Terminal Tower, Winsor watched Harold "Spud" Goldstein, the forty-two-year-old road secretary for the Cleveland Indians, as he waited for the baseball players to appear and board the New York Central overnight train to Boston. In half an hour, the "nine o'clock rattler" was scheduled to depart from Union Terminal. At the invitation of William L. Veeck Jr., the ball club's handsome, thirty-four-year-old owner, Winsor had joined the "small army of camp followers" who traveled to out-of-town games with the team.

"For the first time in history," Spud looked "as if he had something other on his mind beyond peace and composure." Normally, he was "serene" and "unruffled" as he ushered the Indians onto the trains. Tonight's trip, however, was a desperate, last-minute journey that Goldstein had not expected to supervise.

Earlier that morning the road secretary had been sure he would not need to hire a train later in the day. He thought the Indians would spend a champagne-soaked night in Cleveland celebrating their victory in the American League pennant race. Goldstein had two excellent reasons for his assumption: The fifth-place Detroit Tigers and the third-place New York Yankees. At 2:00 P.M. in Cleveland's Municipal Stadium, where "moistened gents," according to Winsor, "gaily paraded the stands in Indian headdresses," Detroit would face a confident team that was leading the American League by a single game over the Boston Red Sox. (In 1948, there were no geographical divisions, hence no division playoffs.)

At the very same hour in Boston, the Red Sox would host the Yankees in Fenway Park. The Indians' fans were counting on the Yankees to humble the Red Sox and on their own team to wallop the Tigers, so that by late afternoon, the Indians would be in first place by two games, the undisputed American League champions for the first time in twenty-eight years.

By 5:00 P.M., Detroit had whipped Cleveland and Boston had pummeled the Yankees. The Indians and the Red Sox each had ninety-eight wins and fifty-eight losses, the first tie for first place in American League history.

Where would the tie be broken? Ten days earlier, Cleveland and Boston had flipped a coin to decide the location. The Red Sox won the toss, so Goldstein phoned the New York Central Railroad, which added two Pullman cars and a second diner to the train to accommodate the team. By the time Winsor had reached Union Terminal, odds for the team beating the Sox in Fenway Park were four to one. The winner would play the Boston Braves, who had clinched their pennant days earlier. The Braves were beginning two days of rest while their future opponent rallied the physical strength and emotional energy for another afternoon of do-or-die innings.

When Winsor finally spotted the Indians, he was standing at the bottom of the stairs that led to the railroad tracks. "The departure following the Sunday catastrophe . . . was hardly festive. Fans crowded the Terminal, autograph books clutched in hand, but as the Tribe descended the staircase they looked to this frayed observer as if they needed something a little more restoring than a 12-hour ride over the New York Central's somewhat unusual roadbed."

Once aboard, "a few of the starving herded into the diner for late sandwiches and coffee." Gordon Cobbledick, the *Plain Dealer*'s forty-nine-year-old sports editor, and his wife, Doris, "settled down to a game of gin rummy." Cobbledick's rival, Franklin A. "Whitey" Lewis, the forty-four-year-old sports editor for the *Press,* who was traveling with his wife, Virginia, began his own game of gin rummy at a separate table. "For the most part," however, "people disappeared behind the swinging curtains, into compartments or drawing rooms," or, in Winsor's case, one of "those solitary torture cells known as roomettes."

In the "few inches of floor space between the sliding door and the descending bed," Winsor tried to "undress without falling into the corridor." He could not brush his teeth after lowering the bed, because "on its tricky descent, the bed automatically locks the wash basin." When he finally climbed between the sheets, he was "roasted and frozen in turn." He endured roomettes because Veeck was one of his heroes.

"Willie came to a slumbering, comatose village with a nearly defunct ball club. He tossed the drab, funereal trappings of the Alva Bradley regime out of the window, installed a wigwam where there had been a funeral parlor, and invited a carnival for dinner." Those raucous evening meals were usually eaten at Gruber's, a new restaurant in suburban Shaker Heights, owned by brothers Max and Roman Gruber, who were assisted by their wives Ruth and Mary Margaret. Shortly after Veeck moved to Cleveland, the Grubers' landlord asked the Indians' owner to help promote his tenants' restaurant. Veeck obliged: "For 100 straight nights, I was always sure to end up at Gruber's and stay until it closed." Midway through the marathon, Ruth Gruber introduced him to Winsor, "a sort of high-class gossip columnist," in Veeck's opinion.

Winsor recalled a "sudden" invitation "to join a dinner with a hilarious little group that included madman Willie Veeck." His close-cropped curly hair had earned him the nickname "Burrhead." Veeck disdained ties. He unbuttoned his sport shirts to provocative depths for the late 1940s, insisting that he, not actress Faye Emerson, introduced the "plunging neckline" to television.

Although Winsor could not "remember anyone's being served dinner" at Gruber's during his first encounter with Veeck. "There was a floorshow of sorts . . . several hours later . . . when the first of a long series of the famous Veeck Follies swung into action at the Alhambra Lounge," Cleveland's classiest "cheat joint," the postwar term for establishments that served beverage alcohol after legal closing hours. The Alhambra was popular with Sunday-night diners at Gruber's. When the restaurant closed at midnight, the Alhambra conveniently opened at 12:01 A.M. the next morning.

Located at East 105th Street and Euclid Avenue, the Alhambra was owned and managed by Alex "Shondor" Birns, a former bootlegger. Prohibition's repeal had forced Birns to change careers. He became a well-publicized gangster, calling himself the Alhambra's "publicity director." Local newspapers labeled him "Public Enemy No. 1." Winsor considered Birns a friend; he found the mobster a generous host, serving drinks "in proper glasses, rather than eye cups." Winsor gave readers directions so they might patronize the hangout: "Simply drive into the E. 105th Market lot, lock the jalopy and then walk through the bowling alley and there you are." If Birns was at the Alhambra on any given night, he often paid the tabs run up by any journalists, lawyers, or off-duty policemen who were on the premises.

When Birns was indicted for bombing a car and killing a competitor in the numbers racket, Veeck was a key defense witness; during the trial, he testified that Birns had been at the Alhambra during the wee hours of a Monday morning when the bombing took place. He was acquitted. Veeck confessed, "I've always found so-called hoodlums to be colorful people." Winsor agreed. He defended Birns to members of his family and took his brother-in-law Char Hickox to the Alhambra and introduced him to the "publicity director" while Hickox was heading the Cuyahoga County Grand Jury. Crooks and crimes were part of any city's nightlife and they made good column items. Winsor wrote: "Six of the toughest" mobsters and "about fifteen bodyguards, took in the opening of *Face the Music*." And

"Julius Lamm of the Uptown Theater is very thankful that the gunmen who drove him all over town after looting the theater . . . neglected to look in his pocket, where all but $5 of his salary was hiding."

In the notorious mobster's "plushy" nightclub, Winsor made his Follies debut. "I was in charge of the slap bass." Ruth Gruber "took over the microphone. She's no Mindy Carson," a twenty-one-year-old popular music singer. Winsor thought Veeck's improvised floorshows demonstrated "the master's touch when it came to dreaming up frolic."

"Smoking nervously," Veeck cast his Follies from a repertory company that included fight promoter Larry Atkins, who had managed the Alhambra Lounge while Birns was in jail; the Cobbledicks of the *Plain Dealer;* Indians' pitching legend Bob Feller and his first wife, Virginia; Indians' farm system director Hank Greenberg and his wife, Carol; Max and Ruth Gruber; knitwear businessman Dick Haber and his wife, Jane; Whitey and Virginia Lewis of the *Press;* broadcaster and record store owner Johnny Lindheim and his wife, Lois; Indians' publicist Marshall Samuel and his wife, Mary Anne; and the *Plain Dealer*'s state house reporter and Sunday columnist Alvin "Bud" Silverman and his wife, Phyllis.

A few of Veeck's performers had limited theatrical experience. Atkins had played pool with Bob Hope, when the comedian was growing up in Cleveland. The forty-four-year-old fight promoter had also been a radio announcer. Whitey Lewis claimed Atkins owned "the worst radio voice ever." Lewis himself had played pool with Hope and Atkins and had also written and published popular songs. The Lindheims were living encyclopedias of Broadway show music. If someone forgot a tune or a lyric, they could hum the melody or recite the words.

During one Follies cast dinner at Gruber's, Winsor recalled that Virginia Lewis looked up from her plate and "remarked in her quiet way, 'Aren't they the jolly ones.'" Her "little five-letter word stuck," and "a small carefree group who refused to let life's darker problems get in the way of fun" became known as the "Jolly Set." (One of the "darker problems" the Jolly Set ignored was Shondor Birns's violent temper, which led him to maim and murder enemies.) The group's raison d'être was the Indians, and Greenberg claimed his colleagues—nine married couples, plus Atkins and Winsor—"lived and ate baseball at the Wigwam and Gruber's on a twenty-four-hour-a-day schedule."

Winsor found himself "stumbling down the Stadium ramps on my bum legs, looking for all the world like a skid-row drunk. I would grab the iron railing in the Stadium's upper deck, cling on for dear life and do my best to understand what was going on. For a while I even attempted scoring, shifting my viewing glasses for reading glasses after each play, but this I

finally had to give up. I learned not only about double plays but also Bob
Feller's unlisted automobile phone number."

For Jolly Set members, who had passed their fortieth birthdays, the
Alhambra Lounge reeked of nostalgia. Remember, they had broken liquor
laws by ordering their first drinks in a speakeasy. Marinated in gin and
tobacco fumes, their amateur floorshows in a former bootlegger's nightclub tasted and smelled like youth. Winsor claimed postwar nightlife had
caused "great despair" among his friends who were saloon keepers. In the
late 1940s, people "seldom ventured beyond their own front doors except to
grab a free meal from the Joneses down the street. Proprietors sat around
their own empty back rooms, dreaming of the days when every block had
its speakeasy and every speakeasy was a gold mine." Veeck gave them a
reprieve.

From April to October, the Indians revived Cleveland's nightlife. "The
strains of gay, brassy music made themselves heard in remote places, people began waking up, to rub their eyes and have a fine time. Restaurants
that used to close annually for the summer began enjoying the novel experience of not only remaining open, but turning the hungry away from their
doors. Special trains began rolling into the city for every conflict, crowding
the hotels to overflowing."

For the 1948 season finale, however, trains were rolling into Boston's
South Street Station. On the October morning of the historic American
League playoff, Winsor awoke in his cramped roomette as the New York
Central rumbled through Massachusetts. He "busted" his "fingernails trying
to return the bed to its closet"; he needed to unlock the washbasin, so he
could make himself presentable before joining the Jolly Set in the diner.

He described the new day with hope: "It was a beautiful, brilliant
autumn morning with the sun smiling over the rusty New England countryside in a manner that seemed full of promise. The same Tribe that had
retired so wearily the evening before filed into the dining car looking like
youngsters getting ready for school. Everyone ate enormous breakfasts."

Winsor's playoff anecdotes featured Jolly Set members. Johnny Lindheim's breakfast consisted of "two soothing brandies, two dozen oysters,
scrambled eggs and bacon, dry toast, a double order of Liederkranz cheese
and six cups of coffee." "Everyone was smiling, even Bob Feller." The dour
pitcher had experienced a slump, but Veeck had remained loyal to him,
even when fans and sportswriters complained he was over the hill.

"Eventually Boston," Winsor wrote, "a metropolis that had gone more
than slightly insane. The lobby of the Kenmore Hotel, where the Indians
make their headquarters, was one solid mass of frustrated humanity crying
for everything from Army cots to those little pasteboards known as ducats."

With items about his new friends, Winsor described a scene sportswriters ignored. Atkins, "wearing a smart, off-white polo coat, decided the only way to clear the foyer was to burst into song. He did and it cleared. The populace was scared to death." Veeck, who was estranged from his wife, could "hardly walk through the foyer without a bath towel to remove the lipstick traces from his handsome pan left by ladies who simply can't resist the impulse."

At Fenway Park the weather was clear, but Winsor's seat, located in the shade behind the third base dugout, was chilly. The Boston Braves attended en masse, gathering intelligence on their opponents. A local newspaper reporter spotted "a flask glinting here and there." Moments before the game began, Lou Boudreau, the Cleveland team's manager and starting shortstop, publicly announced what he had told his teammates a day earlier: Gene Bearden, a six-foot-three, left-handed knuckleballer, with a movie star's profile, would pitch for the Indians. For the first three innings, the twenty-eight-year-old rookie held the Red Sox to a single run. Boudreau had hit a home run in the first inning with no one on base, so when the Indians came to bat at the top of the fourth inning, the score was tied: 1–1. Then third baseman Ken Keltner homered with two men on, and Boston folded. By the ninth inning, the Indians had trounced the Red Sox 8–3.

"After that last delirious out, Bill Veeck made the Indian dugout in one wild leap."

"Wild leap" omitted any mention of the crutches Veeck used.

Anyone who had seen Veeck knew his right leg was a foot shorter than his left one. On Guadalcanal, during World War II, an anti-aircraft gun had recoiled into his leg. The wound became infected, and part of the leg below the knee was amputated in November 1946. When the owner vaulted into the Indians' dugout to congratulate his team, *Press* sportswriter Whitey Lewis said Veeck was "limping as he ran." Winsor didn't mention Veeck's disability, adopting the same policy as reporters who had ignored President Franklin Roosevelt's wheelchair. For Winsor, writing about Veeck's missing limb was taboo. A wife's tears, however, were column fodder.

Sandy Harder was married to Mel Harder, a legendary Cleveland pitcher who once struck out Joe DiMaggio three times in a single game and had recently accepted a coaching job with the Indians. "Sitting a few seats away," Winsor wrote, she had "simply collapsed and then sat on the verge of tears for what must have been but a brief but unbelievable eternity. No one, I think, can blame Sandy Harder for shedding a few tears of relief. Thousands of other people, I imagine were in the same mood. Altogether it was a monumentally appropriate ending to what has been surely one of the most harrowing summers in history."

Male journalists covering the playoff were eventually invited into the visiting team's locker room at Fenway Park. If Winsor attended the news conference, he did not write about what he saw, an omission that raises a question: Was an openly homosexual newspaper reporter welcome in the Indians' locker room? An anecdote about Len Hanna, whose father had played semi-professional ball in Cleveland, and whose enthusiasm for the sport and the Indians was without peer, suggests that he decided not to test his welcome, a decision that would have influenced Winsor.

Charles Schwartz, in a mildly prurient biography of Cole Porter, cites an occasion when Hanna had invited the composer and actor Monty Woolley to attend an Indians' game and had "laid down the law" about how the men were to behave. "Cole and Woolley could be as genial as they wanted" when Hanna introduced them to players on the field, according to Schwartz, "but under no circumstances were they to visit the players' locker room afterwards." Schwartz supposes that Hanna thought his guests "might take a fancy to some members of the Indians team and possibly proposition them." If the anecdote is accurate, it illustrates an odd standard for appropriate behavior. Winsor recalled how Hanna was "pleased as a child when Bill Veeck . . . would take a few players out to Hilo . . . for a swim or tennis." Baseball players were welcome in the locker room at Hanna's pool, but the decision for them to disrobe in the presence of men who found other men physically attractive was left to the athlete, not Hanna or Winsor.

For locker room accounts, *Press* readers relied on Whitey Lewis. According to the sportswriter, Boudreau was about to sit down in front of his locker when Satchel Paige "sauntered past . . . wearing a towel and a grin." Paige was the "ancient" (forty-three-year-old) pitcher Veeck had added to the roster after the season was underway. "Lou turned, whacked Satchel on the bucket and said, 'Satch, you gave us a lot of help. Thanks.'"

Whitey Lewis continued: "As Boudreau was peeling off his heavy outer shirt, Larry Doby sneaked around a post and sidled up to the manager." The twenty-four-year-old centerfielder "stuck out his hand. 'Thanks, Lou, for letting me play. It's been wonderful,' Larry said earnestly."

Lewis singled out Paige and Doby to satisfy his readers' racial curiosity. They were the only black Indians and the only African American players on an American League team. Jackie Robinson had broken the color line in the National League a year earlier, but Veeck doubled the number in 1948.

Earlier, Winsor had noted how fans in Detroit welcomed the spectacle of dark-skinned athletes playing ball with white teammates. "Hundreds upon hundreds" of local Tiger fans celebrated the Indians' racial breakthrough by wearing "brilliant Satch Paige and Larry Doby hats." Winsor did not describe the Tigers' fans or the two Indians with his 1930s lexicon: "black," "brown," "colored," "dark," "Negro," "sepia," or "tan." By 1948, skin color had become a journalistic taboo.

In still another locker room anecdote, Lewis exposed an Indians exhibitionist: Gene Bearden. He "sat on a trunk, wearing a turned up rain hat, period. 'Tired?'" Lewis asked the two-hundred-pound pitcher. "'Naw,' he smiled, 'If you think I'm tired, try following me around at midnight tonight.'"

Boudreau's final words to his players were, "All rules off tonight . . . party at the hotel." By all accounts, the Indians obeyed, proceeding directly to the Kenmore, where they snuck in a side door to avoid a hundred Boston autograph-seekers gathered at the front entrance. Veeck ushered his ecstatic players and their entourage into a "well-guarded" party room. "Roast beef, chicken a-la-king and tiny squabs groaned on the tables and everyone had a fine time although, tragically enough, Satch Paige, grinning under a new gray hat with a handsome snap brim, couldn't be persuaded to work out on his guitar."

If past Veeck parties were prologue, guests would be "acutely dehydrated" Tuesday morning and "wondering what on earth hit them." For readers in Cleveland, Winsor described one of those "moments in life when everyone has to blow off a little steam or else, and the whistles were working on Monday."

Joe Gordon, a five-foot, ten-inch second baseman noted for his humor, and Johnny Berardino, a six-foot utility infielder who had appeared in Our Gang comedies as a child actor, "discovered the piano in the empty ballroom and Joe gave it the full treatment with an accompaniment of some of the finest barber shop quartet harmonizing that has been heard in our century." In the "merry middle" of the victory party, Whitey Lewis admitted that if he had found Bearden, he wouldn't have recognized him. "You couldn't have told the players even with a program." According to Winsor, "no two people were ever able to describe" the event "in similar colors."

True. The color Boston newsmen saw was blood red. "Several of the players became involved in a fight," according to an unsigned article in the *Boston Daily Record*. "Eye-witnesses" claimed "the original participants in the battle were substitute catcher Eric Tipton and first-sacker Eddie Robinson. Joe Gordon stepped in as a peacemaker and had little luck, then was joined by third-baseman Ken Keltner. . . . Only obvious casualty among the celebrating players was Tipton, former football great, who was sporting a scratched face and a badly swollen lip." The *Boston Evening American*'s Bob Ajemian claimed the fisticuffs were the latest sign of "friction in the Cleveland baseball organization, long a hotbed of dissension and unrest." He thought the bad feelings "might be strong enough to hamper the Indians morale."

Winsor cried, Error! "A couple of newspapers in this defeated and disappointed city are bad losers. The *American* and the *Record,* to be blunt about things, both came out yesterday morning with some rather rude cracks about the carnival Veeck . . . tossed for the boys in the Kenmore Hotel. Could be, of course, that they weren't invited and were trying to soothe their own stubbed toes. In any case, they did their best to make it sound like a rout to end them all with a harvest of black eyes."

Actually, the two articles claimed one swollen lip and some scratches, but Winsor was adamant. "Well, a rout it was, and rout it should have been, but I'll pay top prices for any shiners that can be found." Winsor documented "back slapping," "fancy rug cutting in the jitterbug line," and "a lot of necking." In 1948, he defined "necking" as "everyone kissing everyone else's wife."

Over the next several days, his World Series coverage was not about bats, balls, or double plays. For Game 1 he recorded grandstand celebrity athlete fashions: Boxer Joe Louis "arrived an inning late" in a "belted gabardine coat"; Joe DiMaggio "turned up a few minutes later in a double-breasted blue suit." Readers learned elsewhere how the Braves beat the Indians, 1–0.

For Game 2, Winsor explained how Veeck dealt with losing Game 1. "After defeats, Willie Veeck usually retires alone with his sorrows. On Wednesday, however, he was still riding high and after the last frantic inning there was a slight cocktail pouring in his suite." Afterward, "people retired en masse to the Latin Quarter, a huge, gaudy, glittering joint" where many tables were "bordered with Indian fans, including one group who insisted this reporter was Lou Boudreau, no less. So they all have his autograph and I hope I don't go to jail for forgery." Later that day, the Indians beat the Braves, 4–1, to tie the series before they returned to Cleveland.

His coverage of Game 3 described how Veeck entertained baseball writers' wives: "The Hollenden Hotel ballroom was the scene of a twenty-four-hour-a-day floorshow that set a new high for all time in released inhibitions. Every act in town was drafted into service and willingly obliged. The pay was fine, so was the food and drink. Bob Hope showed up, so did Abbott and Costello. Meanwhile the orchestras alternated while the local brass, visiting firemen and inevitable free-loaders washed down mountains of groceries with champagne, sparkling burgundy [Veeck was always a burgundy man], gin, Scotch, whisky, beer and everything else that comes packaged in bottles."

He also told readers about the excitement elsewhere in Cleveland: "The Hollenden . . . wasn't the only madhouse in town. Even the E. Ninth St. honky-tonks drew the carriage trade. Every pub, bar and restaurant in town had its ropes up from sun-up till curfew." Meanwhile, at Municipal Stadium, Gene Bearden faced thirty batters, allowing them only five hits for a 2–0 victory that put the Indians ahead by one game.

After Game 4 Winsor corrected a radio broadcaster: "Will someone please inform [Mel] Allen that Larry Doby hails from Patterson, N. J., NOT Norwalk, O." Before 81,897 fans, a record attendance for a World Series game, Doby hit a four-hundred-foot homer, the decisive run that gave the Indians a 3–1 series lead.

Winsor described how a hapless employee of the Hotel Carter, Johnny Hedenberg, caused the Indians to lose Game 5. The man had "never" seen the Indians win, and "as man and boy, he has sat through better than one hundred contests. You might guess he was in the stands at Lou Boudreau's Sunday afternoon benefit performance for the Braves." Boston massacred Cleveland, 11 to 5. The unlucky Hedenberg forced the Indians to return to Boston, and Winsor to spend another night in a roomette.

Following Game 6, he recorded the train ride back to Cleveland after the Indians beat the Braves 4–3 and won the World Series. "Willie . . . instructed Marsh Samuel and Goldstein to buy up all the champagne and sparkling burgundy available in the Kenmore Hotel." Veeck recalled loading the booze on "the train the way the old time firemen loaded coal." Winsor agreed. "There was quite a lot of it, I might add, and it sparked one of the most spectacular journeys by rail in history." Journalists covering the trip were vague about details. Lewis remembered, "Fizzing and bubbling liquids drowned out the metallic clicking of the wheels."

Winsor wrote, "There was no floorshow, but Johnny Berardino nicely filled the gap with a prolonged impression of Charles Laughton as Captain Bligh of the *Bounty*. As he delivered his lines the grateful audience in the dining car kept shouting, 'Look out! Another wave is on the way!' So there was—another wave of champagne!" In his autobiography, Veeck defined "wave." He had decided to try and "ruffle" Elaine Robinson, the "cool and imperturbable" wife of first baseman Eddie Robinson. Veeck "shook up the half-filled bottle of wine" he held "and just sprayed it gently toward her. Mrs. Robinson turned around, cocked an eye at me, shook up her own full bottle and gave it back to me full blast. From there on into Cleveland, it rained champagne in the diner."

Ironically, the professional journalists censored their own accounts. Their ringleader was more explicit. Veeck remembered asking New York Central's stewards "to find out how much a diner cost because there seemed little doubt that I would have to buy the railroad a new one. We got off cheaply. The railroad was able to fix up the diner as good as new for not much more than $6000." The all-night party ended, according to

Winsor, "with a parade through the sleeping cars, the marchers beating on kitchen pans, waiters' trays and anything else available."

In the morning, there was the official parade in Cleveland, "a grateful, wildly excited city. This one the conquering heroes weren't ready for. Neither were two reporters . . . from the *Detroit Free Press* and the *Chicago Daily News*. Both were eager to catch a train standing in the depot. They never made it. Along with everyone else they were swept up by the cheering multitudes, hurried into cars and paraded up Euclid Avenue. And there ended the notable 1948 series."

But not the Jolly Set: they continued to meet at Gruber's. "It does a restaurant no harm," Veeck maintained, "to have, as a regular clientele, people who get their names in the paper. Some of the biggest restaurants and saloons hired press agents to implant that impression on the public. Almost overnight," the Jolly Set "made Gruber's the best known restaurant in Cleveland and one of the most successful in the country." Winsor was a willing accomplice, because his downtown smoke-and-music beat was sickly. Just weeks before the World Series, he counted only three downtown establishments offering live entertainment: the Alpine Village, Borsellino's, and the Hollenden Hotel's Vogue Room. "The entertainment waters are getting icy," he wrote. "Something is wrong."

In pursuit of fun and column items, Winsor drove to "lush, meticulously manicured" Shaker Heights in his two-seat roadster, a British Alvis with "four, impossible to find, forward speeds." At Gruber's, he was greeted by a car jockey, who parked the car while Winsor entered the restaurant and began a marathon round of table-hopping. His coverage of the Jolly Set's parties raised eyebrows in Cleveland's white Anglo-Saxon Protestant establishment. Most Jolly Set members were Jewish. Greenberg was considered the "first Jewish baseball star." The Habers were prominent members of Oakwood, Cleveland's exclusive Jewish country club. Winsor introduced mainstream Cleveland newspaper readers to the charitable and social life of prominent Jewish Clevelanders, for years the exclusive territory of two local weeklies, the *Jewish Review and Observer* and the *Jewish Independent*. Some of Winsor's gentile readers were appalled. "My old friends began talking about me in whispers or suddenly changing the subject when I came into the room," Winsor wrote. "Since then I seem to have lost track of them, or maybe it is the other way around."

When the Jolly Set partied at Gruber's, the owners pampered its members. Winsor admitted, "I frequently don't see so good at night—but this Max and Ruthie have taken care of." They organized their car jockeys into a "rescue squad" that "learned the intricacies" of Winsor's foreign sports car and drove him to his downtown apartment. On mornings after nights at Gruber's, he woke up "not entirely refreshed," a condition that dulled his literary ambition. Somewhat apologetically, he wrote, "Time was, of course, when like every newspaperman, I had plans for writing That Novel or That Play. But now, I am at last aware, this will never happen. I couldn't possibly spare the time from Gruber's back room; posterity should indeed be very grateful to Max and Ruthie."

Except for Winsor, Veeck, and Atkins, the Jolly Set lived in Cleveland's eastern suburbs, but their "nice, lazy, humdrum pace" bored Winsor and Veeck. They rented apartments in downtown hotels: Veeck at the Hollenden, Winsor at the Carter, a block from the Hanna Theatre. Kellogg Smith remembered the apartment as three adjacent hotel rooms "with two front doors." Elizabeth Luft, one of his colleagues at the *Press,* described the "three tiny rooms" as "jam-packed with his own furniture, some of it priceless antiques." The living room's furnishings included an "early American pine corner cupboard, Florentine chairs," and a modern "brass and glass" bar. "The dominant color in the rooms is green spiked with touches of soft red, mustard yellow and gray." The eclectic mixture of furniture and color palette reflected the taste of Billy Haines, the film actor turned interior decorator who had introduced Winsor to Hollywood in 1934.

He shared his apartment with "Chico, a cockatiel that talks once in a while and Max, a parakeet, that doesn't." Max was a gift from actress Tallulah Bankhead, whose phone number was on Winsor's "regular calling list" for risqué jokes. *Press* television critic Stan Anderson remembered the columnist "rushing to the phone, 'Tallulah,' he will yell, after long-distance contact, 'I must simply tell you about this artist who took a broadie to his apartment. He looked out the window and then rushed frantically to the girl, 'My God,' he said, 'get your clothes off. Here comes my wife.'"

Winsor satisfied his cerebral interests and a passion for collecting first editions at a bookstore half a block from his apartment. Publix, owned and managed by Bob and Anne Levine, catered to "book theorists and collectors" with an inventory of sixty thousand volumes housed on two crowded floors in a building on Huron Road. From the store's front door Winsor could see the Hanna Theatre. (In the 1950s Cleveland's Playhouse Square was still an urbane residential neighborhood.)

He still trekked to Shaker Heights to meet friends at Gruber's. The trips were temporarily interrupted in early 1949, when Cole Porter asked Winsor to visit Linda, who was recuperating in Tucson from chronic lung problems. With Hanna, the columnist traveled to Arizona and entertained the invalid. In May, after Winsor had returned to Cleveland, Joseph Oriel Eaton, seventy-five, died at the family's home in Cleveland Heights. He had been ill for more than a year.

On the *Press* editorial page, Louis Seltzer praised Eaton as one of Cleveland's great industrialists, who helped "put a Cleveland part in every plane and every auto made in this country." In the entertainment section, Winsor apologized. "Frankly, I don't know whether he would like this piece or not. Eulogies he hated and this is not one in any sense. Father had his faults as well as his fine qualities."

Winsor insisted that Eaton had provided "all of the things children should have," like "books by Henty and Alger." George Alfred Henty wrote eighty dull historical accounts of manly soldiers and explorers. Horatio Alger made "strive and succeed" a masculine American credo. A character like Winsor never appeared in either author's "books for boys." Yet Eaton did not shield his sons from unconventional male imagery. He took them to see Vaclav Nijinsky dance *The Specter of the Rose.* Eaton was not homophobic. During the 1930s, he organized the "Racqueteers," an exclusive club for a dozen of his best male business friends who played tennis and cards. He invited Hanna to be a founding member.

In 1949, Winsor wrote of his stepfather, "Now that he is dead it occurs to me that he was a more remarkable man than I perhaps realized." "During the lean years," he wrote, in an anecdote recalled ten years later, "father often made all our toys, working secretly on them for months in the basement." One Christmas, "he made an entire train of wood for one of my brothers, an exact replica of the Lackawanna train we used to take from Montclair to New York as a special treat. My brother Ted, although he was a little dubious about Santa Claus, nonetheless took no chances and had been writing pleading letters for an electric train. I hardly had the courage to look him in the face when he came downstairs to find father's train under the tree. He was up to the situation though. 'This is the best Christmas ever,' he shouted. And it was too, for father, anyway."

The World Champion Indians raised Winsor's spirits when they returned to Municipal Stadium that spring. Cleveland had high expectations for another championship until midsummer, when it became clear the athletes had lost the will to win. Hank Greenberg remembered that as the team fell behind, Veeck "lost interest and rumors that the club was for sale cropped out all over the country."

Without a winning baseball team generating column items, Winsor took to the road. In Saratoga Springs, New York, he described for readers the peculiar environment of the town where he was born. "Vast, wandering houses" exhibited "sudden cupolas like warts on an old woman's face" and "frantic borders of intricate wooden lace" in a confounding landscape. "Scarlet beds of burning cannas" had been "dropped into the middle of lawns without rhyme, reason or design, like blots of wrong-colored ink." Winsor dispelled any notion that his birthplace was inhabited by a classless society. In Saratoga Springs "there is no blending, no crossing of the tracks, or for that matter, even the streets. Each man to his own backyard, please, and no hollering over the back fences or sliding down anyone else's cellar door."

Williamstown was his second stop and included a visit to Buxton Hill, where Linda Porter, after still another long hospital stay, was "relaxing again on her own sun-washed terraces." At night her "bronzed husband" dined "merrily at 8:15 sharp after two glasses of ice cold vodka." Following dinner the composer "drove himself about the country in a new, black Cadillac convertible."

Winsor returned to Cleveland, where the Indians finished in third place, eight games behind the first-place Yankees and seven games behind the Red Sox. According to Greenberg, the rumors of a sale ceased in November 1949, when he and Veeck were in "a bathroom in Chicago. Bill, clad only in a scanty pair of shorts, his left leg draped over the washbasin, was brushing those pearly white teeth. He announced simply that he had sold out to a syndicate headed by Ellis Ryan." The new owner eventually hired Greenberg to be the Indians' general manager.

William Veeck's decision angered many Clevelanders, but not Winsor. "The cold, mean winds of resentment, petty jealousy and harassment have been gathering force in both high and low places," he wrote. "Tempers run short in record time, people are becoming easily petulant and, if you haven't noticed, it is becoming the fashion to kick the conspicuous before they are down." He spent an entire column reminding readers that Veeck had "never lost sight of the little man and, apart from running a ball club, he has found time to help raise money for every conceivable charity that has approached his door."

Veeck's departure from Cleveland did not disband the Jolly Set, which rallied around the Greenbergs. Members persuaded the general manager's wife to give up their New York home. Soon after, "Carol Greenberg sneaked quietly into town, avoided telephones and people, looked at houses and then went quietly back to New York with a new address all but tucked away in her pocket." Bob and Virginia Feller threw a costume ball. Winsor came as a boxer, his plaid woolen bathrobe emblazoned, "Fearless French."

Finally, in November 1949, Winsor found an alternative to publicizing Gruber's: Karamu, the settlement house dedicated to interracial theater. Founders Russell and Rowena Jelliffe had raised $500,000 to build two small theaters at East 89th Street and Quincy Avenue, replacing an auditorium on East 38th Street that had been destroyed by fire in 1939. The single largest donor to the reconstruction fund was Hanna. To provide artistic leadership for the new theaters, the Jelliffes recruited Benno

Frank, a "fat, funny and friendly" German, who had successfully directed chamber dramas in his native Germany. To open the new theaters, Frank organized festival of shows, including Karamu's first musical production, the Cleveland premiere of Gian Carlo Menotti's two-act opera *The Medium,* a historic event in the city's nightlife.

A student of Austrian stage director Max Reinhardt, Frank chose the 233-seat proscenium theater for *The Medium* in a production that reflected his mentor's minimalist and naturalistic style. Instead of a twelve-piece orchestra, Frank used a reduced score for two pianos and hired a thirty-one-year-old Cleveland musician, Frank M. Hruby Jr., to conduct the performances. To portray Madame Flora, the opera's fraudulent spiritualist, he cast Zelma Watson George, an amateur singer who had never acted on the stage. The forty-six-year-old former probation officer was black and weighed three hundred pounds.

Rehearsals began in November. Because her weight caused pain in her knees and ankles, George often used a wheelchair at home. When Frank saw how she whirled about small spaces, he asked her to play Madame Flora in the wheelchair. It would unsettle the audience, he said, and reinforce her characterization.

On the night of December 10, the city's Caucasian musical aristocracy made a rare visit to one of Cleveland's African American neighborhoods. Occupying seats were Cleveland Orchestra music director George Szell and his wife, Helene; legendary violinist Joseph Szigeti, a soloist with the orchestra; director of the Cleveland Institute of Music Beryl Rubinstein and his wife, Elsa; and Marie Simmelink Kraft, the institute's nationally renowned voice teacher. Hanna escorted Congresswoman Frances P. Bolton. Newspapers sent their music and drama critics, society editors, and about-town columnists.

In *The Medium*'s second act, Madame Flora becomes a victim of her own chicanery, imagining that she hears the voices of ghosts. She tries to calm her nerves with whiskey. (Frank had coached his amateur actress, an elegant woman in private life, how to swig rye straight from the bottle.) Madame Flora drinks until she passes out. Meanwhile, Toby, a deaf mute in love with her daughter, whose sweet, silent character had endeared himself to the audience in the first act, reenters Madame Flora's flat and accidentally makes a noise that awakens her. The audience watches as Toby carefully hides behind a curtain. While she tries to discover what made the noise, Madame Flora searches for a gun.

On Karamu's stage, Mrs. George sang hysterically, "Who is it? Who is it? / Speak out or I'll shoot. I'll shoot. I'll shoot."

When she saw the curtain move, the audience watched helplessly as she whirled about in her wheelchair and fired the gun several times at the curtain, killing the "ghost." Over Toby's dead body, Mrs. George asks in a rasping whisper, "Was it you? Was it you?"

Curtain.

The Cleveland critics' reaction?

Omar Ranney, *Press* drama critic: *The Medium* . . . held an audience spell-bound last night. Mrs. Zelma George's singing and playing of the role . . . is positively not to be missed.

Herbert Elwell, *Plain Dealer* music critic: Credit goes to Zelma George for a tour de force. . . . Here was a personation to be remembered for its veracity, and here also was singing of singular power in its broad sweep as well as in its striking parlando effects. [Parlando? Singing as if one is talking.]

Arthur Spaeth, *News* drama critic: Zelma George . . . sings and acts . . . with a skill that is high art, particularly when her craven cheat fancies she's a doomed Frankenstein.

The reviews illustrate three local newspaper taboos: No one mentioned Mrs. George's weight, her wheelchair, or her skin color, although many readers would assume she was black because she was appearing on Karamu's stage. The original schedule of four performances was expanded to satisfy demand for tickets. Early in the run, the Metropolitan Opera's touring company was performing in Cleveland. George remembered that several cast members came to see what Benno Frank was doing at the "little Negro theater." They were stunned. Upon returning to New York, several urged Menotti to see Karamu's production.

For the composer, reviving *The Medium* was problematic. The original Broadway show was only three years old and had run for more than two hundred performances. Marie Powers, a forty-year-old contralto, had created a Madame Flora that New York critics called "magnificent" and "definitive." Could anyone surpass her performance? Plus, Menotti already had another opera, *The Consul,* running in New York City. Could Menotti operas fill two theaters during the same season?

Still, the composer scheduled three trips to Cleveland and cancelled each of them. Meanwhile, *The Medium* filled Karamu's theater sixty-seven times. Two days before the show was to close, Menotti sent his personal assistant, Bill Butler, and a representative of his music publisher, Schirmer's, to Cleveland. Both told the composer to audition Zelma George. He invited her to New York City and arranged for her to sing in a new theater-in-the-round that had been constructed at the Edison Hotel. It would have been convenient for her to stay at the Edison, but she booked a room at the Hotel Theresa in Harlem because she did not know which downtown hotels accepted blacks.

Butler had not been entirely candid with Menotti about her. When the composer entered the Edison Hotel ballroom, he knew the color of her skin but was shocked to find her scooting about the tiny stage in a wheelchair. "My God," Menotti whispered to his assistant, "you didn't tell me she was crippled." In *The Medium,* Toby is terrified of Madame Flora, but Menotti thought an audience would not believe the young man was afraid of a woman in a wheelchair. At the audition, however, he said nothing about his fears. After hearing her, the composer changed his mind. "Broadway has to see this. It's not what we did at all," referring to the production with Powers. "It's a completely different Madame Flora. I didn't see this in my own play."

Menotti's producers financed a two-piano revival for the Arena Stage, which was directly across West 47th Street from the Ethel Barrymore, where Powers was appearing in *The Consul.* For the run of the show, George did move into one of the Edison's thousand rooms, each of which had "bath, shower, radio and circulating ice water." Her debut was scheduled for July 19.

Throughout his career, Winsor used his column to promote talent, especially singers. Zelma George was not the first African American artist he had assisted. In the 1930s, he and his ex-wife had helped local black entertainers secure performances in New York City and Europe. Yet George received special treatment. Winsor understood that an unknown, large black woman in a wheelchair might be ignored or even ridiculed by New York newspapers. Publicity agents who had succeeded in placing items about their clients in Winsor's column suddenly began receiving his calls from Cleveland. He collected chits on her behalf. A week before her opening, he boasted to his readers that her "first publicity releases will hit the Sunday Manhattan papers. Now all Mrs. George has to do is allow lightning to strike."

She was more concerned about how to get on and off the Arena's stage without injuring herself. In Cleveland, Frank had staged *The Medium* behind a proscenium opening with a traditional curtain. At the Arena, the stage was a fifteen-foot-square platform, surrounded on all four sides by banks of chairs. Winsor reported that she was having problems maneuvering her wheelchair on the dark narrow ramps that lead "at terrifying angles to the small, necessarily cluttered stage." The staging was unusual even for Broadway. The *New York Times* music critic believed *The Medium* marked "perhaps the first time in New York history that an opera has been presented under such circumstances."

Winsor kept local readers informed of George's progress. She "was just a little floored when Gian Carlo Menotti, who is directing the production, calmly told her, 'In the history of my directing, I have not given to any artist the freedom I am giving you. I have great confidence and admiration for your acting ability and your good judgment, and except for a casual suggestion here and there, you are on your own.'"

Unable to leave Cleveland, Winsor phoned her on opening night. She had dislocated a shoulder during the dress rehearsal but was pleased with news photographs Winsor had helped arrange. Following his call, flowers began arriving from well-wishers, including a "single bud vase with one very long red rose" from her husband, Claybourne George, president of the Cleveland Civil Service Commission. He had instructed the florist "to see that I get one fresh red rose every day I am here. He is a really sweet guy," she wrote Winsor, "and I love him all the more for that." Before she was called to the stage, Bill Butler, who served as the production coordinator, gave her "a tiny heart pendant set with rubies to wear always as a luck piece." It was underneath her costume as she rolled down the steep ramps to the Arena's darkened stage.

The New York City critics' reactions?

New York Times: Zelma George . . . pulled out so many histrionic stops that not only she, but the stage jangled.

New York Post: Only a superhuman person can sing the score. Marie Powers managed it magnificently in the original production. Zelma George contributes animal ferocity.

Daily Mirror: Zelma George . . . must weigh at least 270 pounds. . . . She plays much of the two acts in a wheelchair. Her performance had the impact and inevitability of Greek tragedy.

Daily News: "Sung and acted by an immense, unusual woman named Zelma George, [she] skates around in a wheel chair so expertly that you can't be sure whether it's a prop or a necessity.

Journal American: Zelma George . . . séances in a wheelchair.

Unlike Cleveland critics, New York City's reviewers felt free to mention the singer's weight and her wheelchair. With one possible exception ("animal ferocity"), they did observe the taboo about noting the woman's race. Newspaper editors' standards for what readers should know about the subject of a news story in a metropolitan daily newspaper and what language was appropriate to describe those facts differed from one city to the next; this dictionary was constantly revised during the period Winsor was a columnist.

Although her original contract was for four weeks, George sang 110 performances throughout the summer and fall. "We could have gone longer," she recalled, "except the theater had been rented out for another production."

While Winsor's most successful protégé thrilled Manhattan, he was enduring Cleveland: "The nocturnal traffic, so to speak, is on the erratic side." At the same time, North Korea's invasion of South Korea had frightened many Clevelanders and provoked an "artificial buying panic. Coffee is stacking up in cowardly kitchens, some grocery stores have found it necessary to limit their customers to 25 lbs. of sugar and an outlying supermarket ran out of soap during the weekend. The hysterical might much better buy a few more government bonds."

He was unimpressed with federal plans to calm the nation's nerves. "In the event of an atomic attack on the United States only three voices would be heard on the air. These would be Bishop Fulton Sheen, Edward Murrow and Arthur Godfrey." All three reflected the growing influence of a new medium that was eroding the power of newspapers to shape opinion. The men were television personalities. Sheen, fifty-nine, hosted a thirty-minute show that promoted the Roman Catholic Church; Murrow, forty-six, was a respected journalist who emceed televised news shows; Godfrey, fifty-one, hosted *Arthur Godfrey's Talent Scouts* and boasted of discovering Pat Boone and Julius La Rosa, two singers who did not meet Winsor's vocal standards. "Well, pardon me," Winsor wrote, "but when my last hours arrive, or perhaps my last split seconds, I don't want to listen to any chatter from Godfrey."

Instead, Winsor urged the fearful to spend money on "pleasure." He did not recommend nightclub entertainment. With World War II levies still on the books, patrons faced "hideous" taxes on their bill that "add up to a mere 26 percent." His preference was foreign travel. "What with the Korean situation, steamship sailings are no longer at a premium. The cancellations, in fact, are staggering and you only have to pick your date, ship and destination and then travel in comfort."

Still another depressing development was the increasing number of obituaries Winsor found himself writing. "One of the last times I saw Lady Mendl (Elsie de Wolfe) was in Paris, shortly after the war and she was already a very, very old if elegant lady, largely dependent upon a wheel chair. 'Never complain, never explain' was the motto she had embroidered everywhere. She never did, either, and she lived a rich full life."

One of the most insightful obituaries Winsor wrote in 1950 concerned Christopher "Topper" Reynolds, the seventeen-year-old son of Libby Holman, who died with a companion while climbing Mount Whitney, in an accident attributed to the young men's lack of experience and training that led them to attempt the ascent in tennis shoes. In his biography of

Holman, Jon Bradshaw at length quoted Winsor, who attempted to explain why Topper, whom he had known since birth, "would want to scale dangerous, snow-clad peaks." He wrote,

> Few youngsters had such sheltered lives. Threatened by kidnappers from the instant of his birth, he was protected twenty-four hours a day by bodyguards who were later replaced by tutors—all in an enormous, remote house in Connecticut that was fortified with burglar alarms. . . . Burglar alarms and bodyguards breed their own particular dreams. Topper's was a soaring character and like the suddenly un-caged eagle, once free, he had to climb a little higher and a little more recklessly than anyone else ever had. He had his mother's utter disregard and contempt for risks of any sort and he deserved something far, far better that such a tragic, wasted ending.

Rather than attempt his own analysis of why the young men had tried the ascent of Mount Whitney without proper clothing and equipment, Bradshaw passed the task to Winsor, quoting the piece he had found in Holman's papers at Boston College. Bradshaw's introduction of the excerpt, which begins, "In his daily column in the New York *Herald Tribune,* Libby's old friend Winsor French," is perhaps the most outrageous example of how Winsor's legitimate journalistic legacy has been carelessly garbled.

In December, as his forty-fifth birthday and the winter holidays approached, Winsor's mood improved. Jerry Zerbe had returned to his hometown on a photographic assignment for *Town and Country* magazine, where he was now society editor. Winsor reflected, "The demand to entertain him is such that if he accepts half the invitations that have been called through the Carter Hotel's switchboard, he will have to leave town on a stretcher."

Winsor generated bookings for his landlord. According to Bea Vincent, who could overhear his conversations from her desk at the *Press,* celebrities frequently phoned him asking where to stay. As in Zerbe's case, he made their reservations. The photographer's visit reminded him how newspaper and magazine publicity had become socially acceptable in the 1940s and '50s. When the photographer was *PARADE*'s art editor and "experimenting with one of the first candid cameras, hostesses used to shudder with apprehension whenever he parked his red Buick in front of their house. Ladies, in those days, gave second thought before allowing themselves to be photographed bending their elbows. In this enlightened era the Zerbe problem is how to separate the wheat from the chaff, as the saying goes. Publicity, it has become abundantly clear, is something that people want these days whether they can use it or not."

During the holiday season, one friend of Winsor's could use all the publicity he could generate. The man was rumored to be considering the lead
in a revival of *The Man Who Came to Dinner* scheduled to open at the
Hanna Theatre on Christmas night. When he finally accepted the offer,
Winsor announced the second coming. "Veeck is back and the Hanna has
him! So does the Carter Hotel." Since selling the Indians, Veeck had remar-
ried. He and his new wife, Mary Frances, were "roughing it in the Honeymoon Suite, several floors below Katharine Cornell, who, as Willie puts it,
is also of the 'theatah.'"

Plugging the Hanna was the least Winsor could do. Milton Krantz, the
theater's manager, who financed the production, told Cleveland historian
John Vacha it was Winsor's idea to cast Veeck as the curmudgeonly drama
critic, a fact that raises suspicions about Winsor's coverage. At the first
rehearsal, he claimed that Veeck surprised his fellow cast members. He
was "letter perfect in one of the longest roles on record." Winsor blatantly
promoted ticket sales. "It looks as if we're in for quite a dinner party and
Milton Krantz of the Hanna would like it known there still are some place
cards left for all performances. If you want to send someone to *The Man
Who Came to Dinner* the Hanna has gift certificates."

In advance of opening night, some newspaper critics were openly skeptical about Veeck's theatrical credentials. Winsor defended his friend with
an item about rehearsals. "I wandered around to the Hanna Theater the
other afternoon, rudely inched my way through the doors and did a brief
Peeping Tom act on *The Man Who Came to Dinner* rehearsing. Brief because
I had to leave the premises before hysteria set in. Willie, if the critics will
permit me a somewhat premature plug, turns out to be quite an actor and
anyone lurking around who thinks a slap-happy clambake is going to be
unveiled Christmas night is in for the shock of his life."

Between rehearsals, the former Indians' owner was still the generous
host: "*The Man Who Came to Dinner* gave one himself for his entire company—a gay, festive flag-raising starting off demurely enough at about 6 in
the evening. Somewhere along the line there was a brief recess for rehearsal
and then action was resumed until the roaring finished about 5 A.M." Winsor saw director Ray Boyles and his wife "carrying home highly-decorated
turkeys and hams in Carter Hotel pillow slips. The slips, it is to be presumed,
were returned."

On Christmas night, the mercury in outdoor thermometers stood at
twenty degrees. Veeck's notices were a degree or two warmer.

Arthur Spaeth, the *News* drama critic, wrote: "At no time . . . did he
come even close to that magic that would make you forget the celebrity
Veeck for the touring genius who turns a small town Ohio household into
a madhouse. It's Bill Veeck who came to dinner."

Omar Ranney, the *Press* drama critic, wasn't much happier, finding Veeck "hardly the sneering fellow Moss Hart and George Kaufman apparently intended. A few liberties have been taken with the script. . . . Lines about Lou Boudreau . . . Max Gruber and Hank Greenberg are all kind of clubby and fun when you're performing in the intimate company of your friends, but it didn't seem to me that the horsing around accomplished much in the way of theater."

The mercury had shrunk to fifteen degrees by the time the audience left the Hanna.

The icy reviews angered Winsor. Stan Anderson, *Press* radio and television critic, explained his colleague's motivation: "Fierce loyalty, genuine in every respect." Winsor hadn't changed since 1938, when Polly Parsons wrote that he had "one outstanding characteristic beyond his sophistication. It's his loyalty to friends—upon whom he bestows the divine right of kings. They can do no wrong."

In Winsor's "unprejudiced" opinion, Veeck was "soft spoken, a stranger to profanity and character assassination. It is probably difficult for people to accept him as the glibly venomous Sheridan Whiteside in *The Man Who Came to Dinner*." The columnist reminded readers that two more of his friends who had played the lead—Monty Woolley and Clifton Webb—were "all famous in their private lives for sarcasm and scathing rebuttal. They had merely to project their own personalities into the role." Veeck had to "rely on an art described as acting. Well, Willie is a born actor and once his astonished friends have relinquished their seats to the general public, it is my opinion that the public is going to have the time of its life. The essential adlibbing . . . gives the play a lift. As always, when *The Man Who Came to Dinner* travels, local names are transplanted to replace Manhattan celebrities that would hardly reduce Ohio audiences to hysterics. This week Lou Boudreau, Hank Greenberg, Larry Atkins, have the darts thrown at them and the audience is gratefully appreciative."

Winsor had no need to defend Roger Stearns, who had played a supporting role. He got good reviews: "Roger Stearns brightens the scene briefly in a Noël Coward turn." At every performance, the pianist played and sang "What Am I to Do?" Cole Porter wrote the ballad for *The Man Who Came to Dinner*, and it captured what the Jolly Set and many Clevelanders felt at Veeck's departure.

What am I to do
Toward ending this madness,
This sadness
That's rending me through?

"Squawks from unexpected places"

CLEVELAND, OHIO

Friday, January 9, 1953, 5 p.m.

In the polished mahogany lobby of the grand dame of Cleveland hotels, the seventy-year-old Hollenden, a short flight of stairs under crystal chandeliers led to the 2-1-6 Club, a "dimly lit haven" expressly created by Hanna for Winsor's friend and frequent companion Roger Stearns. The pianist arrived promptly at 5:00 P.M., "a flower in his button hole," and began playing for a troupe of "regulars" who sipped a "few martinis" while they waited for nightfall, when "life begins to hum a little." One of those regulars was Kellogg Smith, Winsor's colleague at the *Press*, who remembered Stearns as "a charming fellow and a brilliant professional piano player."

Over eighteen years, Stearns had periodically played Cleveland hotel bars, where he had flattered countless customers with personal "umbilical chords." In 1950, when Stearns finally closed the 1-2-3 Club in Manhattan, he once again accepted bookings in hotel lounges. Hanna, however, had another idea. He and Winsor thought downtown Cleveland needed a sophisticated bistro. If Stearns would move to Cleveland, Hanna would build a new club in the Hollenden. Stearns quickly accepted Hanna's financial help; Winsor publicized every step of his friend's new venture. "Roger Stearns . . . drove here from Manhattan last week and since then has been relaxing beside Mentor swimming pools." Winsor was protecting Hanna's privacy: Stearns was a houseguest at Hilo, Hanna's estate in Mentor, which included a spectacular outdoor pool.

Meanwhile, the Hollenden's management was, according to Winsor,

> struggling with painters, cleaners and decorators—all in a frantic effort to dress up a room for the man. So now the dressing has nearly been accomplished and any day Roger will set up shop in the former Artists and Writers Club, the first time those rooms have been opened to the general public in years and years. Long, long ago, when mar-

tinis were only a quarter, [and] when a buck fifty bought a dinner . . .
it used to be quite a place. Full bottles of Scotch and soda siphons
on every table, if Scotch was your drink. It will be interesting to see
what the Stearns personality and his following do to the room now.

The afternoon before Stearns opened, the hotel encountered a hitch. "If
Columbus listens to reason and the Hollenden's requested liquor permit
comes through, Roger Stearns will open in the old Artists and Writers Club
rooms tonight. And when he does the former Sin Room will be retagged
Canasta Corners, with four tables perpetually set up for the addicts." Canasta
is a card game requiring two full decks including jokers; Clevelanders preferred it over gin rummy when they were sipping cocktails.

The permit arrived, and Stearns performed, but Winsor was angry with
the hotel's management. Stearns had "opened cold," without any "advance
publicity" and "no ads." The Hollenden wasn't run by numbskulls. Its management understood the value of publicity, but they didn't need to spend
money to promote Stearns. They knew Winsor, Cleveland's most influential columnist, would help pack the club with item after item about his
friend. The most shameless was a column he wrote while in Paris. It began,
"Dear Roger Stearns: Your 2-1-6 Club, I hear from arriving Americans, is
going great guns."

Jolly Set members and countless wannabes took Winsor's advice and
made the new lounge their early evening headquarters, waiting for "downtown traffic to thin" before they drove to their homes in the suburbs. The
2-1-6 Club courted obsolescence by employing a hatcheck girl, although few
men wore hats in 1953. A young woman named Cele sat in a closet at the
club's front door and, because she seldom saw a hat, spent her time "working
crossword puzzles." Two bartenders traded shifts—Jim and Johnny—and
the waiter was Tommy. Winsor described him as having a "Mae West walk."

Winsor was a regular, but he did not use downtown traffic as an excuse
for lingering over cocktails. At the invitation of the Hollenden Hotel's managers, he had abandoned his suite at the Hotel Carter and moved a few
blocks north and west to the twelve-story, thirty-five-year-old addition,
which occupied half a block on East 6th Street, between Superior and
Vincent Avenues. Smith remembered that the hotel wanted the cachet of
Winsor's name as a permanent resident and that he exploited the commercial value of his celebrity.

Money was not Winsor's sole motivation for accepting the Hollenden's
generosity. His "unreliable" legs had not improved, and now he was closer
to the *Press* offices. Smith recalled that Winsor "gave small dinners" in
his apartment, but "mainly he was entertained by people all over town."

Many of those evenings began in the 2-1-6 Club. The columnist was easily recognized. "He was a tiny man," Smith recalled, "and he smoked and drank ferociously. He had some trouble seeing, though he wore glasses full time." He was always dressed in "a jacket and necktie, except at work. His wardrobe was enormous but nothing ever matched. In his eccentric way, he dressed well but was not elegant."

Two or three nights a week, Winsor would leave the Hollenden to visit what was left of his smoke-and-music beat. By 1953, Cleveland's commercial nightlife couldn't generate enough items to fill his columns, so on Saturdays he began writing about Cleveland's bygone golden age. During an icy January, he gave readers a ten-part series about warm summer evenings at Euclid Beach, an amusement park on Lake Erie's shore owned by the teetotaling Humphrey brothers, Dudley, Harlow, and David. When the brothers purchased the park in 1901, they forbade beverage alcohol on the grounds. "Anyone found to have been drinking was thrown out." Sensing a business opportunity, a "wet" opened a saloon "directly across the street. Men would leave their families at the gates, go across the street and stagger back to the park and become generally obnoxious. Clearly something had to be done. The brothers solved [the problem] by installing a large, roving light at the park entrance, which could be played on the saloon's swinging doors. Guards then could watch patrons coming and going and prevent them from entering the grounds. The saloon went out of business in record time."

The item is Winsor's only published defense of a ban on alcohol, although his favorite Prohibition personalities were constantly reappearing in his columns. When Phil Selznick, the former owner of the Club Madrid, visited Cleveland, Winsor noted he was "balding and a little heavier" but reminded readers that he had "pulled himself up into the Cadillac brackets" by booking the finest entertainers and serving illegal hooch in his popular nightclub. Now he was "selling plastics on the West Coast" and "somehow, it seems a shame."

When a "small, unassuming and blind" piano player named Alex Kallao played the Theatrical Grill, Winsor was reminded of "Tatum and perhaps Rose Murphy," the stars of Cedar Avenue's "dark purlieus" in the early 1930s. When Cleveland Indians' first baseman Luke Easter, "a huge amiable hunk of man," opened a restaurant in the Majestic Hotel, called the Rose Room, Winsor compared him to the African American nightclub owners of the 1930s, when "Mammy Louise Brooks managed the Heat Wave" in the same space. When he visited Johnny Alpino's Club Venice, a few blocks south at Carnegie and East 100th Street, he complimented the chef: "You haven't tasted such spareribs since the days when Mammy Louise Brooks was doing the cooking at the old Turf Club."

In Cleveland's black neighborhoods, Quincy and Scovill were Winsor's "favorite avenues" on summer afternoons. "Radios blare perpetually from every open window, truckloads of sun-ripened watermelons line the curbs, and gents with apparently endless lung power go lazily along with pushcarts, crying out the wonders of soft-shell crabs and crisp, golden skins. Dusty neons waiting for darkness advertise everything from beauty shops to gin joints and street-corner evangelists plead for attention in their shadows. Altogether it's probably the most vibrant and colorful section in town." In the 1930s, he often spent the wee hours in the same neighborhood; now he "would hardly recommend it after nightfall."

During the 1950s, Winsor actually found very little to recommend. "The after dark situation is . . . pretty grim." During those years, local radio personality Bill Randle remembered him as the "original and creative delineator and arbiter of 'who was who' and 'what was what.' He had power that people dream of having. Real power." Winsor's ability to generate a crowd intrigued Irving Hexter, who was chairing the Cleveland Area Heart Society's board of trustees. He wondered if the power of Winsor and his newspaper could be harnessed to raise money. The Heart Society needed funds to train three hundred surgeons, surgical residents, and anesthetists in a new emergency resuscitation technique: quickly opening a patient's chest and massaging the heart. In several cases, patients whose hearts had stopped beating for two, three, or even five minutes had been revived.

Hexter asked Winsor to consider leading a fund-raising event for the society. The columnist proposed a "Heart Dinner" at Gruber's, and the event was "successful beyond the wildest dreams of all of us," Hexter recalled. "No one but Winsor French could have put across the first Heart Dinner." Based on the event's success, Winsor concluded that charity benefits might help resuscitate the city's commercial nightlife. The following year, he helped organize another dinner at Gruber's, this time to raise funds for a non-profit cancer research laboratory, the Jackson Laboratory in Bar Harbor, Maine, run by Dr. Clarence Little, the father of Cleveland architect Robert A. Little, one of Winsor's friends. "One carefree evening between Martinis," Winsor remembered, Max Gruber suggested that Jolly Set members write a book about themselves. "Old Krauthead, as his adoring wife frequently and tenderly refers to him," would pay publication costs. Any proceeds from sales of the book would go to the Jackson Laboratory. The result was that the Jolly Set took a *Curtain Call* in a book of the same title. "Wistful ghosts of a pretty era," Winsor wrote. "As characters go, they may not quite eclipse Damon Runyon's incredible children, but . . . it's a pleasure to see them again, if only for one last, brief flight."

Although the book listed Winsor and Franklin Lewis as its editors, Winsor insisted that his friend Kellogg Smith had "clipped the dangling participles, corrected the split infinitives, added spice when it was needed and rudely reminded dilatory contributors of deadlines." He praised Smith's temperament. "It was a thankless, exhausting job that burned up lots of time and effort," but his colleague "made it all seem a pleasure."

Less than a month after *Curtain Call*'s successful publication, Irving Hexter, Bernard Towell, Roger Stearns, Marshall Samuel, and Winsor were in the 2-1-6 Club counting the large number of worthy Cleveland organizations that were holding annual fund-raising campaigns. Cleveland was not unique. "Some cities in the country," Winsor learned, "have as many as 120 drives a year!" The men wondered if Cleveland could avoid competitive solicitations with "one bang-up project that would support the deserving groups not included in the Red Feather [a predecessor to the United Way] family." Based on the men's previous successes, could they design an event that would grow "over the years . . . into a gigantic gala that would support all the smaller agencies, medical drives and so on"?

What sort of an event would draw thousands of donors? Winsor pushed for a carnival. Where? "Short Vincent," a three-block stretch between East 6th and East 9th Streets that was twice as wide as an alley and lay directly below the windows of Winsor's apartment at the Hollenden Hotel. He claimed Short Vincent was "the only corner in Cleveland that never goes to bed. The bars close every now and then, to be sure, and every now and again things slow down to a lull after the musicians and entertainers have packed up and gone home, but it's never a lonely place for long." About five in the morning, trash collectors entered the street to empty refuse cans lining the sidewalk. "Quite a clatter," he wrote, and "hardly conducive to late sleeping. It's a friendly noise, though, and one you hear the year around on the side streets of Paris. As the little avenue reawakes someone is usually washing down the walk in front of the Tasty Barbecue."

Next door to the restaurant was Frank Ciccia's barbershop, where Winsor got his hair cut and Anne Slavko manicured his nails. "The clearing house for the street's gossip," the shop was frequented by the self-appointed Council of Short Vincent, whose roster included three bookies: "Shoes" Rosen, "Honest Yockum," and "Hymie" Mintz. The latter once ran for the state legislature. When Winsor asked him where he stood on the Taft-Hartley Bill, then before Congress, Mintz replied, "We've paid that."

Then came Kornman's Back Room, where Winsor was a regular at the bar, tended by "pint-sized" Carl Barbitta. The restaurant's owner was Winsor's former bootlegger Billy Weinberger. Behind the bar, *Press* artist Bill Roberts had painted a mural immortalizing Short Vincent in "blazing, uninhibited color, alive with more than several photographic likenesses of its celebrated characters and countless of its prototypes." For Winsor, Kornman's had "all the inducements for a general letting down of the back hair and once it falls, Mone is the perfect accompanist." He was referring to pianist Dick Mone: "Flamboyance and gymnastics he lacks entirely, taste he has in abundance, not to mention an almost inexhaustible library that comes in very handy when people start asking to hear ballads from the long ago."

Two of Kornman's regulars were women who drank without male escorts; Winsor admired this unconventional female behavior. Pat Riley, "the statuesque model for tall, tall girls, who always is dressed as if she had stepped from the pages of Vogue," perched on a barstool. Burleigh Reiff, eighty-two, a former vaudeville star, always chose a table for "a fast toddy before going to bed around midnight. Her perpetual, running conversation sounds like all the old, bound volumes of *Theatre* magazine." Reiff had run a drama school in the Hippodrome building. Her "favorite pupil" was comedian Joe Bova, and she had booked Bob Hope on club dates. Friends frequently reminded her of what an exciting life she had led. "'So I have,' Burl would reply softly, 'but I haven't had enough.'"

Beyond Kornman's was the Theatrical Grill, run by Morris "Mushy" Wexler, who was laundering his substantial gambling income by purchasing real estate on the Strip in Las Vegas. In 1951, the Senate Special Committee to Investigate Organized Crime in Interstate Commerce held hearings in Cleveland. Chaired by Senator Estes Kefauver, the committee took testimony on local gambling operations. Wexler was described as a "tough boy" once involved in local newspaper circulation and taxicab wars. He had "evaded the service of a subpoena," according to a committee report, so he could not be questioned about his ownership of the Empire News Service. "Although there is an attempted façade of respectability, the Empire News Service is primarily engaged in the distribution of gambling information to bookmakers." The Theatrical Grill was literally Wexler's "façade of respectability." Directly across the street, burlesque was making its last stand at the Roxy Theater. In the 1950s, Short Vincent was a haven for the eccentrics Winsor had once found in Cleveland's Lakeside Flats.

Assisted by the 2-1-6 Club's ice-cold gin with a trace of vermouth, Winsor finally convinced his socially prominent friends to join his colorful, tolerant, and disreputable community. Short Vincent was chosen as the site for a street fair called "Fun for Funds." When committee members began asking charities to abandon their own drives for a new joint effort, they heard "squawks from unexpected places."

Trustees on several boards "were horrified at the mere mention of Short Vincent." Ex-bootleggers, unescorted women, "dancers" who bumped and ground in G-strings, to say nothing of Mushy, were too vulgar for their high-minded enterprises. The Lions Club publicly objected to the location and expressed its opposition to sharing a fund-raising event. For years Lions had successfully raised money to prevent blindness. They fought giving up their own campaign. When Marshall Samuel subsequently asked city officials for permission to close Short Vincent for the night of the event, "Fire Chief Elmer Cain wondered if a fire hazard wasn't in the picture." City Council members pestered organizers with questions. Committee members drank more gin.

Over several weeks they recruited local chapters of national groups fighting cancer, cerebral palsy, diabetes, heart disease, muscular dystrophy, multiple sclerosis, and nephritis. Their involvement convinced several Jewish and Catholic hospitals to participate, the latter joining the Maternal Health Association, which advocated Planned Parenthood! As the list grew, arts organizations from the Play House to the Cleveland Heights High School Choir asked if they could benefit from the carnival. The committee accepted all worthy causes. Finally, the Lions growled approval.

When the number of participants neared fifty, the committee held a mass meeting at the Hollenden to announce the date: Monday, June 8. Winsor reported details: "The tickets . . . will be five bucks per person and every last cent will go to the charity designated on the stub by the purchaser. And may I also add that everyone working on the street that evening will have laid five dollars on the line for the privilege. No free riders on this show, and it's going to be quite a show!"

The City of Cleveland not only agreed to close Short Vincent but promised to paint the asphalt in "red and white candy stripes" for a gaudy midway, complete with sideshows reminiscent of the Great Lakes Exposition. *Plain Dealer* columnist George Condon reported the installation of "a tall flagpole," a "roosting place for Richard Tuma, a bartender at Mickey's," another saloon on Short Vincent. "Tuma climbed the pole, and, for a month, remained on his perch to promote the Fair." (Flagpole sitters had been fixtures of the Great Depression.)

Ellis Folph, cohost of the Jolly Set's catered dinner aboard a freight train to Ashtabula, solicited prizes for a drawing—including a round-trip flight to Europe aboard a KLM plane. The Hollenden agreed to open its roof for a nightclub with a continuous floorshow. "Almost every pianist in town will rotate through the Pent House Piano Club." Fun for Funds would not publish a souvenir book like *Curtain Call*. Instead, Mel Tormé, "The Velvet Fog," agreed to write the lyrics, compose the music, and sing the results on a promotional recording to be sold during the fair with proceeds to the charities.

Samuel opened an office in the Hollenden Hotel, from which he was "keeping his fingers on every pulse, meeting every problem that comes along and, somehow, without ever losing his calm." Although Winsor sensed Fun for Funds had "asked for trouble," if June 8 arrived "with no rain, it will have all been worth the stress and strain."

In mid-April, the organizers paused long enough to attend the world premiere of Richard Rodgers and Oscar Hammerstein's newest musical, *Me and Juliet,* a comedy about the perils of backstage love affairs. For days, a cast and crew of 250 had been rehearsing in empty halls throughout Cleveland. The $250,000 production was the most "elaborate and complicated musical play . . . produced in our generation." Scenery for Rodgers and Hammerstein's *Oklahoma* and *South Pacific* had weighed "anywhere from 12 to 15 tons," Winsor wrote. "The trappings for *Me and Juliet* tip[ped] the scales at better than 70 tons" and arrived in Cleveland aboard eleven railroad freight cars. After the production moved into the Hanna and a "full orchestra moved into the pit," rehearsal costs soared to "$8,000 a day." In *Press* photographs, George Abbott, the Broadway legend directing the show, looked glum, but a world premiere of a Rodgers and Hammerstein musical had "tensed and electrified" Cleveland. While Hammerstein was in Cleveland, he stayed in the guesthouse at the home of Winsor's sister and brother-in-law Martha and Char Hickox.

For Winsor, opening night for *Me and Juliet* began at 5:45 P.M. in the 2-1-6 Club, where he met Hanna, Hank and Carol Greenberg, and members of the *Me and Juliet* production staff for a pre-show dinner. Hanna's limousine whisked them to the theater, where they arrived in time for "that moment of wonderful panic as the house lights go down, the coughing and chattering subside, and the curtain slowly rises to salvos of applause."

Winsor's review of what happened on stage was contained in a single sentence: "A production of silken smoothness, beautiful to look at and glitteringly gay." Yes, but what about the lyrics, music, book, and individual performances? Winsor remained silent about a show that critics panned as Rodgers and Hammerstein's least successful collaboration.

After the final curtain, Winsor's party returned to the 2-1-6 for a late supper, then trooped downstairs for after-dinner drinks in the Vogue Room, where Frances Langford, a thirty-nine-year-old singer "sheathed in a gold brocade business that must have been applied to her with wallpaper paste," sang songs from the Broadway shows of Porter and Berlin, what Winsor called a "nostalgic repertoire." After she took a bow, he dropped by a private party for the *Me and Juliet* cast that continued "into the small, small hours with the visiting firemen as well as the local talent whipping up a gala floorshow." It was the sort of party Winsor had attended every few weeks in 1930s Hollywood. In Cleveland, he was lucky if a similar occasion arose every few years, although he hoped Fun for Funds might help fill the void.

During the next several weeks, Winsor and his committee continued to recruit charities. By 4:00 P.M. Monday, June 8, when the fair officially opened, 133 organizations had hopped on the carnival's bandwagon. Despite dark clouds, eight thousand persons quickly descended on Short Vincent. About what happened next on that notable evening in the history of Cleveland's nightlife, Winsor maintained an eerie silence.

William F. McDermott, the *Plain Dealer*'s erudite drama critic and Winsor's competitor and colleague for two decades, reported some details. "People were having fun on a public street in Cleveland. That hasn't happened before in the center of the city, so far as I can remember. . . . Then the rains came. They were not easy rains, but determined and torrential. This rainfall we had Monday night was arrogant and biting."

McDermott's *Plain Dealer* colleague George Condon recalled that the "twilight sky" turned "a sickly yellow." Tuma, the bartender, "shinnied down the flagpole yelling 'Tornado,' and the twister hit. A policeman's horse was picked up, carried through the air and killed. An organ donated by a department store was smashed against a building wall and the street was littered with debris."

McDermott was stunned. "I have lived in Cleveland for more than 30 years. In all that time I do not remember the occurrence of a tornado." Fun for Funds "was betrayed and wrecked in a singularly malicious way by the weather." When police began "warning people to take cover," McDermott was reminded of "wartime London: The same fear, the same scurrying for cover, the same dreadful expectation of unpredictable disaster, the same consolation in the consumption of alcohol."

Ohio's National Guard arrived and enraged McDermott. "Soldiers, with no authority at all, since martial law had not been declared," refused to recognize the drama critic's press card: "Somebody should tell these people that we live in a democracy, and that if a journalist wishes to take a chance, that is his privilege." His defense of press freedoms concluded, McDermott praised Winsor, Stearns, and "the many other people who so carefully and efficiently planned this street fair. . . . They should try it again." In the brief time the fair was open, it raised $35,860. The disappointed organizers were forced to send thirty-six groups checks for $5 each, but they vowed to try again in 1954.

Winsor returned to the smoke-and-music beat and opened another front in his battle to restore Cleveland's nightlife. He was determined to fill the city's struggling nightclubs with teenagers. To do so would require that they be convinced to turn off their radios and television sets and read newspapers. In the 1950s, companies selling vinyl copies of songs recorded by pop musicians considered Cleveland, Detroit, Boston, and Pittsburgh the key "litmus towns" for testing a particular recording's potential national success. If Cleveland's radio audience purchased a singer's latest record in sufficient numbers, companies were willing to invest capital on national distribution. As a result, local broadcasters who selected records to put on the air and the frequency with which they were played became powerful agents in determining entertainers' commercial success. Newspaper columnists covering the smoke-and-music beat had played this role when live performances in nightclubs and theaters were the only profitable venue for singers; radio and television personalities catering to the surge in population born immediately following World War II were eroding newspapers' ability to influence popular culture.

Having listened to radio's earliest broadcasts, Winsor initially held the medium in low regard: "During most of the chain broadcasts whenever they want applause they merely turn it 'on', on a phonograph." And: "The very best radio programs of the coming winter will be recorded on large discs and peddled by the series. And you'll get the advertising ballyhoo thrown in—and that's why the discs will be so cheap!"

Now he recognized that times had changed in Cleveland, "the thriving capital of the popular music world." In his opinion, the city's eight commercial radio stations were "awash with disc jockeys all out for the main chance," and they had "much greater impact on the social life of metropolitan communities than one is likely to imagine. Record spinners can make or break a singer almost overnight. It is also within their power to fall upon a mediocre melody (or cacophony, if you prefer) and catapult it into the front ranks of the hit parades. . . . When it comes to molding public taste, the boys have the power of minor dictators. If they suddenly want to become capricious, watch out!"

In Cleveland, recording industry leaders considered WERE's Phil McLain and Bill Randle—a pair of "personality jocks" whose backing was required for a record's success—the most important broadcasters. McLain's popularity amused Winsor, who saw him "all but swept off his feet by a swarm of nearly hysterical, middle-aged women wanting his autograph. Ladies are mowed down by his voice." He peppered his columns with advice for both men: "Give 'White Christmas' a rest and pay a little attention to Mel Torme's equally beautiful and unhappily neglected 'Christmas Song.'"

To assess another competing medium's impact on teenagers, Winsor watched a single televised broadcast of Dick Clark's *American Bandstand,* which featured singing groups lip-synching their latest records while teenagers danced to the music in the studio, a format that Winsor called "a training school for morons. I caught a brief glimpse the other day and never have I seen a more vapid and pallid group." The columnist blamed "Master

Clark," a twenty-five-year-old former "record spinner," for youthful behavior Winsor considered bizarre, like a female teenager dressed in "Levi's and her old man's shirts," or the male high school student who could "hold a nasal note for a split second" and imagined himself to be Perry Como.

Winsor's antidote for Clark and *American Bandstand* were the teenage matinees of Mindy Carson, a twenty-six-year-old vocalist appearing in the Hollenden's Vogue Room. In December 1953, he suggested "alert adults" should attend her show. "The younger generation, you hear several times daily, has no taste or perception. Well, the teenagers who crowd Miss Carson's matinees must come from a different planet." Carson's audience members were "well dressed, well behaved" and gave the singer "their rapt and quiet attention. She doesn't sing 'Down' to them, neither does she throw away her sophisticated approach or resort to any of the cloying novelties. All going to prove that if you offer them the best there is, they won't merely tolerate it, but cry for more. It would be nice if the record spinners would study their reactions and take the hint."

Bill Randle, who envied Winsor's power to influence public opinion, took his idea and began hosting his own Saturday matinees for teenagers in the Vogue Room. The columnist promoted the events, urging those "who continually complain about the lack of proper entertainment for the young and impressionable" to take their children to Randle's shows. "The price of admission is one buck, and if the youngsters are hungry they can shop from a special teen-age menu on which nothing comes to more than another dollar." Mothers who served as chaperones, "parched though they may be, have to forego martinis. The bar remains hermetically sealed until the last kid has made tracks for home."

While Winsor's television was frequently dark, the Hollenden, which could not ignore the new medium's power, booked its stars. Between telecasts, Dorothy Collins and Snooky Lanson of Lucky Strike's *Your Hit Parade* performed in the Vogue Room, where Winsor saw them for the first time. The singers' contracts required them to each light up a Lucky Strike and do a commercial for the American Tobacco Company toward the end of their acts. Although Winsor, the "ferocious smoker," thought the commercials were "strangely out of place in a supper room," he welcomed kind words for cigarettes, "considering the opinions recently broadcast . . . concerning the weed and cancer. I can think of no . . . more effective sales woman than Miss Collins."

Also, Winsor noted that nightclubs were still forced to charge customers a 20 percent entertainment tax, "a wartime measure," he reminded readers,

> levied in an emergency and supposed to vanish along with rationing
> and traveling restrictions at war's end. Only it didn't. . . . So the aver-

age Joe with ideas of a night on the town thinks twice and finally stays home, turns on his television and raids the icebox for a few cold beers. As a result he wakes up with a little money in his pocket and probably with no hangover either. Meanwhile, artists and musicians all over the land are selling insurance and real estate to make ends meet. If the boys down in Washington would only repeal that staggering tax they would probably all go back to doing what comes naturally to them and most of our cities would lose their provincial after-dark look.

Winsor still had high hopes for downtown's nightlife; these momentarily brightened when the Hollenden booked Mel Tormé, who "sang to feverish standees." He concluded that "if an entertainer has style, taste, the know-how of showmanship and the ultimate talent, the public will beat down the doors to enjoy it." During that same winter week, the Theatrical booked Buddy Greco, "a fine ballad singer . . . trapped by the meretricious tastes of the moment." Winsor blamed the "song writers, if they can be termed such," who were writing "novelties" about "red-nosed reindeer and doggies in windows. Greco, mercifully, prefers such melodies as 'A Foggy Day in London Town,' 'I Have the World on a String,' 'I Get a Kick out of You,'" a more "nostalgic repertoire."

Winsor's favorites were songs from Broadway shows or music many of the same composers wrote especially for favored singers in what would eventually be called the "Golden Era of classic American popular music." Ironically, the nation's teenagers agreed with Winsor and refused to buy records of novelty songs or sentimental ballads, but matinees in the Hollenden's Vogue Room with one's mother was not what they had in mind. In March 1952, twenty-five thousand had attended the "Moon Dog Coronation Ball" in a Cleveland sports arena. Staged by local record spinner Alan Freed, the concert gave rock 'n' roll its first national celebrity. Winsor wasn't present and his columns never mentioned Freed. For his teenage nephews and nieces, he advocated a more sophisticated cultural education. One summer in the 1950s, he convinced a nephew to stage and star in a successful amateur revival of *Design for Living*.

So Winsor's crusade to improve Cleveland's nightlife, whether through Fun for Funds, the 2-1-6 Club, or his newspaper columns, was based on a belief that any city's nighttime activities were among its vital signs. If in the evening downtown sidewalks were empty, a city was sick. From his perspective as an about-town columnist, he diagnosed the terminal illness of his smoke-and-music beat, identifying two federal programs that enabled a post–World War II population boom to abandon central cities. The GI Bill helped veterans buy new homes on raw land at the outer edges of urban areas; federal highway funds provided access to those new communities.

Winsor mourned the loss of the "leafy, lovely city" he had first seen in the summer of 1915. Euclid Avenue was still Millionaires Row, where great mansions belonged to "energetic men and women" who "were not afraid to allow their money to show a little." More important, they spent some of it downtown. "Rather than merely dining in each other's homes or at their clubs, they went to the handsome Pompeian Room at the Statler or the Crystal Room at the Hollenden." Regardless, the city of his youth was "gone forever and I really don't think the gains have been so great. Everyone picked up their money and rushed to the suburbs" leaving behind "sprawling slums."

Retailers followed their customers, building "supermarkets and shopping centers" that were "strangling downtown Cleveland's shops and department stores." Winsor saw a future in Cleveland's Little Italy, a belief he shared with local architect John Terence Kelly. "Little specialty shops mushrooming along Mayfield and Murray Hill Rd., offering such things as imported gloves, fine leather goods, Venetian glass and so on. Well, why not?" He promoted efforts to refurbish the neighborhood's movie theater, "running it as an art house during the winter months, with summer stock taking over for the rest of the year. And again why not? The restaurants would all join forces and offer package deals of dinners plus parking and theater seats."

Another local architect, Robert A. Little, offered him an idea for reviving downtown housing and hoped publication in his column might generate financial backers. Little, who was married to Ann Halle, one of Winsor's childhood friends, asked Winsor to publicize his scheme for constructing town houses on the "broken-off end of the Superior Viaduct," a partially demolished stone bridge near the mouth of the Cuyahoga River. Eighty feet above the valley floor, Little prized the view of "spuming steel mills, the crescendo of the Terminal Tower, the ballet of the lifting bridges, and the ship channel guiding the seven-hundred-foot ore boats out to the cobalt horizon of the lake. No city like it. No place in this city like it, for pure visual excitement. Why not use this old bridge, this exciting location?"

The architect drew "a long low line of twelve town-houses on the deserted bridge, with a narrow street and garages along the North, and private terraces and glass walls along the South." He didn't have a client and "knew of no developer or city official who would do anything but politely listen." Instead, he approached Winsor because he "cared about downtown" and might be interested in buying a town house. Little described Winsor as a "freewheeling bachelor," who "lived securely in a well-furnished dive . . . surrounded by flophouses and vintage smut shops." According to the architect, "Winsor said he would have liked to live in the viaduct project and wrote that the idea might bring a few new residents downtown, but the drawing I sent him and the crazy idea were destined for the bottom drawers of our respective files." Winsor was not surprised by his readers' indifference. He no longer expected an energetic response from local residents. "What actually happened while we were all sleeping is that Cleveland picked up and moved away to other cities."

During this same period, Winsor received two pieces of information that irrevocably changed his life. The first was a gift from Hanna, who had subsidized his taste for most of his adult life. In Smith's words, Hanna "took good care of Winsor, inviting him to Europe a couple of times and spending a lot of other money on him." In 1923, when Hanna was thirty-four years old, he bought "1350 shares of common stock of the Computer-Tabulating-Recording Co.," for which he paid $109,608.75. Less than a year later, the company changed its name to International Business Machines Corp. Hanna's holdings of the company's stock had increased substantially over a quarter century, enriching an already wealthy man. In the 1950s, Hanna shared his good fortune by putting a few thousand IBM shares in a trust for Winsor, "to tide him over when he settled down to serious writing."

The second bit of news was a medical diagnosis. For years, Winsor had known something was wrong with his legs. His worries occasionally surfaced in private correspondence and columns. The car Hanna had given him in 1942 "ran over" him after his "leg gave out." The fall in the darkened stairway of a Paris hotel in 1946 could be blamed on the "bum legs" that caused him to "stumble down the ramps" at Municipal Stadium.

He had worried that a disease that had killed his father and impaired the mental capabilities of a younger sister might have caused his own health problems. He was also concerned that thirty years of daily cocktails might have worsened his health. Typically, he relieved his anxiety with humor. In *Curtain Call,* the book written by Jolly Set members, Winsor titled his own chapter "From Here to Infirmity." During the 1950s, he finally learned that his problem was neither inherited nor caused by drinking. Cerebellar cortical atrophy, an incurable brain disease, was slowly and relentlessly paralyzing his limbs. Useless legs would not stop him. He had role models: Porter had lost the use of both legs in a riding accident; Veeck lost part of one leg to a war injury; Zelma George used a wheelchair to stun theater audiences; brother-in-law Charles Hickox led an active life from a wheelchair. In print, Winsor announced his condition with a jest. When comedienne Bea Lillie, his friend for more than two decades, was frenetically prancing about the Hanna stage, he wrote, "Here I am, leaning on a cane, and when it comes to maturity the lady has the edge on me." He would be forty-nine on Christmas Eve.

Although alcohol didn't cause his disability, it could make weak legs more unreliable. Winsor's surviving sisters believe he was an alcoholic, but none of them could convince this child of Prohibition that he should stop drinking, a privilege for which he had fought long and hard. The fact that one of his sisters drank "three martinis every night" didn't disturb Winsor "too much. I think sometimes it's foolish to try and cure alcoholics. They only develop some other type of trauma."

His columns continued to provide tips for coping with his lifetime obsession. "The booze business is booming," he wrote in 1953, but local cab companies had discontinued their "blotto service, the saving grace for inebriates in their early morning anguish." Throughout the 1930s and '40s, drunks "simply telephoned in their SOS, and in due time along came a taxi, complete with extra driver to pilot home the family car. Well, no longer." Cab company owners were "hard-pressed . . . to get enough drivers for their cabs, much less to provide chaperones for the hopelessly over-served." The customer wasn't responsible; sots were the bartender's fault. In either case, Winsor suggested that "anyone who has bent an elbow once or twice too often remain right on the scene of the disaster; even though the scene happens to be the drawing room of a reluctant hostess. Much better to get on a black list than end up in the clink or on the front pages."

Meanwhile, Winsor was busy worrying about a favorite sister. Anne Dodge, the youngest Eaton, was ensconced at the Desert Inn in Las Vegas waiting for a divorce to be finalized, a process he called "getting the cure." Anne saved his letters to her, a correspondence that reveals his concern for family members, as well as the crème de la crème of Cleveland gangsters. The Desert Inn's owners included Thomas J. McGinty, who "was associated with the biggest gambling operations in Ohio."

In early February, responding to a letter from Anne, Winsor wrote, "I do wish that somehow you could get out of yourself, so to speak, laugh at life and consider your six weeks there as a nightmare with elements of humor that could be put to some use." His sister was a talented artist. "I am positive that if you did a series of pencil or wash drawings of the types in the casino, etc., I could sell them." The casino's owners were not allowing his sister to pay for meals eaten in the hotel, a fact that embarrassed her. Winsor's advice: "Keep right on doing it as long as you can get away with it. Believe me the Desert Inn owners don't hesitate to ask me for publicity. Incidentally Helen and Tom McGinty, who have made all this possible, I think will be showing up before you have finished the 'cure' and for them PLEASE make the supreme effort. I think you should write Tommy, by the way, and thank him."

"The supreme effort" sounded ominous to Anne. After all, she said years later, "They were gangsters." She wrote her brother immediately, asking just what he had in mind. "Honey, what I meant by the 'supreme effort' was this: I know how you feel about people, and I DON'T think Tommy and Helen are your dish of tea." Winsor hoped his sister "would sort of cope with them in an all out way as they have been so very kind. And I know of course you will. Please give my love to Helen and Tommy when they show up, with loads for yourself, Win."

Winsor's willingness to accept a free apartment at the Hollenden and to encourage his sister to accept free meals in a Las Vegas casino illustrate the monetary value hotels placed on the mention of their names in Winsor's column. Accepting the favors offered by these grateful owners, however, violates journalistic ethics, although the practice was a ubiquitous but covert "fringe benefit" for members of the fourth estate who believed their profession was poorly paid. A trust funded with IBM stock did not change Winsor's modus operandi.

In the same correspondence, he described his "regular routine" in Cleveland. It included "trying to see Mother" every afternoon, planning a fourth Heart Fund dinner, and a second book for the Jackson Memorial Lab, called *Full Face,* "the reprint in brochure form of a series of articles I did for Gruber's and so on and so on. I haven't even (and must) write Linda [Porter], who I understand is in desperate condition."

Two weeks later, Winsor was "exhausted. The Heart drive really did me in. But now I am going to try and dream up some sort of trip. Here everything is the same, except Mother, after being *so* well has had a miserable attack of sciatica. She worries about EVERYTHING. And what can you do?"

What Winsor did was amend a will and send an undated letter of instructions to Anne. "The new document, so to speak, leaves everything to you and Martha [Hickox]" (his sister living in Cleveland), "from what I laughingly call my estate. . . . On Len's death my small trust comes to me or my heirs in a lump sum and what you or Martha see fit to do with it is in your hands. I don't want to tie any strings. . . . I am not particularly interested in helping to launch a new husband or a new business and I am more interested in all you girls than in the boys."

Winsor listed the friends who might "like some little gadget of mine": Benny Crowell, Kay Halle, Leonard Hanna, Margaret Sherwin, Roger Stearns, Bernie and Eleanor Towell, Bill Veeck, and Jerry Zerbe. He remembered his nephews: To Joseph Dewey he left "the Thunderbird . . . with unpaid payments"; to Joseph Dewey or Oriel "my books," which meant his collection of first editions. "What Bill Veeck would want, I can't think. Maybe something he gave me, such as the gold wrist watch."

To Anne and Martha he left two oils painted by their grandfather and "two Italian love seats. My God-children are Danny, Oriel, Jennifer, Charles

Hickox and little Winsor. And something surely could be found for all of them. At least I will become the principal topic of conversation for a few minutes every now and then and I hope I will be able to listen from some remote and comfortable outpost."

After writing his will, Winsor planned an escape to Florida with Bernie Towell and Roger Stearns, including a week at the Casa Marina, his favorite resort in Key West. Before deserting Cleveland, he convened the new committee planning the second Fun for Funds at Stearns's 2-1-6 Club. With assignments made, he packed his car, picked up Bernie Towell—a wealthy stockbroker, backgammon champion, and ferocious drinker—and began driving south, away from piles of slush. Stearns would fly down a week later.

If Cleveland's smoke-and-music beat had been more vigorous, Winsor could not have justified his trips. His travel reportage filled the vacuum. He left a week's worth of columns with his editors and didn't wire another until he had reached Route 1 in south Florida, where "tomato and strawberry pickers were crouching in the lush fields and the roadside stands were offering ice cold watermelon, sweet corn." Winsor could be cruel to readers trapped in Cleveland. They wouldn't taste homegrown sweet corn until the Fourth of July.

In Key West, the two men amused themselves with a fishing trip. Winsor was a novice. "Except for one abortive attempt with Cole Porter and Monty Woolley at Ensenada, Mexico, years ago, I have never attempted to catch a fish." For the benefit of readers who shared his inexperience, he listed the provisions required for a party of five: "Box lunches, binoculars, cameras, extra sweaters, 10 bottles of beer, a shaker of Martinis and another of Daiquiris." The results? "I landed a rather annoyed little mackerel."

After a week, Towell departed and Winsor announced Stearns's arrival, "on a brief vacation from the Hollenden's 2-1-6." They sought diversion in risqué joints favored by navy personnel on shore leave. "Sailors and tourists will flock out to Wylk's barroom burlesque to heckle the weary strip-teasers." They also met "bored sailors who wander about aimlessly in wilting 'whites,' looking for the excitement that never comes—unless in unsought barroom arguments that mean trouble and perhaps the clink. To me this is one of the most fascinating and unpredictable cities in the U.S."

After three weeks, Winsor and Stearns drove home, where sad news awaited them. The Jolly Set had lost another founder: Johnny and Rose Lindheim had moved to New York City. And after a long illness, Linda Porter died on May 20, 1954. That summer, downtown "neon belts" disappointed Winsor. Restaurants were "shuttered"; guests in Cleveland hotels "simply sat around the hushed hotel foyers, reading the Sunday papers and looking as if they were in the grip of a deep depression." In the first week of July, when the Cleveland Indians appeared to have regained their will to win, Ruth and Max Gruber invited Veeck to return to the scene of his victory and a reunion of the Jolly Set. Six years later, the restaurant Veeck helped open "seldom served fewer than a thousand customers a day." The Grubers' success led them to join the Hotel Hollenden and publish *Full Face,* a second book to raise money for the Jackson Laboratory. Sounding defensive about his relationship with the restaurant and the hotel, Winsor wrote, "*Full Face* will not in ANY sense be a ballyhoo job for Gruber's or the Hollenden." During the last week of July, when the chance of a tornado was negligible, Fun for Funds reopened on Short Vincent. Neither the book nor the street fair raised as much money as the originals.

The Cleveland Indians saved 1954 by winning the American League pennant. Winsor celebrated by invading the Indians' locker room, the exclusive territory of sportswriters, and violating another journalism taboo. He challenged the news judgment of *Press* sports editor and Jolly Set founder Whitey Lewis by publishing an account of uninhibited affection between male athletes—a "violent outburst of kissing"—that had occurred during the rowdy party in Boston's Kenmore Hotel six years earlier.

Winsor's original account described, "everyone kissing everyone else's wife." In 1954, he revealed players had been kissing each other, too. "In the wigwam, it was a perpetual game of post office and to the violent annoyance of the sportswriters, notably Whitey Lewis, who all but promised public execution to the next photographer who tried to sell him another necking shot." To prove the existence of "necking shots," Winsor illustrated his column with three photos from the *Press* morgue, including handsome Gene Bearden kissing catcher Jim Hegan.

In 1948, none of the local sportswriters explicitly mentioned kissing Indians, although Joe Collier, Winsor's *Press* colleague who had covered the victory party, wrote about "back slappings and explosive greetings" between players. If "explosive greetings" was a euphemism for noisy, man-to-man kisses, Collier had mastered the art of writing between the lines. With hindsight, the 1948 Indians seem notably tolerant of unconventional male behavior, a reflection of the owner's attitude. The owner's affection and respect for Winsor were obvious to all. Veeck's new wife explained why: "Bill had empathy for people that others didn't consider normal."

"Accustomed as I am to off-beat rhythms"

CLEVELAND, OHIO

Sunday, December 20, 1959, 9 p.m.

Following a private black-tie dinner, attorney Joe Coakley was driving his guests west along Carnegie Avenue through a snowstorm. In the front seat was his wife, Patsy. Sitting in the back were Ken Wick; his wife, "Sis"; and Winsor. The columnist had recently heard rumors that certain friends were trying to surprise him with some sort of party. Never one to think small, he hoped he "was being chauffeured to a small pouring at the Arena," the cavernous home of the Cleveland Barons hockey team.

Carnegie was slippery, so Coakley drove slowly while Winsor regaled his hosts with stories about the "gilded gin palaces" that had lined the street during Prohibition. When they reached East 9th Street, Coakley turned north where "a vast klieg light was searching the skies," Winsor recalled, "causing Patsy to ask what was going on."

"We've reached the airport," Winsor replied facetiously.

Then, he reported, "Joe made a handsomely illegal U-turn and we crash landed in front of the Roxy marquee where I was suddenly confronted by larger-than-life posters of myself in what I choose to believe were unlikely poses." His friends had never considered the Arena; they knew any party for Winsor belonged in a burlesque theater.

"A brace of Santa Clauses" (two strong, handsome firemen) opened the car door and lifted Winsor from the back seat. Within the men's warm embrace, the beaming columnist was carried through snowflakes and into the theater where four hundred well-lubricated guests sang "Happy Birthday." In four days, he would be fifty-five.

When the trio reached the stage, the Santas placed Winsor on a throne, where he was "blinded by a spotlight" and "left to the mercy of the merciless" Bill "Smoochie" Gordon, one of the local record-spinners that Winsor criticized. To document the roast of its most popular columnist, the *Press* assigned Joe Collier, whose credentials included the discreet coverage of the Indians' victory party at the Kenmore Hotel. Collier overheard and reported the following exchange from the stage:

"'Are you all right?' cooed Gordon, the master of ceremonies."

"'No,' croaked Winsor, 'I'm likely to have a coronary right now.'"

"'We know you detest this sort of thing,' Gordon said, 'but there's not a chance of getting out of it.'"

"'As long as I don't have to strip,' Winsor managed, finally oriented."

"A uniformed lad handed him a drink," Collier wrote. Winsor welcomed a friend. "George Washington Carter, who normally hustles the trays in Kornman's, hustled a few tall, cool and refreshing glasses" for the guest of honor. "At one point the spotlights veered a bit," Winsor added, "and I was relieved to see a few of my doctors were in the house."

Next came an animal act: "An almost ununiformed young lady came on stage with a plumed trained seal," Collier wrote. "The seal sang 'Happy Birthday.' Winsor, regaining composure, shook flippers with it." His own account of the same event focused on the singer's body odor: "Accustomed as I am to off-beat rhythms, it takes more than . . . 55 years of fortitude to survive being kissed by a seal that has never heard of Chanel No. 5."

One of Winsor's competitors, Peter Bellamy, the about-town columnist at the *News,* noted that "every other row was left open so that waiters and bartenders could bring food and drink to the . . . guests." Collier observed, "Pretty waitresses from Kornman's and the Theatrical Grill went up and down the aisles bearing tidbits of food and large drinks."

Following the seal's serenade, Winsor took a seat in the first row as the stage "swarmed with the regular Roxy burlesque show. It was a stimulating new experience for both the cast and much of the audience," Collier noted. "Miss Brandy Long, Miss Dallas York, Miss Kay Dee and Miss Robin all stripped in the darkened theater as some surprisingly well-informed guests yelled 'Take it off,' and 'more.'"

Between exposures of flesh, musicians from Kornman's, the Theatrical Grill, and the Alpine Village performed. The antics on stage were not what caught the attention of Winsor's newspaper colleagues. Rather, they were stunned by the audience. "Paths crossed," Collier wrote, "that never crossed before."

Kenyon Bolton, son of U.S. representative Frances Payne Bolton, noted philanthropist and former director of protocol at the U.S. embassy in France, partied with Morris "Mushy" Wexler, who ran the Empire News Service, a telegraph service that provided bookies with the latest horse-racing and football information. Dr. George "Barney" Crile, pioneer of new surgical techniques for breast cancer, sipped cocktails with Samuel Gerber, Cuyahoga County coroner.

Architect Robert Little described the party as "the most spectacular urban event of my life in Cleveland." He had heard that the Roxy's dancers had decided to give the society page members of the audience "something to remember." As a result, "a number of guests, before the first intermission, gathered their mates and headed for their homes and the relative tranquility of their own bedrooms." Those who stayed saw the performers "join the audience, and the formal part of the evening closed with interpretive dance on the stage, in the aisles, and in the lobby." Collier reported that partygoers "emptied more than two hundred and fifty fifths of liquor." Any guest with a hangover could have consulted Winsor about potential remedies; he spent a lifetime enabling alcoholic consumption, beginning in the early 1930s, when he thumbed his nose at Prohibition liquor laws by publishing the prices of bootlegged booze and hints about where to find illegal speakeasies. Hangover recipes were his specialty: Grapefruit "Baked." Roll-mop—"A herring wrapped around celery, pickle and onion."

In the *Press,* Winsor asked, "How on earth do you say thank you to 'Pops' and Katie Weinberger, Mushy Wexler, Ruth and Max Gruber, Roman and Mary Margaret Gruber, Jules and Edith Weinberger and Bill and Jean Weinberger who were the committee so-called who planned, plotted and executed all the madness? Not to mention the entertainers and musicians from all over town who gave their all and the some 400 people who skidded through the snowy night and helped . . . render me into a basket case."

During the evening, according to Collier, Winsor stuffed his pockets with "telegrams and letters from the famous and the obscure who couldn't get from East and West Coasts and points between and beyond for the great 'bust out.'" As the sun rose in the East, Winsor finally "crept out of the Roxy to go home."

He did not walk down Short Vincent to his apartment in the Hotel Hollenden. A year after the second Fun for Funds, Winsor and Stearns had moved to the eastern edge of Cleveland and rented an apartment at 19425 Van Aken Boulevard, near Shaker Square. Their L-shaped living room was arranged for entertaining. They served buffet dinners from a "17th-century Italian desk with carving on both sides and drawers that open either way." After guests filled their plates, they seated themselves at a "17th-century Italian dining table." As Elizabeth Luft wrote at the time, "a Waterford crystal chandelier lights the kitchen where Winsor infrequently cooks." For whatever reason, Luft made no mention of Winsor's companion, Roger Stearns, or the pianist's "five-year-old Siamese cat called Geronimo, or Ronny." It was Winsor who revealed that Ronny could "be persuaded to dance sometimes, and even execute . . . *entrechats,* which absolutely fascinated Kay Thompson when she was in town recently." Thompson was a film actress and vocal coach for Lena Horne and Judy Garland, who found time to write a series of children's books about a little girl named Eloise. Winsor insisted, however, that Thompson could not "manage an *entrechat*."

In his new apartment Winsor maintained his vigorous social life, but during the years that immediately preceded the party at the Roxy he had suffered irreparable losses, as certain places where he had acted out his youth changed owners. He and his brothers and sisters had all spent large parts of their childhood in Sam and Blanche Halle's friendly red brick Georgian house at the corner of Harcourt Drive and Cedar Road, once the family home of Winsor's friends the Zerbes. After the Halles died in the early 1950s, their children sold their parents' home. The last act was a house sale of furnishings. Winsor couldn't resist one last look:

> By the time I reached it last Friday the frantic mobs, for the most part, had dispersed. The house itself had that somewhat forlorn, resigned look that sometimes comes to the very ill when they only wish everyone would go away and leave them alone to their aches and pains. The salespeople looked tired and harried. The furnishings, pictures and odd pieces of bric-a-brac seemed strangely unfamiliar and the people pawing over them appeared to be lost and at loose ends, as if they didn't know what on earth they were looking for. But they came and went, while a bored young detective standing at the door asked people to douse their cigarettes.

He regretted the visit. "Going back as I did, to a scene of so many memories, becomes a sort of nightmare. There is not even the relief of nostalgia."

Two months later, the daughters of Aileen Winslow, whose Sunday buffet dinners had been a legendary American salon in the 1930s, arrived in Wickliffe, Ohio. "Patter" (Miss Mildred Winslow) and "Petsey" (Mrs. Aileen Powell) were selling East House, the family home at Nutwood Farms, where after a long illness their mother had died in August 1951. She was fifty-five. Winsor reminisced about Binnie Corrigan, the mistress domo, whose "Irish beauty was a stoplight. Binnie has seen fortunes rise and fall and rise again and no transition has been able to disturb her natural serenity. She could write, if she had the time, a fairly sensational book," including a description of Noël Coward's stay at East House during the world premiere of *Design for Living*.

Peter Winslow, the handsome seventeen-year-old who reportedly caught the eye of the playwright, was employed briefly as society editor for the *Press*. In 1938, he married Alice Wren, a descendant of English architect Sir

Christopher Wren and Scottish novelist Sir Walter Scott. They had a daughter, Wren Winslow. At the time of his mother's death, Peter was thirty-five and employed as an "inspector" on the second shift (3:00 to 11:00 P.M.) at the Tapco plant of Thompson Products, Inc., an auto parts manufacturer. (Thompson is the "T" in TRW, the auto parts company.) Peter eventually moved to the island of Majorca in the Mediterranean Sea, where he died in 1963. He was forty-seven.

With the Halles' house and the Winslows' estate "under new management," as it were, Winsor's last private playground in northeast Ohio was Len Hanna's Hilo. "He ran it like a country club for his friends and their children," Joe Collier wrote in a six-part series for which Winsor was an anonymous source. "An invitation extended once was good for all time unless it was abused."

For years Hanna lived in the gatehouse, but in 1947 he bought an Elizabethan cottage from another wealthy Clevelander who had threatened to demolish the structure, portions of which were constructed in the 1470s. Hanna moved the cottage to Hilo from Hunting Valley, Ohio, and added two wings, "including a sitting room, bedroom and bath for his personal use." Winsor told Collier about Hanna walking "barefooted on the large lawns . . . to savor the possession of the place."

Not long after adding the cottage to Hilo, the illness that had crippled Hanna during his World War II service in London forced him to abandon his walks about his estate as well as his large apartment in Manhattan. He moved to a suite in the Pierre Hotel on 5th Avenue. By 1957, Hanna, Cole Porter, and Winsor shared a disability—bum legs. Before embarking on his annual trip to Europe that year, Winsor "spent two days with Leonard Hanna in his new apartment in the Pierre. . . . People come and go, bringing Leonard, who has been ill, news of the outside world." The columnist had lunch with Cole Porter in his "towering eagle's nest" in the Waldorf-Astoria Hotel. "Cole, still more or less recuperating from a serious operation, is also subdued these days." Winsor didn't describe the surgery, but doctors had amputated one of his legs.

During these dismal months of illness and death among Winsor's life-long friends, he listened to some spiritual advice from his sister Anne and her second husband. They suggested he visit Robert Killam, the local minister who had married Anne and Tony Dodge in a civil ceremony at the Hollenden Hotel. On the first Sunday of May, he "got up at nine, drove all the way out to the end of the Shaker Boulevard world and went to Bob Killam's [Unitarian] church. He was only wonderful. People were standing to hear him speak. Frankly, I felt as if after 50 years of semi-conscious searching I had found the spiritual help I needed. My God but the man's use of expression, command of English, delivery, and his profound and wonderful conception of what religion should be and can be!"

He thanked Anne for bringing "something quite tremendous into my life. He left me absolutely breathless, very moved and very rewarded. . . . I will go often." His datebooks, correspondence, and columns offer no evidence of a second visit. A plausible reason Winsor failed to return is contained in one of his Monday morning columns: "This is being written on a Sunday morning after a Saturday night that ended God knows when."

Winsor escaped to Europe, where he again met Porter in splendid surroundings. At the Gritti Palace Hotel, the composer occupied the "tremendous and somewhat overly ornate rooms" where the Duke and Duchess of Windsor stayed on their annual visits to Venice. The living room in the Gritti suite gave Winsor "the feeling of being in a great, brocade-lined casket. The walls are covered with silk; hanging on them are huge, very bad religious paintings, and the furniture, to put it mildly, is outsized."

Porter was traveling with a handsome film actor, Robert Bray. For those who did not recognize the name, Winsor explained that a year earlier, Bray had played Carl, the bus driver in Marilyn Monroe's first well-received film, *Bus Stop*. Because of Porter's bad legs, Winsor noted that he required "the assistance of two valets and there is a chauffeur as well. And there are two cars. The staff, wheel chair and luggage travel in a station wagon. Cole and Bray, who looks a little like a young Gary Cooper, by the way, lead off in a Cadillac. This is not exactly what one would call roughing it." On a day trip to Vicenza, Winsor became part of Porter's entourage.

He returned to Cleveland late that summer and by September was planning what was becoming an annual visit to New England. He told his sister, however, that he was "dreading Williamstown. I PRAY Cole is not there. Dear God, Linda gone, Cole with one leg, the old house given over to strangers. I think I'll go live with my memories on a mountain peak in Tibet."

On October 5, 1957, exactly a month short of his sixty-eighth birthday, Winsor's patron, Leonard Hanna, died. In various published accounts, chiefly biographies of Cole Porter, Winsor has been identified as "Len Hanna's companion." While their relationship was close and affectionate, the two men were not "companions" in the contemporary sense of a homosexual couple. In fact, Hanna's distaste for personal publicity, which can be attributed to his homosexuality, made it difficult for Winsor to describe their relationship in a daily newspaper. "He would not soon forgive me for what I am doing now," the columnist wrote, as he struggled for words.

"I knew Leonard Hanna intimately for more than thirty years. I have spent winters with him in Florida and California, traveled with him from Rome to Tahiti." He was "the most soft-spoken, truly tolerant and liberal man I have ever known. . . . Anything but soft or unresolved, he had strong, almost violent opinions, but would always listen to the other side of the story and frequently admit himself wrong." Hanna offered Winsor a model for filling his spiritual needs. His friend "had no deep beliefs or religious convictions" but "worshiped the soil, the seasons of the year and the elements. The yields of autumn, the promise of spring, the lush calm of summer and the hush of winter," all observed on the grounds of his beloved Hilo.

The last of Winsor's youthful playgrounds was sold. Hilo's proceeds were added to the substantial assets of Hanna's personal foundation. To the Cleveland Museum of Art, Hanna left $33 million, an endowment that allowed the museum to amass a collection of international significance. The museum also inherited the collection of impressionists that Winsor had admired when they covered the walls of Hanna's Manhattan apartment.

To relieve the gloom and escape Cleveland's cold, wet winter, Winsor and Stearns began planning a trip to California and a return to Hollywood. If anyone could be called Winsor's companion, it was Roger Stearns. The two men had spent extended periods of time with each other since the 1920s. Martha Hickox, Winsor's sister, described Roger as "very gentle," a "cushion for Winsor's more intense emotions." Both men felt too old to drive across country, and Winsor loathed airplanes: "Everyone is in too much of a hurry. Seeing nothing, they are catapulted back and forth through the heavens in jet-propelled test tubes, deep in artificially induced sleep lest they be disturbed by air pockets and sudden changes of currents in the anything but silken skies."

Instead, a few days after Christmas the couple took a train to Chicago, where they boarded the Super Chief for Los Angeles. Winsor's prose expanded to capture the speed of the train and the size of the Western landscape: "The first morning out of Chicago you are in Colorado. Narrow, dirt lanes wind and twist through fenced, empty fields to remote, unpainted ranch houses cowering behind sheltering groves of cottonwood," but "turn a few pages of your book or cat nap, however, and they are behind you." At dusk, the Super Chief stopped at Albuquerque. Winsor had an ear for the absurd: "Here and there were a few traces of Christmas decorations but the church chimes, somewhat off beat, were loudly giving forth with 'Some Enchanted Evening.' By the time we finally pulled out night had fallen, the dining car and bar were already crowded and the heady atmosphere echoed with complaints because the supply of rum had been exhausted and no more daiquiris, thank you."

Winsor had dinner in his bedroom, then "crawled into bed with James Agee's beautiful if disturbing novel, *A Death in the Family.* When I snapped up the window shade in the morning we were in San Bernardino, the mountains were golden in the early morning sunlight, the orange groves backing up to the railroad tracks looked as if each leaf, each orange had been carefully washed and polished." The men checked into the Beverly Hills Hotel, which was "just plushy enough to give you the feeling of living far, far above your income (and heaven knows I am!)." Sounding defensive about his midwinter escape, Winsor added, "P.S. I do not get a rate."

On his second day in Southern California, Winsor lunched with the romantic Hollywood star whose name had filled his datebook in 1935. Former matinee idol Allen Vincent made a nostalgic comeback in his little brown book, but lunch with him did not rate a nostalgic column item. Instead, Winsor catalogued Southern California Christmas decorations: "Two towering royal palms with swags of holly twisted around the full length of the trunks and then, caught amid the fronds, great hair dresses of silver stars. And at night, naturally, they light up. It still strikes me as incongruous and rather touching."

Winsor's copy, however, had not lost its acid content. Female Beverly Hills residents appeared in local supermarkets "wearing toreador pants," their "hair in curlers," their "eyes hidden behind jeweled dark glasses. Those who have to be seen, of course, dress to the nines, flock to Romanoff's and pay astronomical prices for avocado salads."

Hollywood was aging badly. "In the long, long ago of 1934" [actually, it was 1935], Winsor confessed that he had fallen in love with Hollywood. "The movies were a great industry rather than a wan, sickly second cousin to television." Now, however, he had discovered "only 10 feature-length films were being shot in Hollywood, the lowest number since 1922. And now I read in the papers that most of the 20th Century-Fox lot is about to be razed for a $225,000,000 hotel, apartment and business development." As for the nightlife, he wrote, when "I looked in on La Rue and the Mocambo they must have had all of 20 lonely customers." He spotted Victor Mature and acknowledged he was "still quite a hunk of man," but he found the current generation of female stars could not "match the beauty of Garbo's, or the indestructible Dietrich's. And you can have Elizabeth Taylor with my compliments. Tastes are changing, or perhaps I should say taste is vanishing from the scene."

Disappointed, Winsor and Stearns "caught a sleeper out of Santa Barbara in the late evening" and awoke in San Francisco. Waiting on the platform was former Cleveland resident and longtime friend John Tuteur. His wife, Marion, was singer Libby Holman's older sister. Both Stearns and Winsor had followed Libby's career and family for a quarter of a century. From the Tuteurs' house, Winsor wired his readers a classic description of San Francisco weather: "Curtains of mist hung in a light rain that had not quite made up its mind what to do, and then suddenly, gathering force, managed to obliterate the hills, the Golden Gate Bridge and the houses climbing up the slopes of Belvedere in the farther distance. Then the ceiling diminished to zero and all that could be seen was the surf churning on the little crescent beach below us, and a small Coast Guard vessel riding the swells a hundred yards or so off shore."

On a sunnier day, Winsor and Stearns visited his former colleague Kellogg Smith and his wife, Peggy, in their "charming little house" overlooking Richardson Bay in Sausalito. "You have to be a fairly skillful mountain climber, of course, to reach the house from the street," but the view made the columnist "homesick for the Italian Riviera."

In comparison to Cleveland, Winsor found San Francisco's cultural life disappointing. The theater was "very off-Broadway, no George Szell conducts the orchestra and its museums have no Hanna Fund." Furthermore, Winsor had tired of residents' "unending hymn of praise" for themselves. "No society has ever been more scintillating, no climate more benign and nowhere else will you find so many flawlessly dressed women dining so well in such stylish restaurants. Who am I, a simple resident of Shaker Heights, O., to tell them no?"

His verdict pronounced, the "simple resident" and his companion returned to Cleveland and their keyboards: Winsor's typewriter at the *Press* and Stearns's piano in the Sky Chef restaurant at Cleveland's airport. The Hollenden had closed the 2-1-6 Club. In a column devoted to his companion, Winsor described Stearns's career "as hard, grueling work. It is one thing to be the life of a private party and quite another to have to be the life of a saloon night after night." Celebrities passing through Cleveland's airport, however, still made a "bee-line" to the Sky Chef and Stearns's piano to hear their "umbilical chords."

In their apartment, the musician relaxed by "playing solitaire or putting jig-saw puzzles together. Also, six days a week, Stearns locks himself up in his room for hours at a time, recording heavy, ponderous textbooks for the blind. Once, an experience he would not want to live through again, he recorded a suburban telephone book for a blind salesman." When recording books about music, he would "sit down at the piano and illustrate the manuscripts by simply playing along with his reading. He was indefatigable . . . a dedicated man, with no time for the trivia of his salad days."

On February 20, Winsor was up and waiting for Stearns when he returned from the Sky Chef after midnight. He was "watering plants" when he heard a crash, rushed to their living room, and found his companion on the floor unconscious. He called the police, and an ambulance took Stearns to St. Luke's Hospital, where he was pronounced dead of a "coronary attack." He was fifty-six.

The *Press* obituary writer noted that Stearns had died "in the apartment he shared with his close friend, Winsor French. Mr. Stearns was not married." *Variety* called Roger a "nitery pianist" and a "bachelor." A few days after Stearns died, Winsor wrote his sister Anne about his own feelings: "I am still a little numb. Good Lord the shock of running into the living room after hearing the fall and finding him there. Well, perhaps he is well out of it. But this is a damned lonely flat and I am trying to change its character by doing over R's room as quickly as possible."

Cleveland's nightlife offered no comfort. "The Vogue Room is shuttered and the Statler's Terrace Room has dispensed with entertainment." After Stearns died, the Sky Chef restaurants stopped providing entertainment. "It is difficult to believe that once upon a time the town was actually awash with night clubs. . . . Then like a sudden thunder clap, all the lights went out . . . and the town's night life diminished to a few cocktail lounges." Winsor listed them: the Alpine Village, Kornman's Back Room, the Virginian, the Theatrical Grill, and the Empress Room. He was bored by "jazz combos that are imported week after week" but enjoyed "the rash of satirical, small revues dedicated to poking fun at people in high places." And the "sick-sick comedians." To support these efforts, he ordered everyone living in Lakewood, Rocky River, or the Heights "to make at least one trip a week downtown to see what the avenues look like after dark" and everyone living in Gates Mills, Mentor, or Waite Hill to "take apartments downtown."

As rock 'n' roll gained popularity, Winsor spent less and less time in Cleveland. In mid-April, he boarded a New York Central train for one night in Manhattan, a week aboard a refurbished *Queen Mary,* and two months in Europe. He carried "a large jug of leg tranquilizers and still another jug of Vioform as an antidote for the inevitable tourista." On his return, he took another fall trip to New England to visit family and friends, then returned to Cleveland to celebrate his birthday and Christmas with his housebound mother, a source of continuing concern for her children. Winsor wrote to his sister Anne, "When I get so bored I think I will really blow my top, there is Mother, so peaceful and uncomplaining after two and a half years in that bed, looking out of the window at the same dreary view, seeing always the same faces."

To avoid the same fate, Winsor began a month-long trip by himself. Less than a week after Christmas, he boarded a sleeper at the Terminal Tower and woke up in Toronto, the first stop on "a long land voyage that is going to take me across Canada to Vancouver and then down the coast to Beverly Hills." To show him the nightlife in Toronto, he hired a driver, who informed him that the city "goes to bed with the restless sparrows as soon as night falls." In the driver's opinion, "Even the north of Scotland was livelier."

Of his trek across the continent on the Canadian Pacific train, the urbane Winsor warned potential travelers, "It is anything but a picturesque journey." Seated in the Vista-Dome, he saw "a great sea of space of which man obviously wants very little part." In Vancouver, the columnist waited in the station all day for a Great Northern train that would take him to Seattle, "a sophisticated town with a character all its own," then on to Portland, where "the air, if you could call it that, had the tang of wet sheep." In this foul fog, he climbed aboard the Shasta, a Southern Pacific train headed for California. "The huge dome car was filled with whispering and shadows, while in the bar below a noisy poker game was in progress between a brace of brassy dames headed for L.A. and service men en route to a missile base."

On New Year's Eve, the train reached Martinez, California, where Winsor made his last change and caught the Owl, the train that would carry him south to Los Angeles. "Just for the record, I was in Bedroom D, of Car 586, when I looked at my watch and saw it was two minutes before midnight. Fully prepared, I poured a Scotch and soda, snapped up the window shade, looked out into the night and drank a fast, healthy toast to the welcome New Year. And thought for a moment or so of Gruber's and the Theatrical, Kornman's Back Room and the Hollenden's Vogue Room and all the other places where I have sat out the death watch for the tired old year. Bedroom D, of Car 586, seemed a far, far cry."

By late afternoon of New Year's Day, Winsor was in the Polo Lounge of the Beverly Hills Hotel, where he admired "the car park boys," who reminded him of "young Laurence Oliviers." He was surprised to find that coffeehouses had replaced nightclubs. At one called the Unicorn, "darker than any pocket a hand has ever explored," the women wore trousers, and their hair fell in "black, blond or reddish strings to their waists." The men were "bearded and their clothes have remained alien to dry cleaning and pressing since they emerged from the factory. This is the home of the determined beatniks. They drift in from the night, manuscripts under their arms, and beat they are, believe me."

He estimated that more than one hundred coffeehouses were "scattered about the area and not one of them feels any financial pain. Some hang exhibitions of bad contemporary painting, others allow the poets to moon over their verses and still others provide a pianist of sorts, or perhaps try to pick up a little extra loose change selling pastry. . . . Their candles burn in the dusty, determined atmosphere of lost despair far, far into the night."

Winsor was not amused, so he embarked on trips to Palm Springs ("a couple of good hotels, dirt roads that were continually being washed out, and one night club called Roger's Stables") and Tijuana ("Defeated little burros, painted to look like zebras . . . patiently serve as props for the camera fiends"). Enough! He returned to Cleveland but spent part of July, all of August, and most of September in Europe. By November he was in the Berkshires ("the gentle hills are purple now, flecked with gold and troubled by the shadows of scudding clouds"), on his way to Williamstown and his "nephew Joe Dewey's house where a fire crackles on the hearth, there is the sound of a cocktail shaker and with the warm feeling that is probably as close to my own roots as I will ever get."

From Williamstown, Winsor took the New York, New Haven & Hartford Railroad south to Hopewell, New Jersey, where he visited John and Sis O'Hara. O'Hara's colleagues at the *New Yorker* considered him to be "among the greatest short-story writers in English, or in any other language." Mrs. O'Hara was the ex-wife of Joseph Bryan, Winsor's former colleague at *PARADE* magazine and an usher at his wedding to Margaret Perry. Winsor had known "John and 'Sis' O'Hara for most of my mature life."

Because the reclusive novelist didn't get out of bed until early afternoon, Winsor arrived at the O'Haras' residence in the late afternoon. Sis was "still a radiantly beautiful woman with high, wonderful cheek bones, tawny hair and a voice that immediately makes you think of Ethel Barrymore. And with all this goes a brain and as provocative a laugh as a woman was ever blessed with. John, to be sure, now looks a bit of the russet country squire," and far more at peace with the world than during the days when we labored together in the frustrating vineyards of *TIME* magazine, he as a wheel and I as a somewhat glorified office boy."

O'Hara, an "attentive listener," dodged Winsor's questions. "After a long, gay reminiscent hour I went away with no more idea of what his thoughts or writing plans are than when I arrived." One note of interest for Clevelanders was that O'Hara was still interested in writing about O. P. and M. J. Van Sweringen, the bachelor brothers who built Cleveland's Terminal Tower and Shaker Heights, while amassing a great railroad empire only to go spectacularly bankrupt during the Depression.

Winsor returned to Cleveland where his friends surprised him with the party at the Roxy Burlesque. Three days later, he was scheduled to begin a three-month junket "chasing rainbows around Europe." Before leaving town, he visited his bedridden mother. "Oh dear God the searing business of going away," he wrote Anne. "Every time I do it, I swear never again while Mother is still alive. She looks at me in such a lost, pathetic way and I D-I-E. But that's that." With a lovely gesture, Edith Eaton tried to ease her son's anxiety. She ordered a bottle of champagne, which was waiting in Winsor's cabin when he boarded the steamship in Manhattan.

After an uneventful crossing of the Atlantic, with brief dockings at the Azores and Lisbon, Winsor's ship made a leisurely tour of sunny Mediterranean ports including Gibraltar, Naples, and Palermo. He disembarked at Venice and took the train to Rome, where he had reserved a room in the small, luxurious Hotel Hassler at the top of the Spanish Steps next to the Trinita dei Monti. There he would spend a week waiting for Jean and Billy Weinberger.

On an overcast Sunday afternoon, January 24, 1960, Winsor received a long-distance phone call from his sister in Cleveland. In his datebook, he wrote, "Martha called to tell me Mother died yesterday." The woman he most loved in the world was gone. Immediately he felt remorse. "I didn't telephone to say goodbye from New York," he wrote Anne. "I didn't have the courage. And Martha had to remind me to write and thank her for the bottle of champagne she sent," he added. "I mailed the letter . . . from Rome and mother never saw it."

The phone rang a second time; it was his oldest sister, Edith French Dewey. They pondered why they loved their mother so intensely. Too many of Winsor's unconventional male friends had been rejected, even disinherited by angry, bigoted parents. "Lots of people I know hate their mothers," he reminded Edith, "but ours was truly a great woman, with facets of tolerance and understanding that are almost beyond comprehension."

Winsor felt "bereft and perhaps sorry for myself." He had planned to arrange a private memorial service for his mother in Rome, which would be conducted while his brothers and sisters attended their own ceremony in Williamstown. "Now that the time approaches," he wrote Anne, "I find I can't do that either. A total stranger could give me no solace at all. Anne dear . . . . I just can't find the words now to express myself at all."

A relentless daily deadline followed him; he owed the *Press* a column. To ease her brother's grief, Martha had told him their mother's death was a "blessing." He disagreed, which gave him the lead for an obituary he eventually wired Cleveland:

When has death been a blessing, and especially for those left behind with a burden of memories so personal and touching that it is almost impossible to live with them?

All of our lives are punctuated with finalities, and as one grows older you can almost hear their approaching tread. But you are never prepared, never ready; and then at last comes the finality that leaves you inarticulate. Well this for me is that moment. On the other hand,

I cannot let her death go unremarked. It will be weeks before I will be returning to Cleveland again, but life goes on and with it my work, which all too often is of a trivial nature. And with no room in it for a lonely, heavy heart.

The very act of my mother's dying seems somehow to have erased the long, endless years of her illness when no one, even her nurses, ever heard her complain. She has become young and beautiful again, with a high spirit that never left her and a sense of humor that could never be defeated, no matter the odds, and mother knew very well what it required to face life when the chips were down.

Winsor was alluding to Edith Gotti Ide French Eaton's life with her first husband. She was twenty-seven years old in 1899, when she married Winsor Pitcher French, a lawyer from Saratoga Springs, New York. She was thirty-six, the mother of three children—eight, six, and four years old and pregnant with a fourth child—when after a long illness, her husband died in 1908. "Today, as I sit here in Rome, my mind races back over the long, lean and fat years."

In his column, Winsor listed Troy, New York, as his mother's home where she returned with her children after her husband died and Apple Tree Farm, owned by his maternal grandfather, George Ide, an investor and director in the local phone company and a large bank. He mentioned Saratoga Springs, where his family knew actor Monty Woolley's parents, and included Montclair, New Jersey, where his family lived after his mother married Joseph O. Eaton in 1910. Finally, there was "the all-important move to Cleveland," the city Eaton had chosen to locate his new manufacturing business. "Some of those memories are sad, naturally, others are happy." He wrote:

I can see my mother walking through all of them, serene, contained and never afraid. All day as I have walked the streets of Rome, I have been reminded of a long ago morning when father was reading aloud at breakfast the obituary of an old friend. Mother thought it was skimpy and not revealing. "But she was never in the public eye," father said, "to the world at large she was merely Mrs. So and So, and to them her life had been without distinction."

But, believe me, distinction is a quality that does not need describing. When you are fortunate enough to find it in someone you love it leaves a glow in your heart that lasts forever. And you are grateful.

"No one even whimpers"

CLEVELAND, OHIO

Monday, December 25, 1961, 8 p.m.

Winsor was angry. The Baltimore & Ohio Railroad's sleeper between Cleveland and Washington, D.C., was "oversold, overcrowded and understaffed." Union Station was "absolutely mobbed with weary holiday travelers, squalling children and servicemen who had had too much Christmas."

Although the train was scheduled to depart at 9:20 P.M., passengers were normally allowed to board their cars at 8:00 P.M., but for some reason "the conductor at the check-in desk had disappeared and there was no descending to the platform until he reappeared to take our tickets. Other trains, too, were departing for other destinations and there were only two porters on hand to move the mountains of luggage."

Winsor, who never traveled lightly, was more than usually concerned about his pile of luggage. He was carrying one of the Eaton family's oil paintings, a poetic landscape by Alexander Helwig Wyant, a distinguished member of the Hudson River School. Only eighteen inches square, *Glimpse of Lake Champlain* was still a bulky parcel, for the painting was in its original, thick wooden frame that Wyant himself had carved. Winsor's brothers and sisters had decided to offer the hundred-year-old artwork to America's new first lady, Jacqueline Bouvier Kennedy. She had appointed a committee to acquire outstanding eighteenth- and nineteenth-century American art for the permanent collection at the White House. Winsor had volunteered to take the painting to Washington, D.C., on one of his visits to "Hotel Halle," the home in Georgetown owned by his longtime friend Kay Halle.

Since John F. Kennedy had been elected president, Winsor frequently accepted Kay's hospitality. From a settee in her living room or a chair at her dining room table, he could collect items that satisfied the public's insatiable appetite for tidbits about the new president, his glamorous wife, and his large family. To fill columns, he endured the B&O sleeper, but not silently. Saving and improving passenger rail service had become another of his crusades. He believed the goal of the nation's railroads was "to be rid of the passengers. If the railroads can think of anything to make you more uncomfortable, believe me, they will grasp the opportunity to do just that."

Winsor's trip to Washington provided several examples. "In order to reach the club car you had to thread your way through two coaches, crowded with people prepared to pass the long night sitting up, and most were trying to lull themselves to sleep. It was a losing game, I can assure you. Following the coaches you still had to pass through a freezing, empty freight car and then, at last, you reached the cafeteria-bar, smoke-filled and with the usual quota of over-served."

He wasn't finished: "My porter informed me that if the B&O has its way even this train would be taken out of service within a month. In other words, it will only be possible to reach Washington by air, bus, car or perhaps a wagon train." He proposed a "government investigation" of the railroads, or at least "a secretary of transportation in the Cabinet. In any event, for the world's richest and most powerful nation to have its population shuttled about like cattle seems very odd indeed."

Early in the morning on the day after Christmas, the train pulled into Washington's monumental, white marble Union Station and "the exhausted, red-eyed travelers were flushed from these overcrowded coaches onto the platform. And at once spirits soared." Unlike Cleveland, "Porters were everywhere, taxis too." During the ride to Kay's house, Winsor catalogued the virtues of the nation's capital: "The sun shines more often than not, the people are friendly and accessible and if the social whirl is what you want you will find yourself on a merry-go-round almost without equal." More important, "No eyebrows are raised at hermits or eccentrics." (Winsor had mellowed. Twenty-five years earlier, he described "youngish diplomats" that "fluttered" about hotel lobbies "adopting attitudes of self-importance" and "opulent" houses that looked "like over-dressed women at the opera.") Arriving at his destination, he noted that despite freezing temperatures, the "pink camellia hedge" at Kay's house had "burst into delicate bloom." For a moment, he wrote, "exhilaration rode the air and who knows, perhaps 1961 will end on a note of hope after all."

Then Winsor discovered an item on a New Year's greeting card Kay had received from artist Rockwell Kent: "A naked little boy, a new year presumably, standing alone amid a destroyed world—strewn with skeletons." The greeting read, "Not a creature was stirring, not even a mouse. Nevertheless, hope being eternal, Sally and Rockwell Kent wish you and yours and all mankind a happy new year."

A world littered with skeletons was Kent's metaphor for the aftermath of a nuclear war between the United States and the Soviet Union. The

Kennedys' glamour had not dispelled the national anxiety about the cold war. In Washington, Winsor noted that small talk was "almost invariably about 'the Wall,'" the concrete barricade in Berlin that the Soviet Union had erected to separate the U.S. and Russian sectors, a legacy of World War II. East Germany's communist regime was trying to block the escape of men and women risking their lives trying to flee the Soviet satellite. The Berlin Wall seemed to increase the chances for another war in Europe, which could include nuclear warheads and their lethal fallout. In a commercial district of the nation's capital, Winsor saw a fallout shelter on display, "a grisly little affair that looks just about large enough to house at least two people in extreme discomfort and with what appears to be a picture window in its front. The better from which to watch the world crumble, I suppose."

Winsor understood his readers were not interested in his views of U.S.-Soviet relations. They wanted to hear about the Kennedys, so he described lunch with the president's mother-in-law, Janet Lee Bouvier Auchincloss, "the most glamorous baby sitter in all of Washington," and cocktails with Alice Roosevelt Longworth, the daughter of President Theodore Roosevelt, looking "swagger" in "a mink paw coat, tweeds, a stunning broad-brimmed hat and a few casual, very dark, discreet sapphires."

It was during a stay at Hotel Halle that Winsor learned about Jacqueline Kennedy's desire to improve the White House collection of American art. Another Clevelander, Kay's sister-in-law, Helen Halle, had been appointed to the First Lady's Advisory Committee on American Art. Not willing to spend a night on the B&O, Helen Halle had flown to Washington on the same flight with Robert Kennedy, his brother's attorney general. The coincidence gave Winsor an item. According to the decorous lady, the fashion-conscious wife of a department store executive, Ethel Kennedy met her husband, Robert, in odd apparel: "slacks and loafers." Plus, she was "chewing gum."

When Helen Halle described for Winsor the sort of paintings the committee wanted—eighteenth- and nineteenth-century American landscapes, still lifes, marine battles, and portraits of historic figures—he recalled Wyant's *Glimpse of Lake Champlain,* a single tree on a rocky promontory arching above a radiant white mist that obscured the lake's blue water. The small size of the canvas and Wyant's style—an evocative, rather than a precisely detailed depiction of nature—dated the work as being painted after 1853, the year that the thirty-seven-year-old artist suffered a stroke that paralyzed his right side. Wyant subsequently learned how to paint with his left hand and "abandoned the detailed scrutiny of nature that had previously marked his style." (The painting also provides a glimpse of Eaton family history. Joseph Oriel Eaton, father and namesake of Winsor's late stepfather, had studied with Wyant in Cincinnati in 1857, four years after his stroke.)

Having carried the artwork safely to Washington, Winsor arranged its delivery to the White House, an event that generated another column item. "Don't tell me it isn't a neighborly town. The other afternoon I had occasion to call at the White House (service entrance) to deliver a picture to the curator." He was also, he wrote, "carrying a zipper bag," which he hastened to explain to the curator "contained no bomb, but my laundry. She would be delighted, she told me, to send it upstairs and have it washed." Winsor declined the offer and left the painting. His family had offered the Wyant to a college museum, but a "snooty" curator had turned them down. He hoped the work would meet the committee's criteria for acquisition and Jacqueline Kennedy's approval.

Upon his return to Hotel Halle, he found his hostess deep in conversation with Roger Stevens, "a gentleman of infinite vitality and charm." They were discussing how to raise $30 million so the nation's capital could have a first-class performing arts center. Eavesdropping, Winsor collected still another item. "No one anywhere, believe me, is going to be safe once they start shaking their tambourines."

Secondhand reports of Washington's commercial nightlife did not interest Winsor. "What the tired congressmen and lobbyists like are belly dancers. They are all over the place, writhing and undulating like mad (and to mad applause) in such aptly-titled, smoke-filled joints as the Port Said and Suez." Winsor preferred not to undulate. "With dusk, Georgetown draws its blinds, lights the fires on the hearths and settles in. All rather comforting and old world."

After a week at Hotel Halle, Winsor decided to visit the founder of the Jolly Set. He accepted Hank Greenberg's offer of a ride to Maryland, where they found "all the Veecks in high spirits." There, Willy's wife, Mary, "cuts his hair, or rather what is left of it." They reminisced about the changes in their lives. "No more round-the-clock parties, no more Veeck's Follies in basement nightclubs and above all, no more sweating out extra-inning ball games. It is Veeck, the recluse, now." To Winsor, the man seemed "happy enough to keep busy refinishing old furniture for the guesthouse, or exercising his green thumb in a jungle of orchid plants. . . . And the paradox is that he doesn't seem changed at all, except that he now walks on a peg leg which gives him a dashing, romantic air."

Following a short visit to Manhattan, Winsor returned to Cleveland via the New York Central and announced a change in his own life. He had leased an apartment on the seventh floor of the Shoreham at 11800 Edgewater Drive on Lakewood's Gold Coast. "After living some forty-six years on the eastern shores of the Cuyahoga River I finally took the plunge, crossed the bridge and moved to the West Side." He was still breaking taboos. Only someone who has lived in Cleveland for more than a week appreciates his unconventional behavior. Changing riversides was so eccentric that when Winsor gave the *Press* business manager his new address, he said, "I couldn't be more stunned if you told me you had joined the Communist Party!"

In his new apartment Winsor discovered a world of "passing ships and changing skies. Of wild birds, too; violent, sudden storms and nights when the moaning foghorns cause me to suddenly awaken and wonder for a second or two what I am doing in the North Atlantic." To his sister Anne, he wrote, "What a view I have! Easily as dramatic as Portofino—and no language barrier."

He furnished his aerie with the seventeenth-century Italian antiques he had purchased in Europe and added "a wood-burning engine of French porcelain, used for hot chocolate," from Len Hanna's estate, as well as "two little armchairs, upholstered in rough natural linen" from the Halles' house, shelves full of first editions and a new coffee table that held "a petit point backgammon board made by Winsor's mother." On the walls hung portraits autographed by his celebrity friends as well as provocative paintings by his sister Anne, and Augustus Peck, a curator at the Brooklyn Museum of Art. In the 1930s, when a more bohemian Peck illustrated Winsor's book reviews in *PARADE* magazine, he called himself "Gus."

Winsor boasted in another letter to Anne, "Already I have had several little sit down dinners with great success." He also established his social standing with the Lakewood post office. A small, cream-colored envelope had arrived addressed to him. The return address was embossed in gold: "The White House, Washington."

> Dear Mr. French: I cannot tell you how delighted I am to accept the charming landscape by Alexander Wyant. It will be a great addition to The White House permanent collection. Thank you very much for your thoughtfulness and spontaneous generosity. Jacqueline Kennedy

With renewed enthusiasm and a classic hardwood cane, Winsor returned to his typewriter on the fourth floor of the two-year-old editorial offices and printing plant the *Press* had built at East 9th and Lakeside Avenue. The site had been cleared of structures like Winsor's apartment at Sin Shanty as part of the city's "urban renewal" efforts. Winsor's office was only "ten minutes and two traffic lights away" from his new apartment. An important change in local newspaper ownership had also occurred. After years of declining circulation and increased productions costs, Forest City Publishing, owners of the *Plain Dealer,* had sold the *News* to the *Press,* now

Cleveland's only afternoon daily. Similar newspaper mergers, sales, or closings occurred in many urban markets. Typically two newspapers survived: One published in the morning, another in the evening. In the 1960s, people had more time to read the evening newspaper than they do today, so it often had a larger circulation and greater advertising revenues.

To help explain his change of address, the columnist immediately began a series headlined "Winsor Goes West," travel reportage written to acquaint his former East Side neighbors with West Side cultural landmarks. He had no vanity about the cane. It appeared prominently in photos of him at Lakewood Civic Auditorium, the Zoo, the Baldwin-Wallace College campus, and the Metropolitan Park system, which Clevelanders called "the Emerald Necklace" and Winsor compared to the Vienna Woods. "Littered with campers and with its infrequent views of the anything but blue Danube," the Austrian landmark "pales into insignificance in comparison to the gardens, wooden slopes, bridle paths and camping sites that surround Cleveland. And how we neglect them! All of our beaches are polluted. Family picnic groups disperse with no thought of the litter they leave behind. And who dares to park along some leafy, dead-end lane."

Winsor was off on another crusade: Saving the region's parklands. For two years, he pestered public officials with critical columns. "It wouldn't be a bad idea for the Gordon Park gardeners to get about their spring cleaning. What with the refuse cascading down the slopes, the place is beginning to look like a landscaped city dump." He remembered when it was "illuminated by gas street lamps and attended to nightly by a lamplighter on a bicycle. Primitive, perhaps, but at least the boulevard led to a broad, white beach lapped by unpolluted waters."

Yet the neglected Gordon Park was "a Garden of Eden compared to the view from the Rapid Transit windows between E. 55th and the Terminal. This, surely, must be one of the happiest hunting grounds for rats in the nation, as well as one of the most disgraceful corners of the city. Down these hillsides are tossed discarded bedsprings, abandoned iceboxes, egg crates, garbage and you name it."

When city officials proposed selling another park, White City Beach, "because it drifts into dunes and requires raking which costs a few bucks," Winsor called the plan "madness. This is the last halfway decent beach on our lakefront, and as it is smack up against the filtering station, probably the least polluted. And no one even whimpers."

In Cleveland neighborhoods, he missed "the little traveling carnivals" that once were fixtures of urban summer nightlife. "Those rickety Ferris wheels that used to blossom suddenly for two or three evenings on corner lots were probably lethal, but they were also one of the summer's prettiest sights. And is there any more nostalgic music than the sounds issuing from a merry-go-round calliope."

Following Winsor's scolding columns on Cleveland's landscape and his breathtaking move to the West Side, editor Louis Seltzer felt he should try and explain his newspaper's best-known personality to new readers of the *Press*. Seltzer assigned Bill Dvorak to the difficult task, who called Winsor's column "a 20th-century Pepys Diary" containing "equal parts O. O. McIntyre, F. Scott Fitzgerald, Lucius Beebe and Elsa Maxwell . . . plus a dash of Puck."

Pepys wrote about London in diaries during the mid-1600s; McIntyre wrote about New York City in newspapers during the 1920s and '30s, and Fitzgerald wrote class-conscious short stories and novels during the same period; Beebe wrote about society, including Winsor's wedding, in 1933; Elsa Maxwell hosted parties, some of which Winsor attended; and Puck was the fairy who created mischief in Shakespeare's *A Midsummer Night's Dream,* 1595 or 1596.

In newspaper city rooms, where occupants boasted about their capacity for liquor, stories steeped in alcohol enhanced one's status. In this contest, Winsor was a top seed. On any night, he confided to his sister, he could "toss off a fifth of Scotch with no effort" and the subsequent hangovers were legendary.

Stan Anderson remembered one afternoon, when a "Lilliputian elephant once walked through the city room" accompanied by an advance man for the Grotto Circus. "Winsor French was engaged busily in a phone conversation with a companion of the previous night. French was telling his friend that his head was 'simply splitting and please don't speak harshly,' when his side vision permitted him a glimpse of the creature with the prehensile trunk."

The former member of Stuart Walker's acting company, who believed that "a little ham is a good thing in life," sensed an opportunity for improvisational theater. "My God," he screamed, "I've got to hang up. There's a goddamn elephant plunging through the office." Anderson maintained that it took "some time before a crew of sympathetic colleagues could calm down French and convince him there was only one elephant in the room and that that elephant was very small, indeed—and not pink."

His competitors at the *Plain Dealer* no longer sniggered about his footwear. George Condon, whose column was as broad a canvas as Winsor's, said, "Newspaper people love a good storyteller and Winsor was positively captivating."

Newspaper readers, according to radio's Bill Randle, never used the columnist's last name. "It was just 'Did you see what Winsor had in his column today?' or 'Wait 'til Winsor hears about that!' Or, mostly, 'What does Winsor think of it?'" He was "like God or Mahatma Gandhi or Frank Sinatra."

What really aroused his colleagues' curiosity, however, was the size of his wallet.

Dvorak: "Winsor devotes considerable time and column space to the entertainment bistros. He is continually hurt because everybody doesn't eat (and drink) out every night, hang the expense."

Anderson: While searching trash baskets for column notes, Winsor may "run across a paycheck or dividend payment which he also has relegated to the basket."

Dvorak: "Winsor's standards concerning money and people are peculiarly his own. He wrote: 'To charter a yacht is not nearly as fracturing as you might think. They come from $250 a day up.'"

Renting yachts was unimaginable for reporters who complained about salaries limited by union contracts. Yet Winsor understood that the cost of a yacht divided by nine would be less per night than a first-class hotel room. So in May 1962, he and eight compatible family members and friends chartered a yacht to tour the Greek Islands. They met in Athens on the first of June.

His companions included Kay Halle, Eve Hexter, Eddy and Mickey Joseph, Margaret "Mag" Sherwin, Charles and Martha Hickox (Winsor's sister), Connie Macomber, a rowdy theater friend of his, and "enough books to furnish a library, histories of ancient and modern Crete, Rhodes and all of the thousands of islands dotting these waters."

They had chartered the *Thendara* on the advice of Constantine Nicoloudis, a guide who accompanied them on the week's cruise. Margaret Sherwin thought Constantine "extremely attractive." In letters to her family, she described their accommodations: "two double cabins (one very small), and three tiny single ones." Constantine slept in the "lounge, Winsor in the Steward's cabin, the steward on the dining room floor. Two heads for all, and one head is in the Hickox's cabin."

On the first two days, a wind-blown, roller-coaster sail to the island of Hydra unsettled Eve Hexter and the cook. The former left the yacht and returned to Cleveland. To calm his stomach, the latter "drank gin," Margaret wrote. The remaining voyagers persevered on becalmed seas, pampered by eight crewmembers. Winsor's dispatches from four islands describe the shenanigans.

At Paros, everyone but the columnist went ashore "to visit the church of Our Lady of a Hundred Gates," where one could "buy little tin impressions of a leg, an arm, a heart, or whatever part of your body needs attention, leave it on the altar and then pray for the best." When Eddy Joseph returned to the *Thendara,* he brought aboard "a small tin leg, which, with an offering, he left on the altar for me. What I could really use is a brand new stomach."

Taking a page from Cole Porter's travel handbook, in Patmos the party found a "likely-looking tavern" that was "immaculately clean and absolutely bare except for wine racks and a tin water tank hanging above a tin wash basin, a roll of toilet paper beside in lieu of towels." After ordering a dinner of "lobster, sea urchins and red mullet" they went in search of

> local musicians. All this accomplished, we then decided to let come what may and what came was a party for the entire village. . . . First came the islanders with their children, little boys and girls bearing gifts of flowers. Then the passengers from a cruise ship in the harbor, Swedes, Danes and Germans. . . . As soon as the musicians commenced playing their curious wailing music the dancing began. Sometimes a single man would go it alone, later to be joined by a friend. Many were ritual dances, born in antiquity and vaguely erotic. . . . The sailors from our boat got in on the act as well.

When Winsor was presented the bill, he discovered that dinner for nine, drinks for more than thirty extra people and the fee for the musicians all came to less than twenty-five dollars. At this, he wrote, "What are we doing living in the best location in the nation?"

In Mykonos, "Cocktail parties suddenly blossom on after-decks, eventually growing into dinners as ours did for the John Steinbecks." That author and his wife were traveling with sons Tom and John, a tutor ("a young man called Terrance"), and the fashion designer Jean Dessès. He had draped both the Duchess of Windsor and Elsa Maxwell in gowns of chiffon and mousseline that resembled the robes of ancient Greeks and Egyptians. "As in Patmos, practically the entire town came to join us. Dancers emerged from nowhere, less pagan here and more stylized. Even the beautiful Saroya, the ex-queen of Iran, with her haunted eyes, appeared out of the night, followed by a battery of photographers. And the next morning, naturally, the papers gave her full credit for having staged the gala, but the proprietor of the tavern gave us the check."

Finally, Winsor reported, Aegina was the "last port of call and just as well. I was beginning to think . . . being hauled up and down dizzying rocky cliffs would never end." He appreciated the "guide at Rhodes who wanted to carry me on his back up the staircase in the Palace of the Grand Master when I couldn't make it on my own. And still another who lit a cigarette for me by simply holding it under his eyeglasses in the brilliant sun." Believing there were countless Cleveland readers wanting to follow his footsteps, he advised them, "Assemble a party of four or six, start bargaining well in advance for a small, sturdy vessel, then you will be master of your own imagination and for far less money than you might expect." After contemplating his advice, *Press* readers could turn to the grocery ads and see if anyone could beat Stop & Shop's price for ground beef.

What Winsor's colleagues and readers didn't appreciate was that Leonard Hanna's gift of IBM stock did not make him a man of unlimited means. He was asset rich and cash poor. To finance his European trips, he borrowed money using Hanna's gift as collateral. To his sister Anne, he wrote, "My expenses are extraordinary and I also must try and reduce my bank loan." However, loan proceeds did allow Winsor to spend a week in southern Italy and Adriatic ports after his companions flew home from Athens, and before he sailed on the *Leonardo da Vinci*. An erratic U.S. stock market had made wealthy American passengers nervous. With his outstanding loan, even Winsor followed the daily swings of the IBM share. When the price finally stabilized at $298 a share, he and his traveling companions were "a little less freighted with gloom."

After docking in New York, he taxied to Grand Central Station. By early evening he was on "the Cleveland Limited, rolling along beside the Hudson in the gathering twilight." From his train window, he saw "the old excursion boats were still plying their way between New York and Troy and Albany. Only yesterday it seems I used to ride them with Cole Porter and wonderfully gay little cruises they were, too, with wonderful diversions always going on around you, both on shore as well as on the river. But, as they say, you can never go back."

But Winsor fought hard to save what was left of the past, especially where the railroads were concerned. Two months after returning from Europe, he returned to the Terminal Tower station to catch a train to Washington. "There were no redcaps in sight and people of all ages were struggling up and down the stairs with their luggage." Once again, "the conductor had failed to show up at the check-out desk. . . . I was told it was impossible to go aboard. The porter, I was informed, would not show up until just before departure time, the car was dark."

Winsor was skeptical. Armed with folding money, he "snagged a redcap who led me through a maze of dimly lit, draughty baggage rooms, then into the elevator and down to the platform. There was my car, a blaze of lights, and standing beside it was the porter, my old friend Charlie Bell who has been with the line some 35 years."

With Bell's help, Winsor stowed his luggage, crawled into his berth, fell asleep and awoke in Washington, D.C., where he found a city preparing for "the most glittering gala this anything but socially retiring village has seen in many a season." The centerpiece was a performance of Irving Berlin's new musical comedy, *Mr. President,* at the National Theater. Proceeds from $100 patron tickets would benefit two Kennedy family charities. Kay Halle asked Winsor to be her escort, for an evening that promised at least four or five columns.

The last time Winsor had covered the opening of a Berlin musical was in September 1933, when he and his fiancée Margaret Perry attended the New York City premiere of *As Thousands Cheer,* an event so popular it led Margaret's mother to postpone her daughter's wedding by a week. Twenty-nine years later, Berlin had "emerged from his long retirement to write the words and music" for *Mr. President,* but he could no longer command the audience he once had. Winsor had been following the show's tryouts in Philadelphia: "The critics were anything but kind and the attendance anything but sensational." Yet when the White House announced that President Kennedy and his wife would attend opening night at the National Theater, "mail orders had poured in with a cascade of blank checks."

Before the performance, he and Kay dined at Katherine and Phillip Graham's "historic R Street house." Katherine was Kay's personal friend; her family owned the *Washington Post* and *Newsweek* magazine. Among others, Winsor sipped champagne with Justice Arthur Goldberg and Secretary of Agriculture Orville and Jane Freeman. "Of protocol there was none. You helped yourself to dinner from the groaning buffets . . . and then everyone who had been unable to produce a chauffeur-driven car was driven away in chartered buses."

In the president's box, Winsor recognized Jackie Kennedy's mother and Alice Longworth, two formidable women he'd met earlier at Hotel Halle. The first lady joined the group, but not the president, although his rocking chair was "waiting for him . . . having been sent over earlier in the day from the White House." The theater was "crawling with the Secret Service and there were those who wished they had been far away." The air conditioning had been turned off, and the Secret Service would not allow anyone to crawl out on the roof and turn it on. "The mighty as well as the meek sweltered."

After the curtain went up on the second act, John F. Kennedy entered the presidential box in darkness. Nanette Fabray, who portrayed the show's first lady, watched "as a constant stream of aides came and went. Neither she nor Winsor and the rest of the audience knew that the first stages of the Cuban missile crisis were "commanding Kennedy's attention."

In the steaming auditorium, "the final curtain at last flushed the multitudes into the street, sending some six hundred of them on to the British

Embassy where the Ambassador and Lady Ormsby Gore presided over a dazzling reception." There Winsor met the president's sister Eunice Shriver, who impressed him. Berlin's *Mr. President?* "Disappointing."

Ignoring Winsor's pleas, in November the B&O announced plans to discontinue its "direct train to the nation's capital from Cleveland." Winsor did not like the alternative: "Hopping the Toonerville Trolley the B&O still operates. On this streamlined job you will be flushed out at Harrisburg, Pa., and, as I understand it, will have to walk quite a distance over an open platform, and very likely carrying your own luggage. . . . And, may I ask, is this progress?"

One reader wrote Winsor to say it wasn't: "When you go to Detroit now by rail it takes all day and two railroads! To Pittsburgh, or Akron, or Lima etc., you don't go at all. In the unlikely event you can find any train to take, you travel in filthy coaches filled to the brim with half-dressed, haggard, sweating humanity sprawling in each other's laps. To participate in this nightmare you pay almost as much as it costs to fly, or if you are willing to be robbed blind in broad daylight you pay the ludicrous Pullman rates."

Winsor conceded that the "airplane is here to stay. Railroads on the other hand, also have their valid points and in times of crisis are absolute necessities. . . . A nation of our size and blessed with our wealth should be able to maintain rail communications at least between the major cities. And if the companies themselves can't do it and still keep their heads above water, why not a government subsidy? Heaven knows we subsidize everything else."

The rival New York Central sensed a public relations opportunity. When Winsor boarded their train for Manhattan in November, there were redcaps at the East Cleveland Terminal, and "drinks were served," two guarantees of a friendly column: "For once sleep came swiftly. I was not aware of any shunting about during the night. In fact the ride was smooth as silk and I can only suppose the New York Central people have laid down a new roadbed when I wasn't looking. The next morning I was awakened by a gentle tapping at my door and there if you please was a waiter bearing a tray with coffee, orange juice and the morning paper, compliments of the steward."

The railroad had bamboozled Winsor. He wrote, "Things are changing."

On his way to the dock where the *Queen Mary* was waiting, he witnessed more than one illegally parked Rolls-Royce that seemed "immune from parking tickets." Could a Rolls intimidate policemen? There was no time to dawdle in Manhattan. Much to Winsor's dismay, steamships no longer departed at midnight. They lifted anchor in the middle of morning, no time for champagne. Once aboard, he was told "fewer than 150 people were traveling first class." Like passenger trains, steamships were an endangered species. "The slot machines the Cunard Line was experiment-ing with the last time I was aboard have vanished and these I miss. It has long been my belief that if the luxury liners want to snatch the air-minded from the planes they are going to have to come up with some sort of Las Vegas touch."

If the Cunard's owners hoped Winsor's columns would boost bookings, they were to be disappointed. For the first forty-eight hours, "driving rains, followed by gale-force winds" had the *Queen Mary* pulling "every trick she knows—pitching, lurching, quivering and creaking." In the corridors pas-sengers staggered "like so many drunks." At night, Winsor "undressed sit-ting on the floor" and then hoisted himself into bed, where he was "conked sharply on the head by a soda bottle, an overflowing ashtray and a plate of soda biscuits."

During cocktails on the voyage's third day, "the purser announced to all and sundry that between the hours of noon and five P.M. we had passed through the eye of the hurricane." The storm had upset "Mrs. John F. C. Bryce, of the Huntington-Hartford fortunes, who came aboard with her maid and ninety-two pieces of luggage!" The *Queen Mary*'s instability had sent Mrs. Bryce's maid to bed, so the heiress had to unpack her own lug-gage. Readers expected to hear more about colorful passengers, but Win-sor wasn't allowed to finish his story.

On the night of November 29, 1962, truck drivers at the *Plain Dealer* walked off the job, followed by twenty-four hundred employees in eleven different unions at both the *Press* and *Plain Dealer,* forcing both news-papers to cease publication. Almost simultaneously, employees struck New York City newspapers as well.

Winsor was in London "blissfully unaware I was unemployed . . . every-thing going out and nothing coming in, only I didn't know it." That same week, he had purchased a Rolls-Royce, succumbing to a passion he first described thirty years earlier in *PARADE* magazine. "We know where you can buy a Rolls-Royce touring car, all in A1 condition, for $888.88—but not a cent less. Dark maroon, black running-gear, five wire wheels, four new tires. Free ad? We've been promised a weekend's use of it. (P.S. $777.77 will close the deal.)"

Subsequent envy the columnist expressed for the Rollses owned by Bar-bara Hutton and Lady Mendl as well as the automobile's apparent immu-nity from parking tickets were over. He owned a Silver Cloud, but before it could be loaded aboard the *Queen Mary* and accompany him to the United States, the car had to be "deloused. England, it appears, has a potato bug the United States is not eager to import." After his auto took a "steam bath," it and Winsor boarded the ship together, "but there were dark omens." A dock strike that had crippled New York's harbor threatened to delay the *Queen Mary*'s departure. Winsor did not return to the United States until January, and when he arrived in Manhattan, striking longshoremen refused to unload his prize. "The Rolls Royce made four round trips over the Atlantic before the coast strike was settled."

Meanwhile, his editorial colleagues in Cleveland had continued to picket their employers throughout January, February, and a bitterly cold March. George Condon remembered colleagues from both newspapers pulled stocking caps over their ears and foreheads to protect themselves. The *Plain Dealer* columnist and his fellow union members trudging back and forth across the entrance to the parking lot at the *Press* building had "scrunched-up shoulders and the pinched look that comes from standing in the cold." They had been out of work for more than 120 days, the longest strike in Cleveland newspaper history.

Suddenly, a gleaming black Rolls-Royce, chauffeured by a noble African American man in elegant black livery, "swept grandly into the parking lot." The pickets "dipped their placards and grinned at the slender man who waved to them from the back seat." Winsor was visiting the city room to "go through his mail." The striking unions' leadership had given him permission "to drive through the picket line."

Pickets had heard stories about problems Winsor encountered taking possession of his new automobile. Condon was glad to see it finally had arrived. Winsor's chauffeured entrance through motley picket lines quickly became part of his legend. Condon remembered that he "rode his Rolls with panache." Ironically, at the same time as he was driven into the parking lot, Seltzer, the newspaper's editor, drove himself out in "a nondescript Ford. The contrast," Condon wrote, "was more than enough to cheer the hearts of all the newspaper working stiffs. The patrician and the proletariat: brothers in arms."

On April 8, 1963, newspaper owners finally settled with employees. Winsor was "well aware that both Cleveland and New York were awash with cynics only too happy to tell you they had learned how to get along without papers. Well, the entertainment and restaurant worlds didn't. A long, dreary hibernation," he wrote, "and may there never be another one."

"I cannot use my hands to write"

LONDON, ENGLAND

Saturday, September 7, 1963, 4 p.m.

Winsor waited for Lady Melchett in the art deco opulence of the drawing room at Mulberry House, where the walls were covered with silver foil and great slabs of green marble. Lady Melchett had inherited the Regency residence on Smith Square from her late husband, Henry Mond, Lord Melchett, the heir to his father's chemical fortune. In the drawing room, Lady Melchett—"Gwen" to Winsor—poured "tea or drinks for statesmen, actors, writers and artists." English aristocrats labeled her a "colonial from an unknown South African family"; Winsor called her a "connoisseur of everything from Renaissance and modern painting to food, wines, jazz and people."

Whenever Winsor was in London, Lady Melchett entertained him. On this particular occasion, he noted that she was wearing "slacks," a garment that for Winsor revealed a woman who broke taboos.

He often asked Gwen if he could bring a guest to Mulberry House, "a small elegant museum." Over the years, she had been "very generous about allowing me to take friends to see her famous collection of Grecian marbles, Augustus John paintings, Blakes and so on."

Lady Melchett's "so on" included two remarkable artworks: a relief and a fire basket, which celebrated the Monds design for living. In the drawing room over the green marble fireplace hung *Scandal,* the gilded bronze relief by Charles Sargeant Jagger. "Two lovers" (Lord and Lady Melchett) "stand naked before outraged onlookers who peer at them with hands raised in horror," according to art historians.

In the fireplace, a cast-iron fire basket continued the story. "Two snarling cats are depicted hiding behind female masks to signify the 'double face' and 'cattiness' of society gossip." The Monds had commissioned these pieces as humorous references to their early ménage à trois with an English writer, Gilbert Cannan. Over tea, Winsor and Lady Melchett's conversation veered between "sheer frothy gossip" and "a serious discussion of art or politics."

On this same trip, Winsor had renewed a friendship with another prominent English personality who had pursued an unconventional "design for living." Two days earlier, he had lunched with Harold Nicholson at Sissinghurst Castle, the estate he had created with his late wife, one of Winsor's favorite novelists, Vita Sackville-West. The seventy-five-year-old retired diplomat and critic had greeted Winsor in a "battered old slouch hat and clothes that had seen better days a generation ago." Sir Harold was "recovering from a stroke," but he insisted on taking Winsor for a tour of the gardens, "a monument to the late Miss Sackville-West who had to commence with a barren wilderness."

In the 1920s, Winsor had visited the Nicholsons shortly after the couple had bought Sissinghurst. "Wanting the yew and box hedges to mature quickly," Sackville-West "literally fed them ox blood," Winsor recalled. What Winsor didn't know was that the busy couple found time to pour tea for Winsor during a period that Nicholson was keeping a male lover and Sackville-West was satisfying her romantic interests with two females: Violet Keppel Trefusis, the daughter of Alice Keppel, Edward VII's mistress, and the novelist Virginia Woolf. Meanwhile, Sackville-West bore two sons by Sir Harold and nurtured the yews.

After his remarkable wife died, Sir Harold opened the estate to what Winsor called "day-trippers." Visitors could tour the grounds for a contribution that helped maintain the gardens. "Whatever the Nicholson family problems may be, new life has been given to what might have remained forever a fallen and forgotten ruin."

Winsor's admiring, but selective, miniature profiles of Lady Melchett and Sir Nicholson exemplified how he expressed his approval for individuals who had the courage to break society's rules without violating their privacy or his own and his newspaper's sense of propriety. During that same trip, however, Winsor also wrote about how the mere suggestion of unconventional sexuality could be cruelly exploited, in his review of Terrence Rattigan's play *Man and Boy*, "a long and rather unpleasant discussion involving a little group of utterly amoral people." The production starred Charles Boyer and included "what must be one of the most evil scenes yet conceived by a modern playwright." Boyer's character "tries to persuade a deviate associate that his son, a perfectly normal young man, is a homosexual."

For the first time in thirty years, Winsor used the word "homosexual" in print. The clinical term had entered the vocabulary acceptable in general circulation newspapers. Using the words "perfectly normal" to describe the heterosexual male character suggests that the middle-aged Winsor still felt some ambivalence about his own unconventional desires, a faint echo of the word "effeminate" he had used to describe himself in the 1920s, when he was Briton Hadden's secretary at *TIME*.

Soon after the performance of *Man and Boy*, Winsor departed for Paris and a shocking experience. "After more than 27 years the famous Ritz Bar has been entirely redecorated. No longer comfortable as an old shoe, it has been transformed into a fantasy of crystal, elaborate, engraved mirrors that cast no reflections and extraordinary arrangements of blatantly artificial flowers." Fortunately, "beaming Georges, of the world's longest memory for names and faces, still watches over his clients as if they were children that at any moment might wander into danger." Winsor left Georges in charge of Europe and returned to Cleveland in time to celebrate his fifty-ninth birthday.

The year 1964 brought recognition for Winsor and his colleagues. *TIME* called the *Cleveland Press* one of "America's 10 Best Newspapers." Its circulation hit four hundred thousand in the 1960s, leading the *Plain Dealer,* but publishing in the afternoon was no longer an advantage. Families had turned to another medium for their evening news: television. Morning papers reacted by increasing the number of sections designed expressly for women, which substantially boosted their circulation figures.

Winsor found himself spending less and less time in the city room. "My life has become really vicarious," he wrote Anne. "Nothing but an hour or so at the office." He arrived at the *Press* in the passenger compartment of his Silver Cloud, driven by Sam Hill, a tall, sixty-year-old gentleman who served Winsor as "chauffeur, caretaker and man Friday." Canes eventually failed to help the columnist. Hill helped him into a wheelchair and pushed him into the building where he would deliver his copy, pick up his mail, and joke with colleagues. On one visit, a colleague noticed a change. In addition to the wheelchair, Winsor was now "obliged to hang an orthopedic collar around his neck."

Friends he had known since Prohibition left town. On Short Vincent, Kornman's was closed. Billy Weinberger had moved to Las Vegas, where he was running Caesar's Palace. Shoes Rosen followed him west the same year. Fire destroyed the Theatrical in 1960. Wexler rebuilt his fabled establishment, but it was never the same. Yet Winsor found downtown residents to champion: "I see the police are chasing the shoeshine boys off the streets, confiscating the tools of their trade. . . . Shining shoes is a lot more healthy than stacking pool cues. Furthermore, nearly every man I know badly needs a shine."

He also recorded the passing of his lifelong female friends, like Josephine Grasselli, "'Aunt Jo' to legions," and her companion Frances "Quinnie" Quinlan, whose lives were cushioned by income from thousands of shares of stock in the E. I. du Pont de Nemours Company, which had bought the family's Cleveland-based chemical company in 1928. When Winsor was in his early twenties, Aunt Jo had hosted gambling parties, at which she passed out crisp dollar bills to her guests so they could play roulette or craps with "onyx and diamond dotted dice." Grasselli and her companion enjoyed "the wonderful times that only people can who love the good things of life; food, wine, the theater, beautiful surroundings (but no phony trappings) and flowers."

Winsor also lamented the passing of "Bessie Brown, the great blues singer," who "soared gracefully to fame and what in those days was described as the 'big time.' It was not to last forever, but then nothing does. . . . I remember she worked as a matron in a women's jail and loved it. But then she always loved people, no matter their weaknesses."

Winsor's night people were now more likely to be characters in books, although he "loathed" the men he met in Ernest Hemingway's *Moveable Feast*. The author was "a phony both in personal and literary ways, while Scott [Fitzgerald] was a historian, a poet, far, far, too sensitive and will be read long after Hemingway's silly little bull fighters and calvados drinkers have had their flies zipped up for them by posterity."

While his wits were sharp, Winsor was losing control of his hands. He could no longer write a "W" with one looping line. Instead, he printed the initial with four straight-angled strokes. In an attempt to regain control of his limbs, Winsor was receiving drug therapy. "Time out," he wrote his sister. "Dr. Seymour just came to give me my bi-weekly shot. I am becoming a passionate devotee of drugs. So divine. Just to float all day."

The doctor had also banned beverage alcohol. Cerebellar cortical atrophy presents symptoms similar but not identical to alcoholic brain disease. Winsor worried that his thirst for Scotch had caused his problems. Dr. Seymour wanted to make sure alcohol was not a contributing factor, so had told Winsor to stop drinking. Playwright Eugene O'Neill had faced a similar dilemma. When his "handwriting became shaky and he began to have difficulty walking," O'Neill initially blamed his "alcohol-ravaged youth." Both men were eventually diagnosed as having the rare genetic disorder, which progressively destroys that part of the brain that controls muscles and coordination. Eventually, victims have trouble feeding themselves and speaking, although their minds remain clear. Winsor didn't dwell on the prognosis.

Life on the wagon soured Winsor's view of Cleveland. "In the days when I could still toss off a fifth of Scotch with no effort it wasn't so bad—but to view these people cold, stone sober is something else again." The high point of his week came on Sundays, when Hill packed the columnist into the back seat of his Rolls and drove him to Pepper Pike for dinner with his sister Martha Hickox and her family. When they were away, he felt "a little bit lost."

To relieve his monotonous existence, Winsor decided to visit the New York World's Fair with Kay Halle, before boarding the *Queen Mary* and another trip to Europe. At the World's Fair, Winsor discovered the difficulties of life in a wheelchair. "The guards quickly reminded me that Americans can be the rudest people on earth. They would do nothing to help us through the turnstile with my wheelchair . . . , and when we ducked out of the rain into the Hertz offices our reception, if anything, was icier." Furthermore, the fair was "tawdry" and "Jerry-built." Later that same evening in a suite at the St. Regis Hotel, Winsor received old friends, including Libby Holman, who looked "absolutely terrific with almost pure white hair."

When on the following day the *Queen Mary* pulled away from its dock, Winsor noted the presence of "women in slacks who looked miserable, hot and sloppy" as opposed to "women in beautifully tailored suits who looked cool, collected and well-dressed." If Dr. Seymour read Winsor's column he learned that his patient was not following orders. "Someone had sent me a bottle of champagne. Turtle, my faithful steward of many crossings, had it on ice and we cracked it at once, even though as far as I am concerned it is forbidden."

In his wheelchair, Winsor followed "the same path; from my cabin to the smoking room, on to the Verandah Grill for lunch and dinner and then the return trip." On this route, he discovered the Cunard Line was trying to woo a younger generation with "the Beachcombers Room, which is open all day from morning until midnight for anyone between the ages of 13 and 20." Meanwhile, first-class passengers were "rattling around like peas in a half empty pod." Despite his weakness for tinkering with clichés, Winsor did find fresh phrases to describe his trips. At Cherbourg, "the air smelled (wonderfully to me) of fish and oil and Gauloise cigarettes." When he awoke a day later in London, he heard "the wheezing, itinerant street bands made up of veterans growing older and shorter of breath by the day."

To his delight, one of his nieces, Deborah Hickox, arrived in London by plane and "turned up at the Berkeley for coffee and rolls." They drove south to Lewes and visited Shelley's Hotel, owned by friends Martin and Peggy Heriot. Their establishment, he reported, "glows with the personality shed on it by Heriot (who at times can be difficult) and his lovely wife Peggy, who doesn't even know the meaning of the word difficult."

Shelley's unique attraction for Winsor was its "comfortable little bar where all the town characters assemble twice a day" for "pink gins" mixed by "the bar lady," Gladys Williams, a "high cheek-boned woman of impeccable manners." One never tipped her: "On paying your bill it is polite to invite her to have a drink with you. She profusely thanks you, but as far as I can gather never takes the drink, so I suppose it all adds up to a tip in the end with no one's feelings being hurt." Shelley's regulars included "rugged, tweedy old gentlemen smoking pipes" and "much younger and exceedingly pretty women who somehow never look the type to me who would frequent bars in the forenoon, downing a half dozen gins as if they were so many glasses of water."

Winsor's niece continued her own trip, leaving him seeking help navigating London. "I have been unable to find anyone who would like to push a wheelchair around. This has made getting any place other than a precise destination by hired car something of a drag, as they say." Peggy Heriot eventually rescued Winsor. As she pushed him through one of London's parks, "a man jumped up from his folding chair and insisted on taking over. . . . When I thanked him he said, 'I wasn't thinking of you sir, but your missus.' So at my very ripe age I have had a young and beautiful wife wished on me. This I felt called for a celebration so we went into the Ritz and had large, ice cold, dry martinis. Forbidden to me, which gave them even greater zest in these elegant surroundings." Neither useless legs nor a doctor's orders would change Winsor's behavior. A few days later, his sister Martha Hickox arrived with "an architectural student from Cleveland and Kent State University, who has taken over my wheelchair and widened my horizons" for the remainder of the trip.

Shortly after Winsor's return to America, Cole Porter died in California. The composer was seventy-three. Winsor's own health problems made him more dependent on his family and friends, all of whom lived on the east side of the Cuyahoga River. He abandoned Lake Erie's shore and rented an apartment at 13900 Shaker Boulevard, near Shaker Square. By the end of the year, he was sixty and no longer able to type. He dictated columns and personal letters to a secretary, whose collaboration did not censor the content of his correspondence with Anne Parker: "It's freezing cold, snowing, I'm fighting what feels like walking pneumonia and wondering how I can get out of having a 6:30 dinner this evening with Barbara Stanwyck," a fifty-seven-year-old actress trying to revive her movie career. "I thought she had gone to her reward years ago but it appears she has just completed a new movie with her ex-husband, Robert Taylor, called *Night Walker*. I made the fatal mistake of calling it *Street Walker* in print and she didn't appreciate it." If Winsor and Stanwyck dined, the encounter did not rate an item.

As his physical health declined, Winsor wrote "about-town" columns without leaving his apartment. A telephone call from chilly Florida provided an item for him, housebound in snowy Cleveland: "I talked to a friend of mine in Palm Beach the other day who informed me the ladies were all wearing furs." He still documented downtown's struggle for survival: "For the first time in the history of Cleveland, so they tell me, a downtown movie theater is offering FREE INDOOR parking to its patrons. This is the Palace . . . and it should be a boon to teenagers who find dating costs reaching astronomical proportions."

From the back seat of his Rolls-Royce, Winsor cast a critical eye on Public Square: "You would have to travel the world over to find an uglier open spot of ground in any large city . . . a playground for pigeons and a sort of dreary outdoor 'office' for the bums who occasionally sit alone on the scattered benches." On another chauffeured trip, he visited Jean's Fun House, a surviving neighbor of Sin Shanty, Winsor's 1930s apartment in the Lakeside Flats. The hardy enterprise was owned by Gertie ("Mrs. Jean") Gevaras, whose "pet monkey, Angelo . . . was an East Ninth Street character. Not so long ago he went to his rest, but his cage still hangs there empty and Gertie is bereft—as are the regular customers who used to stop by to have daily chats with him and poke little snacks through the bars. The joint smells fresher, though."

The postman brought items, including a letter from the Automobile Club offering Winsor the opportunity to renew his driver's license by mail. "I am now about as able to handle a car as a child of three. With no control of my legs and almost none of my hands I would practically be Public Enemy No. 1 to city traffic, or even on a country lane. No matter, a 5-cent stamp plus the fee would have bought me a new driving permit and no questions asked. Obviously this is ridiculous."

The idiocy of the Automobile Club and difficulties navigating the World's Fair and London in a wheelchair provoked Winsor into a series of columns promoting the rights of the "handicapped, paraplegics, cardiacs, the people who must live in wheelchairs and who all find their lives are made unnecessarily more difficult simply because the architects who design so many of our important buildings never give a thought to ramps."

Buildings without adequate means for wheelchair entry were a form of job discrimination. "A man could be a genius, but if he was in a wheelchair and couldn't get to work, then he could not obtain the employment for which he was qualified." Schools without ramps were worse: "Recently I talked with a woman [Mrs. Anton Zverina] whose teen-aged daughter is paralyzed from the waist down and must depend on a wheelchair. Extremely ambitious as well as bright, she has her heart set to go to college and, eventually, to teach art. Well, in order to teach anything, you must first learn it and this child is not even able to get inside the Art Institute building. In other words she is even being denied the privilege of a fair chance."

Writing from experience, Winsor continued: "The handicapped do not wish to be considered objects of pity and, as all normal human beings would, they try to remain as independent and self-sufficient as possible. All too often they just can't make it. The very least of their problems, however, should be the right to become decently educated, able to take advantage of our public schools just as easily as more fortunate children. Well, please don't think for a moment they can and it is a matter that many school boards should give careful thought to, and not in some remote future. Heaven knows that once out in the world even the most brilliant of the handicapped finds it difficult enough to gain employment. The untrained and uneducated might just as well go on relief."

Of Winsor's many crusades, his columns on behalf of persons dealing with physical handicaps generated the most passionate letters from readers.

My husband was stricken [with polio] fifteen years ago and left paralyzed from the waist down . . . a flight of stairs is a most unwelcome sight. In some stores we have been allowed, reluctantly, to use the freight elevator.

Because some one is physically handicapped, everyone takes it as a matter of course that he is mentally retarded.

Do you honestly believe that you would have gotten the job that you hold now if you had become handicapped prior to getting it? Maybe and maybe not.

People don't let anyone that is paralyzed from stroke be near normal in public. . . . I wish you would write more on this maybe it will help. About us being only paralyzed, not sick or a nut.

The campaign mobilized groups who used Winsor's columns to get the attention of Cleveland mayor Ralph Locher, who in March 1966 ordered that entrances to all public buildings be made accessible to handicapped persons. He said, "I had no idea it was so difficult for a physically handicapped person to get into City Hall until Winsor French began writing about it in the *Press*. We'll either build ramps or make arrangements for using special elevator entrances or lifts so people in wheelchairs can get in and out. That includes not only City Hall but all city-owned buildings like police and fire stations."

No longer willing to take his chances on his own in London and Paris, a revitalized Winsor hired a young Cleveland artist, David Parkinson, to be his "keeper" and push his wheelchair through his annual European trek. They boarded the USS *United States* in June 1966, another crossing that produced items about celebrity passengers. In the Promenade Restaurant at a table next to Winsor's, the Duke and Duchess of Windsor dined. The columnist strained to hear their conversation, "no luck. From here on I think I'll carry an ear trumpet." Toward the end of the voyage, as Parkinson was wheeling him out of the room, Winsor "noticed the Duchess of Windsor beckoning me to her table." Years earlier, Aileen Winslow, whose Sunday suppers had been such an important source of early column items, introduced Winsor to the former Wallis Simpson and the former King of England. Winsor recalled, "David I thought was going to faint, but he remained on his feet" while the two listened to the duke reminisce about two visits to Cleveland.

Although Winsor had equipped his wheelchair with a horn, in London he avoided crowds and watched the changing of the guard on a television set in his hotel room while Parkinson joined throngs of tourists on the sidewalk. But when the former Louise Albritton, the "gay, blond and beautiful" wife of CBS correspondent Charles Collingwood, offered Winsor and his "keeper" a tour of Portobello Road, the columnist quickly accepted her invitation.

Louise Collingwood, a former television and movie actress, led the men through "an insane, perpetual carnival" where "the beats of both sexes gather, usually dressed almost exactly alike, although sometimes the girls wear 'mini' skirts, and all with shoulder length hair. You wonder . . . who on earth would dream of hiring such extraordinary creatures." (Family members' hair was not exempt from criticism. Winsor invited his sister Anne and her husband, Tony Parker, to visit Cleveland and stay in his apartment, but Tony wasn't welcome "if he still has a beard. I know I sound two thousand years old and I love all my nieces and nephews as well as their generation, but the beatnik bit I can't cope with.")

On the assumption that newspaper readers were always curious about seedy sexual exhibits, Winsor persuaded Louise Collinwood to take him to Soho to "see one of those famous strip tease joints that open up early in the morning and grind on wearily throughout the entire day and evening." He found them "smoky, sordid little honky-tonks smelling of beer, cheap whiskey and down-at-the-heels humanity. The audiences consist largely of men, half asleep over their tepid beers. The artists, shall we say, have long since forgotten their youth, and none of them really strip."

After a day of slumming, Winsor bought drinks for his entourage at Claridge's, in a bar where "watchful waiters thread their way silently between the marble-topped tables, thanking you for everything, even if you tip over the drink that cost you perhaps $2, as I did." Winsor's hands had betrayed him, and he felt a need to tell readers. On the following days, Winsor hired a driver to take him and Parkinson to Shelley's Hotel to see the Heriots, to Mulberry House for tea with Lady Melchett, and to a production of Noël Coward's *A Song at Twilight,* in which the playwright portrayed "an aging, tired author of great prominence," a self-conscious casting decision he had used in *Design for Living.* A former mistress of the Coward character was trying to blackmail the playwright with a packet of love letters he had "written to another man." Winsor thought their dialogue "rather boring and repetitious." Winsor thought Coward looked "exhausted and frequently went up on his lines, which seemed strange to me considering he wrote them."

Winsor repeated the "backstage gossip" that *Twilight* was "based on episodes in the life of the late W. Somerset Maugham," who had died in January. Coward had firmly denied the rumors, and Winsor wrote, "I am inclined to believe him." At the time of Maugham's death, he had written his own critical assessment of Maugham and for the first time revealed the details of his meetings in the 1920s and 1930s with the author and Haxton, to whom who he referred as Maugham's "secretary and closest friend."

The man he once called "almost my favorite person," Winsor now described as "humorless." Maugham disliked "most people," according to Winsor, who doubted "if many got to know him really well. Tortured by an impediment in his speech, he was inclined to be rather silent." Winsor believed him "a bitter and unhappy man, despite his great fame and wealth." However, he described Haxton, who was eighteen years younger than Maugham, as "a rather dashing figure who used to ride horseback in the Bois" whenever Maugham gave him "a morning free."

After his lunch at the Villa Mauresque, Winsor remembered, Maugham "retired to his room for a siesta, but the guests usually stayed on for a swim in his marble pool, fringed by a grove of pines (or were they palms or avocados? Memory falters.)." Maugham's biographers agreed that "palms" surrounded the pool; "avocados" bordered a lower terrace. Robert Calder, who wrote a sympathetic biography of Maugham, described the Villa Mauresque as a "great literary pilgrimage point" during the mid-twentieth century, and "never so lively as during the thirties when Haxton presided over activities as Maugham's companion-secretary and lover." Bryan Connon, a less kindly biographer, wrote, "Beautiful but obscure young men were part of the scenery" at Villa Mauresque.

Winsor provides one unpublished anecdote about the author. At a luncheon with Lady Ribblesdale (mother of the late Vincent Astor), Maugham was "extremely subdued. His friend Gerald Haxton was dying in a New York hospital [1944] and once I heard him complain about what a long and expensive process it was." Winsor was appalled. "My mind raced back over the years to Paris, the Riviera and an era when Haxton was the indispens-able man. . . . I had had enough. I never saw Maugham again except once, across the bar in the Hotel de Paris in Monte Carlo. He did not see me and no pleasantries were exchanged." (After Haxton's death, Maugham wrote Coward that his companion of thirty years was "my pleasure and my anxi-ety and without him I am lost, lonely and hopeless.") Winsor also doubted "if much of [Maugham's] work will survive"; he was notably wrong.

On another evening, Winsor was enraged by a performance of *Funny Girl*, a musical comedy "allegedly based on the career of the late Fanny Brice (whom I knew). Absolutely none of her material has been included in the book and Julie Styne's score contains only one song that could be remembered more than half an hour. This, of course, is 'People.' It is sung by Miss Streisand in a voice coming right out of her nose and sounded to me exactly like a fingernail scratching a classroom blackboard."

And on that cranky note, Winsor departed for France and the pleasures of the Ritz Bar, where he learned that the fabled Georges had retired and been replaced by "Paul," who had become the "emperor of this exclusive small domain." He was upholding standards of which Georges and Winsor approved. "Women in slacks or men without neckties would not be admit-ted. This is one of the last citadels of elegance on earth and the manage-ment means to keep it that way."

Peggy Heriot took a holiday from Shelley's and joined Winsor and Par-kinson in Paris. On a shopping trip, they parked Winsor in his wheelchair on the sidewalk outside the Hermes boutique, then they went inside. "To my astonishment, a woman hurrying by attempted to press a five franc note in my hand. I have been taken for a lot of things in my time, but never before for a beggar and I am beginning to think I should perhaps revise my thinking and use my chair a bit more profitably."

By the time Winsor had returned to Cleveland, his journalism patron, Louis Seltzer, had retired after thirty-eight years. The columnist's circle of friends was growing smaller and smaller. Jules Weinberger died. A son of "Pop" Weinberger, Winsor's Prohibition bootlegger and Billy's brother, he "simply liked people and didn't ask or expect perfection of them." Winsor now spent many nights trying to refresh his memories of Cleveland night-spots, including speakeasies supplied by the Weinbergers. Chauffeur Sam Hill remembered Winsor "would be with some friends and they'd get into an argument over some restaurant . . . and I would have to drive them to wherever it was they were arguing about to settle the matter."

For years, Winsor tried to find his first speakeasy, "the east 30's or 40's, almost on the edge of the Pennsylvania railroad tracks. It had all the charm of a skid row flop house. To get in you rang a bell at the side door, and muttered 'Halsey sent me' to the gent who came to the grilling. There was sawdust on the floor, the atmosphere reeked of stale beer and a gasping crystal radio set tortured the air." On these trips, the passengers' compartment of the Silver Cloud became a small, mobile saloon. In cold weather, Winsor sipped Scotch, in warm weather, vodka and tonic. Hill drove the party "downtown, or all around town until two and three in the morning."

Winsor was not alone in searching for the relics of his youth. Another such hunter was Archibald MacLeish, whose poetry and critique of capitalism in 1932 had earned Winsor's praise at *PARADE*. "The truth is that we left the twenties without choice and against our wills," MacLeish wrote. "The speculative hysteria of 1929 and the speculative collapse of 1930 interrupted one of the few hopeful periods of American history."

On these trips to recapture the past, Winsor sometimes had Hill stop and push him inside a memorable watering hole to visit an old friend, like "Mike," the owner and bartender at the Harbor Inn "down in the flats." Winsor preferred to visit Mike in the winter when "the freighters [a]re tied up until spring" and "sailors, with time on their hands, gather there in the evenings to gossip, drink a few beers and play the pinball games. As you might imagine, the conversation can become a bit salty."

A conversation with Mike, "a storehouse of memories," filled a column. "Whiskey Island when he knew it was notorious as a sort of nudist beach. Those days have vanished forever, and anyway, who would want to swim in that water, nude or not." Winsor noted a tiny benefit of aging. Mike's "hearing, to be sure, is not quite what it used to be, but could be a blessing. That juke box never stops caterwauling from the minute the inn opens until curfew."

Winsor had not lost his clout. In November 1966, Cleveland's city council passed legislation "calling for a pedestrian ramp leading into City Hall from the back parking lot. That will make it possible for those in wheelchairs to get into City Hall without having to negotiate the steps." The *Press* gave credit to its plucky columnist. "Winsor has utilized his infirmities to champion the causes of the handicapped. Yesterday at the Mayor's Committee for the Employment of the Handicapped lunch, Winsor was awarded a presidential citation for his efforts. The *Press* proudly shines in his reflected glory." Although his column was not appearing every day, the *Press* still received letters from readers curious about his personal life. "Is he really confined to a wheelchair? Is he married?" An anonymous editor responded, "It's true that he's confined to a wheelchair. . . . French is a bachelor."

He spent the summer of 1967 in Europe, traveling again with Parkinson and filing columns from his familiar path. During the following winter, however, Winsor continued to decline. In a letter dictated to his sister, he said, "Reading has become very difficult for me. In fact, after I have gotten through the morning paper, that is just about it for the day." But he wasn't too tired to give career advice to his artist sister who was trying to generate interest in her painting. "Call Sherman Lee," then director of the Cleveland Museum of Art, "and tell him you are my sister. . . . He is a very shy and quiet man, and I don't think he is very fond of me, but that shouldn't make any difference. . . . He liked your work very much and I feel sure he would enjoy meeting you and seeing more of it." Anne ignored her brother's advice.

In 1968, Winsor managed another European jaunt, but when he returned, he told Seltzer's replacement, Tom Boardman, he was ready to retire. On September 25, 1968, Boardman assigned Joe Collier, who had covered Winsor's birthday party at the Roxy, to write the story. "After thirty-one wonderful years of reporting for *Press* readers on the famous, the naughty and the hard-core rich, Winsor French has decided to call it a day and get on with his memoirs. The memoirs will be irresistibly fashioned from the doings of spectacular times, as were his *Press* columns, beautifully written as always."

Two months later, Winsor wrote Anne, "I cannot use my hands to write any more, and it is very difficult to dictate." His world was shrinking. "Cleveland grows more and more dull. I take a little ride almost every day whenever the weather is fine, and that is about the full extent of my life, nor do I seem to show much sign of improvement, but I still have hope." Another sister relieved his monotony. "Martha usually sticks her head in every day to say hello, and she is a welcome sight."

For the next two years, Winsor established a routine. "I try and go every afternoon usually to Martha's, with the exception of Mondays when she has a group of women in to study English History, and that is something I don't need. I am still planning on going to London June 10th, leaving here on the 8th, and spending a day in New York. I must say I really admire my courage!" To make the trip possible, two of Winsor's teenage nephews, Fayette and Patrick Hickox, accompanied him, helping him dress, feeding him, and pushing his chair. Patrick sailed with Winsor aboard the *Queen Elizabeth II*. Turtle, who had transferred from the *Queen Mary,* pampered the men. Fayette relieved his brother in Paris, and Winsor took his nephew for drinks at the Ritz Bar. Fayette held Winsor's glass as he sipped a martini. A man in a wheelchair who required help sipping his cocktails was an unacceptable tableau in "one of the last citadels of elegance on earth." The men were told to leave immediately. As Fayette wheeled Winsor from the room, his uncle chided the manager, listing for him a quarter century of contretemps that paled in comparison to being fed a drink. The Ritz Bar, Winsor's Parisian headquarters since the 1920s, had evicted one of its most loyal patrons and generous customers.

After more than four years of its absence from the *Press,* readers missed his column. In October 1972, friends persuaded Cleveland mayor Carl Stokes to visit Winsor and present him with a proclamation: "Whereas Winsor French's byline was a guarantee of delightful intelligence and civilized comment in the *Cleveland Press* for more than 30 years, and whereas he has been a friend and confidante not only to the rich and famous and the Short Vincent handicappers, but also to the poor and nondescript and to Cleveland's handicapped . . . I, Carl B. Stokes, borrowing Cole Porter's song title, do hereby proclaim October 16 as 'Winsor French Night and Day.'"

Newspaper publicity about the mayor's proclamation prompted Bill Randle to reminisce in a weekly newspaper. He called Winsor's columns "little prose masterpieces . . . opulent and plush pillows of praise that boosted unknowns to overnight fame and fortune . . . and lightning swift thrusts that burst pretty balloons of press agent hot air." If Winsor had the energy to read Randle's article, he might have gagged on the purple prose.

In what seems like an unusual burst of candor for the late 1960s, Randle wrote that Winsor's male friends were "drinking buddies and lovers and gossips and real swingers. They had time, money, creativity to burn and a kind of 'candle at both ends' attitude . . . a lot of people having a never-ending international party and not really caring much whether anybody likes it or not." For Randle, Winsor represented the "fast-and-loose, devil-may-care" attitude of pre–World War II newspapermen. The disc jockey had one regret. Younger generations would never appreciate Winsor's legacy. "There is no major collection of Winsor's writing that's available that I can recommend to you. You know, his best pieces over the years. Winsor could edit it himself. He's still extant. Not as chipper as he was a few years ago—but still around. Somebody, by all means, do it and have it illustrated photographically by Jerome Zerbe, please. Nobody else will do."

Randle's wish went unfulfilled, and Winsor's health continued to deteriorate. On Christmas Eve he was sixty-eight years old. As news spread of his rapid decline, friends journeyed to Cleveland to say goodbye. Margaret Perry visited Shaker Square to reminisce with her first husband. Paralysis never interrupted Winsor's nightly cocktail hours. Sam Hill held the glasses that were filled with vodka and tonic. Kay Halle came up from Washington, D.C., to have drinks with her lifetime friend. "He couldn't speak, but I could see in his eyes that he recognized me."

Patsy Coakley, who helped organize Winsor's birthday party at the Roxy, remembered "a wistful bit of a smile that would cross his face when some amusing thought was spoken. He proved over and over again in these last agonizing and humiliating years, what a lion-hearted giant of a man he really was! I've missed him for so long while he was imprisoned in that decaying shell, but I always felt he was still there—somewhere in there was Winsor."

On Tuesday morning, March 6, 1973, he died. The *Press* was prepared. Weeks earlier, Boardman had commissioned an obituary from retired reporter Joe Collier. "French was famed for his chronicles of the wealthy and how they lived and played," he wrote. "The late Leonard Hanna, years ago, gave Winsor some shares of stock . . . [that] happened to be IBM and . . . helped make Winsor very well off. In his affluence he made substantial gifts to various organizations, including Rainbow Hospital and Karamu House. But he never talked of his charities, which, it appears, were multitudinous. On one occasion a man found his way to Winsor's desk, and mumbled thanks. 'Aw, that's all right forget it,' a desk companion heard Winsor say."

"'Who was that?' Winsor asked when the man was gone."

"'That was the father of the boy you bought an artificial leg for,' he was reminded."

Collier obscured the ugly reality of cerebellar cortical atrophy. "This morning he had talked with friends on the telephone," he wrote. For the previous three years, Winsor had seldom been able to talk. Family and friends called him, so he could at least hear how much they cared for him. The *Press* editorial page described Winsor

> as a diminutive man with a large heart. His public knew he was a fine prose stylist, and his friends knew he had few peers as a raconteur and wit. At home he chronicled the affairs of the high, the mighty, the swingers, the eccentric. It didn't matter really who they were, just as long as they were colorful enough to provide grist for the French mill. . . . The columns of Winsor French reflected a cultivated gentleman who had the rare gift of knowing how to enjoy life. And in his quest of enjoyment and fulfillment he was determined that as many others as possible should accompany him . . . a talented and compassionate man, he enriched and brightened this community. His death at age 68 is our loss.

Newspapers don't like to publicize the competition, even in death. Nevertheless, the *Plain Dealer* could not ignore Winsor's demise. Its reporter wrote that Winsor "lived and wrote in the glittering world of the famous, the naughty and the hard core-rich," a bald-faced plagiarism of Joe Collier's story about Winsor's retirement that recalled his "wonderful years of reporting for *Press* readers on the famous, the naughty and the hard-core rich." The *Plain Dealer* quoted his advice for exploring the Greek Islands: "'To charter a yacht is not nearly as fracturing as you might think. They come from $250 a day up.'" The sentence betrayed the fact that reporters at both newspapers were most interested in Winsor's reported wealth.

Henry Lavine, a lawyer at Squire, Sanders and Dempsey who had prepared Winsor's will, tried to minimize *Press* stories about the size of his estate. In a letter to Boardman, Lavine wrote, "Winsor's family would very much like to have a minimum of publicity. . . . I suppose when I say a minimum of publicity, I really mean no publicity. I understand you have a very able reporter at the Probate Court who does a fine job of ferreting out such information. I hope that you will be able to do something but, if not, the family will certainly understand."

Lavine's request was ignored. When his law firm filed an inventory of Winsor's estate in probate court, the *Press* published excerpts on the front page:

Cash	$ 29,470
Stocks and securities	
IBM (3,728 shares)	$1,642,184
AT&T (804 shares)	$ 400,000
First National City Corp (644 shares)	$ 49,668
U.S. Treasury Bonds	$ 400,000
Total:	$2,521,322

Five sisters, one brother, three nephews, and two nieces shared the estate, with cash gifts to Mrs. Dorothy Rogers (domestic employee, $10,000), Sam Hill (chauffeur, $10,000), Billy Weinberger ($5,000), and Kay Halle ($2,000).

Wire services picked up the story. *Variety* was stunned by the size of an estate amassed by "a former society gossip and theatrical columnist. . . . Some of his bequests came as a surprise to many Clevelanders," especially "$5,000 to one of his life-long friends, a former Cleveland restaurant-nitery owner who is now President of Caesar's Palace in Las Vegas." The *New York Times* consulted its files and repeated the error that Winsor, a "film critic and travel columnist," was "a graduate of St. Paul's School."

In 1968, the year Winsor retired, the *Press* surrendered its circulation lead to the *Plain Dealer*. Ten years later *Press* circulation had dropped to three hundred thousand, down 25 percent from its heyday in the 1960s. In 1982 the *Plain Dealer* purchased the *Press* subscription list, and the afternoon daily ceased publication; this was part of the trend occurring in many American cities, where morning newspapers first dominated then eliminated their afternoon rivals. Despite the *Press*'s demise, Winsor's colleagues did not forget him. In 1985, Cleveland's Press Club elected the columnist to its Hall of Fame, enshrining the falsehood that in 1946 Winsor had interviewed Noël Coward, Beatrice Lillie, and Somerset Maugham as average Europeans coping in the aftermath of World War II.

In his memory, friends donated $100,000 to the Playhouse Square Foundation, to create a nightspot named after Winsor. In 1995 Playhouse Square Center opened a new Wyndham Hotel on a point between Huron Road and Euclid Avenue, about halfway between Winsor's apartment at the Carter Hotel and the Hanna Theatre, where he spent so many evenings. Called "Winsor's," the restaurant, since renamed, was decorated with copies of his celebrity pictures. At the time of his death, both daily newspapers reported that Winsor rejected Cleveland as the site for his burial, preferring instead a family plot in Williamstown with his mother and stepfather.

Neither paper remembered *PARADE,* the irreverent magazine Winsor founded, nor the pranks of his alter ego, Noel Francis, at the *News.* Winsor's pioneering coverage of Hollywood celebrities, Cleveland's African American entertainers in the 1930s, and Jewish social life in the 1950s and '60s were forgotten or ignored, as were his provocative theater and movie reviews. Obituaries were silent about his attempts to revive Cleveland's nightlife with Fun for Funds and the 2-1-6 Club. No one mentioned his sexual preference or that he had overcome the prejudices of homophobic colleagues, sources, and readers. Winsor covered American and European nightlife from the last year of Prohibition (1932) to a year before the Stonewall riots (1969), a notable era of repression for gay men. Yet during those intolerant times, he won respect and affection from thousands of readers. Tom Boardman wrote, "Winsor was an amazing guy who, among other things, had nothing but friends."

And when they eventually learned of his death, friends and readers wrote condolence letters that arrived at his empty apartment near Shaker Square. Actor and film writer Allen Vincent, a romantic interest of Winsor's in the 1930s, wrote: "I've been ashamed of myself for not writing to him for several months—a writing job has been keeping me tied down so that I hate the sight of a typewriter, but that is no excuse for not communicating with a friend as dear to me as he was. He had a spirit that I've never met anywhere else, and he made me laugh more than anybody. I've known and loved him for about thirty years. He was a true and generous friend and I'm only one of many people who will miss him greatly. Thirty years, hell—it's more like forty-five. I'll grieve about Winsor."

Margaret Perry wrote,

My feelings for him were very special and very lasting. I've always been so proud to have been a part of his life, and will miss him deeply. The anguish of being so confined is over for him now—and he goes, surrounded by affection from everyone he knew. That is an awful lot to take with you. I am glad of one thing—that it is to be Williamstown. He took me there 40 years ago to meet his mother—and I remember vividly how much he loved it there. I've missed him for a long, long time. It won't stop now.

Ruth Glick, a friend and loyal reader, repeated an anecdote that told how Winsor ranked with newspaper readers. "Once a long time ago I said to a friend, 'Have you ever been in Winsor French's column?' and she said, 'Hell, I've never even made it to Milton Widder.'" Winsor would have appreciated her letter. At his retirement, Joe Collier interviewed him in his apartment and noted that when the notoriously unsentimental writer talked about ending his daily column, he shed a tear at cutting ties with readers and colleagues.

"It was my whole life."

Permissions

Notes

Sources are listed on the page they first occur. The initials "WF" identify newspaper articles written by Winsor French. When no name is given, the author is unknown. Citations without quotation marks paraphrase the source.

INTRODUCTION

xiv "isolated" Chauncey, *Gay New York,* 2–6.
xv "post-newspaper era" Frank Rich, *New York Times,* 10 May 2009.

"THE PLOT IS VERY, VERY DARING"

1 "Every time a . . ." Polly Parsons, *News,* 22 Jan. 1938.
1 "There were hard . . ." Jake Falstaff, *Press,* 3 Jan. 1933.
2 Radio Act of 1927 . . . , Teel, *Public Press,* 113, 132.
2 "nasal twanging" WF, *PARADE,* 28 July 1932, 12.
2 "has never missed . . ." WF, *News,* 11 July 1933.
2 "some shooting or . . ." George Davis, *Press,* 4 Jan. 1933.
2 "whoopee beat" *Plain Dealer,* 28 Feb. 1983.
2 "younger set" *Plain Dealer,* undated [1928], Eleanor Clarage Sutton file, *Cleveland Press* Collection, Cleveland State University (hereafter CPC).
3 "luncheon at a . . . " *Press,* 27 Sept. 1963.
3 "free and easy . . . " Teel, *Public Press,* 25–26.
3 "dreadful sense of . . . " ibid.
3 Clarage was the . . . , *Press,* 27 Sept. 1963.
3 on-the-job-training . . . , Teel, *Public Press,* 10.
3 two hundred colleges . . . , ibid., 118.
3 yet only one . . . *Press,* 9 Oct. 1939.
3 George Davis, the bespectacled, Collier, *Scripps Howard News,* undated, George Davis file, CPC.
3 "force, virility, sparkle . . ." Louis Seltzer, *Press,* 1 Nov. 1926.
3 "Jake Falstaff" *Scripps Howard News,* Dec. 1932; *Press,* 23 Apr. 1932; Stafford, *Press,* 24 Nov. 1960.
4 He had chosen . . . , Martha Eaton Hickox (hereafter MEH) interview with author, 28 Aug. 1997.
4 uncovered a smallpox . . . , *New York Stage,* Mar. 1932; *Cleveland Leader,* undated, Archie Bell file, CPC.

4 "The plot and . . ." Helen Allyn, *Press,* 2 Jan. 1933.

5 price of its premium . . . , *News,* 3 Jan. 1933.

5 "Man after man . . ." WF, *PARADE* 24 Sept. 1931, 10.

5 "questioned whether the . . ." Teel, *Public Press,* 121.

5 "a concise and brilliant . . ." WF, *PARADE,* 28 Jan. 1932, 31.

5 "the one really . . ." WF, *PARADE,* 19 May 1932, 33.

5 "voices of a thousand . . ." MacLeish, "To the Young Men of Wall Street," 453–54.

6 "bleakness" Peeler, *Hope among Us Yet,* 10.

6 "the gaunt and . . ." WF, *PARADE,* 1 Oct. 1932, 26.

6 "If you can't afford . . . summer . . ." WF, *News,* 28 Apr. 1933.

6 "Fifteen-cent haircuts . . ." WF, *News* 7 Dec. 1932.

6 "One of the . . ." WF, *News.* 30 Dec. 1932.

6 "most sworn at . . ." *PARADE,* 14 Apr. 1932, 16.

6 In the 1920s . . . , Chauncey, *Gay New York,* 274.

6 "created a raised . . ." Parsons, *News,* 22 Jan. 1938.

7 flasks hidden . . . , Kovach, *Plain Dealer,* 23 Jan. 1981.

7 Andorn had pasted . . . , WF, *News,* 24 Jan. 1933.

7 Winsor preferred the "Idehaven" . . . , invoice, 11 Dec. 1936, WF to Joseph O. Easton (hereafter JE), Hickox Papers; *PARADE,* 9 June 1932, 21.

8 He chose the . . . , Hoare, *Noël Coward,* 249.

8 Britain's official censor . . . , Lahr, *Coward the Playwright,* 85.

8 "one of a handful . . ." Chauncey, *Gay New York,* 321–27.

8 "Gay," ibid., 17–23.

9 "Noël Coward is . . ." WF, *News,* 20 Dec. 1932.

9 "Somehow, by a . . ." Archie Bell, *News,* 3 Jan. 1933.

9 "a wildcat report . . ." Davis, *Press,* 4 Jan. 1933.

9 "three rather peculiar . . ." Ralph Kelly, *Plain Dealer,* 2 Jan. 1933.

10 "The play is . . ." Hoare, *Noël Coward,* 248.

10 "Although chairs are . . ." WF, *News,* 10 Jan. 1933.

10 short, blond, blue-eyed . . . , Hoare, *Noël Coward,* 88.

10 great-grandson and namesake . . . , *TIME,* 21 Mar. 1927.

10 "intimate" *Plain Dealer,* 2 Jan. 1933.

10 "sort of two-pronged . . ." Amherst, *Wandering Abroad,* 57.

10 playwright was disappointed . . . , Hoare, *Noël Coward,* 89.

10 personal favorite . . . , Payn and Day, *My Life with Noël Coward,* 259.

10 "Everything's glandular . . ." Coward, *Design for Living,* 18.

11 "What's the truth . . ." ibid., 19.

11 "stormed off the . . ." Amherst, *Wandering Abroad,* 199.

11 "mumbled most of . . ." Davis, *Press,* 4 Jan. 1933.

11 "too low pitched" William McDermott, *Plain Dealer,* 3 Jan. 1933.

11 "People will tell . . ." WF, *News,* 3 Jan. 1933.

11 "Mr. Coward writes . . ." Brooks Atkinson, *New York Times,* 25 Jan. 1933.

11 "a serious, though . . ." John Mason Brown, *Evening Post,* 20 May 1933.

11 "Shaking her finger . . ." Amherst, *Wandering Abroad,* 199.

11 "Small of stature" Hoare, *Noël Coward,* 86.

12 "Our lives are . . ." Coward, *Design for Living,* 58.

12 "Will you forgive . . ." ibid., 82–83.

12 "astounded . . . in spots . . ." Falstaff, *Press,* 3 Jan. 1933.

12 "Dress, of course . . ." Dorothy Harman, *News,* 3 Jan. 1933.

12 "Nearly every smart . . ." Cornelia Curtiss, *Plain Dealer,* 3 Jan. 1933.

12 Katherine, called . . . , Personal Papers of Kay Halle, John F. Kennedy Presidential Library.

13 "Kay Halle gaily . . ." WF, *News,* 5 Jan. 1933.

13 "two of the . . ." Kelly, *Plain Dealer,* 3 Jan. 1933.

13 "horticultural lads" Chauncey, *Gay New York,* 315.

13 "We have our . . ." Coward, *Design for Living,* 128.

13 "Coward's comedy poses . . ." Davis, *Press,* 4 Jan. 1933.

13 "An unconventional variation . . ." McDermott, *Plain Dealer,* 3 Jan. 1933.

13 "A strangely different . . ." Bell, *News,* 3 Jan. 1933.

13 Because personal experience . . . , Unidentified clipping, Archie Bell file, CPC; *Plain Dealer,* 17 Nov. 1958; *Press,* 30 Dec. 1960.

14 playwright didn't object . . . , Bell, *News,* 3, 4, 5 Jan. 1933.

14 "What has gone . . ." Abel, "Staging Heterosexuality," 187.

14 "Coward's comic revenge . . . ," Lahr, *Coward the Playwright,* 83.

14 "always believed that . . ." Robert Hurwitt, *San Francisco Chronicle,* 5 Apr. 2009.

15 "odor of sin" Atkinson, *New York Times,* 25 Jan. 1933.

15 "silken obscenities" Percy Hammond, *Herald Tribune,* 25 Jan. 1933.

15 "essentially rotten" Euphemia Wyatt, *Catholic World,* March 1933.

15 "One of the two . . ." WF, *Press,* 6 Dec. 1937.

15 "the greatest dandy . . ." *Bachelor,* Apr. 1937, 57; *Variety,* 9 Feb. 1966.

"RUDDERLESS IN A . . . SEA OF HOSPITALITY"

16 Mrs. Winslow's birthplace . . . , *Press,* 6 Aug. 1951.

16 she became fluent . . . , *Cleveland Press,* 19 Dec. 1931.

16 "Victorian museum" WF, *Press,* 25 June 1955; WF, *PARADE,* 26 Nov. 1931, 25, and 18 Feb. 1932, 12.

17 "latest parlor game . . ." WF, *News,* 9 Jan. 1933.

17 "Noël was staying . . ." Hoare, *Noël Coward,* 250.

17 "calmly nicked Noël . . ." WF, *News,* 11 Jan. 1933.

17 salary of reporters . . . , Teel, *Public Press,* 173.

17 salary of schoolteachers . . . , Eliassen and Anderson, "Investigations of Teacher Supply and Demand," 12–16.

17 "Private parties were . . ." Gill, *New York Life,* 188.

17 "provided her with . . ." WF, *PARADE,* 16 June 1932, 14.

17 "detested school" Gill, *Happy Times,* 14.

18 "first class . . . dinner clothes" ibid., 49.

18 "Without an invitation . . ." Zerbe, *Art of Social Climbing,* 44.

18 "You don't have . . ." ibid., 19.

18 "exceptionally strenuous . . ." Gill, *Happy Times,* 10.

18 "most brilliant" Wilner, *Man Time Forgot,* 59.

19 sorted, condensed, and . . . , ibid., 83–84, 86–87.

19 "flippant urbanity" ibid., 197.

19 "serious and entertaining writing" Teel, *Public Press,* 13.

19 transport the publication from . . . , Wilner, *Man Time Forgot,* 155–57.

19 "sole purpose was . . ." ibid., 197.

19 "lived quietly" WF, *Press,* 16 Feb. 1952.

19 "lost and lonely . . . roared . . . " Busch, *Briton Hadden,* 174.

19 "speakeasy and honky-tonk . . ." ibid., 105–6.

19 "a few carefully . . ." ibid., 173–74.

19 "outlandish, questionable or . . ." ibid., 104.

19 Crescent Athletic Club, Wilner, *Man Time Forgot,* 164.

19 "a written examination . . ." WF, *Press,* 9 Feb. 1952.

20 "thought nothing of . . ." WF, *Press,* 2 Feb. 1952.

20 "They were a . . ." WF, interview, TIME Inc. Archive (hereafter TIA) 26 June 1956.

20 "full-blown alcoholic" Wilner, *Man Time Forgot,* 166.

21 they rented space . . . , ibid., 192.

21 "Mad as I get . . ." ibid., 193; WF to Halle, quoted in Katherine Halle to Noel F. Busch, June 20, 1948, TIA.

21 "Take it or . . ." WF to JE, 12 Oct. 1927, Hickox Papers.

21 "a high school dropout . . ." Wilner, *Man Time Forgot,* 192.

21 "I am working . . ." WF to JE, 12 Oct. 1927, Hickox Papers.

21 "insulting movie reviews," Wilner, *Man Time Forgot,* 202.

21 "shows for several . . . " WF to JE, 12 Oct. 1927, Hickox Papers.

21 "B.H. and I . . ." WF to JE, 14 Nov. 1927, Hickox Papers.

21 "You must have . . ." JE to WF, 8 Oct. 1928, Hickox Papers.

21 "I was put . . ." WF, *Press,* 9 Feb. 1952.

22 "French thought Hadden . . ." WF, TIA.

22 "Some time later . . ." WF, *Press,* 23 Feb. 1952.

22 "robust curiosity" WF, TIA.

22 "effeminate young man" WF, TIA.

22 "advertising agent" WF, *PARADE,* 31 Dec. 1931, 1.

22 "disciples" Chase, *Past Imperfect,* 52.

23 "charm of expression . . ." Walker, Program, Portmanteau Theater, Jan. 8, 1917; *New York Times,* 14 Mar. 1941; *Variety,* 19 Mar. 1941.

23 "soprano" Wilner, *Man Time Forgot,* 170.

23 "used to express . . ." Chauncey, *Gay New York,* 102.

23 not the whirlwind . . . , Wilner, *Man Time Forgot,* 225–26.

23 "cultural attributes of . . ." Gill, *Happy Times,* 16.

23 convinced Zerbe to . . . , Gill, *New York Life,* 188.

23 $35 a week . . . , Terkel, "Recordings from 'Hard Times.'"

23 "the most entertaining . . ." *New York Times,* 5 July 1930; 5 Oct. 1930.

23 *Vanity Fair* had . . . , *PARADE,* 8 Oct. 1931, 1.

24 For *Fortune,* Jackson . . . , *PARADE,* 3 Dec. 1931, 1.

24 "been complaining bitterly . . ." WF, *PARADE,* 25 June 1931, 17.

24 "trim, well-mounted . . ." *TIME,* 15 June 1931.

24 "rumored," WF, *PARADE,* 18 June 1931, 17.

24 "a large down-at-the-heels . . ." WF, *Press,* 2 July 1950.

25 *"PARADE* sincerely regrets . . ." WF, *PARADE,* 2 July 1931, 4.

25 "dreamily poetic," WF, *PARADE,* 29 Oct. 1931, 32.

25 "manuscript play," WF, *PARADE,* 21 Apr. 1932, 31.

26 "Broken-down old . . ." WF, *PARADE,* 23 July 1931, 12–14.

26 "From the very . . ." WF, *PARADE,* 6 Aug. 1931, 14–16.

26 "Radio, aviation and . . ." WF, *PARADE,* 11 June 1931, 18.

26 "great crowds of . . ." WF, *PARADE,* 4 June 1931, 33.

26 "one who has . . ." *Webster's International Dictionary* (1924).

26 "to start a . . ." Glenn Pullen, *Plain Dealer,* 23 Mar. 1933; *Plain Dealer,* 28 Feb. 1983.

27 "clippings of photographs . . ." WF, *News,* 27 Mar. 1933.

27 "W.W. announced . . ." WF, *News,* 18 Jan. 1933.

27 "Ruth Cambridge, Winchell's . . ." WF, *News,* 10 July 1933.

27 "there wasn't a . . ." Gabler, *Winchell,* 410.

27 "Among the current . . ." Walter Winchell, *New York Mirror,* 5 Oct. 1933.

27 "Like many foreigners . . ." WF, *News,* 18 Nov. 1932.

27 "Jean Malin, who . . ." WF, *News,* 9 Jan. 1933.

28 "I am not . . ." WF, *News,* 30 Nov. 1932.

28 "That's all for . . ." WF, *News,* 29 July 1933.

28 "They would let . . ." WF, *News,* 16 Aug. 1933.

"PLEASE BEAR WITH MY INCOHERENCE"

29 "squadrons of police," WF, *News,* 4 Oct. 1933.

29 "a beautiful . . . tawny-haired . . ." WF, *Press,* 7 June 1952.

29 "fairy tale and sex," Jacobs, *Christmas in July,* 81.

29 "mumps" or "chicken pox," Sturges, *Preston Sturges,* 253.

30 "four rehearsals," Cleveland Play House, *Criminal at Large* program, 19 Dec. 1933.

30 "over-sized handbag," Brock Pemberton, *New York Times,* 7 July 1946.

30 "a cigar band," WF, *News,* 22 Jan. 1938.

30 "Her perpetual coyness . . ." WF, *News,* 11 Sept. 1933.

31 "Silver foxes," WF, *News,* 4 Oct. 1933.

31 "an erotic and aggressive," Bach, *Marlene Dietrich,* 118–19.

31 "embody the fantasy . . ." Kimball, *You're The Top,* 72.

31 "greatest song-and-dance man" Hemming and Hajdu, *Discovering Great Singers,* 74.

31 Berlin measured the . . . , P. McNutt, *Collier's,* 18 Aug. 1934.

31 "a freak tonsil" WF, *News,* 16 Nov. 1932.

31 "guttural, dusky voice" WF, *PARADE,* 10 Dec. 1931, 28.

31 "unreliable pitch" Kimball and Sudhalter, *You're the Top,* 21.

31 Reynolds was . . . , Bradshaw, *Dreams that Money Can Buy,* 180.

32 "Let's have the . . ." WF, *News,* 16 Aug. 1933.

32 "the people who . . ." WF, *News,* 18 Jan. 1933.

32 "plastered with magnified . . ." Richard Lockbridge, *New York Sun,* 2 Oct. 1933.

32 "Man Bites Dog" by Irving Berlin, © 1970 by Irving Berlin. © Renewed International Copyright Secured. All Rights Reserved. Reprinted by Permission; Kimball and Emmet, *Complete Lyrics of Irving Berlin,* 283; Jablonski, *Irving Berlin,* 160.

32 "ultimate target" Bergreen, *As Thousands Cheer,* 321.

32 "built their show . . ." Atkinson, *New York Times,* 15 Oct. 1933.

32 "journalistic design" Stark Young, *New Republic,* 18 Oct. 1933.

33 "How's Chances" by Irving Berlin, © 1933 by Irving Berlin. © Renewed International Copyright Secured. All Rights Reserved. Reprinted by Permission; Kimball and Emmet, *Complete Lyrics of Irving Berlin,* 284.

33 "her marriage be . . ." WF, *News,* 6 Oct. 1933.

34 "sat us down . . ." MEH; Anne Eaton Parker (hereafter AEP) interview, 28 Aug. 1997.

34 "run as a . . ." WF, *News,* 15 Aug. 1933.

34 "the so-called Hemingway . . ." WF, *News,* 4 Oct. 1933.

34 "a mere mass . . ." WF, *PARADE,* 18 June 1931, 45.

35 "bleeding hearts tattooed . . ." WF, *News,* 5 Oct. 1933.

35 "glass collection from . . ." WF, *PARADE,* 7 Jan. 1932, 18.

35 black satin . . . , WF, *News,* 29 Aug. 1933.

35 blue artificial eyelashes . . . , WF, *News,* 9 Oct. 1933.

36 "of fashion are . . ." WF, *News,* 5 Oct. 1933.

36 "only purpose . . . was . . ." Kriendler, *21,* 35–36.

36 "sensitive about publicity" Pemberton, *New York Times,* 7 July 1946.

36 "came of a . . ." *Variety,* 3 July 1946.

36 "great house" Pemberton, *New York Times,* 7 July 1946.

36 "member of the . . ." *News,* 21 Aug. 1933.

37 "a talented portrait . . ." *New York Times* 9 Feb. 1875.

37 "helped save the . . . " Britten, "Chronicles of Saratoga."

37 "graduate of St. Paul's" *New York Times; Press,* 21 Aug. 1933.

37 "As a young . . ." WF to Louis Seltzer (hereafter LS), 1 Oct. 1946, WF, microfiche, CPC.

37 "Most kids wore . . ." WF, *Press,* 20 Nov. 1954.

38 "goodness outweighs knowledge" St. Paul's School, www.sps.edu, Oct. 24, 2001.

38 "more or less . . ." WF, *Press,* 21 June 1952.

39 "chafed under the . . ." *PARADE,* 3 Sept. 1931, 12.

39 Andorn . . . earned, Kovach, *Press,* 23 Jan. 1931.

39 Fetzer earned . . . , *Scripps Howard News,* Dec. 1932.

39 "Walter Murray's sunken . . ." WF, *News,* 2 Dec. 1933.

39 "The gentlemen of . . ." WF, *News,* 22 Aug. 1933.

39 "reporter's badge No. 6" WF, *News,* 22 Mar. 1934.

40 "Winsor called . . . . The . . . " J. Carroll (hereafter JC) to JE, 19 July 1932, Hickox Papers.

40 "More than one . . ." WF, *News,* 18 Aug. 1933.

40 "Money meant nothing . . ." Pemberton, *New York Times,* 7 July 1946.

40 "Practically the entire . . ." WF, *News,* 7 Oct. 1933.

41 "King Leer" *Variety,* 2 Dec. 1959.

41 "world-weary" WF, *Press,* 1 June 1954.

41 "Broadway is holding . . ." WF, *News,* 24 Aug. 1933.

41 "Chuck Wilson, one . . ." WF, *News,* 31 May, 1933.

41 "Jean Pearson . . ." WF, *News,* 28 Nov. 1932.

41 *The Green Bay Tree,* Loughery, *Other Side of Silence,* 86; Chauncey, *Gay New York,* 357.

41 "a serious depiction . . ." Chauncey, *Gay New York,* 311.

41 Winsor's stepfather hosted . . . , JE to Hotel Pierre, 2 Oct. 1933, Hickox Papers.

42 writing profiles . . . , WF, *News,* 23 Nov. 1933.

42 "Trevelyan Higgins" WF, *News,* 21 Nov. 1932.

42 one of Libby . . . , Bradshaw, *Dreams that Money Can Buy,* 78; *New York Times* 20 June 1965.

42 "the second-handsomest . . ." Gill, *New York Life,* 189.

42 "the right people" *TIME,* 10 Dec. 1934.

42 "outstanding athlete" *New York Times,* 10 Mar. 1934.

42 "a 20-game losing . . ." WF, *Press,* 16, 23 Feb. 1952.

42 "the world's funniest . . ." WF, *Press,* 2 Oct. 1934.

42 "crisp observations" WF, *Press,* 22 Nov. 1934.

42 "a medley of . . ." WF, *News,* 4 Sept. 1933.

42 his own one-man . . . , WF, *News,* 25 Oct. 1933.

42 "Sunday Night Supper . . ." WF, *News,* 6 Oct. 1933.

42 "from his sometimes . . ." WF, *News,* 16 Nov. 1933.

42 "Cleveland's best known . . ." Moats, *Town and Country,* Jan. 1937, 40–43.

43 "permanent fixture in . . ." WF, *News,* 19 Jan. 1933.

43 "honey blonde" Zerbe, *People on Parade,* 41.

43 "most of the year" *New York Times,* 26 Mar. 1937.

43 Benjamin Holt married . . . , Zerbe, *Society on Parade,* 10.

43 "Winsor's posse" ibid.

43 "quarts of tomato . . ." WF, *News,* 9 Oct. 1933.

43 collection of poems, WF, *PARADE,* 25 Feb. 1933, 21.

43 "On the way . . ." WF, *News,* 10 Oct. 1933.

43 "played godfather to . . ." Parsons, *News,* 12 Feb. 1938.

43 "a somewhat pretentious . . ." R. Davis to WF, undated, Hickox Papers.

44 "cornflower blue velvet" Helen Worden, *New York World Telegram,* 9 Oct. 1933.

44 "since she had . . ." WF, *Press,* 7 June 1952.

44 "hands trembled so . . . " WF, *News,* 22 Jan. 1938.

44 "Take any big . . ." Worden, *New York World Telegram,* 9 Oct. 1933.

44 $18,000 . . . , *Press,* 20 Dec. 1933.

44 "But the part . . ." Worden, *New York World Telegram,* 9 Oct. 1933.

45 "This New York" Gill, *New York Life,* 189.

45 "news pictures of . . ." Zerbe, *People on Parade,* 7.

45 "The Park Lane reception . . ." ibid., 10.

45 "came upon some . . ." WF, *News,* 28 Nov. 1932.

45 "Winsor, no one's . . ." Parsons, *News,* 22 Jan. 1938.

45 "Instead of throwing . . ." Bradshaw, *Dreams that Money Can Buy,* 184.

"WHAT PRICE REPEAL?"

46 "gilded gin palaces" WF, *News,* 10 Nov. 1933.

46 "Night and Day" (from *Gay Divorce*). Words and Music by Cole Porter © 1932

(Renewed) WB Music Corp. All Rights Reserved. Used by Permission of Alfred Publishing Co. Inc.; Kimball, *Complete Lyrics of Cole Porter,* 152–53.

46 "$3,500 of exceedingly . . ." WF, *News,* 4 Dec. 1933.

47 "Every other spot . . ." ibid.

47 "Those airplanes that . . ." WF, *News,* 7 Feb. 1933.

47 "interminable lines of . . ." WF, *PARADE,* 10 Sept. 1931, 13.

47 "They now go . . ." WF, *PARADE,* 6 Aug. 1931, 13.

47 "An escorted truck . . ." WF, *News,* 16 Jan. 1933.

47 broke the law . . . , WF, *News,* 28 Oct. 1933.

47 "Champagne can be . . ." WF, *News,* 18 Nov. 1932.

48 "you were presented . . ." WF, *PARADE,* 11 Feb. 1932, 24.

48 "Blotto. It consists . . ." WF, *PARADE,* 31 Dec. 1931, 20.

48 "the town's oldest . . ." WF, *News,* 6 Dec. 1932.

48 "a six-foot boxing . . ." WF, *News,* 9 Dec. 1932.

48 "how many downtown . . ." WF, *News,* 29 Nov. 1932.

48 "ordered a glass . . ." WF, *News,* 6 Dec. 1932.

48 "In the midst . . ." WF, *PARADE,* 11 Feb. 1932, 24.

49 "astonished" WF, *News,* 2 Jan. 1934.

49 "slicked-down jet . . ." Grafton, *Red, Hot, and Rich,* 65.

49 "single-handedly provide . . ." ibid., 2.

49 316-acre estate . . . , *Plain Dealer,* 27 Sept. 1963.

49 Since 1924 . . . , Parsons, *News,* 12 Feb. 1938.

49 "Every period of . . ." WF, *PARADE,* 18 June 1931, 17.

50 "largest allowance of . . ." Eells, *Life that Late He Led,* 36.

50 *Cora,* a musical . . . , Schwartz, *Cole Porter,* 272.

50 their many biographers . . . , Gill, *New York Life,* 216–17, 322–23.

50 "finishing touches" WF, *PARADE,* 5 Nov. 1931, 20.

50 "insufficient for the . . ." WF, *PARADE,* 3 Dec. 1931, 13.

50 "string of wonderful . . ." McBrien, *Cole Porter,* 141.

50 "abandoned because a . . ." Kimball and Sudhalter, *You're the Top,* 5.

50 "rumor" WF, *PARADE,* 24 Dec. 1931, 22.

50 "withdrawn from production" *PARADE,* 7 Jan. 1932, 25; Schwartz, *Cole Porter,* 121.

51 "a privileged few" WF, *News,* 2 Jan. 1934; McBrien, *Cole Porter,* 197.

51 "Anything Goes" (from *Anything Goes*). Words and Music by Cole Porter © 1934 (Renewed) WB Music Corp. All Rights Reserved. Used by Permission of Alfred Publishing Co. Inc.; Kimball, *Complete Lyrics of Cole Porter,* 171.

51 a large house . . . , WF, *Press,* 18 Sept. 1954.

51 appeared deserted, WF, *News,* 13 Feb. 1934.

51 "snappiest" WF, *News,* 11 Sept. 1933.

51 The owners . . . , WF, *News,* 26 Aug. 1933; 30 Sept. 1933.

51 "No one can . . ." WF, *News,* 5 June 1933.

71 "brandy and Benedictine" WF, *News,* 5 Jan. 1934.

51 "huge black musical . . ." WF, *News,* 11 Sept. 1933.

51 Harold Simpson, WF, *News,* 11 Jan. 1934.

51 "one of the real . . ." WF, *News,* 18 Sept. 1933.

51 "bronze Helen of Troy" WF, *Press,* 4 Sept. 1954.

51 "frantic" WF, *News*, 1 June 1933.

52 "a phony British . . ." WF, *News*, 2 Jan. 1934.

52 "interest a New York . . ." WF, *News*, 18 Sept. 1933.

52 "Perhaps someone will . . ." WF, *News*, 2 Feb. 1934.

52 "Hot-house peaches . . ." WF, *News*, 17 July 1933.

52 "tiny dance floor" WF, *News*, 2 Jan. 1934.

52 "one gay little group . . ." WF, *News*, 3 Jan. 1934.

52 "the commonplace hours . . ." WF, *News*, 15 June 1933.

52 "they were searching . . ." WF, *News*, 3 Jan. 1934.

53 "Winsor and his . . ." Parsons, *News*, 22 Jan. 1938.

53 "zip-zowie, hair-raising . . ." Bell, *News*, 20 Dec. 1933.

53 "an overwrought young . . ." McDermott, *Plain Dealer*, 20 Dec. 1933.

53 "running broad jump" *Los Angeles Times*, 10 Oct. 1934.

53 "For your private . . ." WF, *News*, 14 Dec. 1933.

53 "his evenings touring . . ." WF, *News*, 16 Nov. 1933.

54 allowance of $2,225 . . . , *Plain Dealer*, 2 Dec. 1933.

54 "expense account . . . the . . . " WF, *Press*, 20 Dec. 1933.

54 Margaret's trousseau cost . . . , *Plain Dealer*, 21 Dec. 1933.

54 "back in New York . . ." Paul Yawitz, *New York Mirror*, 13 Jan. 1934.

54 "depravity" Chauncey, *Gay New York*, 324.

54 "the innermost stations . . ." Yawitz, *New York Evening Graphic*, 25 Aug. 1931.

54 "In spite of Paul . . ." WF, *News*, 13 Jan. 1934.

54 "nothing about selling . . ." WF, *News*, 2 May 1933.

54 "more restaurants are . . ." WF, *News*, 9 May 1933.

54 "beer garden proprietors" WF, *News*, 25 Sept. 1933.

55 "fork out a tidy . . ." WF, *News*, 23 Feb. 1933.

55 "When winter comes . . ." WF, *News*, 20 Sept. 1933.

55 "The prices for your . . ." WF, *News*, 10 Nov. 1933.

55 "afraid people may not . . ." WF, *News*, 13 Nov. 1933.

55 "Stricken by conscience" WF, *News*, 8, 11 Dec. 1933.

55 "Murph's, and now . . ." WF, *News*, 9 Dec. 1933.

55 "If and when . . ." WF, *News*, 16 Dec. 1933.

55 "hard liquor would . . ." *Plain Dealer*, 20 Dec. 1933.

56 "That picture . . . was . . ." WF, *News*, 22 Jan. 1934.

56 "The first weekend . . ." WF, *News*, 23 Jan. 1934.

56 "I'm very amused . . ." WF, *News*, 24 Jan. 1934.

56 "Save your sympathy . . ." WF, *News*, 26 Jan. 1934.

57 "I wonder . . ." WF, *News*, 28 Jan. 1933.

57 "At the Avalon . . ." WF, *News*, 1 Feb. 1934.

57 "Foldups of 1934," WF, *News*, 4, 11 Jan. 1934; 3, 6 Feb. 1934.

57 "Dim lights, bead curtains . . . and . . . " WF, *Press*, 11 Sept. 1954.

57 "reservations . . . stacked up . . ." WF, *News*, 21 Sept. 1933.

57 "murky speakeasies . . ." WF, *Press*, 4 Sept. 1954.

58 "sit or dance . . ." WF, *News*, 26 Jan. 1934.

58 "Prohibition went out . . ." WF, *News*, 7 Dec. 1933.

58 "write a world-shattering . . ." WF to LS, 1 Oct. 1946, CPC.

59 "The letter of credit . . ." JE to WF, 22 July 1926, Hickox Papers.

59 "went off to Paris . . ." Gill, *Happy Times,* 15.

59 "I have received . . ." JE to WF, 12 Aug. 1926, Hickox Papers.

59 "smartly in black" WF, *Press,* 25 June 1946.

59 "a picturesque if . . ." WF, *Press,* 25 July 1946.

59 "I assume from . . ." JE to WF, 26 June 1927, Hickox Papers.

59 "slight, blond and . . ." WF, *Press,* 5 July 1946.

60 "war in earnest" WF, *News,* 14 Feb. 1934.

60 "practically impossible to . . ." ibid.

60 "a small intimate bar . . ." WF, *News,* 2 Feb. 1934.

60 "Before she struts . . ." WF, *News,* 14 Feb. 1934.

60 "dropped into the . . ." ibid.

61 "an extraordinary orchestra" WF, *News,* 21 Feb. 1934.

61 "maintaining a public nuisance" Chauncey, *Gay New York,* 312–13.

61 "five-day, forty-hour week" WF, *News,* 20 Feb. 1934.

62 awarded $750,000 . . . , Bradshaw, *Dreams that Money Can Buy,* 180.

62 "Bicycle polo . . ." WF, *News,* 2 Mar. 1934.

62 "a substantial hit . . ." WF, *News,* 21 Mar. 1934.

62 "LOVE AND GOOD . . ." JE to Mrs. WF, 7 Apr. 1934, Hickox Papers.

62 "a last minute leap . . ." WF, *News,* 11 Apr. 1934.

62 "a great secret" JE to Mrs. WF, 25 Apr. 1934.

63 "I should like . . ." JE to WF, 23 May 1934.

63 "rushed through the customs" WF, *Press,* 14 June 1946.

63 "the very top . . ." WF, *Press,* 28 June 1946.

63 "open window, looking . . ." WF, *Press,* 3 July 1946.

63 "songs are fairly tuneless" WF, *Press,* 27 June 1946.

63 "a gilt and crystal restaurant" WF, *Press,* 3 July 1946.

63 "theater seats, a . . ." WF, *Press,* 5 July 1946.

64 "pencil slim" Rule, *New York Times,* 21 Feb. 1981.

64 somber, son of, Eells . . . , *Life that Late He Led,* 133.

64 "intelligent, charismatic, cultured . . ." Mulholland, *International Herald Tribune,* 2 May 2008; McBrien, *Cole Porter,* 158.

64 "best jewelry designer" Nathan, *New York Times,* 22 Nov. 1998.

64 "snatched" WF, *Press,* 5 July 1946.

64 sad letter . . . , MEH, AEP interview, 28 Aug. 1997.

64 "radical, Socialist, Wobbly . . ." Teel, *Public Press,* 5–7.

65 "By midnight the . . ." WF, *Press,* 6 Oct. 1934.

65 "As a city . . ." WF, *Press,* 17 Oct. 1934.

65 "By universal consent" WF, *Press,* 6 Oct. 1934.

65 "Once again Martinis . . ." WF, *Press,* 13 Oct. 1934.

65 "too risqué" WF, *Press,* 15 Oct. 1934.

65 Repeal had been . . . , Chauncey, *Gay New York,* 335.

66 "the Beebe of . . ." Parsons, *News,* 22 Jan. 1938.

66 "Luscious Lucius" *Variety,* 9 Feb. 1966.

66 "A small army . . ." WF, *Press,* 1, 3 Nov. 1934.

66 "Dispatches from Reno . . ." WF, *Press,* 5 Nov. 1934.

66 "CORRECTING, if I may . . ." WF, *Press,* 12 Nov. 1934.

67 "erroneous, absolutely erroneous . . ." ibid.

"THE MEN WEAR ANYTHING THEY PLEASE"

68 "asked for 5 P.M.," WF, *Press,* 27 May 1935.

68 Benedict "Benny" Crowell Jr., . . . , WF, *Press,* 1 Mar. 1935.

68 English manor with . . . , Mann, *Wisecracker,* 124–25.

68 "exactly like a birdhouse" WF, *Press,* 25 May 1935.

68 "a new kind . . ." WF, *Press,* 8 May 1935.

68 "taking an interview . . ." WF, *Press,* 18 July 1935.

69 "was almost the . . ." WF, *Press,* 27 May 1935.

69 "Los Angeles . . . stretches . . ." WF, *Press,* 25 May 1935.

69 pencil sketch of, WF, *PARADE,* 2 Feb. 1932, 1.

69 "dynamic circle" Mann, *Wisecracker,* 175.

69 "Her wit has . . ." WF, *Press,* 14 June 1935.

69 "staring through old" WF, *Press,* 27 May 1935.

69 "an enormous picture hat . . ." ibid.

70 "If you don't . . ." WF, *News,* 2 Jan. 1933.

70 "Haines picked up . . ." Mann, *Wisecracker,* 256.

70 "to see Rufus" WF, Datebook, 17 May 1935, Hickox Papers.

71 "a young Detroit socialite . . ." WF, *Press,* 25 May 1935.

71 "sickly, heavy odor" WF, *Press,* 24 May 1935.

71 "badly in need . . ." WF, *Press,* 27 Feb. 1936.

71 "Fulco's" WF, Datebook, 13 May 1935.

71 "curb-link bracelet . . ." Mulholland, *International Herald Tribune,* 2 May 2008.

72 "cut-ups" WF, *News,* 24 Apr., 4 May, 15 July, 26 Sept. 1933.

72 "most of his . . ." WF, *PARADE,* 26 May 1932, 22.

72 Crowell and Young's . . . , WF, *News,* 14 Nov. 1933, 1 Feb. 1934.

72 "fabulous restaurant" WF, *Press,* 25 May 1935.

72 dined again with Vincent . . . , WF, Datebook, 15 May 1935.

72 thirty-two-year-old . . . , Truitt, "Allen Vincent," *Who Was Who on Screen,* 732.

72 "second lead" Ragan, "Allen Vincent," *Who's Who in Hollywood,* 2:739.

72 "very good as . . ." WF, *News,* 3 Mar. 1933.

72 "It is about time . . ." WF, *News,* 9 Sept. 1933.

72 "He never tries . . ." WF, *News,* 30 Jan. 1933.

72 "dinner with Allen" WF, Datebook, 16 May 1935.

73 "The boys make . . ." WF, *Press,* 15 July 1935.

73 "Allen's (Spent the night)." WF, Datebook, 18 May 1935.

73 "I wildly enjoyed . . ." Allen Vincent to S. Warner, Mar. 1973, Hickox Papers.

73 "It was a . . ." WF, *News,* 21 Jan. 1933.

73 "was never born . . ." WF, *News,* 8 Dec. 1933.

73 "insipid" Wilner, *Man Time Forgot,* 202.

73 Alice White . . . , *Variety,* 23 Feb. 1983.

73 "cute blondes" WF, *News,* 26 Dec. 1933.

73 "If *Employee's Entrance* . . ." WF, *News,* 10 Feb. 1933.

73 Sidney "Sy" Bartlett, . . . , *Variety,* 7 June 1978.

73 "I have just . . ." WF, *News,* 8 Mar. 1933.

74 "You can buy . . ." WF, *News,* 11 Mar. 1933.

74 "effeminate" ibid.

74 "too, too purple . . ." WF, *Press,* 5 Mar. 1936.

74 "I have always . . ." WF, *News,* 26 Dec. 1933.

75 "It's about a . . ." *Press,* 28 Feb. 1933.

75 "The action is . . ." WF, *News,* 28 Feb. 1933.

75 "afraid to screen . . ." WF, *News,* 6 May 1933.

76 When Allen . . . , WF, *News* 5 June 1933.

76 "practically a sell-out. . . . So . . . " WF, *News* 15 Sept. 1933.

76 "terrific demand for . . ." WF, *News,* 16 Sept. 1933.

76 "If you have not . . ." WF, *News,* 29 Sept. 1933.

76 "subversive anti-Fascist, . . . " Elsner-Sommer, *"Mädchen in Uniform,"* International Dictionary of Films and Filmmakers, 601–2.

76 "In discussing the . . ." WF, *Press,* 3 July 1935.

76 "Inane and stupid" WF, *Press,* 29 May 1935.

76 "Simply an enormous . . ." WF, *Press,* 25 May 1935.

76 "At the first . . ." WF, *Press,* 17 June 1935.

76 "Take any and . . ." WF, *Press,* 29 May 1935.

77 "Keen Camp with . . ." WF, Datebook, 25 May 1935.

77 "gilded restaurants where . . ." WF, *Press,* 18 June 1935.

77 "the most expensive . . ." WF, *Press,* 3 June 1935.

77 "conspicuously seated" WF, *Press,* 20 Feb. 1936.

77 "Carole Lombard in . . ." WF, *Press,* 3 June 1935.

77 "Car broke down" WF, Datebook, 30 May 1935.

77 used Winsor's sister . . . , Margaret (Peggy) Eaton Taplin (hereafter PT) and
MEH interviews, 28 Aug. 1997.

77 "Hollywood with its . . ." WF, *Press,* 6 June 1935.

78 "sprawling in the . . ." WF, *Press,* 24 Jan. 1935.

78 "Olympian-sized" Mann, *Wisecracker,* 249–56.

78 "victims" WF, *News,* 6 Mar. 1933.

78 lesbians or sexual rebels . . . , Mann, *Wisecracker,* 258–59.

78 "restrain women from . . ." WF, *News,* 19 Dec. 1932.

79 "celluloid land" WF, *Press,* 18 July 1935.

79 "actors and actresses . . ." WF, *Press,* 20 June 1935.

79 "Fieldsie" WF, *Press,* 8 July 1935.

79 "old clothes" WF, *Press,* 15 June 1935.

79 "hundreds of curious" WF, *Press,* 20 June 1935.

79 "will go to any end . . ." WF, *Press,* 2 July 1935.

80 "crawl out of . . ." WF, *Press,* 22 June 1935.

80 a movie scenario . . . , WF, Datebook, 1 July 1935.

80 "Samuel Goldwyn will . . ." WF, *Press,* 29 May 1935.

80 "One highly paid . . ." WF, *Press,* 13 June 1935.

80 "During one emotional . . ." WF, *Press,* 13 June 1935.

80 "murder story" WF, Datebook, 4 June 1935.

80 "Cary Grant were . . . " Gill, *New York Life,* 190.

81 "were obliged to . . ." Gill, *New Yorker,* 2 June 1997.

81 "once one of . . ." WF, *Press,* 4 Mar. 1936.

81 to audition talent . . . , WF, *Press,* 24 June 1935.

81 "magnificently corseted" WF, *Press,* 4 July 1935.

82 "Crying jag" WF, Datebook, 12 July 1935.

82 "This city can . . ." WF, *Press,* 17 July 1935.

82 "Home drunk and . . ." WF, Datebook, 2 May 1935.

82 "turned in such . . ." WF, *Press,* 24 June 1935.

82 "His agents already . . ." WF, *Press,* 19, 25 July 1935.

82 "row with Allen" WF, Datebook, 15 July 1935.

82 "Hollywood apartment house" *New York Times,* 17 July 1935.

82 "one of the most . . ." WF, *Press,* 22 July 1935.

83 "Rufus phoned drunk" WF, Datebook, 1 June 1935.

83 "leaving unhappily a . . ." WF, *Press,* 25 July 1935.

83 "round of parties" WF, *Press,* 24 July 1935.

83 "amazing evening" WF, Datebook, 20 July 1935.

83 two quarts of Scotch . . . , WF, *Press,* 25 July 1935.

83 "indifferent ugliness" WF, *Press,* 26 July 1935.

83 "A very tan . . ." *Press,* 30 July 1935.

83 "descended" Parsons, *News,* 22 Jan. 1938.

84 "chronicler of the . . ." Collier, *Press,* 26 Sept. 1968; Collier, *Press,* 6 May 1973.

84 "rich and talented . . ." William Randle, *Sun,* 26 Oct. 1972.

84 "$15.00 for room . . ." JE to WF, 5 Feb. 1935, Hickox Papers.

84 "WOULD LIKE TO . . ." WF to JE, 16 Oct. 1935, Hickox Papers.

84 "2 cases of . . ." JE to WF, 11 Aug. 1938, Hickox Papers.

85 "Darkened shop windows . . ." WF, *Press,* 31 July 1935.

85 Margaret Moore, . . . , Grafton, *Red, Hot, and Rich,* 139.

85 Zerbe . . . photographs, *TIME,* 10 Dec. 1934.

85 who had met Porter . . . , McBrien, *Cole Porter,* 251–52; Schwartz, *Cole Porter,* 277; WF, *Press,* 20 Feb. 1958.

86 wealthy hostesses . . . , WF, *Press,* 7 Dec. 1957, WF, *PARADE,* 1 Oct. 1931, 20; 24 Dec. 1931, 22.

86 long-distance, JE to WF, 28 Feb. 1936, Hickox Papers.

86 "Winsor French . . . has . . ." J. Carroll to To Whom It May Concern, 13 Feb. 1936, Hickox Papers.

87 "A heaven-sent . . ." WF, *Press,* 29 Feb. 1936.

87 "The only way . . ." WF, *Press,* 31 Jan. 1940.

87 "the most charming . . ." WF, *Press,* 4 Mar. 1936.

87 "Liquor, . . . postage stamps" Eells, *Life that Late He Led,* 131–32.

87 with those of Placid . . . , Mallillin to WF, undated, Hickox Papers.

87 "average day " WF, *Press,* 6 Mar. 1936.

87 "can be a . . ." WF, *Press,* 11 July 1935.

87 "giving Cole Porter . . ." WF, *Press,* 4 Feb. 1936.

88 "After hanging around . . ." WF, *Press,* 3 Feb. 1936.

88 "that rambles over . . ." WF, *Press,* 6 Mar. 1936.

88 "A touch timidly" WF, *Press,* 7 Mar. 1936.
88 "I bumped into . . ." WF, *Press,* 4 Mar. 1936.
88 "I must have . . ." WF to JC, 9 Mar. 1936, Hickox Papers.
89 "all his hosts . . ." WF, *Press,* 7 Jan. 1966.
89 "almost my favorite . . ." WF, *Press,* 10 Mar. 1936.
90 "whipped up a . . ." WF, *Press,* 11 Mar. 1936.
90 Messel was a . . . , WF, *PARADE,* 14 July 1932, 25.
90 "Do I really . . ." WF, *News,* 11 June 1936.
91 "I shall be . . ." JC to WF, 13 Mar. 1936, Hickox Papers.
91 "I notice that . . ." JE to WF, 13 Mar. 1936, Hickox Papers.
91 "Enclosed is a . . ." WF, to JE, 17 Mar. 1936, Hickox Papers.
92 Hoffenstein, *Complete Poetry,* 13.
92 "scatological and obscene" Kimball, *Cole;* Gill, *Cole,* xvi.
92 "Rap Tap on Wood." Words and Music by Cole Porter © 1936 (Renewed) Chappell & Co., Inc. All Rights Reserved. Used by Permission of Alfred Publishing Co., Inc.; Kimball, *Complete Lyrics of Cole Porter,* 198.
92 "unfortunate habit" Eells, *Life that Late He Led,* 132.
92 "Sudden departure from . . ." WF, *Press,* 2 May 1936.
92 "left the opulent . . ." WF, *Press,* 5 May 1936.
93 "The mercury soared . . ." WF, *Press,* 8 May 1936.
93 "Mr. Pepys of . . ." Siegel, *Press,* 13 May 1936.
93 "Contrary to all . . ." WF, *Press,* 12 May 1936.
93 "morose" Parsons, *News,* 22 Jan. 1938.

"YOU'VE NEVER HEARD SUCH MUSIC"

94 "Cleveland" Kimball, *Cole;* Gill, *Cole,* 26–27; Kimball, *Complete Lyrics,* 70; Schwartz, *Cole Porter,* 274.
94 "maddest hat . . ." WF, *Press,* 11 June 1936.
95 "The boys serve . . ." WF, *Press,* 26 June 1936.
95 "Give yourself a . . ." WF, *News,* 5 June 1933.
95 "sitting big as life . . ." WF, *Press,* 10 June 1936.
95 "A tip to editors . . ." WF, *Press,* 21 Feb. 1936.
95 "better known nightclubs . . . screaming . . . " WF, *News* Mar. 6, 1933.
96 about 12 million, WF, *PARADE,* 15 Oct. 1931, 29.
96 "in an area . . ." Miggins and Morgenthaler, "Ethnic Mosaic," 130–31.
96 white racial attitudes . . . , Davis, *Black Americans in Cleveland,* 129.
96 "restaurants, bars, theaters . . ." Miggins and Morgenthaler, "Ethnic Mosaic," 133.
96 "if you like . . ." WF, *News,* 17 Nov. 1933.
96 "I think it . . ." Giddens, *PARADE,* 19 May 1932, 3.
96 Harlem Steppers . . . , WF, *News,* 30 Mar. 1933.
96 "gave away groceries . . ." WF, *News,* 3 Feb. 1933.
96 "black and tan . . ." WF, *News,* 31 Oct. 1933.
96 "dark stretches of . . ." WF, *News,* 24 Oct. 1933.
96 "Clara Smith hangs . . ." WF, *News,* 14 Oct. 1933.
96 "Jim Williams, an . . ." WF, *News,* 8 Dec. 1932.

97 "who brushes your . . ." WF, *News,* 28 Dec. 1932.

97 "cellars and purlieus" WF, *Press,* 4 Sept. 1954.

97 Musicians' Club, WF, *News,* 30 Jan. 1934.

97 "One study of . . ." Simpson, *Negro in the Philadelphia Press;* Gist, "Negro in the Daily News"; Martindale and Dunlap, "African Americans," 71.

97 "only Negro . . . who . . . " Villard, *Nation* 16 Apr. 1930, 430–44.

97 "race weeklies" Martindale and Dunlap, "African Americans," 71.

97 two struggling weeklies . . . , *"Cleveland Call & Post,"* Encyclopedia of Cleveland History, 208.

97 "tables where you . . ." WF, *News,* 19 Apr. 1933.

97 "Go late, order . . ." WF, *News,* 4 Jan. 1933

98 "I am waiting . . ." WF to JE, 14 Nov. 1927, Hickox Papers.

98 "I am sorry . . ." JE to WF, 18 Nov. 1927, Hickox Papers.

98 "NEGROES," "WOMEN," and . . . , *TIME,* May–July, 1927.

98 reviewed *Brown America* . . . *PARADE,* 15 Oct. 1931, 29.

99 "those qualities . . ." Martindale and Dunlap, "African Americans," 64.

99 "a group of . . ." WF, *PARADE,* 10 Dec. 1931, 28.

99 "and request that . . ." WF, *PARADE,* 17 Dec. 1931, 18.

99 "Ethel Waters in . . ." WF, *PARADE,* 24 Dec. 1931, 25.

99 "the first black . . ." Hemming and Hajdu, *Discovering Great Singers,* 19.

99 "news media are . . ." Martindale and Dunlap, introduction to *Minorities,* 3–4; "African Americans," 65.

100 black-owned nightclubs . . . , Chauncey, *Gay New York,* 248–67.

100 "Look in at . . ." WF, *PARADE,* 14 Jan. 1932, 23.

100 "Dinker—salesman of . . ." WF, *PARADE,* 17 Mar. 1932, 16–19.

100 "illicit drinking in . . ." Teel, *Public Press,* 121.

101 "a drink except . . ." WF, *PARADE,* 17 Mar. 1932, 16–19.

101 "come into its . . ." WF, *Press,* 11 Sept. 1954.

101 "White intellectuals of . . ." Peeler, *Hope among Us Yet,* 9.

101 "our finest period . . ." Thomson, *American Music since 1910,* 9.

101 "It took 'intestinal fortitude' . . ." Zucker, *PARADE,* 31 Mar. 1932, 3.

102 "Bessie Brown, a . . ." Elliott, *PARADE,* 24 Mar. 1932, 3.

102 "knew all the . . ." WF, *Press,* 25 Sept. 1954.

102 "shrimp gumbo" WF, *News,* 13 May 1933.

102 "Virginia ham in . . ." WF, *News,* 13 Jan. 1934.

102 "dug deeply into . . ." WF, *News,* 13 Jan. 1933.

102 "ran entirely out . . ." WF, *Press,* 11 June 1936.

102 "fastest show" WF, *Press,* 18 June 1936.

102 "a smoky little . . ." WF, *Press,* 25 Sept. 1954.

103 "her inimitable technique . . ." WF, *Press,* 18 June 1936.

103 "Evelyn Chevillat makes . . ." WF, *Press,* 13 Nov. 1940.

103 "small but select . . ." WF, *PARADE,* 22 Sept. 1932, 25.

103 "Fleet's Inn" WF, *Press,* 25 May 1937.

103 "immaculately clean little . . ." WF, *Press,* 1 Oct. 1945.

103 "two very inebriated . . ." WF, *Press,* 20 May 1937.

104 "gypsy fortune tellers . . . looking . . . " WF, *Press,* 25 May 1937.

104 "to be terrified . . ." WF, *News,* 1 June 1933.

104 "young, literally starving . . ." WF, *Press,* 7, 21 Nov. 1953.

104 "the lad in plaid" *News,* 3 July 1933.

104 "brisk little walks . . ." *Press,* 24 May 1954.

104 "Looking right at you . . ." *News,* 22 Jan. 1938.

104 "people without any . . ." *News,* 13 May 1933.

104 "managed to find . . ." WF, *Press,* 23 June 1936.

105 Porter entertained . . . , WF, *Press,* 17 June 1936; McBrien, *Cole Porter,* 197.

105 "socially prominent tenor . . ." WF, *News,* 25 Jan., 10 Feb. 1933.

105 his wife's loathing . . . , Eells, *Life that Late He Led,* 132–33.

105 "incredible to pass . . ." WF, *Press,* 16 June 1936.

105 "a modern Garden . . ." *Press,* 3 Feb. 1936.

105 "unpredictable" WF, *Press,* 9 Jan. 1937.

105 "bar barge" Williamson, *Press,* 4 Mar. 1936.

105 "society column" Peckham, *Gentlemen for Rent,* 13–16.

106 "Guide Escort Service," *Literary Digest,* 12 Dec. 1936; Cunningham, *News* 8 Feb. 1937.

106 "the flower of American . . ." Peckham, *Bachelor,* Apr. 1937, 27–28.

106 "vaguely reminiscent . . ." *Encyclopedia of Cleveland History,* 468.

106 "some 24 women . . ." WF, *Press,* 11 June 1936.

106 "The sudden decision . . ." WF, *Press,* 26 June 1936.

106 "plutocratic sensation . . ." WF, *Press,* 30 June 1936.

107 "grounds, flooded with . . ." WF, *Press,* 10 June 1936.

107 "winterize, refurbish and . . ." WF, *Press,* 8 Oct. 1936.

107 "a giddy honky-tonk . . ." WF, *Press,* 7 Oct. 1936.

107 "beginning to look happier" WF, *Press,* 1 Oct. 1936.

108 pre-Broadway tryouts . . . , WF, *Press,* 2 Oct. 1936.

108 "a cold gray . . ." WF, *Press,* 3 Oct. 1936.

108 "a wise-cracking . . ." WF, *Press,* 2 Oct. 1936.

108 "wearing a costume . . ." WF, *Press,* 8 Oct. 1936.

109 "in the first row . . ." WF, *Press,* 10 Oct. 1936.

109 "just in time . . ." ibid.

109 "White pigskin!" WF, *Press,* 19 Aug. 1963.

110 "everything in their . . ." WF, *Press,* 12 Oct. 1936.

110 "living their too . . ." WF, *Press,* 13 Oct. 1936.

110 "no longer the . . ." WF, *Press,* 14 Oct. 1936.

110 "arrived carrying an . . ." WF, *Press,* 19 Oct. 1937.

110 "A reporter goes . . ." WF, *Press,* 16 Oct. 1936.

111 "The cast has . . ." WF, *Press,* 31 Oct. 1936.

111 "much better show" WF, *Press,* 2 Nov. 1936.

111 "too ill to . . ." McBrien, *Cole Porter,* 203.

111 "a floor show . . ." WF, *Press,* 7 Jan. 1937.

112 "spare ribs littered . . ." WF, *Press,* 9 Jan. 1937.

112 "the land of the . . ." WF, *Press,* 2 Feb. 1937.

112 "three cars with . . ." WF, *Press,* 8 Feb. 1937.

112 "Across the lawn . . ." WF, *Press,* 11 Feb. 1937.

112 "Life is simply . . ." ibid.

112 "poked [his] nose . . ." WF, *Press,* 10 Feb. 1937.

112 "Chain gangs" WF, *Press,* 12 Feb. 1937.

113 "the most dangerous . . ." WF, *Press,* 13 Feb. 1937.

113 "was too ill . . ." McBrien, *Cole Porter,* 203.

113 "owned by Billy Wilkerson . . ." WF, *Press,* 22 Feb. 1937.

114 "decided it would . . ." WF, *Press,* 24 Feb. 1937.

114 "where everyone beat . . ." WF, *Press,* 3 May 1937.

114 "had reached another . . ." WF, *Press,* 22 May 1937.

114 "considering delivering an . . ." Eells, *Life that Late He Led,* 173.

"I MAY HAVE BEEN A LITTLE HARSH"

115 "flying miraculously . . . " Zerbe, "The House on Harcourt," 35.

115 "three safety-pins" Mary Louise Brown Curtiss to WF, March 22, 1956, Hickox
   Papers.

116 "loin cloth . . . " WF, *PARADE,* 4 Feb. 1931, 1.

116 "spectacular" Vacha, *Showtime in Cleveland,* 105.

116 "Always the eager . . ." WF, *Press,* 10 Nov. 1937.

116 "had GREAT chances" WF to JE, 14 Nov. 1927, Hickox Papers.

116 "hardly anyone in . . ." WF, *Press,* 13 Jan. 1937.

116 "with his dinner . . ." WF, *News,* 22 Jan. 1938.

117 "A young girl" WF, *Press,* 7 Dec. 1937.

117 "She is one . . ." WF, *Press,* 14 Oct. 1936.

118 Harry Richman "is . . ." WF, *News,* 14 Oct. 1933.

118 Frances Stevens "has . . ." WF, *News,* 17 Feb. 1933.

118 "the art she . . ." Arthur Spaeth, *News,* 7 Dec. 1937.

118 "Her technique is . . ." McDermott, *Plain Dealer,* 7 Dec. 1937.

118 "Completed weeks ago . . ." WF, *Press,* 8 Dec. 1937.

118 "The modern actress . . ." Warfel, *Press,* 9 Dec. 1937.

118 "personal property . . . a . . . " WF, *Press,* 15 Oct. 1937.

119 "The Carl Hannas . . ." WF, *Press,* 11 Dec. 1937.

119 "was delivered to . . ." WF, *Press,* 13 Dec. 1937.

120 "kill 'em with . . ." Allan Temko to author, UC Berkeley, 1961.

120 "Dear Queenie" J. Bennett to WF, 13 Dec. 1937, Hickox Papers.

120 "not a swimming . . ." Riggin, Olympian's Oral History, 54.

121 "I'm a lousy . . ." *Press,* 20 May 1937.

121 "If Johnny Weissmuller . . ." WF, *Press,* 22 May 1937.

121 "roaring" WF, *Press,* 27 May 1937.

121 "At the moment . . ." WF, *Press,* 29 May 1937.

121 "dirty" Kevin Leigh to WF, 24 Feb. 1959, Hickox Papers.

121 "paid a streetcar . . ." John Silvey to WF, 7 Mar. 1959, Hickox Papers.

121 nightclub on a barge, WF, *Press,* February 15, 1936.

122 Despite Winsor's promotion . . . , WF, *Press,* 7, 8 Jan. 1937.

122 "putting the Aquacade . . ." WF, *Press,* 28 May 1937.

122 "The stage, at . . ." Schneider, *Press,* 13 May 1937.

122 ticket sales . . . , WF, *Press,* May 20, 1937.

122 "to throw a . . ." WF, *PARADE,* 25 June 1931, 46.

122 "one outstanding characteristic . . . " Parsons, *News,* 22 Jan. 1938.

122 "Billy Rose's not . . ." WF, *PARADE,* 28 Apr. 1932, 31.

122 "up to her . . ." Goldman, *Fanny Brice,* 152.

123 "he fell in . . ." ibid., 172–75.

123 "careless play writing" WF, *Press,* 6 Dec. 1937.

123 "wholesale slaughter" WF, *Press,* 17 Oct. 1936.

123 "fast fading interest . . ." WF, *Press,* 13 Oct. 1937.

123 "Each year shows . . ." WF, *PARADE,* 24 Dec. 1931, 25.

124 "the world's most . . ." WF, *Press,* 20 Oct. 1936.

124 "shied at some . . ." Gill, *Cole,* xvi–xvii.

124 "Although still angry" Eells, *Life that Late He Led,* 173.

124 "tall, broad-shouldered" McBrien, *Cole Porter,* 212.

124 "the Porters and . . ." Grafton, *Red, Hot, and Rich,* 102–3.

125 "party of friends" Gill, *Cole,* xiv.

125 "appropriately disrespectful book" WF, *Press,* 8 Dec. 1939.

125 "put words into . . ." WF, *Press,* 7 Dec. 1939.

125 "But in the Morning, No" (from *Du Barry Was a Lady*). Words and Music by Cole Porter © 1939 (Renewed) Chappell & Co., Inc. All rights reserved. Used by permission of Alfred Publishing Co., Inc.; Kimball, *Complete Lyrics of Cole Porter,* 259.

125 "slatternly" Eells, *Life that Late He Led,* 190–91.

126 "big and brassy" Hemming and Hajdu, *Discovering Great Singers,* 77–79.

126 "vocal sound" Henry Pleasants, *Great American Popular Singers,* 334.

126 "I don't bother . . ." Merman and Martin, *Who Could Ask For Anything More,* 10.

126 "outright hostility" Merman with Eells, *Merman,* 198–99.

126 "coarse . . . but enjoyable" Thomas, *I Got Rhythm!* 70–71.

126 promoted a recording . . . , WF, *Press,* 26 Dec. 1939.

126 "Ignoring the negative . . ." Merman with Eells, *Merman,* 108–9.

126 "too much of . . ." WF, *Press,* 12 Dec. 1939.

126 she had divorced . . . , *Plain Dealer,* 20 June 1938.

126 "dingy, waterfront saloon . . . shrouded . . . " WF, *Press,* 11 Dec. 1939.

127 "an extremely fine actor" WF, *Press,* 27 Dec. 1940.

127 "sordid laundry" WF, *Press,* 15 Dec. 1939.

127 "the most outrageous, . . ." WF, *Press,* 14 Dec. 1939.

127 "master of the . . ." Harbin, "Public and Private Man," 262.

128 "The theater has . . ." *Press,* 12 Jan. 1940.

128 "shared a love . . . " Harbin, "Public and Private Man," 267.

128 *Panama Hattie* . . . , Ewen, *Cole Porter Story,* 102–3.

128 "complete score and . . ." *New York Herald Tribune,* 12 Jan. 1935.

128 "a black bandage . . ." WF, *Press,* 12 Oct. 1957.

128 "seldom arose . . ." Collier, *Press,* 19 Aug. 1963.

128 "Yalie and great . . ." McBrien, *Cole Porter,* 177–78; Eells, quoted in Howard, *Travels,* 9.

129 "Renee, wearing no . . ." WF, *Press,* 24 Dec. 1935.

129 "As an actor . . ." WF, *Press,* 5 Jan. 1940.

129 "A little pie . . ." WF, *Press,* 8 Jan. 1940.

129 "In my sentimental . . ." WF, *Press,* 18 Jan. 1940.

129 "one of the most depressing, . . ." WF, *Press,* 2 Jan. 1940.

"NIGHTS ARE . . . A BACCHANALIAN ROUT"

130 "Shivering, apprehensive passengers . . ." WF, *Press,* 29 Jan. 1940.

130 "Music played, multi-colored . . ." WF, *Press,* 18 July 1955.

131 "The Swastikas go . . ." WF, *News,* 26 Aug. 1933.

131 "Because Jewish books . . ." WF, *News,* 11 May 1933.

131 "the famous Duke . . ." WF, *News,* 5 Oct. 1933.

131 "feel sorry for . . ." WF, *Press,* 18 Oct. 1937.

131 "dark and terrible . . ." WF, *Press,* 15 Dec. 1939.

131 "shattering . . . letdown for . . ." WF, *Press,* 11 July 1951.

131 "We are off . . ." Howard, *Travels,* 14.

132 Paul Sylvain . . . , ibid.; Eells, quoted in Howard, *Travels,* 9.

132 "slipped into the . . ." WF, *Press,* 29 Jan. 1940.

132 "aboard the *Franconia*" Grafton, *Red, Hot, and Rich,* 92.

133 "a perfectly appalling . . ." WF, *Press,* 4 Jan. 1941.

133 "daiquiris were the . . ." WF, *Press,* 1 Feb. 1940.

133 "as if they . . ." WF, *Press,* 2 Feb. 1940.

133 "mothered" McBrien, *Cole Porter,* 236.

133 "lanky, dark-skinned . . ." WF, *Press,* 1 Feb. 1940.

134 "The night we . . ." WF, *Press,* 2 Feb. 1940.

135 "You get a . . ." WF, *News,* 29 July 1933.

135 "The crowd is . . ." WF, *News,* 18 Aug. 1933.

135 "Heaven must be . . . " Eells, *Life that Late He Led,* 191.

135 "None of them . . ." WF, *Press,* 17 Feb. 1940.

135 "Crowded with opportunists . . ." WF, *Press,* 20 Feb. 1940.

135 "Everyone we came . . ." WF, *Press,* 22 Feb. 1940.

135 "the national pastime . . ." WF, *Press,* 26 Feb. 1940.

135 "We were served . . ." WF, *Press,* 27 Feb. 1940.

136 "The freshwater showers . . ." WF, *Press,* 21 Feb. 1940.

136 "more suitors than . . ." Isaac Edward Emerson Papers, Library of the University of North Carolina at Chapel Hill.

136 "slender bronzed Polynesian . . ." WF, *Press,* 18 Mar. 1940.

137 "Inevitable" WF, *Press,* 19 Mar. 1940.

137 "Supposed to be . . ." WF, *Press,* 20 Mar. 1940.

137 "gin, vanilla ice cream . . ." WF, *Press,* 21 Mar. 1940.

137 "clad only in . . ." WF, *Press,* 22 Mar. 1940.

138 "lunching with Maugham . . ." WF, *Press,* 23 Mar. 1940.

138 "Samoan singers . . ." WF, *Press,* 25 Mar. 1940.

140 "the little pilot boat . . ." WF, *Press,* 26 Mar. 1940.

140 "Surrounded by French . . ." WF, *Press,* 27 Mar. 1940.

141 "the Porter party . . ." McBrien, *Cole Porter,* 236.

141 "Make It another Old Fashioned, Please" (from *Panama Hattie*). Words and Music by Cole Porter © 1940 by Chappell & Co., Inc. Copyright Renewed and Assigned to John F. Wharton, Trustee of the Cole Porter Musical & Literary Property Trusts. Chappell & Co., owner of publication and allied rights throughout the World. All Rights Reserved Used by permission of Alfred Publishing Co., Inc.; Kimball, *Complete Lyrics of Cole Porter,* 288.

141 "deserted at various . . ." WF, *Press,* 28 Mar. 1940.

142 "suffered from rootlessness . . ." Eells, *Life that Late He Led,* 191–92.

142 "The only menacing . . ." WF, *Press,* 28 Mar. 1940; McBrien, *Cole Porter,* 235.

142 "the most savage, . . ." WF, *Press,* 29 Mar. 1940.

143 "brass fortissimo" Ewen, *Cole Porter Story,* 102–3.

143 "old and new friends . . ." WF, *Press,* 30 Mar. 1940.

143 "The Wheel Inn . . . serves . . . " WF, *Press,* 1 Oct. 1940.

143 "of the places . . ." Eells, *Life that Late He Led,* 192.

144 "At this point . . ." WF, *Press,* 1 Oct. 1940.

144 "scrawled her name . . ." WF, *Press,* 29 Oct. 1940.

144 "This campaign of . . ." *Plain Dealer,* 1 Oct. 1940.

144 "sent 30 telegrams . . ." WF, *Press,* 29 Oct. 1940.

144 "an extremely disturbing . . ." WF, *Press,* 26 Oct. 1940.

145 "gay and frothy . . . " WF, *Press,* 13 Nov. 1940.

145 "weightless . . . irresponsible gayety . . ." McDermott, *Plain Dealer,* 13 Nov. 1940.

145 "dusting off party" Spaeth, *News,* 13 Nov. 1940.

145 "At the time . . ." WF, *Press,* 14 Nov. 1940.

145 "pace-and-style setter" Parsons, *News,* 12 Feb. 1938.

146 "He has written . . ." WF, *Press,* 27 Dec. 1940.

146 "In this reporter's . . ." WF, *Press,* 28 Oct. 1940.

146 "aimless and without . . ." WF, *Press,* 31 Dec. 1940.

147 "The honky-tonks . . ." WF, *Press,* 2 Jan. 1941.

147 "the Hanna Theater . . ." WF, *Press,* 3 Jan. 1940.

147 "I am about . . ." WF, *Press,* 12 Sept. 1941.

"OUR OWN DESIGN FOR LIVING"

148 "Dear Father, Len . . ." WF to JE, 2 Dec. 1941, Hickox Papers.

148 "seeing a great deal" WF, *Press,* 6 June 1964.

148 "ice blue hair" WF, *Press,* 1 Sept. 1951.

149 "Everyone's reason seems . . ." WF to AEP, 12 Dec. 1941, Parker Papers.

149 "asked for duty . . ." Collier, *Press,* 2 Aug. 1963.

149 "I wish something . . . " WF to AEP, 12 Dec. 1941.

149 "Having Benny here . . ." WF to JE, 18 Dec. 1941, Hickox Papers.

149 "I am wondering . . ." JE to WF, 22 Dec. 1941, Hickox Papers.

150 "I have had . . ." JE to WF, 20 Jan. 1942, Hickox Papers.

150 "There have only . . ." WF to AEP, 18 Mar. 1942, Parker Papers.

150 "a lean, lanky guy" French and Lewis, *Curtain Call,* 6.

150 "We soon became . . ." Smith to author, 17 July 2001.

151 "most attractive and . . ." Johnson, *New York Sun,* 13 Feb. 1942.

151 gold-standard investors . . . , Widder, *Press,* undated, Mar. 1947.

151 Dwight Deere Wiman, *New York Times,* 21 Jan. 1951; *Variety,* 20 Jan. 1951.

151 "Being a bar . . ." Stearns, "The Umbilical Chord," *Curtain Call,* 74.

152 "gin rummy" *New Yorker,* 13 June 1942, 4.

152 "You had better . . ." JE to WF, 27 Apr. 1942, Hickox Papers.

152 "I hope I . . ." WF to AEP, 3 May 1942, Parker Papers.

153 "I have written . . ." JE to WF, 11 May 1942, Hickox Papers.

153 "Deprived of bulls . . ." WF to AEP, 25 July 1942, Parker Papers.

154 "You owe me . . ." WF to AEP, 26 Aug. 1942, Parker Papers.

154 "diametrically opposed to . . ." Coward, *Design for Living,* 58.

154 "Perhaps, if I . . ." WF to AEP, 26 Aug. 1942.

154 "It would have . . ." AEP interview, 28 Aug. 1997.

155 "EVERYTHING BREAKS . . ." WF to AEP, 25 July 1942, Parker Papers.

155 "earn some money" WF to JE, 20 Nov. 1943, Hickox Papers.

155 "Very amusing" WF to AEP, 26 Aug. 1942.

155 "characters are merely . . ." WF, *PARADE,* 28 July 1932, 28.

155 "verse seems only . . ." WF, *PARADE,* 5 Nov. 1931.

156 "no more literary . . ." WF, *PARADE,* 31 Dec. 1931, 30.

156 "bitten off in . . ." WF, *PARADE,* 14 Jan. 1932, 28.

156 "eliminate every unnecessary . . ." WF, *PARADE,* 26 Nov. 1931, 30.

156 "a genius for . . ." WF, *PARADE,* 4 Feb. 1932, 26.

156 "with one line . . ." WF, *PARADE,* 31 Dec. 1931, 30.

156 "suspense, wit, tragedy," WF, *PARADE,* 6 Aug. 1931, 48.

156 "that neither contradict . . ." WF, *PARADE,* 11 June 1931, 43.

156 "handle a quiet . . ." WF, *PARADE,* 24 Sept. 1931, 31.

156 "cloyingly sentimental" WF, *PARADE,* 13 Aug. 1931, 32.

156 "complete depravity and . . ." WF, *PARADE,* 14 Jan. 1932, 28.

156 "His brain may . . ." WF, *PARADE,* 31 Dec. 1931, 30.

156 "a novel for . . ." Isabel M. Patterson, *New York Herald Tribune,* 15 Nov. 1931.

156 "unquestionably the great . . ." WF, *PARADE,* 17 Dec. 1931, 25.

156 "brilliant" WF, *PARADE,* 29 Oct. 1931, 30–32.

157 "clear, bright, burnished . . ." Luis Kronenberger, *New York Times* (*Early City Edition*), 25 Oct. 1931, 5.

157 "To have a . . ." Harwood, *Saturday Review* 152 (10 Oct. 1931): 462.

157 "Mrs. Woolf's new form . . ." West, *New York Herald Tribune,* 1 Nov. 1931, 1.

158 "Thanks for the soap . . ." WF to JC, 7 June 1943, Hickox Papers.

158 "Winsor French still . . ." Howard, *Travels,* 18.

158 "Peg and I are . . ." WF to JE, 20 Nov. 1943, Hickox Papers.

158 "a lonesome watch" WF, *Press,* 26 Sept. 1968.

158 "pints of Scotch . . ." WF, *Press,* 25 Oct. 1966.

158 "established one hundred clubs" Collier, *Press,* 2 Aug. 1963.

158 In 1944, Stearns . . ." WF, *Press,* 20 Feb. 1958.

158 "did an hour-long . . ." Stearns, "The Umbilical Chord," *Curtain Call,* 75.

159 purchased a six-room, . . . , undated clipping, Hickox Papers.

159 "Mr. French's volatile . . ." Seltzer, *Press,* 1 Oct. 1945.

"SOLID GOLD FROM WRIST TO ELBOW"

160 "I was born . . . " WF to LS, 1 Oct. 1945.
160 "Through the grime . . ." WF, *Press,* 1 Oct. 1945.
161 "you could walk . . ." ibid.
161 "cellars and purlieus" WF, *Press,* 4 Sept. 1954.
161 "You were just . . ." WF, *Press,* 10 Oct. 1945.
161 "What has happened . . ." ibid.
161 "The bereft and . . ." WF, *Press,* 24 Aug. 1946.
161 more interested in . . . , WF, *Press,* 26 Mar. 1962.
162 "initials carved into . . ." WF, *Press,* 24 May 1946.
162 "If you are going . . ." WF, *Press,* 27, 28 May 1946.
162 "In less than . . ." WF, *Press,* 31 May 1946.
162 "battle dress" WF, *Press,* 1 June 1946.
162 " The visitor in . . ." WF, *Press,* 29 May 1946.
162 "I can count . . ." WF, *Press,* 3 June 1946.
162 "Everyone is tired, . . ." WF, *Press,* 8 June 1946.
163 "Most people arrive . . ." WF, *Press,* 1 June 1946.
163 "only permitted two . . ." WF, *Press,* 4 June 1946.
163 "created as beautiful . . ." WF, *Press,* 7 June 1946.
163 "All the available . . ." WF, *Press,* 5 June 1946.
163 "More sleek, highly . . ." WF, *Press,* 3 June 1946.
163 "one of the few . . ." WF, *Press,* 14 June 1946.
163 "Trees, clipped so . . ." WF, *Press,* 15 June 1946.
164 "A German soldier . . ." WF, *Press,* 3 July 1946.
164 "When I walked . . ." WF, *Press,* 5 July 1946.
164 "crowded with Americans . . ." ibid.
164 "very simply in . . ." WF, *Press,* 2 July 1946.
164 "They sit on . . ." WF, *Press,* 18 June 1946.
164 "You step into . . ." WF, *Press,* 22 June 1946.
165 "I myself feel . . ." WF, *Press,* 21 June 1946.
165 "were still there, . . ." WF, *Press,* 25 June 1946.
165 "This morning my . . ." WF, *Press,* 29 June 1946.
166 "at least once . . ." WF, *Press,* 9 July 1946.
167 "far from brief . . . merely . . ." WF, *Press,* 10 July 1946.
167 "the fashionable folk" WF, *Press,* 12 July 1946.
167 "designed so that . . ." WF, *Press,* 16 July 1946.
168 "hoping they will . . ." WF, *Press,* 17 July 1946.
168 "I reached the . . ." WF, *Press,* 22 July 1946.
169 "They float huge, . . ." WF, *Press,* 24 July 1946.
169 "It must have . . ." WF, *Press,* 29 July 1946.
169 "went right through . . ." WF, *Press,* 25 July 1946.
170 "a really superb . . ." WF, *Press,* 24 July 1946.
170 "the little bals . . ." WF, *Press,* 26 July 1946.
170 "most expensive and . . ." WF, *Press,* 1 Aug. 1946.
171 "Right at the . . ." WF, *Press,* 31 July 1946.

172 "I may be much . . ." WF, *Press,* 2 Aug. 1946.

172 "everywhere, towering to . . ." WF, *Press,* 7 Aug. 1946.

172 "It is all . . ." WF, *Press,* 9 Aug. 1946.

172 "Sent to Europe . . ." Van Tassel and Grabowski, *Encyclopedia of Cleveland History,* 424.

173 "With the exception . . ." WF, *Press,* 3 June 1946.

173 "repaired with metal . . ." WF, *Press,* 17 June 1946.

"BLOW OFF A LITTLE STEAM"

174 "nine o'clock rattler" WF, *Press,* 4 Oct. 1948.

174 "For the first . . ." WF, *Press,* 5 Oct. 1948.

174 "serene" WF, *Press,* 25 Sept. 1948; Gibbons, *Press,* 12 July 1947.

174 "moistened gents" WF, *Press,* 28 Sept. 1948.

175 "The departure following . . ." WF, *Press,* 5 Oct. 1948.

175 "few inches of . . ." WF, *Press,* 21 Jan. 1954.

175 "Willie came to . . ." WF, *Press,* 30 Aug. 1949.

176 "For 100 straight . . ." Veeck, *Veeck as in Wreck,* 200–201.

176 "sudden" French, "From Here to Infirmity," *Curtain Call,* 18.

176 "Burrhead," Greenberg, "Pied Piper of the Wigwam," *Curtain Call,* 23.

176 "plunging neckline," Hanna Theatre, *The Man Who Came to Dinner,* program, 25 Dec. 1950.

176 Alhambra Lounge, Veeck, *Veeck as in Wreck,* 204.

176 Winsor considered Birns . . . , MEH to author, 28 Aug. 1997.

176 "in proper glasses, . . . " WF, *Press,* 2 July 1954.

176 "I've always found . . ." Veeck, *Veeck as in Wreck,* 204.

176 "Six of the . . ." WF, *News,* 11 Jan. 1933.

177 "Julius Lamm of . . ." WF, *News,* 2 May 1933.

177 "the master's touch . . ." French and Lewis, *Curtain Call,* 52–53.

177 "Smoking nervously" ibid., Greenberg, "Pied Piper of the Wigwam," 23.

177 "the worst radio . . . , Franklin Lewis, *Press,* 3 Mar. 1948.

178 "The strains of gay, . . ." WF, *Press,* 30 Aug. 1949.

178 "fingernails trying to . . ." WF, *Press,* 21 Jan. 1954.

178 "It was a beautiful, . . ." WF, *Press,* 28 Sept. 1948.

178 "Everyone was smiling, . . ." WF, *Press,* 5 Oct. 1948.

179 "hardly walk through . . ." WF, *Press,* 6 Oct. 1948.

179 "a flask glinting . . ." *Boston Daily Record,* 5 Oct. 1948.

179 knee was amputated . . . , Ira Berkow, *New York Times,* 20 Oct. 2005.

180 father had played . . . , WF, *Press,* 12 Oct. 1957.

180 "laid down the . . ." Schwartz, *Cole Porter,* 196.

180 "pleased as a . . ." WF, *Press,* 19 Aug. 1963.

180 "sauntered past . . . wearing . . . " Lewis, *Press,* 5 Oct. 1948.

180 "Hundreds upon hundreds" WF, *Press,* 28 Sept. 1948.

181 "All rules off . . ." Lewis, *Cleveland Indians,* 268.

181 "well-guarded" WF, *Press,* 5 Oct. 1948.

181 "Roast beef, . . . " WF, *Press,* 25 Sept., 6 Oct. 1948.

181 "acutely dehydrated" WF, *Press,* 28 Sept. 1948.

181 "moments in life . . ." WF, *Press,* 5 Oct. 1954.

181 "You couldn't have . . ." Lewis, *Press,* 5 Oct. 1948.

181 "Several of the . . ." *Boston Daily Record,* 5 Oct. 1948.

181 "friction in the . . ." Bob Ajemian, *Boston Evening American,* 5 Oct. 1948.

182 "A couple of . . ." WF, *Press,* 6 Oct. 1948.

182 "arrived an inning . . ." WF, *Press,* 7 Oct. 1948.

182 "After defeats, Willie . . ." WF, *Press,* 8 Oct. 1948.

182 "The Hollenden Hotel . . ." WF, *Press,* 2 Oct. 1954.

182 "The Hollenden . . . wasn't . . ." WF, *Press,* 12 Oct. 1948.

183 "Willie . . . instructed Marsh . . ." WF, *Press,* 2 Oct. 1954.

183 "shook up the . . ." Veeck, *Veeck as in Wreck,* 207.

184 "It does a restaurant . . ." ibid., 200–201.

184 "The entertainment waters . . ." WF, *Press,* 24 Sept. 1948.

184 "four, impossible to . . ." French, "From Here to Infirmity," *Curtain Call,* 18.

184 Veeck at the Hollenden, . . . , Veeck, *Veeck as in Wreck,* 199.

185 "with two front . . ." Smith to author, 17 July 2001.

185 "three tiny rooms" Luft, undated *Press* clipping, Hickox Papers.

185 "regular calling list" Anderson, "The Man at the Next Desk," *Curtain Call,* 62.

185 "book theorists and . . ." WF, *Press,* 6 Feb. 1954.

185 Cole Porter asked . . . , Howard, *Travels,* 22.

186 "put a Cleveland . . ." *Press,* 16 May 1954.

186 "Frankly, I don't . . ." WF, *Press,* 16 May 1949.

186 He took them . . . , Zerbe, "The House on Harcourt," 35.

186 "Racqueteers," an exclusive . . . , Wood, *The Tavern,* 121.

186 "During the lean . . ." WF, *Press,* 23 Dec. 1961.

186 "lost interest and . . ." Greenberg, "Pied Piper of the Wigwam," 23.

186 "Vast, wandering houses" WF, *Press,* 9 Aug. 1949.

187 "The cold, mean . . ." WF, *Press,* 30 Aug. 1949.

187 "Carol Greenberg sneaked . . ." WF, *Press,* 10 Dec. 1949.

188 "fat, funny and friendly" Paterson, *Solid Seasons.*

188 a reduced score . . . , Arthur Loesser, *Press,* 7 Dec. 1949.

188 often used a . . . , Standifer and George, interview transcript.

188 Caucasian musical . . . , Herbert Ellwell, *Plain Dealer,* 10 Dec. 1949.

188 Hanna escorted . . . , WF, *Press,* 10 Dec. 1949.

188 "Who is it? . . ." Menotti, *The Medium,* 118–21.

188 "*The Medium* . . . held . . ." Ranney, *Press,* 10 Dec. 1949.

189 "Credit goes to . . ." Elwell, *Plain Dealer,* 10 Dec. 1949.

189 "Zelma George . . . sings . . ." Spaeth, *News,* 10 Dec. 1949.

189 "little Negro theater" Standifer and George, interview transcript.

189 *The Medium* filled . . . , Hruby to author; Garland, *Journal American,* 20 July 1950.

189 Menotti sent his . . . , Standifer and George, interview transcript.

190 Hotel Theresa in Harlem, Zelma George (hereafter ZG), Menotti interview with author, December 20, 1982.

190 "bath, shower, radio . . ." ZG to WF, 20 July 1950, Hickox Papers.

190 "first publicity releases . . ." WF, *Press,* 13 July 1950.

190 "perhaps the . . ." Harold Schonberg, *New York Times,* 20 July 1950.

191 "was just a . . ." WF, *Press,* 13 July 1950.

191 "Zelma George . . . pulled . . ." Schonberg, *New York Times,* 20 July 1950.

191 "Only a superhuman . . ." Vernon Rice, *New York Post,* 20 July 1950.

191 "Zelma George . . . must . . . " Robert Coleman, *Daily Mirror,* 20 July 1950.

191 "Sung and acted . . ." Robert Sylvester, *Daily News,* 20 July 1950.

191 "Zelma George . . . séances . . . " Robert Garland, *Journal American,* 20 July 1950.

192 "We could have . . ." Standifer and George, interview transcript.

192 "The nocturnal traffic, . . ." WF, *Press,* 20 Dec. 1950.

192 "artificial buying panic . . ." WF, *Press,* 18 July 1950.

192 "In the event . . ." WF, *Press,* 23 Feb. 1954.

192 "add up to . . ." WF, *Press,* 7 Dec. 1949.

192 "What with the . . ." WF, *Press,* 12 July 1950.

192 "One of the last . . ." WF, *Press,* 15 July 1950.

193 "would want to . . ." WF, *Press,* 16 Aug. 1950.

193 "In his daily . . ." Bradshaw, *Dreams that Money Can Buy,* 288.

193 "The demand to . . ." WF, *Press,* 10 Dec. 1949.

194 "Veeck is back . . ." WF, *Press,* 19 Dec. 1950.

194 Winsor's idea . . . , Vacha, *From Broadway to Cleveland,* 76.

194 "I wandered around . . ." WF, *Press,* 22 Dec. 1950.

194 *"The Man Who . . ."* WF, *Press,* 26 Dec. 1950.

194 "At no time . . . did . . . " Spaeth, *News,* 26 Dec. 1950.

195 "hardly the sneering . . ." Ranney, *Press,* 26 Dec. 1950.

195 "Fierce loyalty, genuine . . ." Anderson, "The Man at the Next Desk," *Curtain Call,* 62.

195 "one outstanding . . ." Parsons, *News,* 22 Jan. 1938.

195 "soft spoken, a . . ." WF, *Press,* 27 Dec. 1950.

195 "Roger Stearns brightens . . ." Spaeth, *News,* 26 Dec. 1950.

195 "What Am I to Do" (from *The Man Who Came to Dinner*). Words and Music by Cole Porter © 1942 (Renewed) Chappell & Co., Inc. All Rights Reserved. Used by Permission of Alfred Publishing Co., Inc.; Kimball, *Complete Lyrics of Cole Porter,* 277.

"SQUAWKS FROM UNEXPECTED PLACES"

196 "dimly lit haven" WF, *Press,* 5 July 1954.

196 "a charming fellow . . ." Smith to author, 17 July 2001.

196 "umbilical chords" Stearns, "The Umbilical Chord," *Curtain Call,* 74–75.

196 "Roger Stearns . . . drove . . . " WF, *Press,* 6 July 1950.

196 "struggling with painters . . ." WF, *Press,* 14 July 1950.

197 "If Columbus listens . . ." WF, *Press,* 12 July 1950.

197 "opened cold" WF, *Press,* 14 July 1950.

197 "Dear Roger Stearns:" WF, *Press,* 28 July 1951.

197 "downtown traffic to thin" WF, *Press,* 5 July 1954.

198 "Anyone found to . . ." WF, *Press,* 10 Jan. 1953.

198 "balding and a . . ." WF, *Press,* 22 July 1950.

198 "small, unassuming and blind" WF, *Press,* 12 May 1954.

198 "a huge amiable . . ." WF, *Press,* 16 Dec. 1953.

198 "You haven't tasted . . ." WF, *Press,* 21 July 1950.

199 "The after dark . . ." WF, *Press,* 6 July 1950.

199 "original and creative . . ." Randle, *Sun,* 26 Oct. 1972.

199 "successful beyond the . . ." Hexter, "The Heart of the City," *Curtain Call,* 61.

199 "One carefree evening . . ." WF, "From Here to Infirmity," *Curtain Call,* 18.

199 "Wistful ghosts of . . ." French and Lewis, *Curtain Call,* 53.

200 "Some cities in . . ." WF, *Press,* 16 May 1953.

200 "the only corner . . ." WF, *Press,* 11 July 1955.

200 "We've paid that." Collier, *Press,* 21 Dec. 1979.

200 "blazing, uninhibited color, . . ." WF, *Press,* 25 June 1954.

201 "the statuesque model . . ." WF, *Press,* 12 July 1955.

201 "a fast toddy . . ." WF, *Press,* 11 July 1955.

201 "'So I have,' . . ." WF, *Press,* 29 May, 5 June 1954.

201 "tough boy" U.S. Senate, Special Committee, 71.

201 "squawks from unexpected . . ." WF, *Press,* 25 Apr. 1953.

202 "The tickets . . . will . . ." WF, *Press,* 1 July 1954.

202 "red and white . . ." WF, *Press,* 16 May 1953.

202 "a tall flagpole" Condon, *Cleveland,* 251.

203 "elaborate and complicated . . ." WF, *Press,* 25 Apr. 1953.

203 eleven railroad freight . . . , WF, *Press,* 9 Apr. 1953.

203 While Hammerstein was . . . , MEH to author, 10 Dec. 2003.

203 "that moment of . . ." WF, *Press,* 25 Apr. 1953.

203 "A production of . . ." WF, *Press,* 22 Apr. 1953.

204 "People were having . . ." McDermott, *Plain Dealer,* 9 June 1953.

204 "twilight sky" Condon, *Cleveland,* 252.

205 "litmus towns" Whiteside, *Cry,* 70–71.

205 "During most of . . ." WF, *News,* 1 July 1933.

205 "The very best . . ." WF, *News,* 9 Oct. 1933.

205 "the thriving capital . . ." WF, *Press,* 11 Dec. 1954.

205 "all but swept . . ." WF, *Press,* 4 Dec. 1954.

205 "Give 'White Christmas' . . ." WF, *Press,* 10 Dec. 1953.

205 "a training school . . ." WF, *Press,* 3 May 1960.

206 "Levi's and her . . ." WF, *Press,* 8 May 1954.

206 "hold a nasal . . ." WF, *Press,* 4 Dec. 1954.

206 "alert adults" WF, *Press,* 11 Dec. 1953.

206 "who continually complain . . ." WF, *Press,* 7 June 1954.

206 "strangely out of place . . ." WF, *Press,* 23, 30 June 1954.

206 "a wartime measure" WF, *Press,* 8 Apr. 1960.

207 "sang to feverish . . ." WF, *Press,* 11 Feb. 1954.

207 "a fine ballad . . ." WF, *Press,* 10 Feb. 1954.

207 "Golden Era of . . ." Hemming and Hajdu, *Discovering Great Singers,* 10–11; WF, *Press,* 12 May 1960.

207 convinced a nephew . . . , J. Dewey to author, 3 July 2003.

208 "leafy, lovely city" WF, *Press,* 25 Nov. 1961.

208 "Little specialty shops . . ." WF, *Press,* 12 Apr. 1960.

208 "broken-off end of . . ." Little, *Second Love,* 43.

209 "took good care . . ." Smith to author, 17 July 2001.

209 "1350 shares of . . ." Collier, *Press,* 20 Aug. 1963.

209 "to tide him . . ." Collier, *Press,* 6 Mar. 1973.

209 "Here I am, . . ." WF, *Press,* 23 Dec. 1953.

210 Winsor's surviving sisters . . . , MEH, AEP, PT, to author 28 Aug. 1997.

210 "three martinis . . ." WF to AEP, 27 Feb. 1961.

210 "The booze business . . ." Collier, *Press,* 30 Dec. 1953.

210 "was associated with . . ." U.S. Senate, Special Committee, 92.

210 "I do wish . . ." WF to Anne Eaton Dodge (hereafter AD), 4 Feb. 1954.

211 "Honey, what I meant . . ." WF to AD, 16 Feb. 1954.

211 "regular routine" WF to AD, 4 Feb. 1954.

211 "exhausted. The Heart . . ." WF to AD, 16 Feb. 1954.

211 "The new document . . ." WF to AEP, undated.

212 "tomato and strawberry . . ." WF, *Press,* 17 Apr. 1954.

212 "Except for one . . ." WF, *Press,* 29, 31 Mar. 1954.

212 "Sailors and tourists . . ." WF, *Press,* 5 Apr. 1954.

212 "bored sailors who . . ." WF, *Press,* 8 Apr. 1954.

212 Johnny and Rose Lindheim . . . , WF, *Press,* 14 Jan. 1954.

212 "simply sat around . . ." WF, *Press,* 6 July 1954.

213 reunion of the Jolly Set . . . , WF, *Press,* 9 July 1954.

213 "seldom served fewer . . ." WF, *Press,* 2 Jan. 1954.

213 "*Full Face* will . . ." WF, *Press,* 20 Nov. 1953.

213 Fun for Funds reopened . . . , WF, *Press,* 1 July 1954.

213 "violent outburst of kissing" WF, *Press,* 2 Oct. 1954.

213 "everyone kissing everyone . . ." WF, *Press,* 6 Oct. 1948.

213 "back slappings and . . ." WF, *Press,* 5 Oct. 1948.

213 "Bill had empathy . . ." Berkow, *New York Times,* 20 Oct. 2005.

"ACCUSTOMED AS I AM TO OFF-BEAT RHYTHMS"

214 "was being chauffeured . . ." WF, *Press,* 22 Dec. 1959.

214 "blinded by a spotlight" Collier, *Press,* 21 Dec. 1959.

215 "every other row . . ." Bellamy, *News,* 21 Dec. 1979.

216 "the most spectacular . . ." Little, *Second Love,* 44.

216 Grapefruit "Baked. . . . ," WF, *Press,* 26 Mar. 1935.

216 "A herring wrapped . . ." WF, *Press,* 26 Nov. 1934.

216 "17th-century Italian desk . . ." Luft, *Press,* undated.

217 "By the time . . ." WF, *Press,* 1 Mar. 1955.

217 "Irish beauty was . . ." WF, *Press,* 25 June 1955.

217 Peter Winslow . . . , *Plain Dealer,* 12 Aug. 1951.

218 "He ran it . . ." Collier, *Press,* 19, 23 Aug. 1963.

218 "spent two days . . ." *Press,* 23 Apr. 1963.

218 "got up at nine, . . ." WF to AEP, 1 May 1955.

219 "This is being . . ." WF, *Press,* 30 May 1960.
219 "tremendous and somewhat . . ." WF, *Press,* 22 May 1957.
219 "dreading Williamstown . . ." WF to AEP, 9 Sept. 1957, Parker Papers.
219 "Len Hanna's companion" McBrien, *Cole Porter,* 197.
219 "He would not . . ." WF, *Press,* 12 Oct. 1957.
220 Hanna's personal foundation . . . , WF, *Press,* 19 Aug. 1963.
220 collection of impressionists . . . , WF, *Press,* 28 Apr. 1960.
220 "very gentle" MEH to the author, 28 Aug. 1997.
220 "Everyone is in . . ." WF, *Press,* 1 Jan. 1958.
220 "Here and there . . ." WF, *Press,* 14 Jan. 1958.
221 "Two towering royal . . ." WF, *Press,* 3 Jan. 1958.
221 "wearing toreador pants" WF, *Press,* 8 Jan. 1958.
221 "In the long, . . ." WF, *Press,* 4 Jan. 1958.
221 "only 10 feature-length . . ." WF, *Press,* 15 Jan. 1958.
221 "I looked in . . ." WF, *Press,* 16 Jan. 1958.
221 "match the beauty . . ." WF, *Press,* 12 May 1960.
221 "caught a sleeper . . ." WF, *Press,* 18 Jan. 1958.
222 "charming little house" WF, *Press,* 21 Jan. 1958.
222 "very off-Broadway, . . ." WF, *Press,* 20 Jan. 1958.
222 "as hard, grueling . . ." WF, *Press,* 7 Dec. 1957.
222 "playing solitaire or . . ." WF, *Press,* 9 Feb. 1958.
223 "coronary attack" *Press,* 20 Feb. 1958.
223 "nitery pianist" *Variety,* 26 Feb. 1958.
223 "I am still . . ." WF to AEP, 1 Mar. 1958.
223 "The Vogue Room . . ." WF, *Press,* 12 May 1960.
223 "to make at least . . ." WF, *Press,* 28 Dec. 1958.
223 "a large jug . . ." WF, *Press,* 18 Apr. 1958.
223 "When I get so . . ." WF to AEP 4 Aug. 1956.
223 "a long land voyage . . ." WF, *Press,* 31 Dec. 1958.
224 "It is anything . . ." WF, *Press,* 3 Jan. 1959.
224 "a sophisticated town . . ." WF, *Press,* 7 Jan. 1959.
224 "The huge dome car . . ." WF, *Press,* 8 Jan. 1959.
224 "darker than any . . ." WF, *Press,* 14 Jan. 1959.
225 "a couple of good . . ." WF, *Press,* 10 Jan. 1959.
225 "Defeated little burros, . . ." WF, *Press,* 17 Jan. 1959.
225 "the gentle hills . . ." WF, *Press,* 2 Nov. 1959.
225 "John and 'Sis' O'Hara . . ." WF, *Press,* 25 May 1960.
225 "among the greatest . . ." Gill, *Here at the* New Yorker, 117.
225 "Oh dear God . . ." WF to AEP, 8 Aug. 1956.
226 "I didn't telephone . . ." WF to AEP, 24 Jan. 1960.
226 "When has death . . ." WF, *Press,* 25 Jan. 1960.

"NO ONE EVEN WHIMPERS"

228 "oversold, overcrowded and . . ." WF, *Press,* 30 Dec. 1961.
228 thick wooden frame . . . , *Milwaukee Journal,* 25 Mar. 1962.

229 "The sun shines . . ." WF, *Press,* 4 Jan. 1962.

229 "youngish diplomats" WF, *Press,* 8 Feb. 1937.

229 "pink camellia hedge" WF, *Press,* 1 Jan. 1962.

230 "almost invariably about . . ." WF, *Press,* 5 Jan. 1962.

230 "the most glamorous . . ." WF, *Press,* 7 Dec. 1961.

230 "swagger" WF, *Press,* 8 Dec. 1961.

230 "slacks and loafers" WF, *Press,* 6 Dec. 1961.

230 "abandoned the detailed . . ." "Wyant," *Who Was Who in American Art,* 3:3652.

231 "a gentleman of . . ." WF, *Press,* 6 Jan. 1962.

231 "What the tired . . ." WF, *Press,* 6 Dec. 1961.

231 "all the Veecks . . ." WF, *Press,* 9 Dec. 1961.

231 "After living some . . ." WF, *Press,* 26 Dec. 1961.

232 "I couldn't be . . ." WF to AEP, 28 Sept. 1960.

232 "What a view . . ." WF to AEP, 25 Jan. 1961.

232 "a wood-burning engine . . ." Luft, *Press,* undated.

232 "Already I have . . ." WF to AEP, 27 Feb. 1961.

232 "Dear Mr. French: . . . " Jacqueline Bouvier Kennedy to WF, 8 Feb. 1962.

232 "ten minutes and . . ." WF, *Press,* 27 Mar. 1961.

233 "the Emerald Necklace " ibid.

233 "Littered with campers . . ." WF, *Press,* 7 May 1960.

233 "It wouldn't be . . ." WF, *Press,* 29 Apr. 1960.

233 "illuminated by gas . . ." WF, *Press,* 25 Nov. 1961.

233 "because it drifts . . ." WF, *Press,* 16 May 1960.

234 "a 20th-century . . ." Dvorak, *Press,* 26 Mar. 1962.

234 "toss off a fifth . . ." WF to AEP, 29 May 1964.

234 "Lilliputian elephant once . . ." Anderson, "The Man at the Next Desk," *Curtain Call,* 62.

234 "a little ham . . ." WF, *Press,* 6 Mar. 1973.

234 "Newspaper people . . ." George Condon to Mrs. Alfred McNulty, undated.

234 "It was just . . ." Randle, *Sun,* 26 Oct. 1972.

235 "Winsor devotes considerable . . ." Dvorak, *Press,* 26 Mar. 1962.

235 "enough books to . . ." WF, *Press,* 1 June 1962.

235 Constantine Nicoloudis . . . , WF, *Press,* 29 May 1962.

235 "extremely attractive" Wood, "Summer Snapshots," *Cleveland Magazine,* June 1984, 54–57, 147–48.

235 "to visit the church . . ." WF, *Press,* 4 June 1962.

236 "likely-looking tavern" WF, *Press,* 12 June 1962.

236 "Cocktail parties suddenly . . ." WF, *Press,* 14 June 1962.

236 "last port of . . ." WF, *Press,* 15 June 1962.

236 "guide at Rhodes . . ." WF, *Press,* 18 June 1962.

237 "Assemble a party . . ." WF, *Press,* 9 June 1962.

237 "My expenses are . . ." WF to AEP, 27 Feb. 1961.

237 "a little less . . ." WF, *Press,* 30 June 1962.

237 "the Cleveland Limited, . . ." WF, *Press,* 1 July 1962.

237 "There were no . . ." WF, *Press,* 25 Sept. 1962.

238 "the most glittering . . ." WF, *Press,* 27 Sept. 1962.

238 "mail orders had . . ." *New York Times,* 26 Jan. 1986.

239 the president's sister . . . , WF, *Press,* 28 Sept. 1962.

239 "direct train to . . ." WF, *Press,* 6 Nov. 1962.

239 "When you go . . ." J. A. Casper to WF, 6 July 1965.

239 "drinks were served" WF, *Press,* 10 Nov. 1962.

239 "immune from parking tickets" WF, *Press,* 14 Nov. 1962.

239 "fewer than 150 . . ." WF, *Press,* 28 Nov. 1962.

240 "driving rains, followed . . ." WF, *Press,* 26, 27 Nov. 1962.

240 "blissfully unaware I . . ." WF, *Press,* 8 Apr. 1963.

240 "We know where . . ." WF, *PARADE,* 28 Apr. 1932, 29.

240 "deloused. England, it . . ." WF, *Press,* 9 Apr. 1963.

241 "The Rolls Royce made . . ." WF, *Press,* 6 Mar. 1973.

241 "scrunched-up shoulders . . ." Condon, *Plain Dealer,* 25 Mar. 1980.

241 "well aware that . . ." WF, *Press,* 11 Apr. 1963.

"I CANNOT USE MY HANDS TO WRITE"

242 "tea or drinks . . ." WF, *Press,* 17 Sept. 1963.

242 "colonial from an . . ." C. H. Reilly, *Country Life,* 6 June 1931, 736–38.

242 "very generous about . . ." WF, *Press,* 29 June 1966.

243 "battered old slouch . . ." WF, *Press,* 14 Sept. 1963.

243 "a long and rather . . ." WF, *Press,* 27 Sept. 1963.

244 "After more than . . ." WF, *Press,* 4 Oct. 1963.

244 "My life has become . . ." WF to AEP, 29 May 1964.

244 "chauffeur, caretaker and . . ." McLaughlin, *Press,* 9 Mar. 1973.

244 "obliged to hang . . ." *Press,* 14 Oct. 1966.

244 "I see the police . . ." WF, *Press,* 26 May 1964.

244 "'Aunt Jo' to legions" WF, *Press,* 30 May 1964.

245 "onyx and diamond . . ." WF, *PARADE,* 8 Oct. 1931, 19.

245 "Bessie Brown, the great . . ." WF, *Press,* 29 May 1964.

245 "a phony both . . ." WF to AEP, 29 May 1964.

245 "handwriting became shaky . . ." Grady, *New York Times,* 13 Apr. 2000.

246 "a little bit lost" WF to AEP, 23 July 1960.

246 "The guards quickly . . ." WF, *Press,* 20 June 1964.

246 "absolutely terrific with . . ." WF, *Press,* 22 June 1964.

246 "women in slacks . . ." WF, *Press,* 23 June 1964.

246 "the same path; . . ." WF, *Press,* 24 June 1964.

246 "rattling around like . . ." WF, *Press,* 26 June 1964.

246 "the wheezing, itinerant . . ." WF, *Press,* 29 June 1964.

246 "turned up at . . ." WF, *Press,* 30 June 1964.

246 "glows with the . . ." WF, *Press,* 4 July 1964.

246 "the bar lady" WF, *Press,* 2 July 1964.

246 "high cheek-boned woman . . ." WF, *Press,* 1 May 1957.

247 "I have been . . ." WF, *Press,* 7 July 1964.

247 "an architectural student . . ." WF, *Press,* 16 July 1964.

247 "It's freezing cold, . . ." WF to AEP, 14 Jan. 1965.

247 "I talked to . . ." WF, *Press,* 14 Feb. 1966.
248 "For the first . . ." WF, *Press,* 8 Feb. 1966.
248 "You would have . . ." WF, *Press,* 16 Feb. 1966.
248 "pet monkey, Angelo . . . was . . . " WF, *Press,* 22 Dec. 1965.
248 "I am now . . ." WF, *Press,* 8 Dec. 1965.
248 "A man could . . ." WF, *Press,* 9 Feb. 1966.
249 "My husband was . . ." Mrs. Robert C. Lord to WF, 23 Feb. 1966.
249 "Because some one . . ." Mrs. B. G. Odiorne to WF, 22 Feb. 1966.
249 "Do you honestly . . ." Mrs. Leonard R. Roesch to WF, 9 Mar. 1966.
249 "People don't let . . ." Mrs. E. P. Linder to WF, 28 Jan. 1966.
249 "I had no idea . . ." *Press,* 9 Mar. 1966.
250 "no luck. From . . ." WF, *Press,* 17 June 1966.
250 "gay, blond and beautiful" WF, *Press,* 23 June 1966.
250 "if he still . . ." WF to AEP, 14 Jan. 1965.
251 see the Heriots . . . , WF, *Press,* 29 June 1966.
251 "an aging, tired . . ." WF, *Press,* 24 June 1966.
251 "secretary and closest . . ." WF, *Press,* 7 Jan. 1966.
251 "great literary pilgrimage . . ." Calder, *Willie,* 206.
251 "Beautiful but obscure . . ." Connon, *Somerset Maugham and the Maugham Dynasty,* 86.
252 "my pleasure and . . ." Day, *Letters of Noël Coward,* 229–30.
252 "allegedly based on . . ." WF, *Press,* 28 June 1966.
252 "emperor of this . . ." WF, *Press,* 12 July 1966.
252 "To my astonishment, . . ." WF, *Press,* 18 July 1966.
252 "simply liked people . . ." WF, *Press,* 11 Nov. 1966.
252 "would be with . . ." McLaughlin, *Press,* 9 Mar. 1973.
252 "the east 30's or 40's, . . . " WF, *Press,* 11 Sept. 1954.
253 "The truth is . . ." MacLeish, *Saturday Review of Literature,* 16 Jan. 1932, 453–54.
253 "the freighters . . ." WF, *Press,* 3 Jan. 1967.
253 "calling for a . . ." *Press,* 29 Nov. 1966.
253 "Winsor has utilized . . ." *Press,* 14 Oct. 1966.
253 "Is he really . . ." *Press,* 11 Apr. 1967.
254 "Reading has become . . ." WF to AEP, 9 Feb. 1968.
254 "After thirty-one . . ." Collier, *Press,* 26 Sept. 1968.
254 "I cannot use . . ." WF to AEP, 11 Nov. 1968.
254 "Cleveland grows more . . ." WF to AEP, 17 July 1969.
254 "Martha usually sticks . . ." WF to AEP, 25 Apr. 1969.
254 "I try and go . . ." WF to AEP, 17 May 1971.
254 Turtle, who had . . . , F. Turtle to WF, 6 Nov. 1970.
255 "Whereas Winsor French's . . ." Mayor Carl Stokes, City of Cleveland Proclamation, October 1972.
255 "little prose masterpieces . . . opulent . . ." Randle, *Sun,* 26 Oct. 1972.
255 "fast-and-loose, . . ." Paul E. Steiger, *Wall Street Journal,* 29 Dec. 2007.
255 "He couldn't speak, . . ." K. Halle to MEH, 14 Mar. 1973.
255 "a wistful bit . . ." P. Coakley to MEH, 6 Mar. 1973.
256 "French was famed . . ." Collier, *Press,* 6 Mar. 1973.

256 "as a diminutive man . . ." *Press,* 6 Mar. 1973.

256 "lived and wrote . . ." *Plain Dealer,* 7 Mar. 1973.

257 "Winsor's family would . . ." H. Lavine to T. Boardman, 26 Mar. 1973.

257 the *Press* published . . . , Bergen, *Press,* 29 May 1963.

257 "a former society gossip . . ." *Variety,* 30 May 1973.

257 "film critic and . . ." *New York Times,* 7 Mar. 1973.

258 "Winsor was an . . ." T. Boardman to H. Lavine, undated.

258 "I've been ashamed . . ." A. Vincent to S. Warner, undated.

258 "My feelings for . . ." M. Perry to MEH, 26 Mar. 1973.

259 "Once a long . . ." R. Glick to MEH, undated.

259 "It was my whole life." Collier, *Press,* 26 Sept. 1968.

Select Bibliography

BOOKS

Alpert, Hollis. *The Barrymores.* New York: Sun Dial, 1964.

Amherst, Jeffery John Archer. *Wandering Abroad: The Autobiography of Jeffery Amherst.* London: Secker & Warburg, 1976.

Bach, Steven. *Marlene Dietrich: Life and Legend.* New York: Morrow, 1992.

Bergreen, Laurence. *As Thousands Cheer: The Life of Irving Berlin.* New York: Viking, 1990.

Bird, George L., and Frederic E. Merwin. *The Press and Society.* New York: Prentice-Hall, 1951.

Bradshaw, Jon. *Dreams that Money Can Buy.* New York: Morrow, 1985.

Brown, Eve. *Champagne Cholly: The Life and Times of Maury Paul.* New York: Dutton, 1947.

Brown, Jared. *The Fabulous Lunts: A Biography of Alfred Lunt and Lynn Fontanne.* New York: Atheneum, 1986.

Brown, John Mason. *Two on the Aisle: Ten Years of the American Theater in Performance.* New York: Norton, 1938.

Busch, Noel. *Briton Hadden: A Biography of the Co-Founder of* TIME. New York: Farrar, Straus, 1949.

Calder, Robert. *Willie: The Life of W. Somerset Maugham.* New York: St. Martin's, 1990.

Campbell, W. Joseph. *Yellow Journalism: Puncturing the Myths, Defining the Legacies.* Westport, Conn.: Praeger, 2001.

Chase, Ilka. *Free Admission.* Garden City, N.Y.: Doubleday, 1948.

——. *Past Imperfect.* Garden City, N.Y.: Doubleday, Doran, 1942.

Chauncey, George. *Gay New York: Gender, Urban Culture, and the Making of the Gay Male World.* New York: HarperCollins, 1994.

Citron, Stephen. *Noel & Cole: The Sophisticates.* London: Sinclair-Stevenson, 1992.

Condon, George. *Cleveland: The Best Kept Secret.* Garden City, N.Y.: Doubleday, 1967.

Connon, Bryan. *Somerset Maugham and the Maugham Dynasty.* London: Sinclair-Stevenson, 1997.

Coward, Noël. *Play Parade: Design for Living.* New York: Garden City, 1933.

Davies, David R. *The Postwar Decline of American Newspapers, 1945–1965,* No. 6 of the History of American Journalism Series. James D. Startt and William David Sloan, series editors. Westport, Conn.: Praeger, 2006.

Davis, Russell H. *Black Americans in Cleveland: From George Peake to Carl B. Stokes, 1796–1969.* Washington, D.C.: Associated Publishers, 1972.

Day, Barry. *The Letters of Noël Coward.* New York: Knopf, 2007.

Eells, George. *The Life that Late He Led: A Biography of Cole Porter.* New York: G. P. Putnam's Sons, 1967.

Elsner-Sommer, Gretchen. *International Dictionary of Films and Filmmakers,* Vol. 1, *Films.* Detroit: St. James Press, 2000.

Embree, Edwin R. *Brown America: The Study of a New Race.* New York: Viking, 1931.

Ewen, David. *The Cole Porter Story.* New York: Holt, Rinehart, Winston, 1965.

Falstaff, Jake. *The Bulls of Spring: The Selected Poems of Jake Falstaff.* New York: G. P. Putnam and Sons, 1937.

Fisher, Clive. *Noël Coward.* New York: St. Martin's, 1992.

Fiske, Dwight. *Without Music.* New York: Chatham, 1933.

French, Winsor, and Franklin Lewis, eds. *Curtain Call.* Cleveland: Gruber Foundation, 1952.

Fulco, di Verdura. *The Happy Summer Days: A Sicilian Childhood.* London, Weidenfeld & Nicolson, 1976.

Furia, Philip. *Irving Berlin: A Life in Song.* New York: Schirmer Books, 1998.

Fury, David A. *Johnny Weissmuller: Twice the Hero.* Minneapolis: Artist's Press, 2000.

Gabler, Neal. *Winchell: Gossip, Power, and the Culture of Celebrity.* New York: Knopf, 1995.

Gill, Brendan. *Cole: A Biographical Essay.* New York: Delta, 1992.

———. *Happy Times.* New York: Harcourt, Brace, Jovanovich, 1973.

———. *Here at the* New Yorker. Random House, 1975.

———. *A New York Life.* New York: Poseidon Press, 1990.

Goldman, Herbert G. *Fanny Brice: The Original Funny Girl.* New York: Oxford University Press, 1992.

Grafton, David. *Red, Hot, and Rich: An Oral History of Cole Porter.* New York: Stein and Day, 1987.

Hecht, Ben, and Charles MacArthur. *The Front Page.* New York: Covici-Friede, 1928.

Hemming, Roy, and David Hajdu. *Discovering Great Singers of Classic Pop.* New York: Newmarket, 1991.

Hoare, Philip. *Noël Coward: A Biography.* New York: Simon & Schuster, 1995.

Hoffenstein, Samuel. *The Complete Poetry of Samuel Hoffenstein.* New York: Modern Library, 1954.

Howard, Jean. *Travels with Cole Porter.* New York: Harry N. Abrams, 1991.

Jablonski, Edward. *Irving Berlin: American Troubadour.* New York: Henry Holt, 1999.

Jacobs, Diane. *Christmas in July: The Life and Art of Preston Sturges.* Berkeley: University of California Press, 1992.

Kimball, Robert, ed. *Cole.* New York: Delta, 1992.

———. *The Complete Lyrics of Cole Porter.* New York: Da Capo, 1992.

Kimball, Robert, and Linda Emmet, eds. *The Complete Lyrics of Irving Berlin.* New York: Knopf, 2000.

Kimball, Robert, and Richard M. Sudhalter. *You're the Top: Cole Porter in the 1930s.* Indianapolis: Indiana Historical Society, 1992.

Kriendler, Peter. *21: Every Day Was New Year's Eve.* Dallas: Taylor Publishing, 1999.

Kusmer, Kenneth L. *A Ghetto Takes Shape: Black Cleveland, 1870–1930.* Urbana: University of Illinois Press, 1976.

Lacey, Robert. *Little Man: Meyer Lansky and the Gangster Life.* Boston: Little, Brown, 1991.

Lahr, John. *Coward the Playwright*. London: Methuen, 1982.

Lesley, Cole. *Remembered Laughter: The Life of Noël Coward*. New York: Knopf, 1976.

Lewis, Franklin. *The Cleveland Indians*. New York: G. P. Putnam's Sons, 1949.

Little, Robert A. *Second Love*. Cleveland: Robert A. Little, 1992.

Loughery, John. *The Other Side of Silence: Men's Lives and Gay Identities: A Twentieth-Century History*. New York: Henry Holt., 1998.

Mann, William J. *Wisecracker: The Life and Times of William Haines*. New York: Viking, 1998.

Maxwell, Gilbert. *Helen Morgan: Her Life and Legend*. New York: Hawthorne, 1974.

McBrien, William. *Cole Porter: A Biography*. New York: Knopf, 1998.

Menotti, Gian-Carlo. *The Medium*. New York: G. Schirmer, 1947.

Merman, Ethel, with George Eells. *Merman: An Autobiography*. New York: Simon and Schuster, 1978.

Merman, Ethel, as told to Pete Martin. *Who Could Ask for Anything More?* Garden City, N.Y.: Doubleday, 1955.

Milstein, Nathan, and Solomon Volkov. *From Russia to the West: The Musical Memoirs and Reminiscences of Nathan Milstein*. New York: Henry Holt, 1990.

Morella, Joseph, and George Mazzei. *Genius and Lust: The Creative and Sexual Lives of Cole Porter and Noël Coward*. New York: Carroll & Graff, 1966.

Morgan, Ted. *Maugham: A Biography*. New York: Simon and Schuster, 1980.

O'Donnell, Doris. *Front-Page Girl*. Kent, Ohio: Kent State University Press, 2006.

Oliver, Donald. *Greatest Revue Sketches*. New York: Avon Books, 1982.

Neff, James. *Mobbed Up: Jackie Presser's High-Wire Life in the Teamsters, the Mafia, and the FBI*. New York: Atlantic Monthly Press, 1989.

Parker, Dorothy. *Death and Taxes*. New York: Sun Dial, 1931.

Payn, Graham, and Barry Day. *My Life with Noël Coward*. New York: Applause, 1994.

Peckham, Ted. *Gentlemen for Rent*. New York: Frederick Fell, 1955.

Peeler, David P. *Hope among Us Yet: Social Criticism and Social Solace in Depression America*. Athens: University of Georgia Press, 1987.

Pleasants, Henry. *The Great American Popular Singers*. London: Victor Gollancz, 1974.

Porter, Cole. *The Cole Porter Story: As Told to Richard G. Hubler*. Cleveland: World, 1965.

Ragan, David. *Who's Who in Hollywood,* Vol. 2, *M–Z*. New York: Facts on File, 1992.

Reid, Ed, and Ovid Demaris. *The Green Felt Jungle*. New York: Trident, 1963.

Rose, William Ganson. *Cleveland: The Making of a City*. Kent, Ohio: Kent State University Press, 1990.

Schwartz, Charles. *Cole Porter: A Biography*. New York: Dial, 1977.

Shaw, Archer H. *The* Plain Dealer: *One Hundred Years in Cleveland*. New York: Knopf, 1942.

Short, Bobby. *Black and White Baby*. New York: Dodd, Mead, 1971.

Simpson, George. *The Negro in the Philadelphia Press*. Philadelphia: University of Pennsylvania Press, 1936.

Sturges, Preston. *Preston Sturges*. New York: Simon and Schuster, 1990.

Styne, Jule. *Funny Girl: A New Musical*. New York: Random House, 1964.

Teel, Leonard Ray. *The Public Press, 1900–1945,* No. 5 of the History of American Journalism Series. James D. Startt and William David Sloan, series editors. Westport, Conn.: Praeger, 2006.

Thomas, Bob. *I Got Rhythm! The Ethel Merman Story.* New York: G. P. Putnam's Sons, 1985.

Thomson, Virgil. *American Music since 1910.* New York: Holt, Rinehart Winston, 1970.

Truitt, Evelyn Mack, ed. *Who Was Who on Screen,* 2d ed. New York: R. R. Bowker, 1983.

Vacha, John. *From Broadway to Cleveland: A History of the Hanna Theatre.* Kent, Ohio: Kent State University Press, 2007.

———. *Showtime in Cleveland: The Rise of a Regional Theater Center.* Kent, Ohio: Kent State University Press, 2001.

Van Tassel, David D., and John J. Grabowski. *The Encyclopedia of Cleveland History.* Bloomington: Indiana University Press, 1987.

Veeck, Bill. *Veeck as in Wreck.* New York: G. P. Putnam's Sons, 1962.

Villard, Oswald Garrison. *The Disappearing Daily: Chapters in American Newspaper Evolution.* New York: Knopf, 1944.

Weaver, John V. A. *Trial Balance: A Sentimental Inventory.* New York: Farrar & Rinehart, 1932.

Whiteside, Jonny. *Cry: The Johnnie Ray Story.* New York: Barricade, 1994.

Wilner, Isaiah. *The Man Time Forgot.* New York: HarperCollins, 2006.

Wilson, Clint C., II, and Félix Gutiérrez. *Race, Multiculturalism, and the Media: From Mass to Class Communication,* 2d ed. Thousand Oaks, Calif.: Sage, 1995.

Wood, James M. *Halle's: Memoir of a Family Department Store.* Cleveland, Ohio: Geranium Press, 1996.

———. *The Tavern.* Cleveland: Tavern Co., 2003.

Zerbe, Jerome. *The Art of Social Climbing.* New York: Doubleday, 1965.

———. *People on Parade.* New York: David Kemp, 1934.

Zuro, Owen, and Marshall Wright. *The History of Eaton Corporation, 1911–1985.* Cleveland: Eaton Corporation, 1985.

ARTICLES AND CHAPTERS

Abel, Samuel D. "Staging Heterosexuality: Alfred Lunt and Lynn Fontanne's Design for Living." In *Passing Performances: Queer Readings of Leading Players in American Theater History,* edited by Robert A. Schanke and Kimberley Bell Marra. Ann Arbor: University of Michigan Press, 1998.

Ainsworth-White, Marion. "The Higher Education of Women: Women in Journalism." *Arena,* June 1900, 669–72.

Anderson, Stan. "The Man at the Next Desk." In French and Lewis, *Curtain Call.*

Bish, Louis E. "What Is a Bachelor?" *Bachelor,* April 1937, 9.

Bok, Edward. "Is the Newspaper Office the Place for a Girl?" *Ladies' Home Journal,* February 1901.

Britten, Evelyn Barrett. "Chronicles of Saratoga." Saratoga Historical Society, Saratoga, New York.

Connolly, Charles B. "The Ethics of Modern Journalism." *Catholic World* 75 (July 1902), 453–54.

Eliassen, R. H., and Earl W Anderson. "Investigations of Teacher Supply and Demand Reported in 1933." *Educational Research Bulletin* 13 (January 17, 1934), 12–16.

French, Winsor. "From Here to Infirmity." In French and Lewis, *Curtain Call.*

Gist, Noel. "The Negro in the Daily Press." *Social Forces* 10 (March 1933), 405–11.

Graves, W. Brooke. "Public Reporting in the American States." *Public Opinion Quarterly* 2 (April 1938), 211–28.

Greenberg, Hank. "Pied Piper of the Wigwam." In French and Lewis, *Curtain Call.*

Harbin, Billy J. "The Public and Private Man from Saratoga Springs." In *The Gay and Lesbian Theatrical Legacy: A Biographical Dictionary of Major Figures in American Stage Figures in the Pre-Stonewall Era,* edited by Billy J. Harbin, Kimberley Bell Marra, and Robert A. Schanke. Ann Arbor: University of Michigan Press, 2005.

Hexter, Irving. "The Heart of the City." In French and Lewis, *Curtain Call.*

Krinsky, Charles. "Cornell, Katherine (1893–1974) and Guthrier, McClintic (1893–1961)." *Encyclopedia of Gay, Lesbian, Bisexual, Transgender and Queer Culture.* www.glbtq.com.

MacLeish, Archibald. "To the Young Men of Wall Street." *Saturday Review of Literature* (January 16, 1932), 453–54.

Martindale, Carolyn, and Lillian Rae Dunlap. "The African Americans." In *U.S. News Coverage of Racial Minorities: A Sourcebook, 1934–1996,* edited by Beverly Ann Deepe Keever, Carolyn Martindale, and Mary Ann Weston. Westport, Conn.: Greenwood, 1997, 63–144.

McNutt, Patterson. "Musical Comedy Express." *Collier's,* August 18, 1934, 17, 47–48.

Miggins, Edward M., and Mary Campbell Morgenthaler. "The Ethnic Mosaic: The Settlement of Cleveland by the New Immigrants and Migrants." In *The Birth of Modern Cleveland, 1865–1930,* edited by Thomas F. Campbell and Edward M. Miggins. Cleveland, Western Reserve History Society, Associated University Presses, 1988.

Moats, Alice-Leone. "To Eat and Not to Mate." *Town and Country,* January 1937, 104–40.

St. Paul's School, "In-Depth Description," www.sps.edu, Concord, N.H., October 24, 2001.

Stearns, Roger. "The Umbilical Chord." In French and Lewis, *Curtain Call.*

Villard, Oswald Garrison. "The Press Today: The Associated Press." *Nation,* April 23, 1930, 486–87.

Wickham, Ben. "The Russian Rear Admiral." In French and Lewis, *Curtain Call,* 25–26.

"Wyant, Alexander." *Who Was Who in American Art.* Edited by Peter Hastingstalk. Madison, Conn.: Sound View Press, 1999, Vol. 3, 3652.

Zerbe, Jerome. "The House on Harcourt." In French and Lewis, *Curtain Call.*

MANUSCRIPTS AND UNPUBLISHED MATERIAL

Carroll, J. JCarroll (JC) to JE, 19 July 1932, Hickox Papers. Private collection.

Cleveland Play House. Program, *Criminal at Large,* December 19, 1933.

Curtiss, Mary Louise Brown (MLBC) correspondence, Hickox Papers, Cleveland, Ohio.

Davis, Roger (RD) correspondence, Hickox Papers, Cleveland, Ohio.

Eaton, Joseph O. (JE) correspondence, Hickox Papers, Cleveland, Ohio.

Emerson, Isaac Edward. Isaac Edward Emerson Papers, Library of the University of North Carolina at Chapel Hill.

French, Winsor (WF). Corporate Records and Reminiscences, *TIME* Inc. Archives, New York: New York.

———. Datebook 1935, Hickox Papers, Cleveland, Ohio.

———. WF to Louis Seltzer (LS), 1 October 1946, WF microfiche, *Cleveland Press* Collection, Cleveland State University Library.

Halle, Kay (1895–1989). Kay Halle Personal Papers, John F. Kennedy Presidential Library, Boston.

Hanna Theatre. Program, *The Man Who Came to Dinner,* December 25, 1950. Cleveland Public Library Theater Collection.

Kranz, Harry. Interview with Christopher Iannicelli. Oral History Archives of World War II, New Brunswick History Department, Rutgers, State University of New Jersey, April 29, 1996.

Paterson, William. Solid Seasons: My Forty-five Years at Two Resident Theaters. San Francisco, San Francisco Performing Arts Library and Museum, 1996.

Riggin, Aileen. An Olympian's Oral History. Los Angeles: Amateur Athletic Foundation of Los Angeles, 2008.

Standifer, Jim, and Zelma Watson George. Interview transcript, African-American Music Collection, University of Michigan, Ann Arbor.

Stuart Walker's Stock Company. Program, Portmanteau Theater, January 8, 1917. Cleveland Public Library Theater Collection.

Terkel, Studs. "Recordings from 'Hard Times.'" Studs Terkel Collection. Chicago Historical Society, 2002.

U.S. Senate Special Committee to Investigate Organized Crime in Interstate Commerce Report, 1951. Records of Senate Select and Special Committees, 1789–1988. In *Guide to Federal Records in the National Archives of the United States,* bicentennial edition. Washington, D.C.: National Archives and Records Administration, 1989.

Wye, Christopher. "Midwest Ghetto: Patterns of Negro Life and Thought in Cleveland, Ohio, 1929–1945." Ph.D. diss., Kent State University, 1973.

INTERVIEWS

Dewey, Joseph. Cleveland, July 3, 2003.

George, Thelma, and Gian-Carlo Menotti. Cleveland, December 6, 1982.

Hickox, Martha Eaton. Cleveland, August 28, 1997.

Parker, Anne Eaton Dodge. Cleveland, August 28, 1997.

Taplin, Margaret Eaton Sichel. Cleveland, August 28, 1997.

Index